Cheeky Angel™

Vol. 5
Story and Art by
Hiroyuki Nishimori

Cheeky Angel
Vol. 5
Action Edition
Story and Art by
HIROYUKI NISHIMORI

Translation/Joe Yamazaki
English Adaptation/Gary Leach
Touch-Up Art & Lettering/Gabe Crate
Cover and Interior Design/Izumi Evers
Editor/Michelle Pangilinan

Managing Editor/Annette Roman
Director of Production/Noboru Watanabe
Editorial Director/Alvin Lu
Sr. Director of Acquisitions/Rika Inouye
VP of Sales & Marketing/Liza Coppola
Executive VP/Hyoe Narita
Publisher/Seiji Horibuchi

Printed in the U.S.A.

Published by VIZ, LLC
P.O. Box 77010
San Francisco, CA 94107

Action Edition
10 9 8 7 6 5 4 3 2 1
First printing, February 2005

store.viz.com

RATED T+ FOR OLDER TEENS

PARENTAL ADVISORY
CHEEKY ANGEL is rated T+ for Teen Plus. Contains strong language, violence and sexual themes. Recommended for older teens (16 and up).

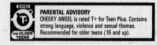

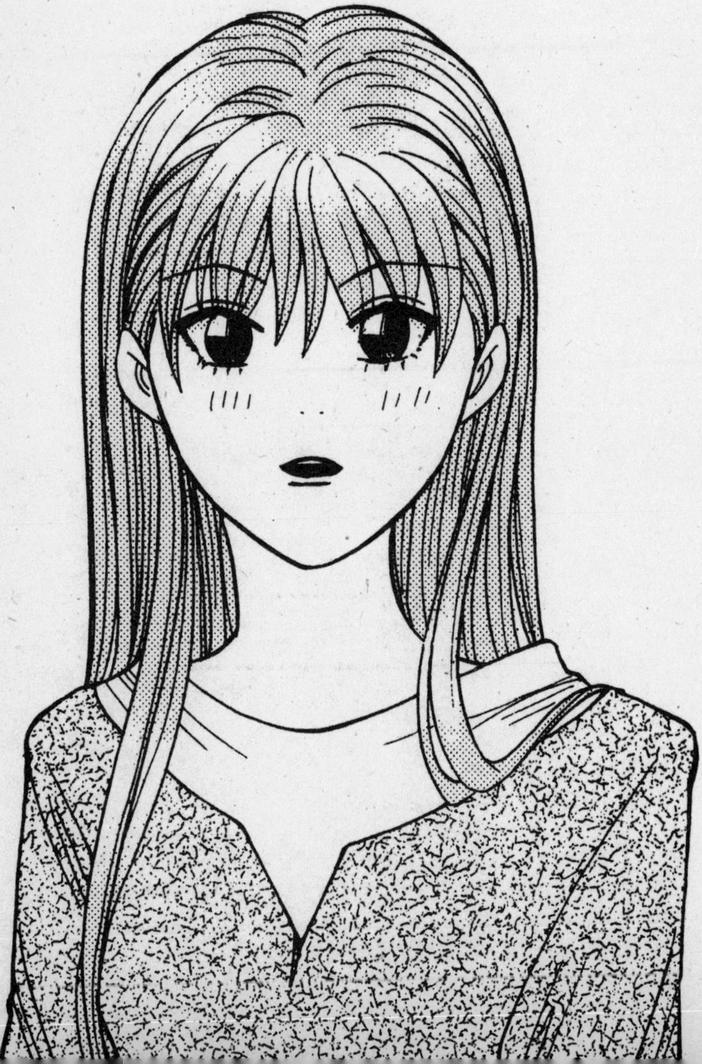

STORY THUS FAR

Lovely Megumi Amatsuka, cursed by a demonic clown, finally finds the "Evil Book" from which it sprang. Genzo and his friends—"Meg's Musketeers"—are powerless against the string of "accidents" that always seem to happen around her. Yet they press on, even though they really annoy Megumi more than help her. Then, for no particular reason, Megumi decides to go to Osaka with her father. There she meets a female burglar and gets involved in a shenanigan involving the yakuza... But Genzo, who trails Megumi all the way to Osaka, arrives and helps Meg escape. The situation appears to have been resolved, but...

Contents

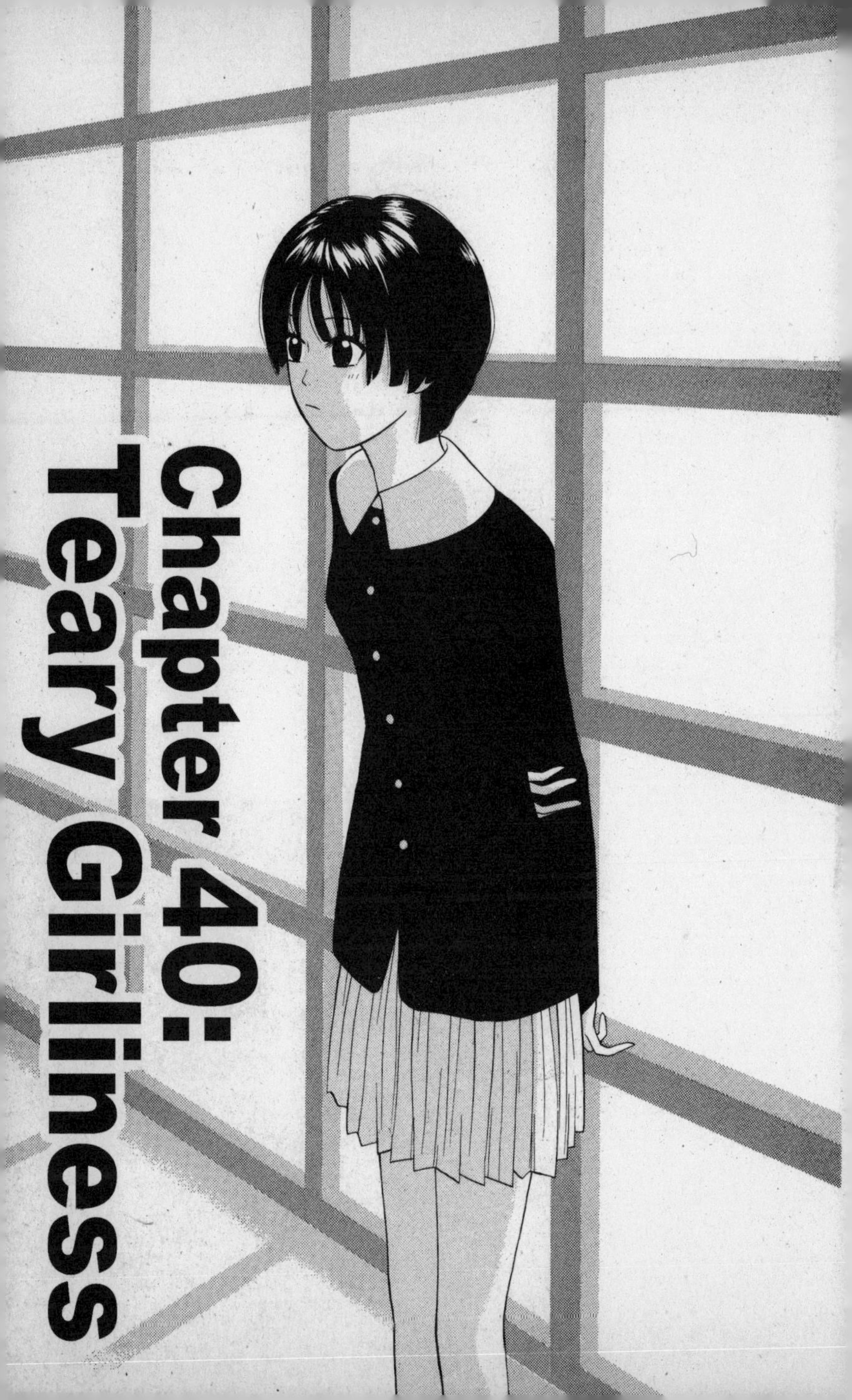
Chapter 40:
Teary Girliness

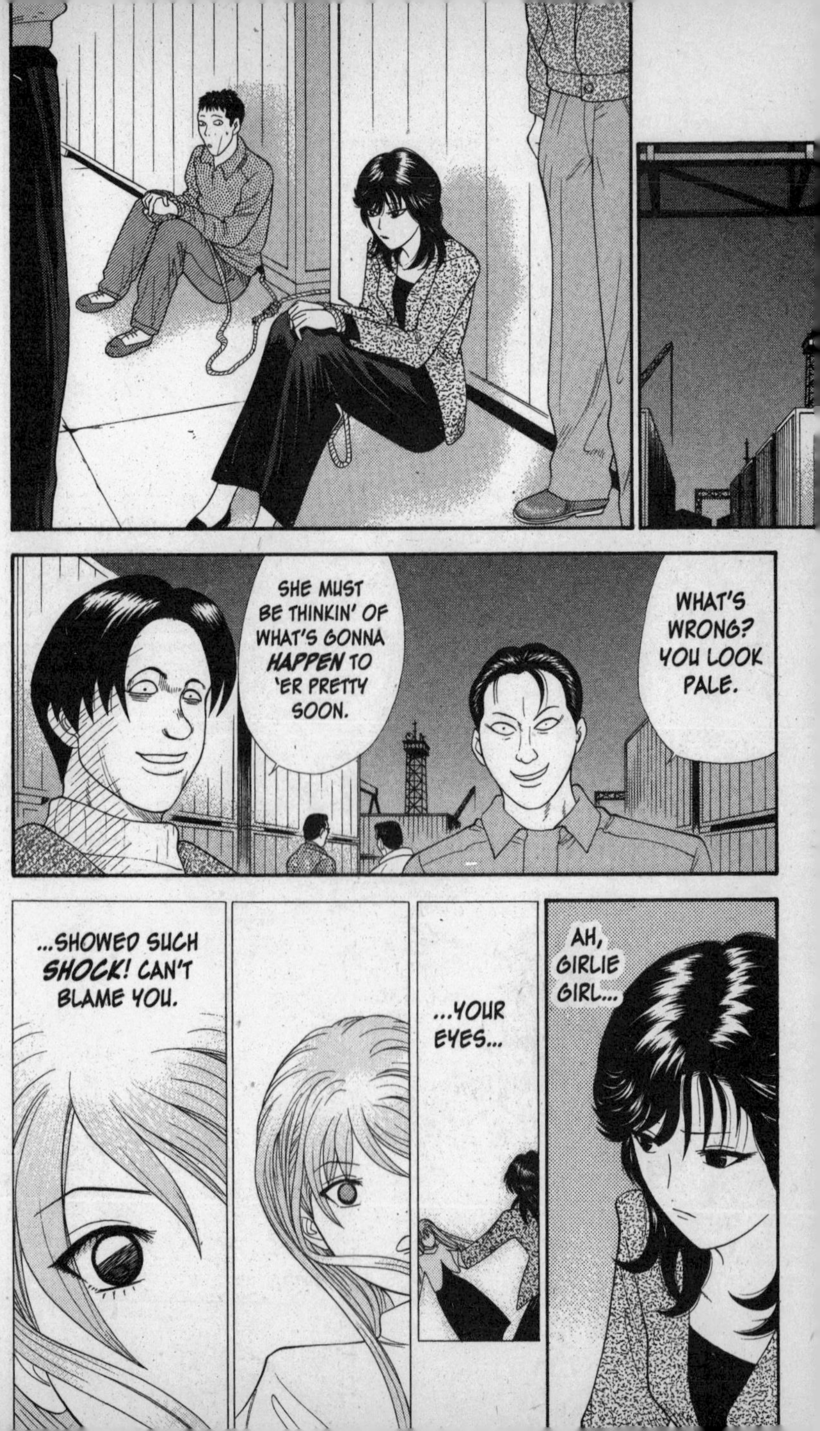
WHAT'S WRONG? YOU LOOK PALE.
SHE MUST BE THINKIN' OF WHAT'S GONNA HAPPEN TO 'ER PRETTY SOON.
AH, GIRLIE GIRL...
...YOUR EYES...
...SHOWED SUCH SHOCK! CAN'T BLAME YOU.

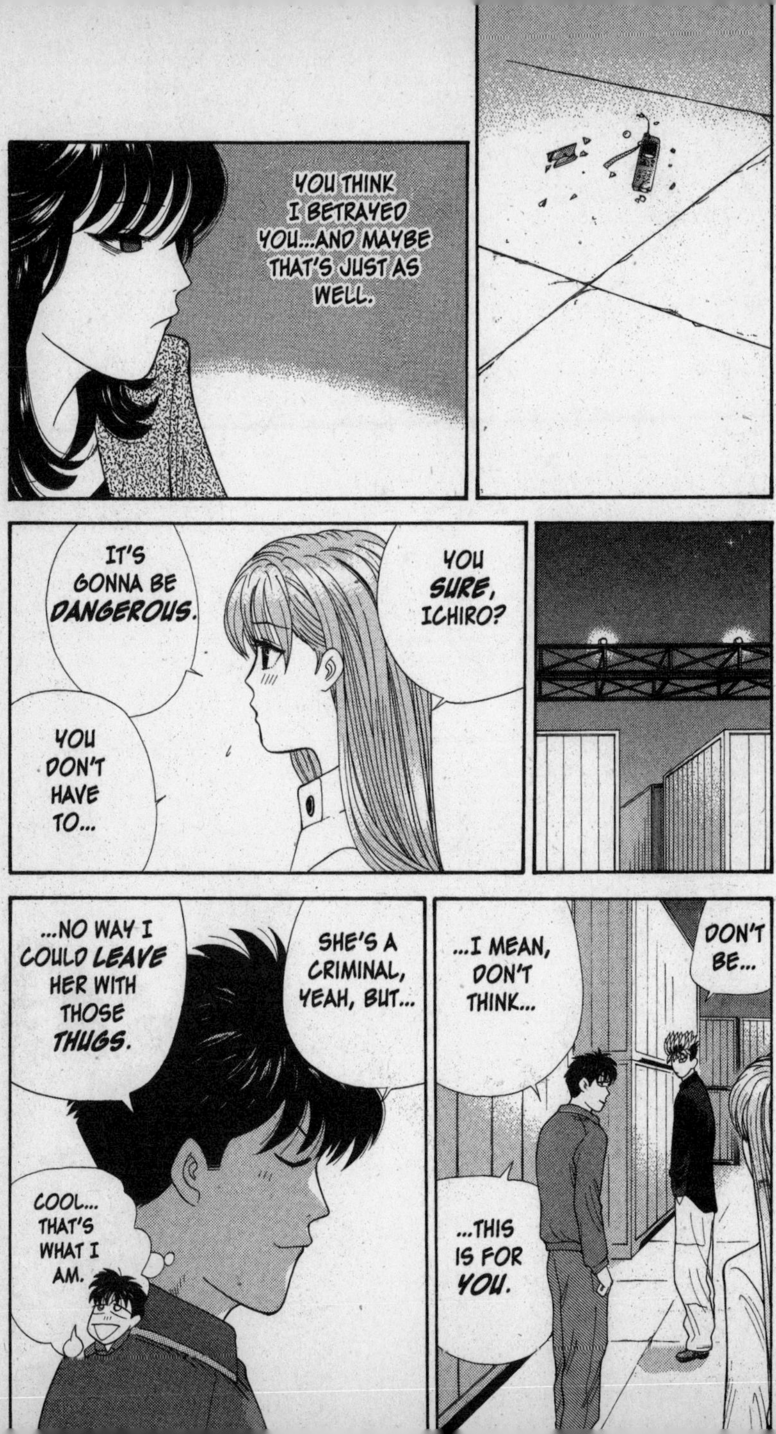
YOU THINK I BETRAYED YOU...AND MAYBE THAT'S JUST AS WELL.
YOU SURE, ICHIRO?
IT'S GONNA BE DANGEROUS.
YOU DON'T HAVE TO...
DON'T BE...
...I MEAN, DON'T THINK...
...THIS IS FOR YOU.
SHE'S A CRIMINAL, YEAH, BUT...
...NO WAY I COULD LEAVE HER WITH THOSE THUGS.
COOL... THAT'S WHAT I AM.

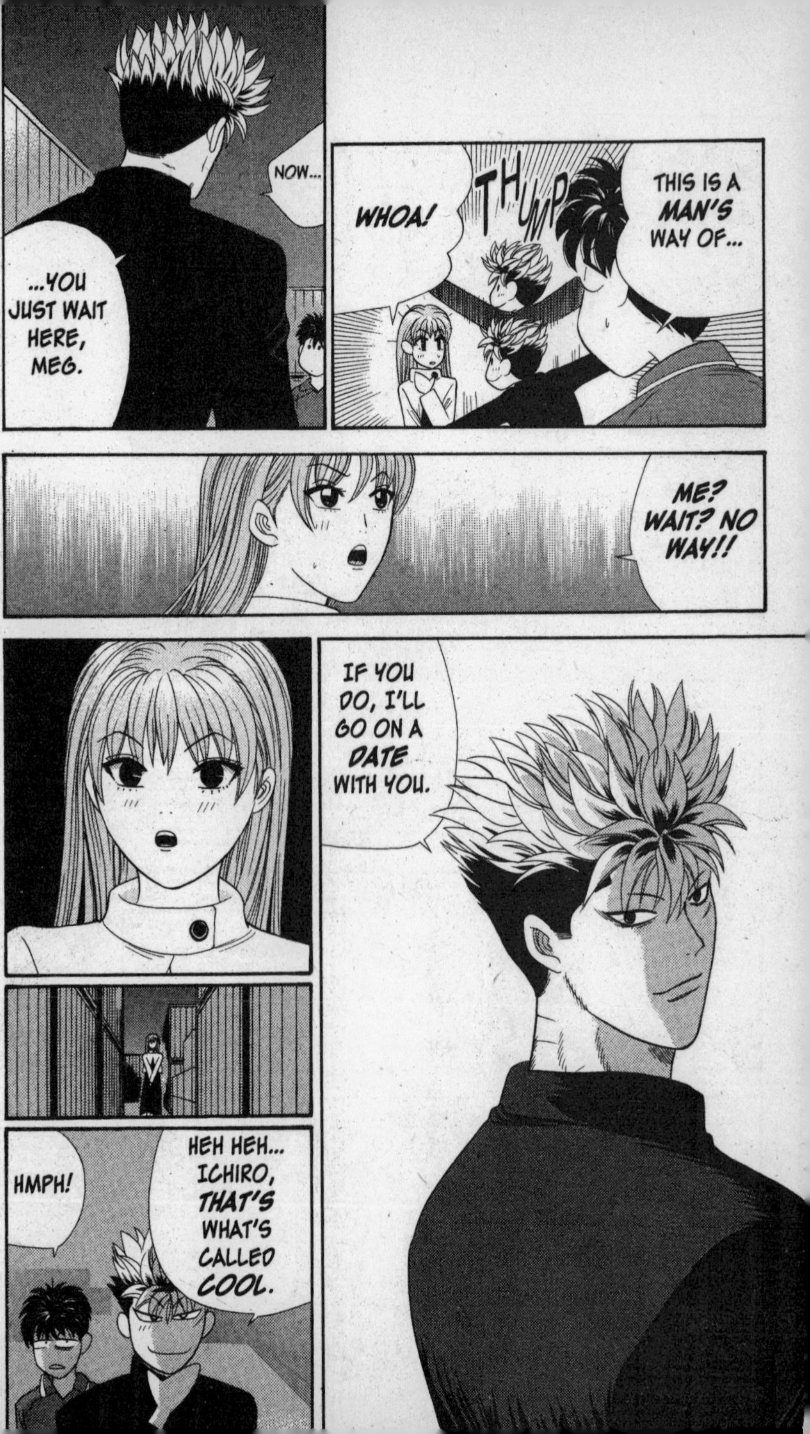
THIS IS A MAN'S WAY OF...
THUMP
WHOA!
NOW...
...YOU JUST WAIT HERE, MEG.
ME? WAIT? NO WAY!!
IF YOU DO, I'LL GO ON A DATE WITH YOU.
HEH HEH... ICHIRO, THAT'S WHAT'S CALLED COOL.
HMPH!

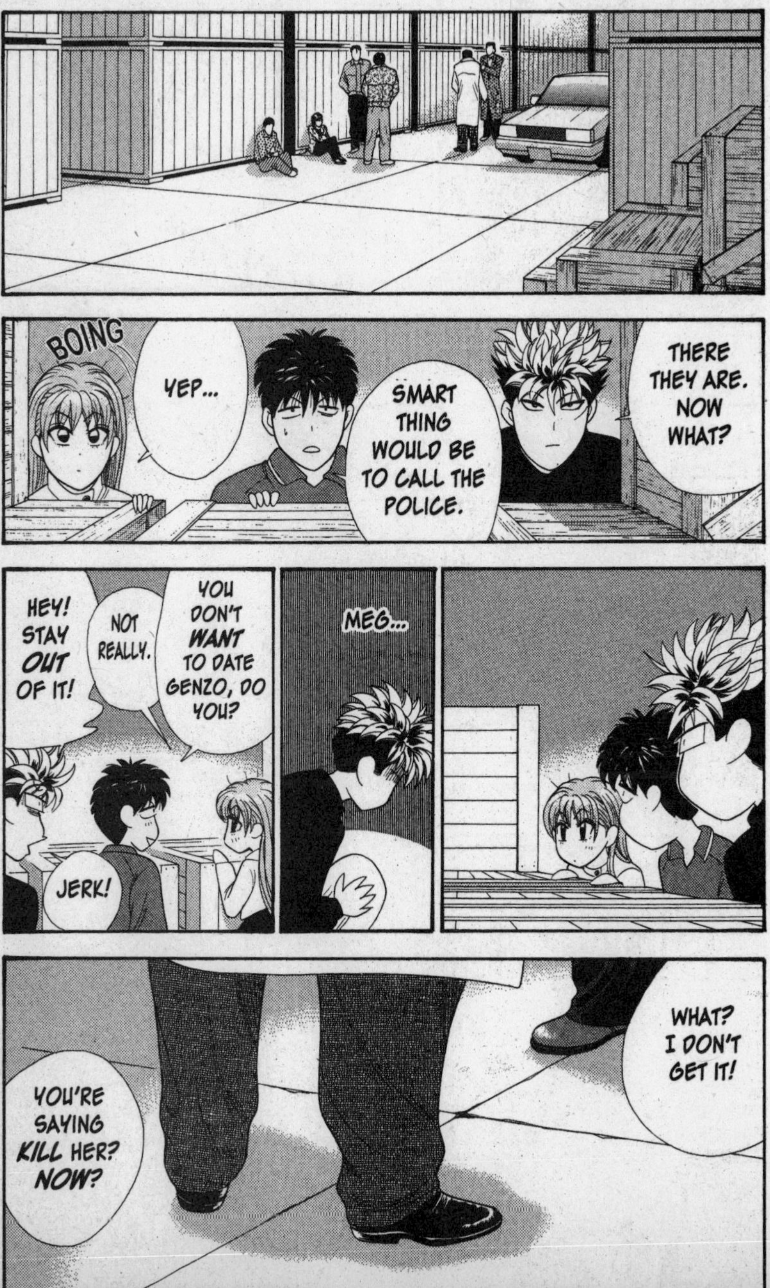
THERE THEY ARE. NOW WHAT?
SMART THING WOULD BE TO CALL THE POLICE.
YEP...
BOING
MEG...
YOU DON'T *WANT* TO DATE GENZO, DO YOU?
NOT REALLY.
HEY! STAY *OUT* OF IT!
JERK!
WHAT? I DON'T GET IT!
YOU'RE SAYING *KILL* HER? *NOW*?

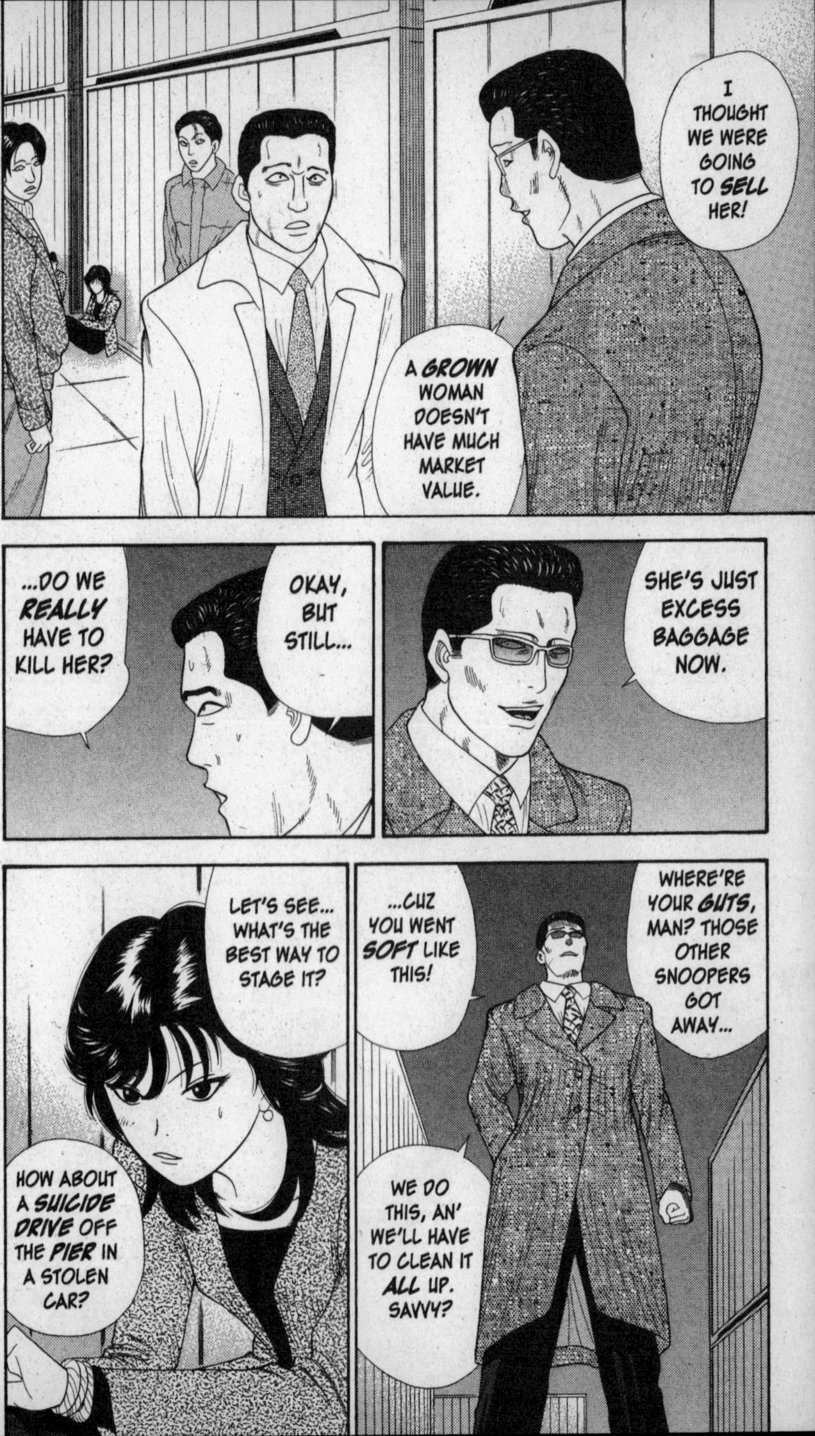
I THOUGHT WE WERE GOING TO SELL HER!
A GROWN WOMAN DOESN'T HAVE MUCH MARKET VALUE.
SHE'S JUST EXCESS BAGGAGE NOW.
OKAY, BUT STILL...
...DO WE REALLY HAVE TO KILL HER?
WHERE'RE YOUR GUTS, MAN? THOSE OTHER SNOOPERS GOT AWAY...
...CUZ YOU WENT SOFT LIKE THIS!
WE DO THIS, AN' WE'LL HAVE TO CLEAN IT ALL UP. SAVVY?
LET'S SEE... WHAT'S THE BEST WAY TO STAGE IT?
HOW ABOUT A SUICIDE DRIVE OFF THE PIER IN A STOLEN CAR?

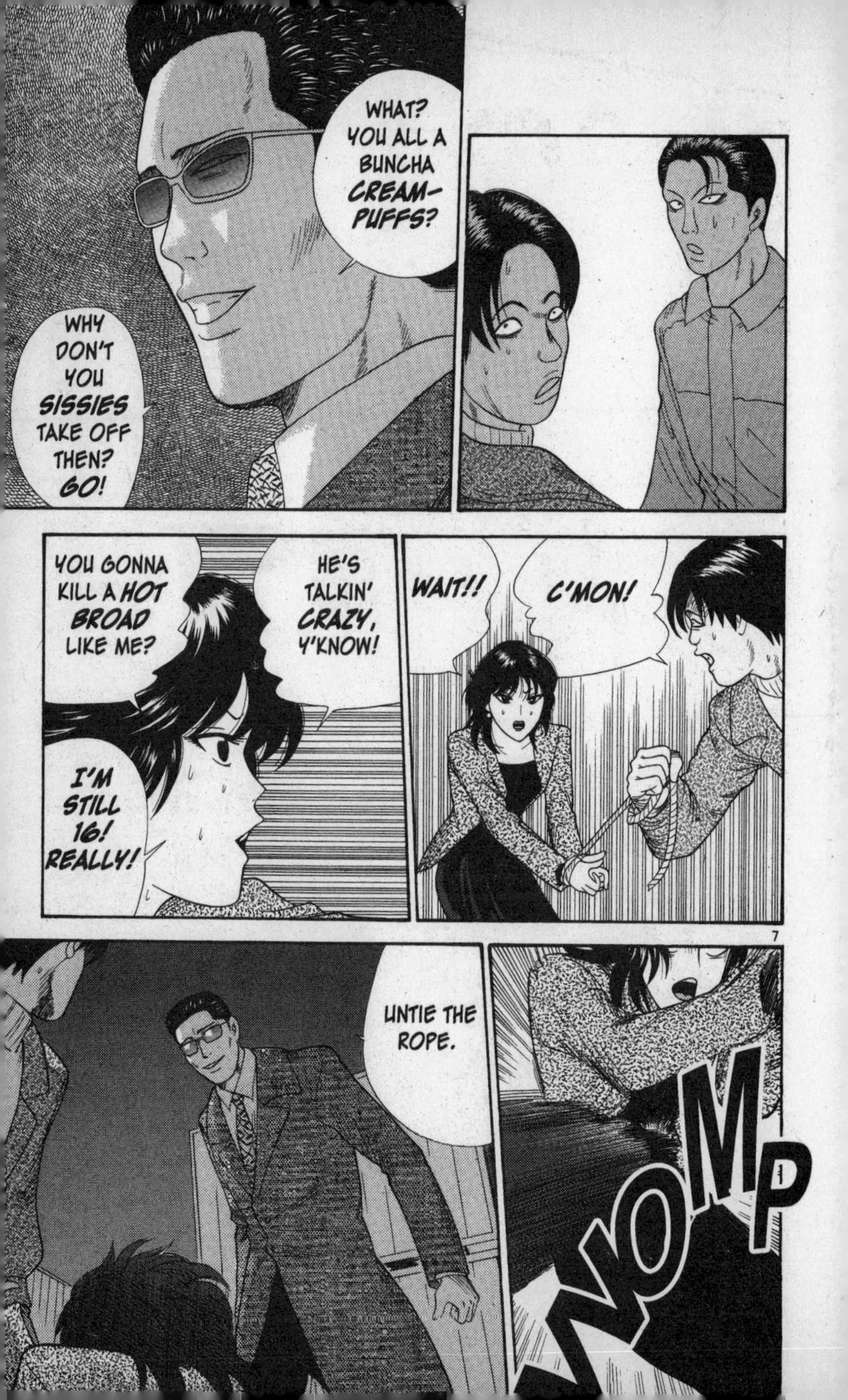
WHAT? YOU ALL A BUNCHA CREAM-PUFFS?
WHY DON'T YOU SISSIES TAKE OFF THEN? GO!
C'MON!
WAIT!!
HE'S TALKIN' CRAZY, Y'KNOW!
YOU GONNA KILL A HOT BROAD LIKE ME?
I'M STILL 16! REALLY!
WOMP
UNTIE THE ROPE.

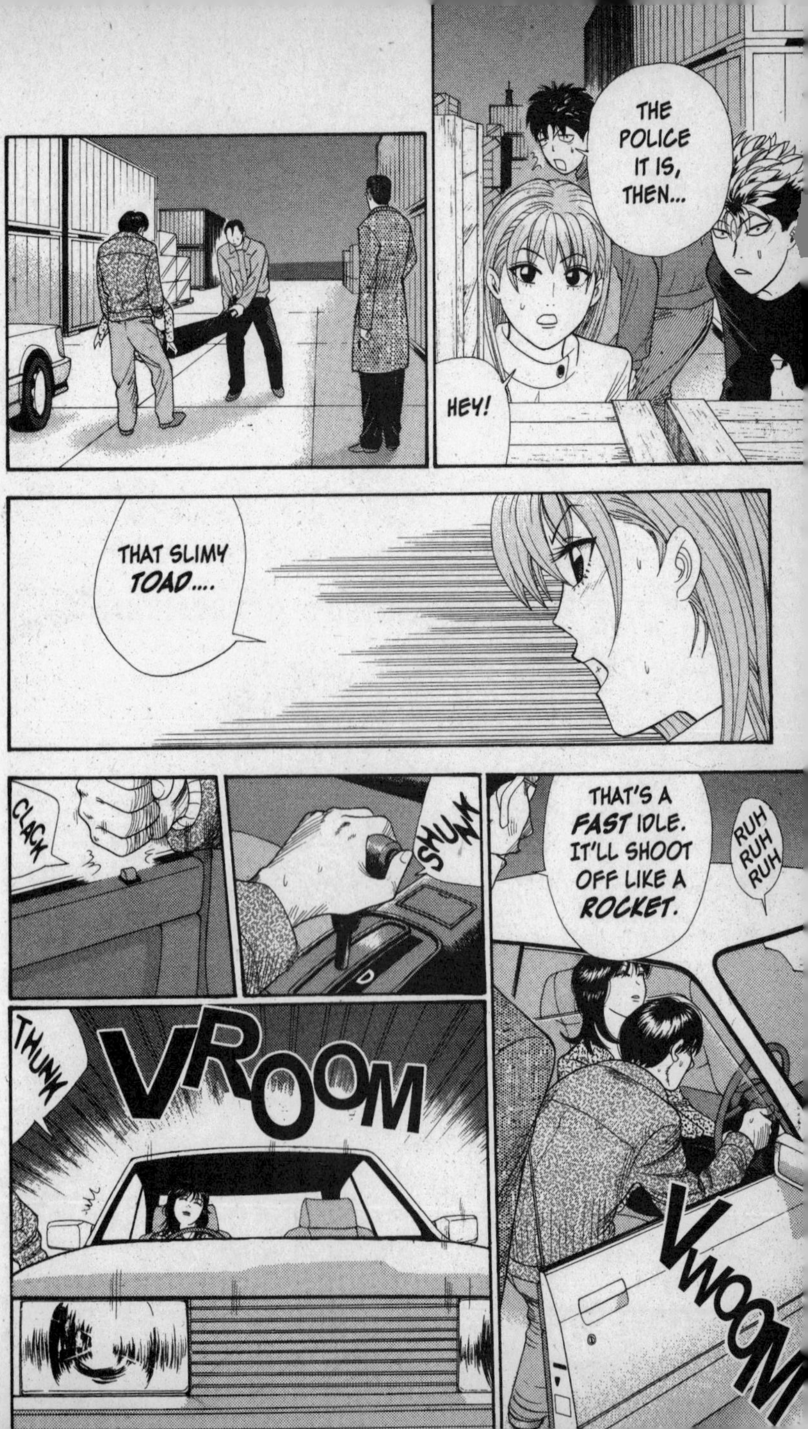
THE POLICE IT IS, THEN...
HEY!
THAT SLIMY TOAD....
THAT'S A FAST IDLE. IT'LL SHOOT OFF LIKE A ROCKET.
RUH RUH RUH
VWOOM
SHUNK
CLACK
THUNK
VROOM

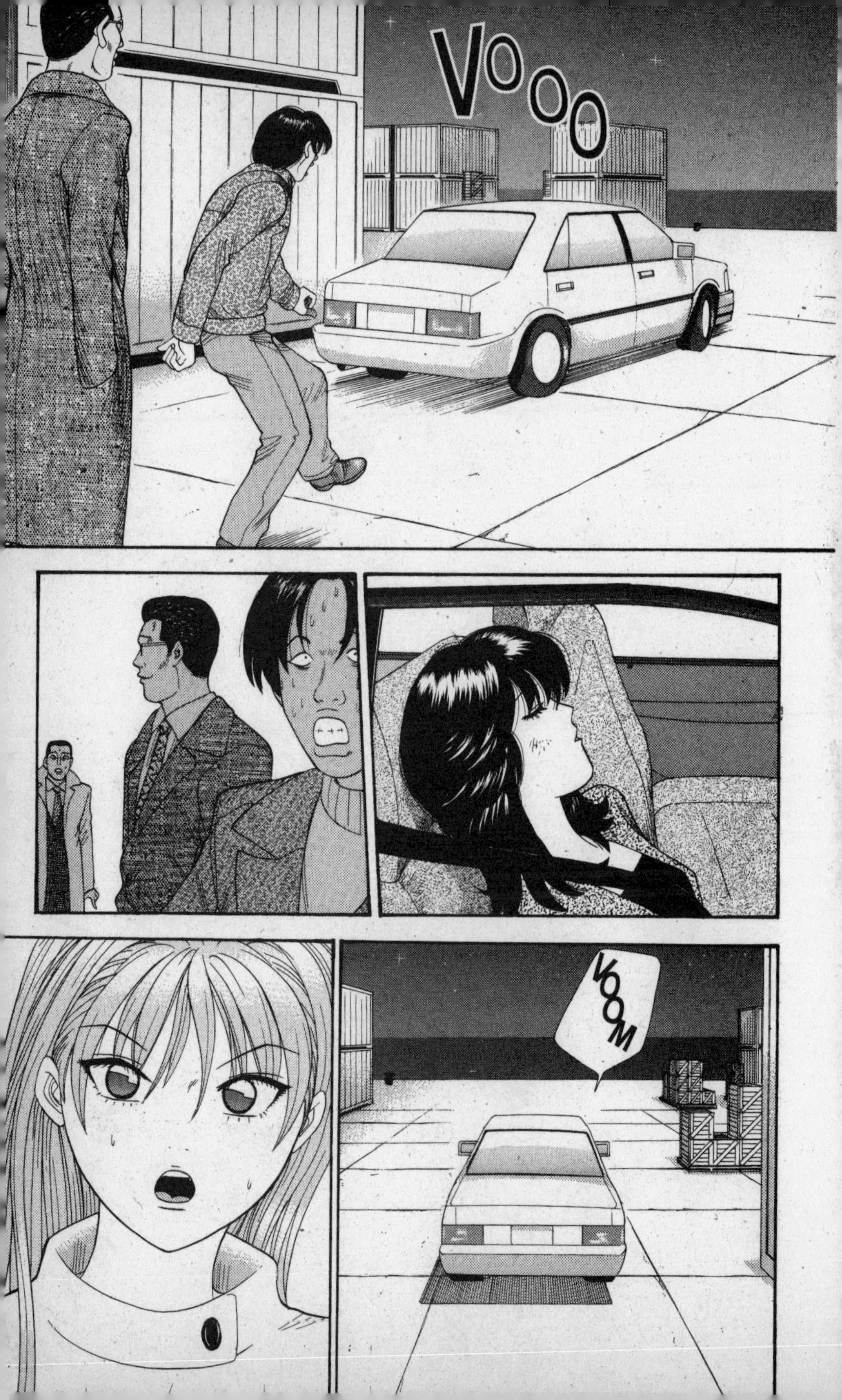
VOOO
VOOM

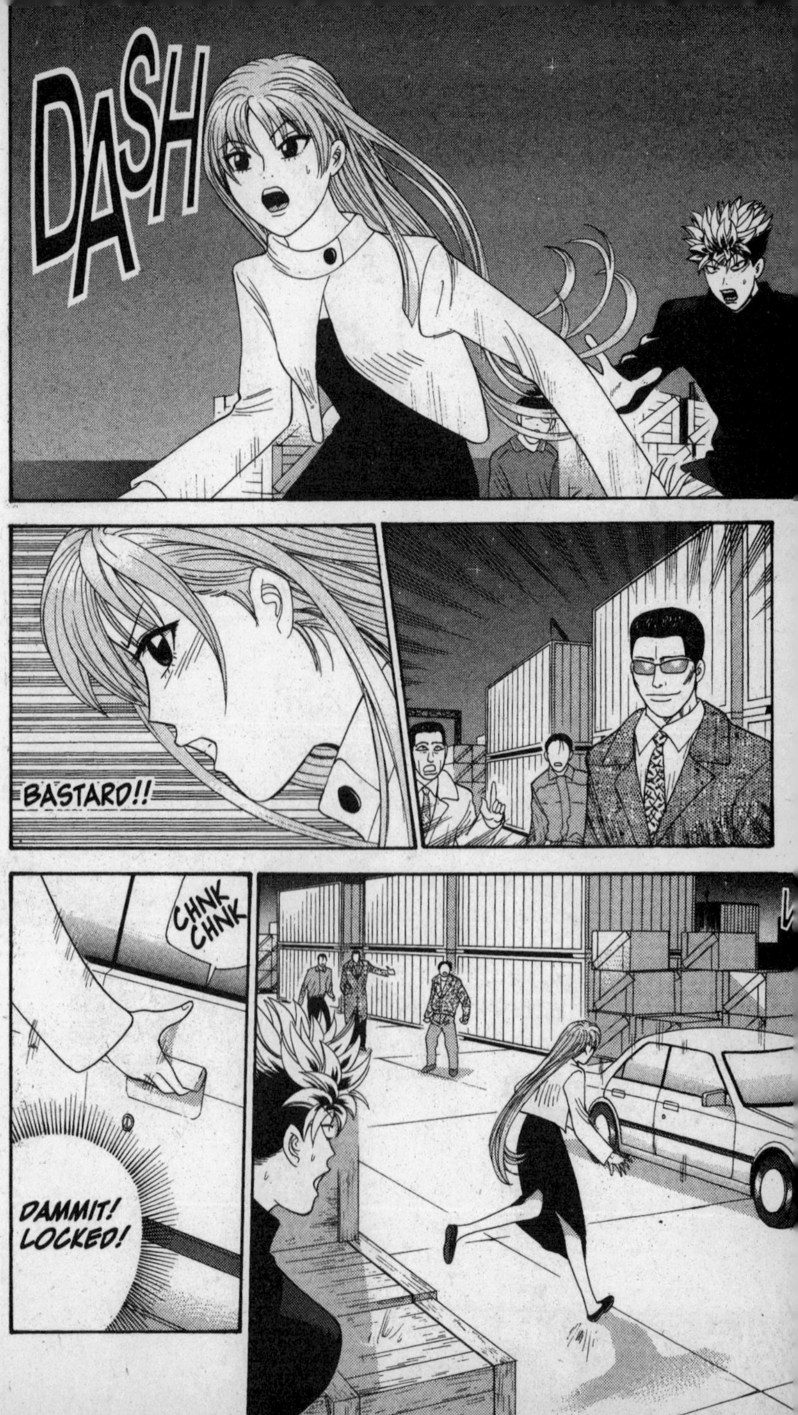
DASH
BASTARD!!
CHNK CHNK
DAMMIT! LOCKED!

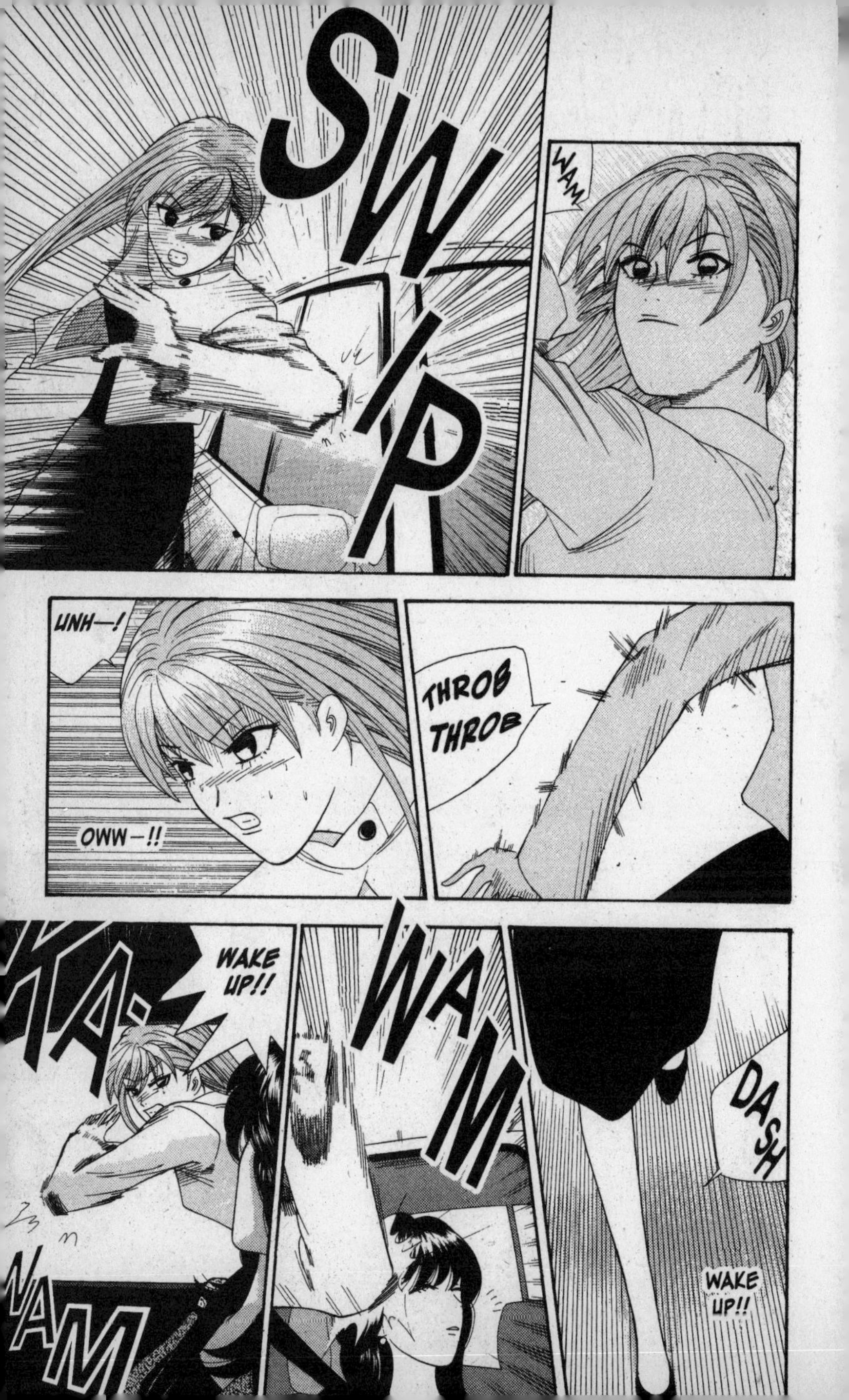
WAM
SWIP
THROB THROB
UNH—!
OWW—!!
DASH
WAKE UP!!
WAM
KA-
WAKE UP!!
WAM

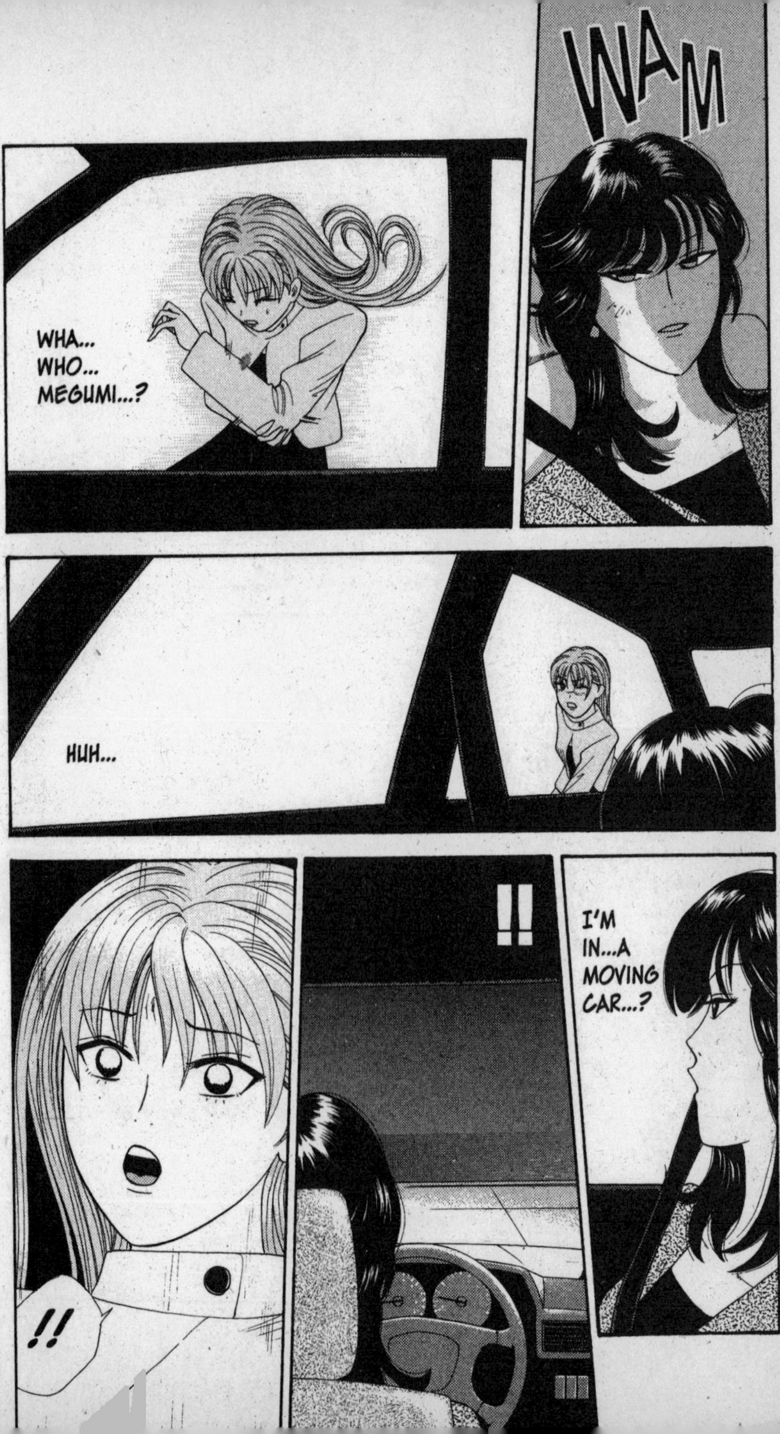
WAM
WHA... WHO... MEGUMI...?
HUH...
I'M IN...A MOVING CAR...?
!!
!!

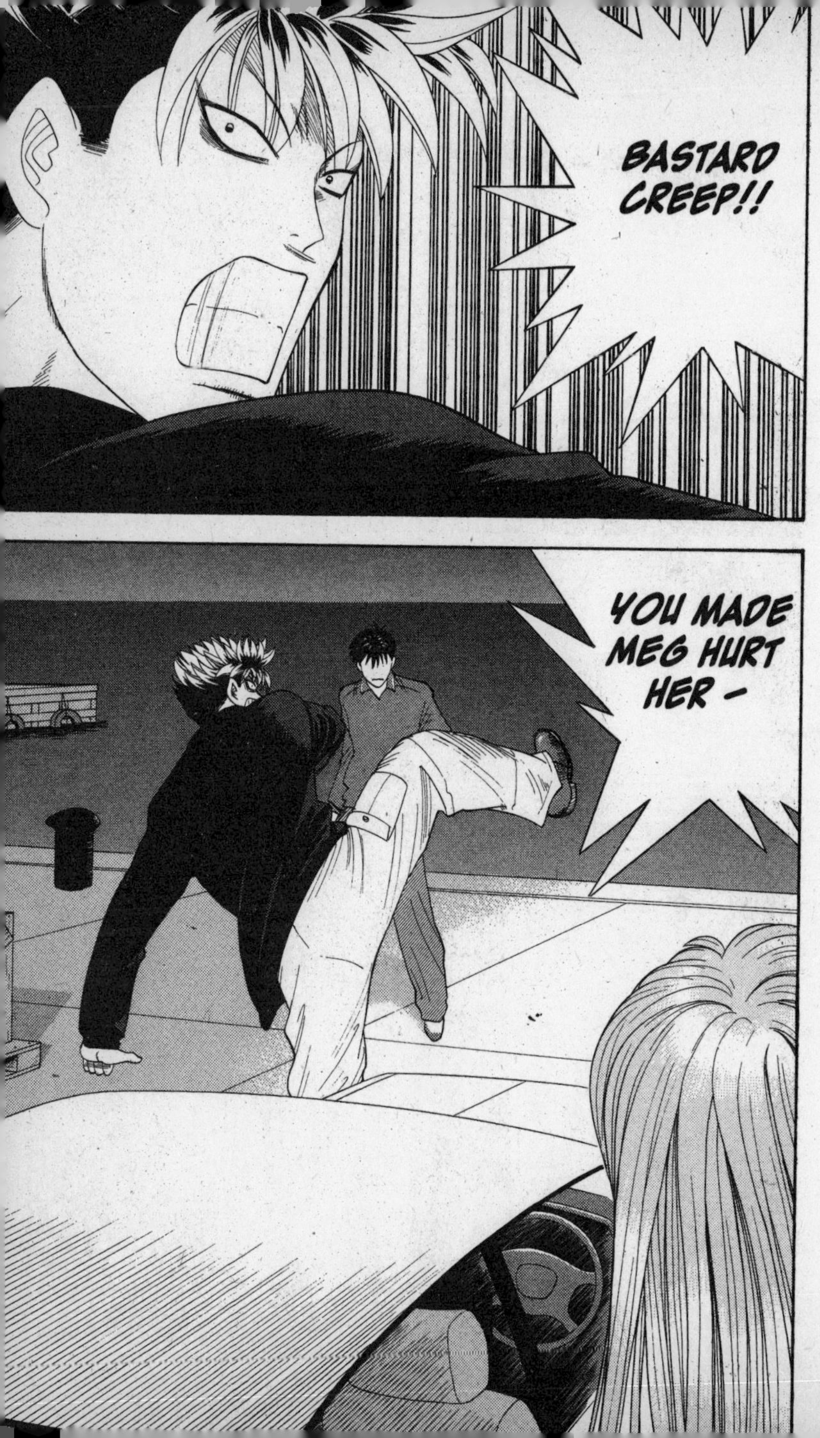
BASTARD CREEP!!
YOU MADE MEG HURT HER -

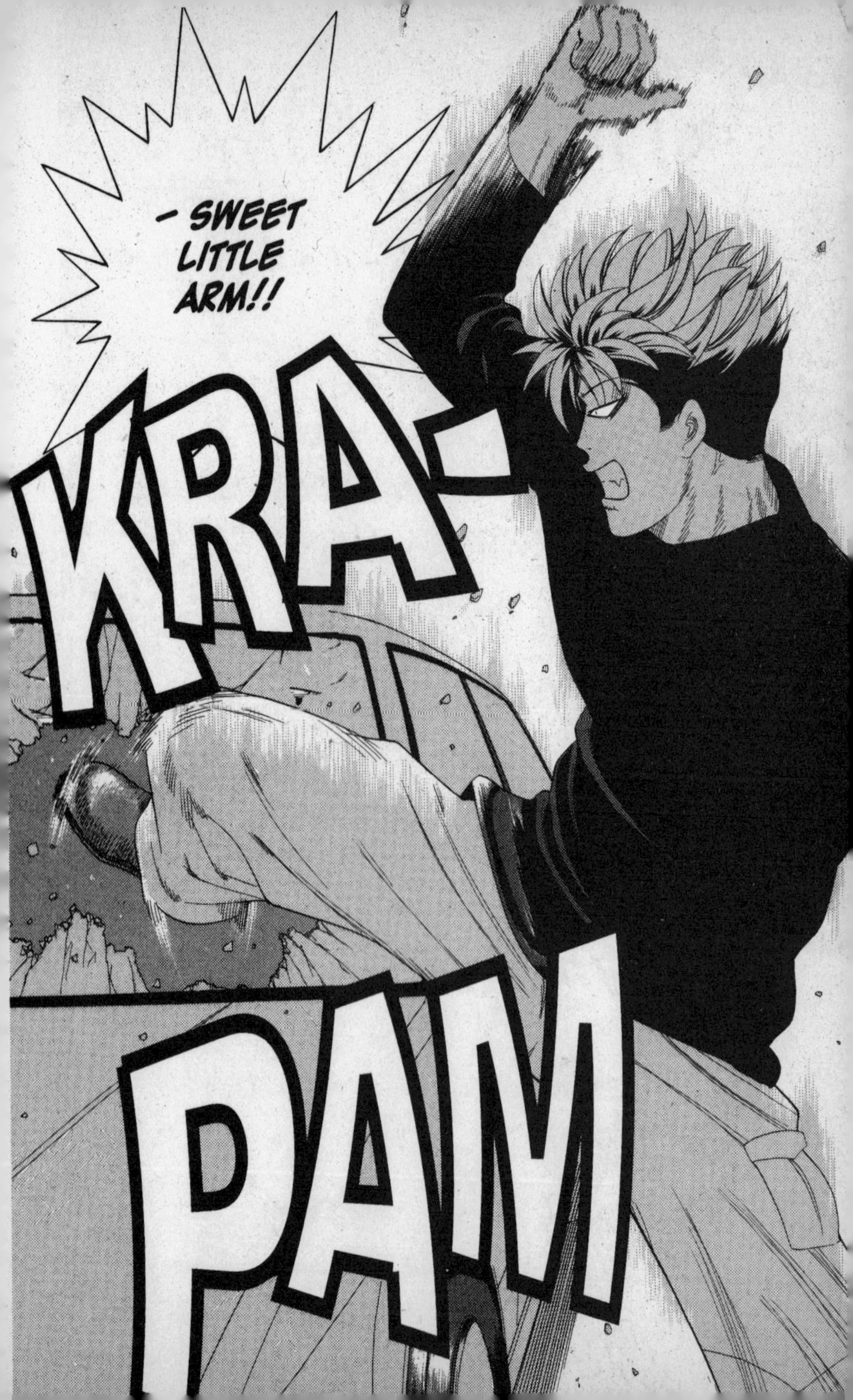
- SWEET LITTLE ARM!!
KRA-
PAM

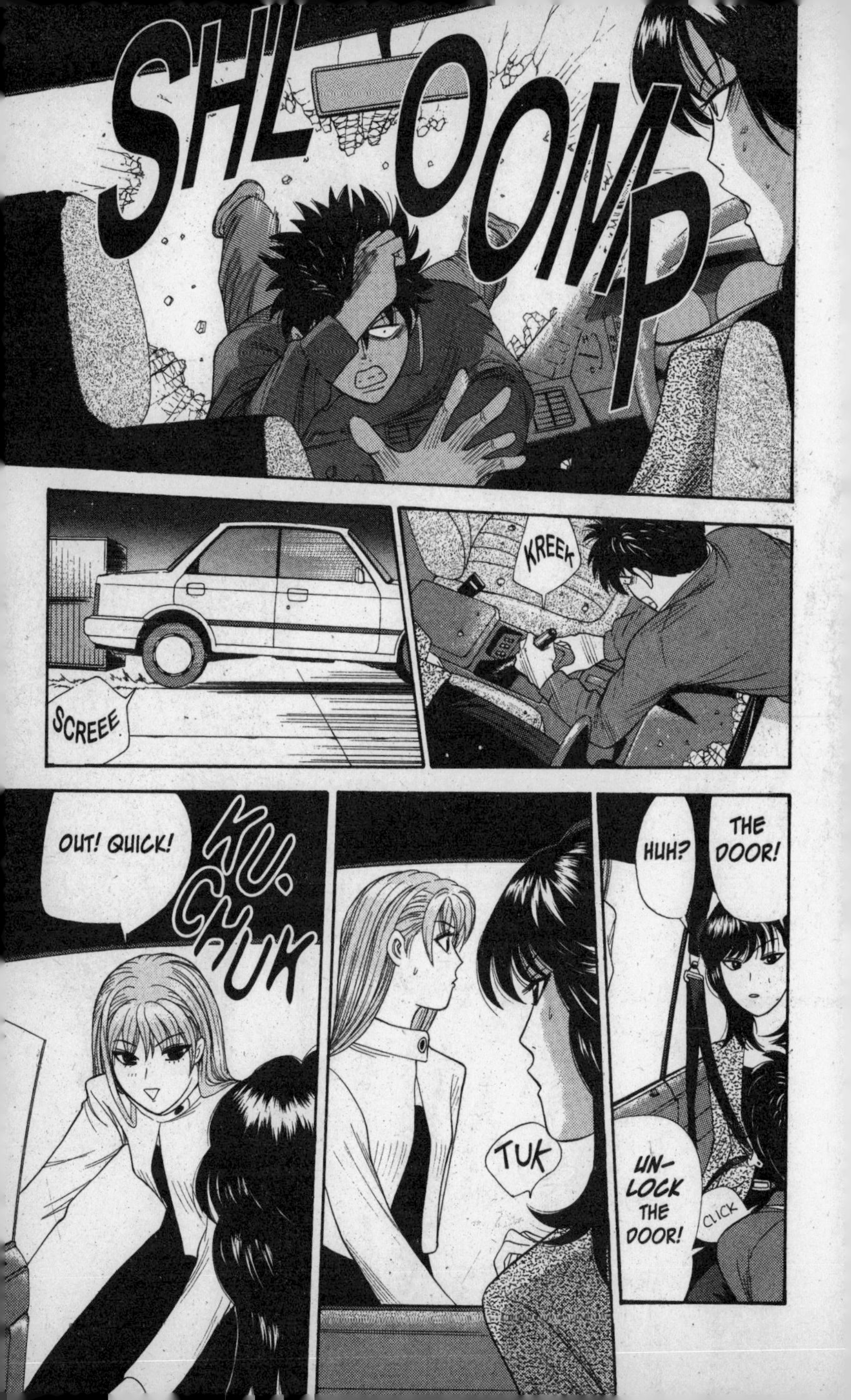
SHL'OOMP
KREEK
SCREEE
THE DOOR!
HUH?
UN-LOCK THE DOOR!
CLICK
TUK
KU-CHUK
OUT! QUICK!

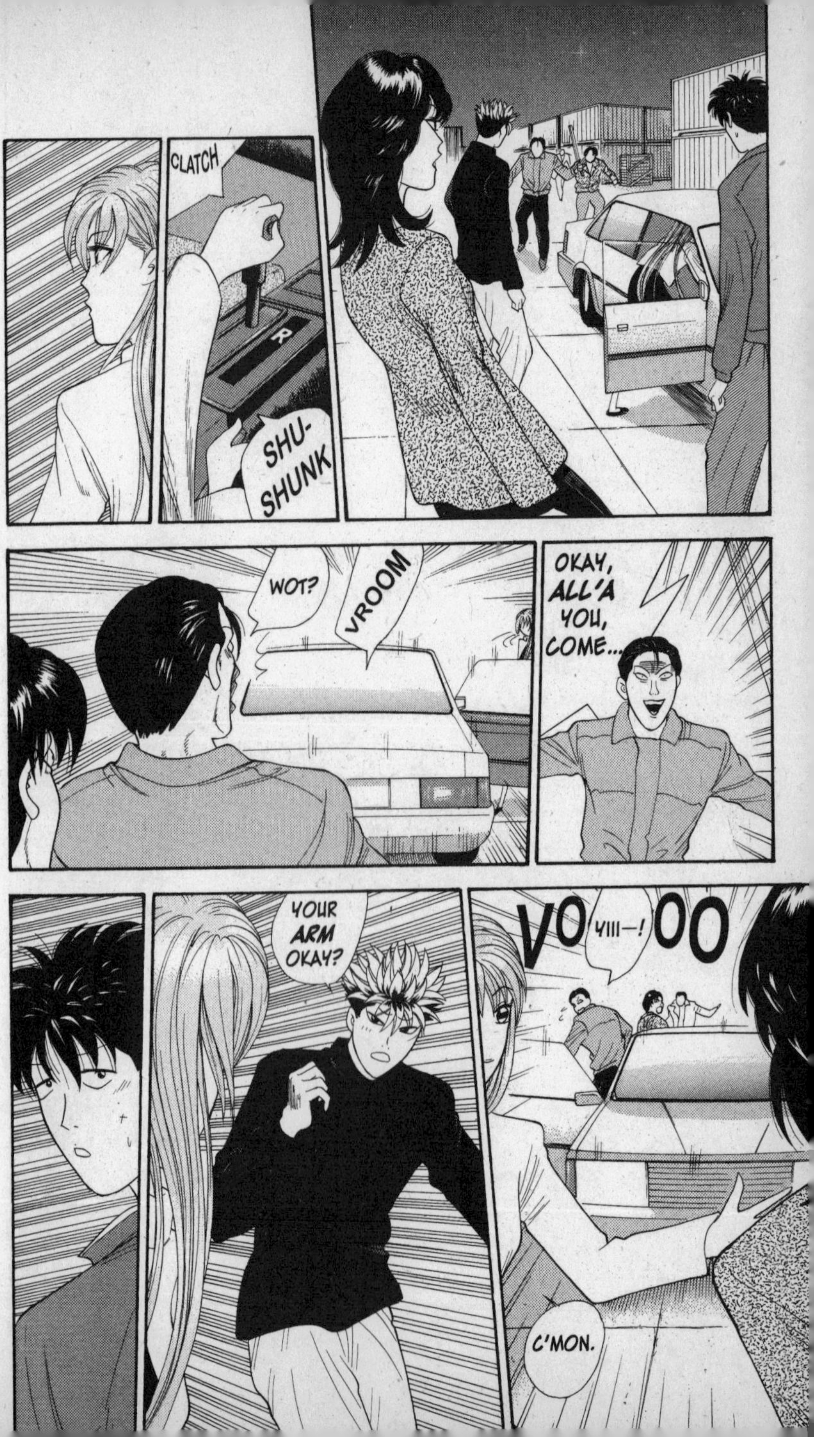
CLATCH
SHU-SHUNK
OKAY, ALL'A YOU, COME...
WOT?
VROOM
VOOO
YIII—!
C'MON.
YOUR ARM OKAY?

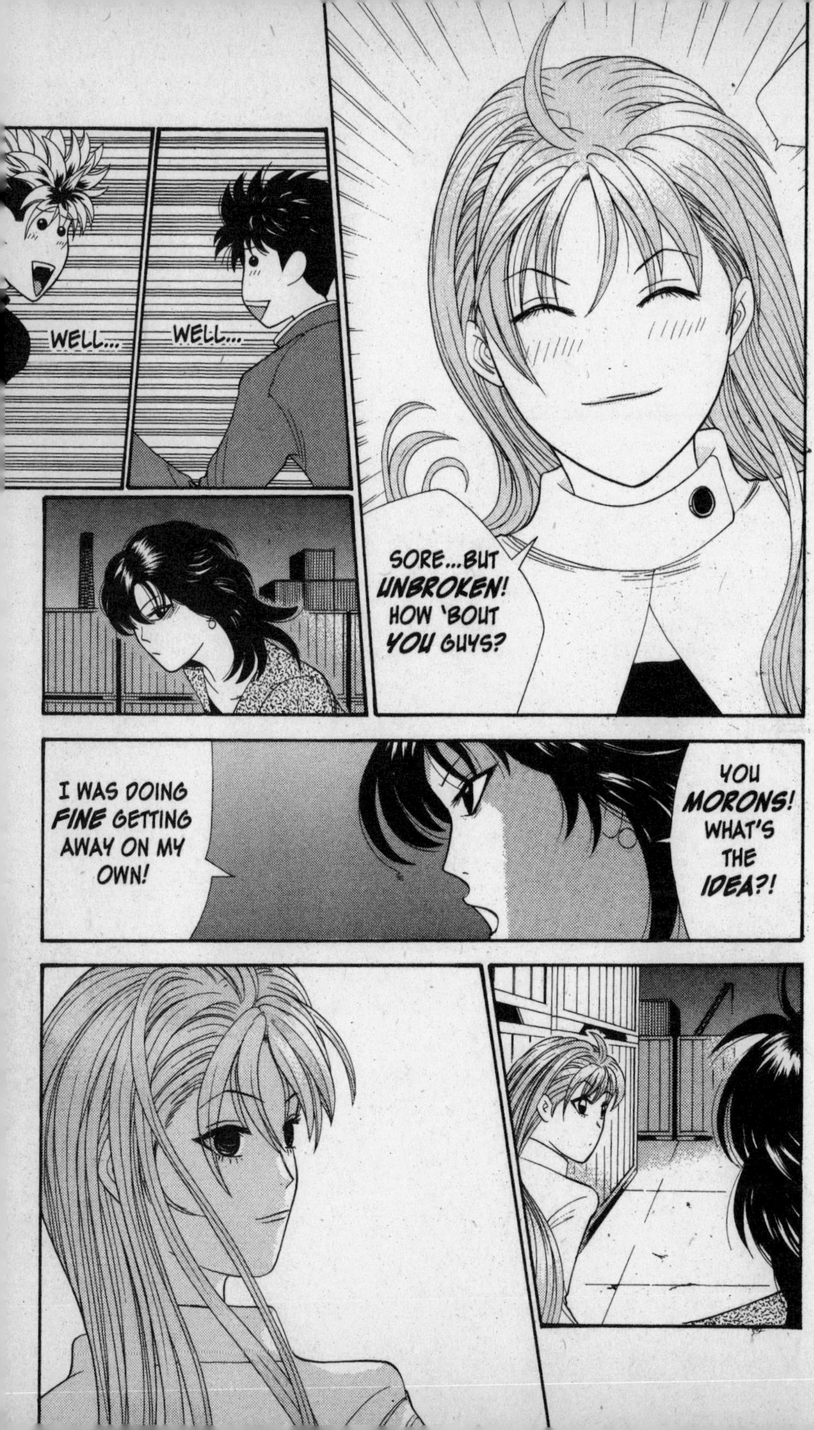
SORE...BUT UNBROKEN! HOW 'BOUT YOU GUYS?
WELL...
WELL...
YOU MORONS! WHAT'S THE IDEA?!
I WAS DOING FINE GETTING AWAY ON MY OWN!

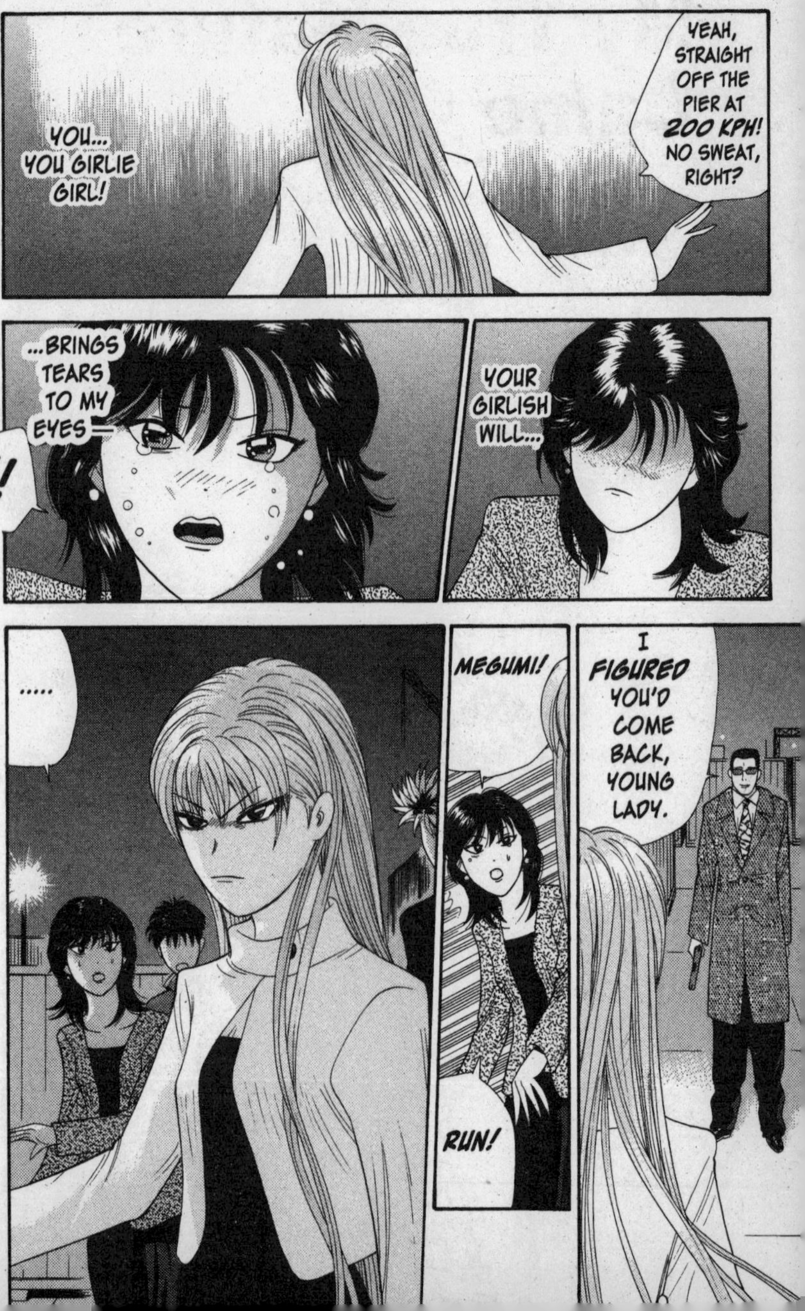
YEAH, STRAIGHT OFF THE PIER AT 200 KPH! NO SWEAT, RIGHT?
YOU... YOU GIRLIE GIRL!
YOUR GIRLISH WILL...
...BRINGS TEARS TO MY EYES
!!
I FIGURED YOU'D COME BACK, YOUNG LADY.
MEGUMI!
RUN!
.....

Chapter 41: My True Nature Came Out!

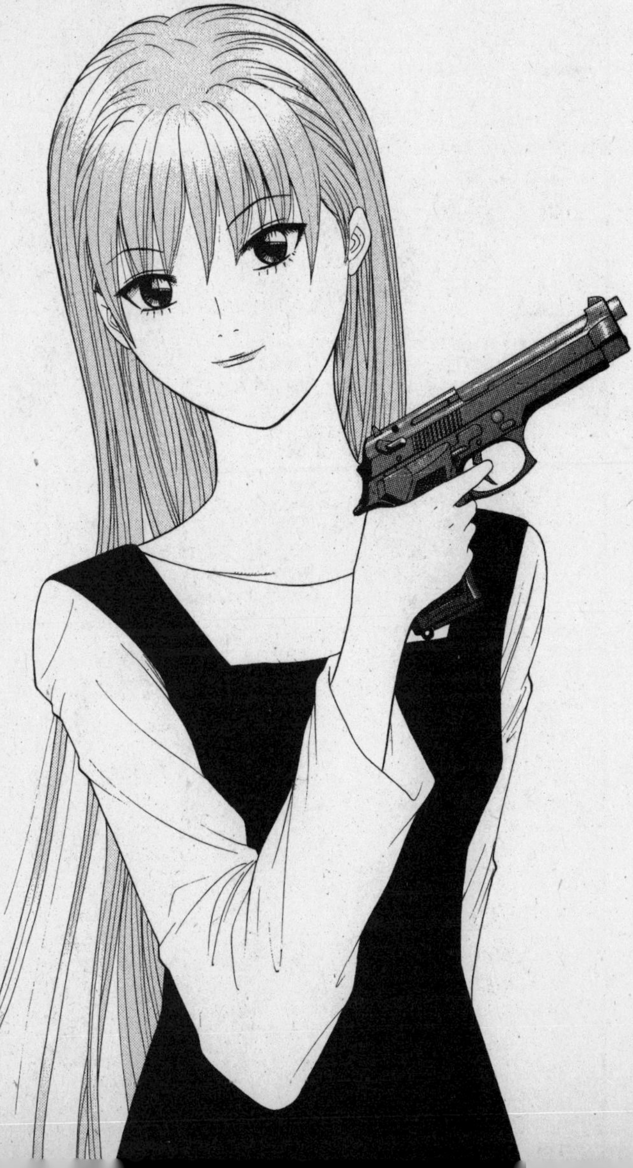

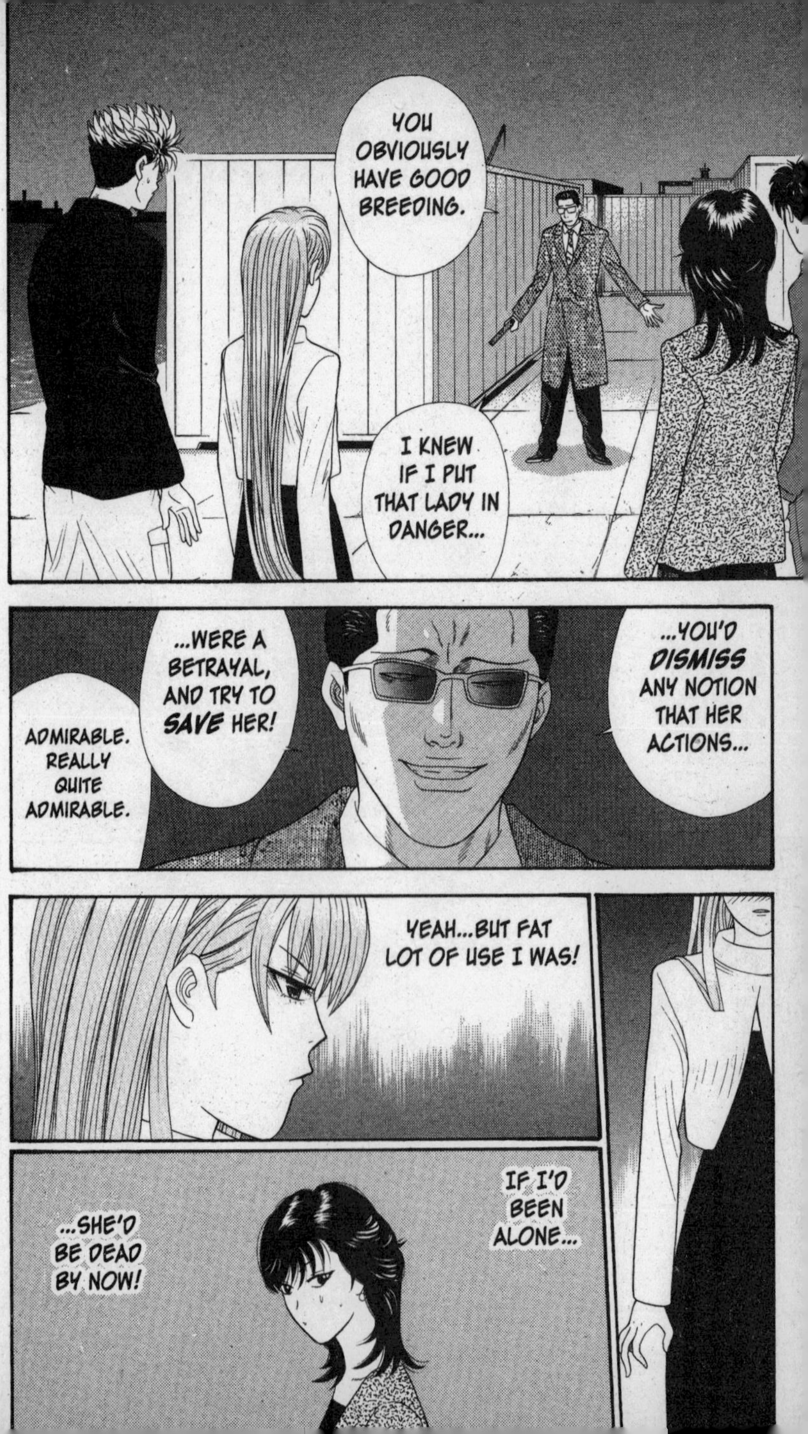
YOU OBVIOUSLY HAVE GOOD BREEDING.
I KNEW IF I PUT THAT LADY IN DANGER...
...YOU'D DISMISS ANY NOTION THAT HER ACTIONS...
...WERE A BETRAYAL, AND TRY TO SAVE HER!
ADMIRABLE. REALLY QUITE ADMIRABLE.
YEAH...BUT FAT LOT OF USE I WAS!
IF I'D BEEN ALONE...
...SHE'D BE DEAD BY NOW!

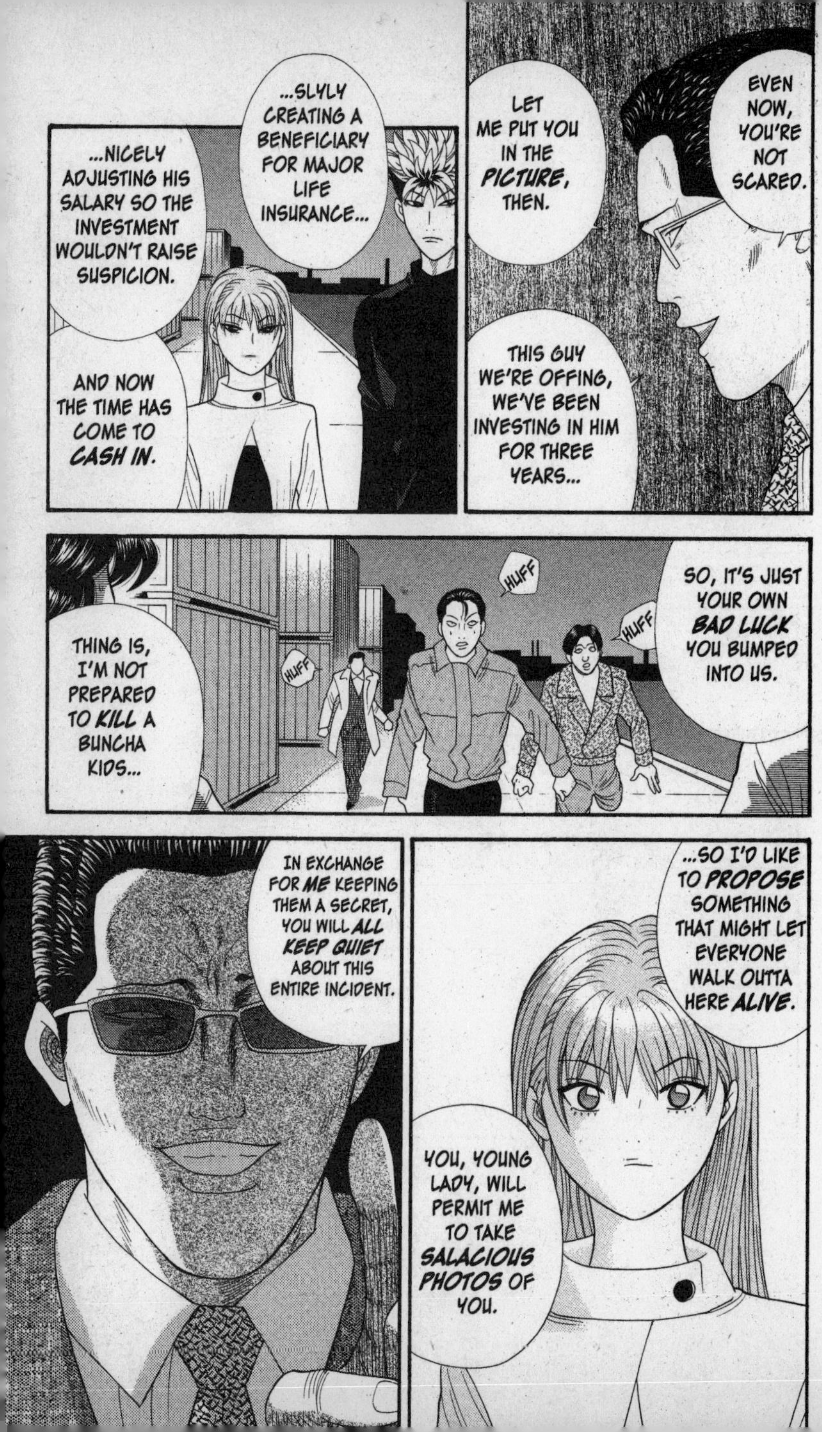
EVEN NOW, YOU'RE NOT SCARED.
LET ME PUT YOU IN THE PICTURE, THEN.
THIS GUY WE'RE OFFING, WE'VE BEEN INVESTING IN HIM FOR THREE YEARS...
...SLYLY CREATING A BENEFICIARY FOR MAJOR LIFE INSURANCE...
...NICELY ADJUSTING HIS SALARY SO THE INVESTMENT WOULDN'T RAISE SUSPICION.
AND NOW THE TIME HAS COME TO CASH IN.
SO, IT'S JUST YOUR OWN BAD LUCK YOU BUMPED INTO US.
HUFF
HUFF
HUFF
THING IS, I'M NOT PREPARED TO KILL A BUNCHA KIDS...
...SO I'D LIKE TO PROPOSE SOMETHING THAT MIGHT LET EVERYONE WALK OUTTA HERE ALIVE.
YOU, YOUNG LADY, WILL PERMIT ME TO TAKE SALACIOUS PHOTOS OF YOU.
IN EXCHANGE FOR ME KEEPING THEM A SECRET, YOU WILL ALL KEEP QUIET ABOUT THIS ENTIRE INCIDENT.

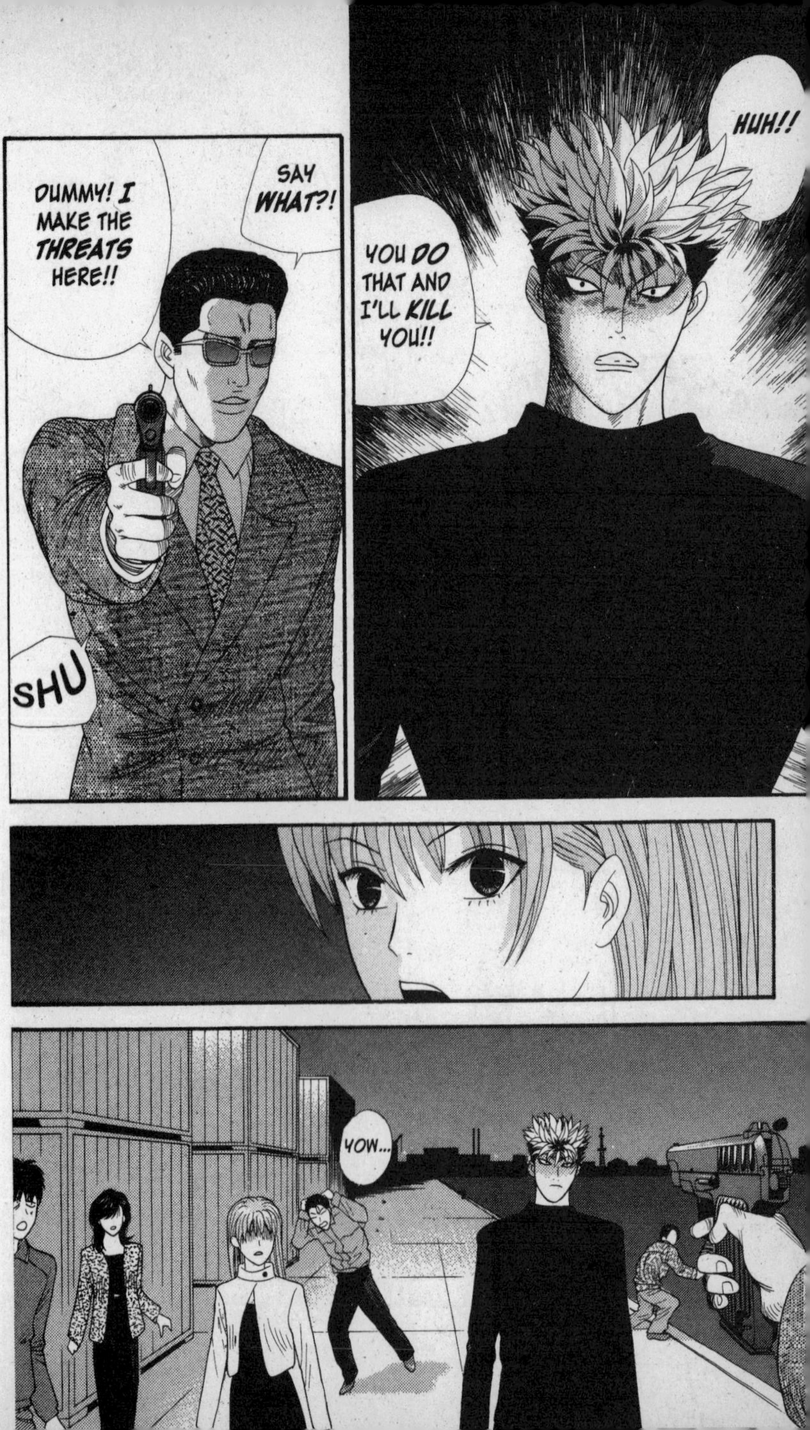
HUH!!
YOU DO THAT AND I'LL KILL YOU!!
SAY WHAT?!
DUMMY! I MAKE THE THREATS HERE!!
SHU
YOW...

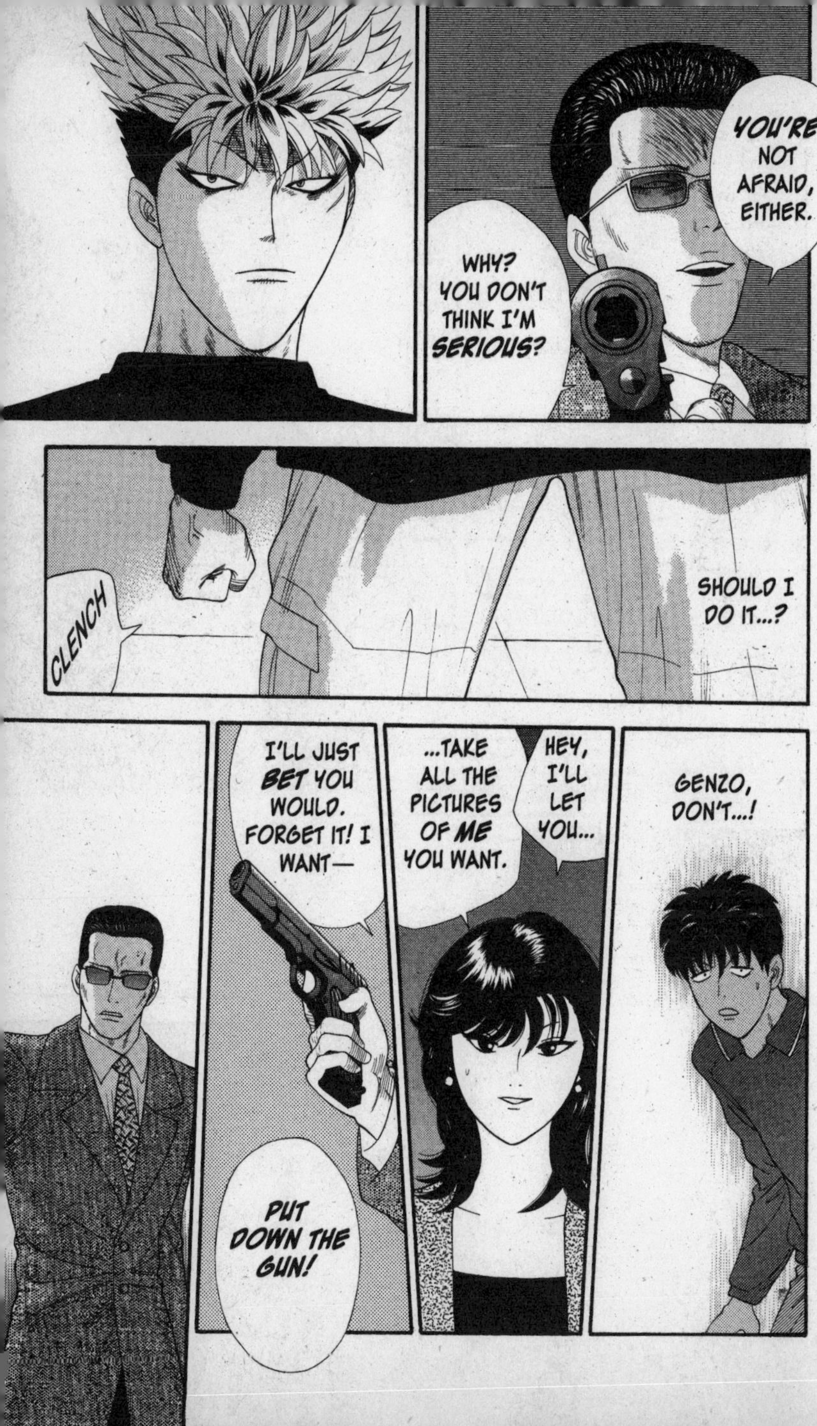
YOU'RE NOT AFRAID, EITHER.
WHY? YOU DON'T THINK I'M SERIOUS?
SHOULD I DO IT...?
CLENCH
GENZO, DON'T...!
HEY, I'LL LET YOU...
...TAKE ALL THE PICTURES OF ME YOU WANT.
I'LL JUST BET YOU WOULD. FORGET IT! I WANT—
PUT DOWN THE GUN!

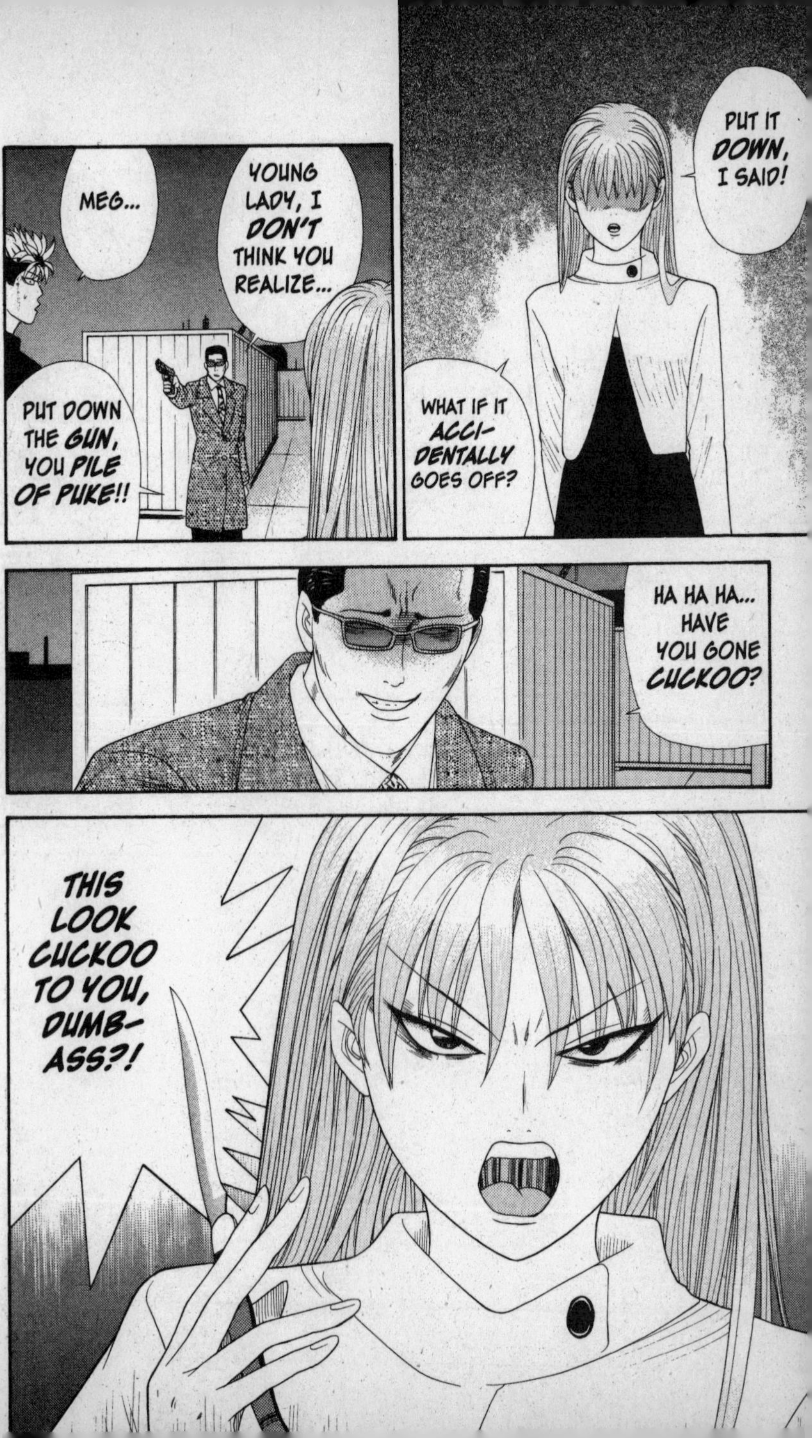
MEG...
PUT DOWN THE GUN, YOU PILE OF PUKE!!
YOUNG LADY, I DON'T THINK YOU REALIZE...
WHAT IF IT ACCI-DENTALLY GOES OFF?
PUT IT DOWN, I SAID!
HA HA HA... HAVE YOU GONE CUCKOO?
THIS LOOK CUCKOO TO YOU, DUMB-ASS?!

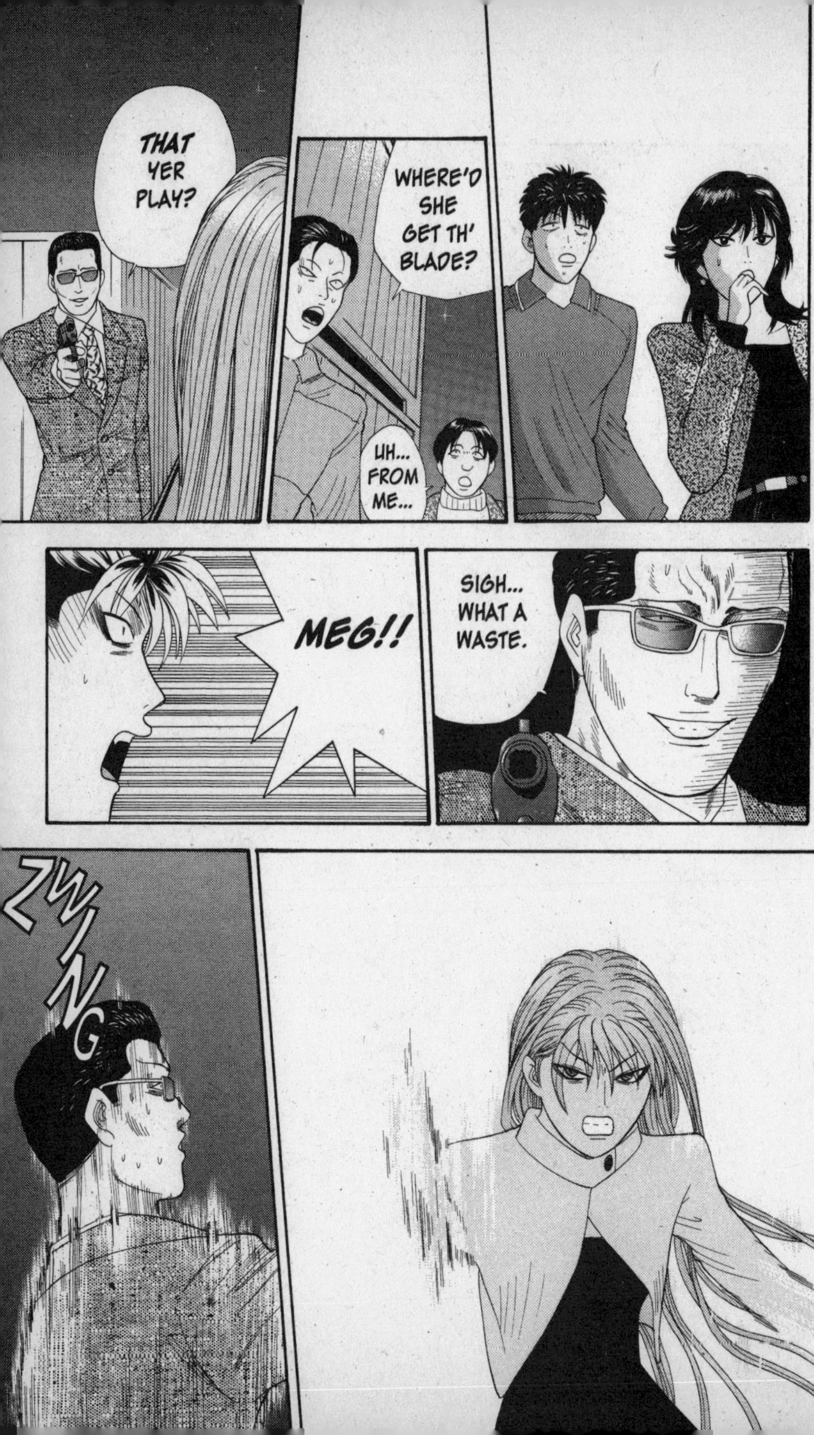
WHERE'D SHE GET TH' BLADE?
UH... FROM ME...
THAT YER PLAY?
SIGH... WHAT A WASTE.
MEG!!
ZWING

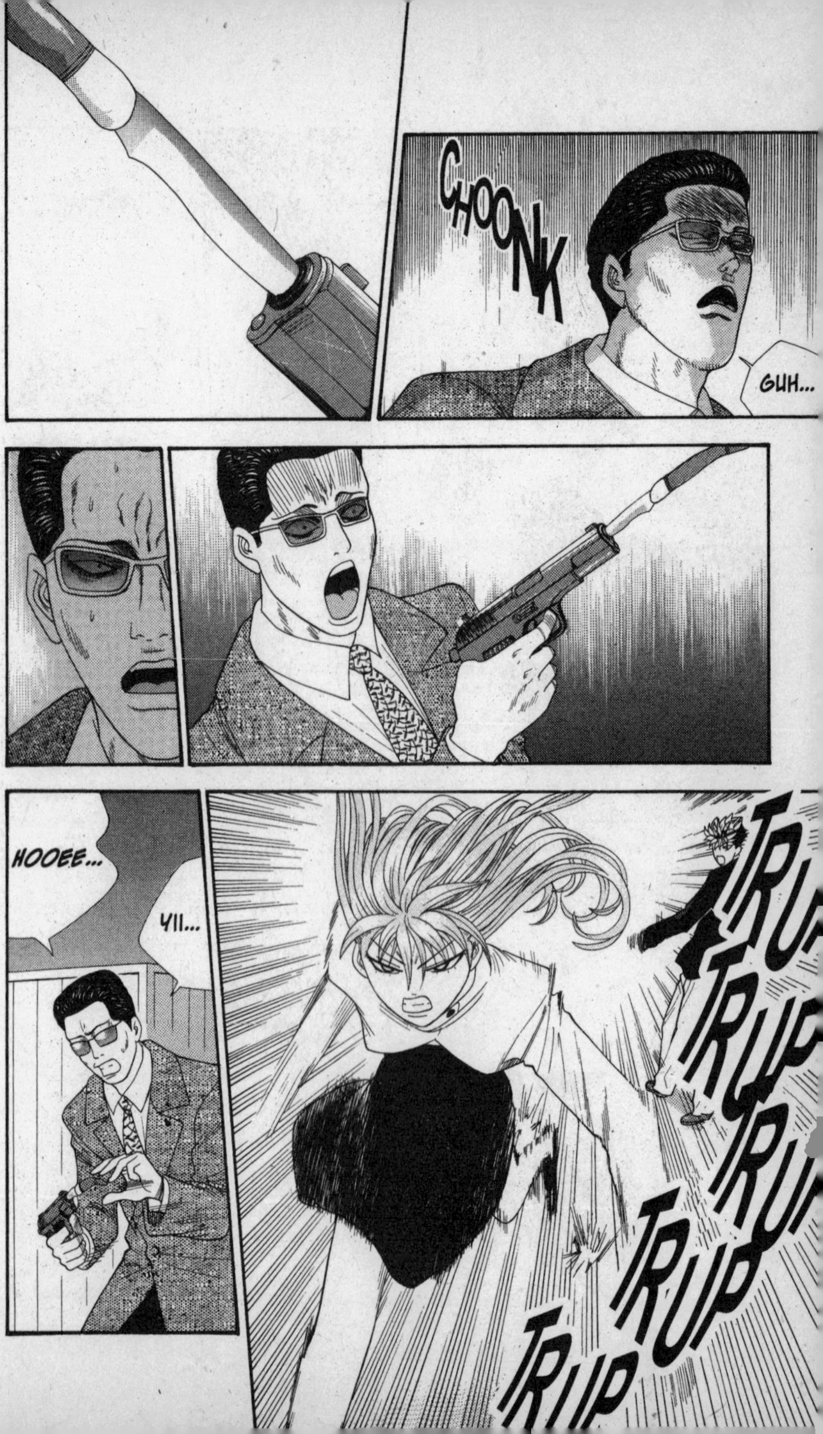
CHOONK
GUH...
HOOEE...
YII...
TRUP TRUP TRUP TRUP TRUP TRUP

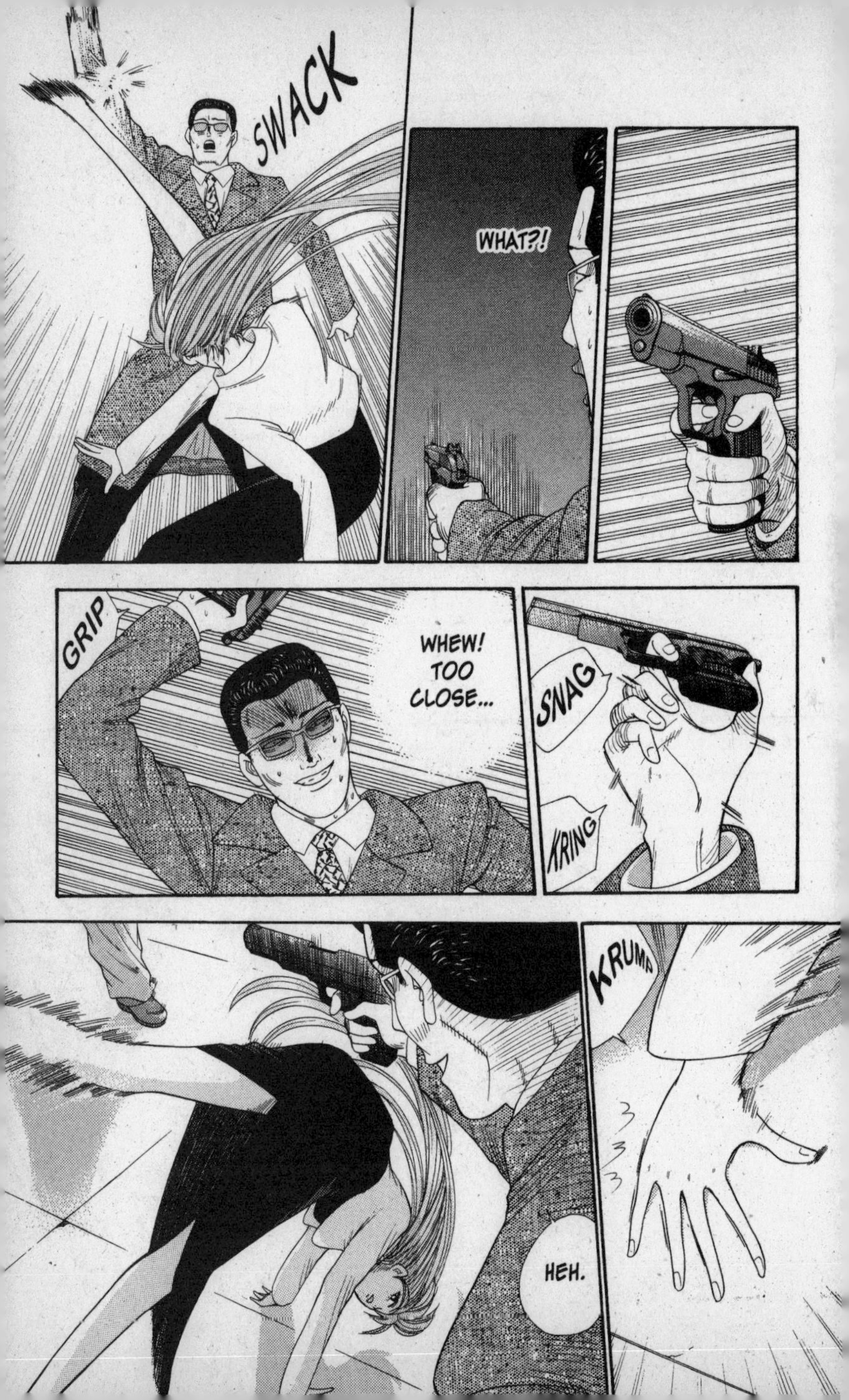
WHAT?!
SWACK
SNAG
KRING
GRIP
WHEW! TOO CLOSE...
KRUMP
HEH.

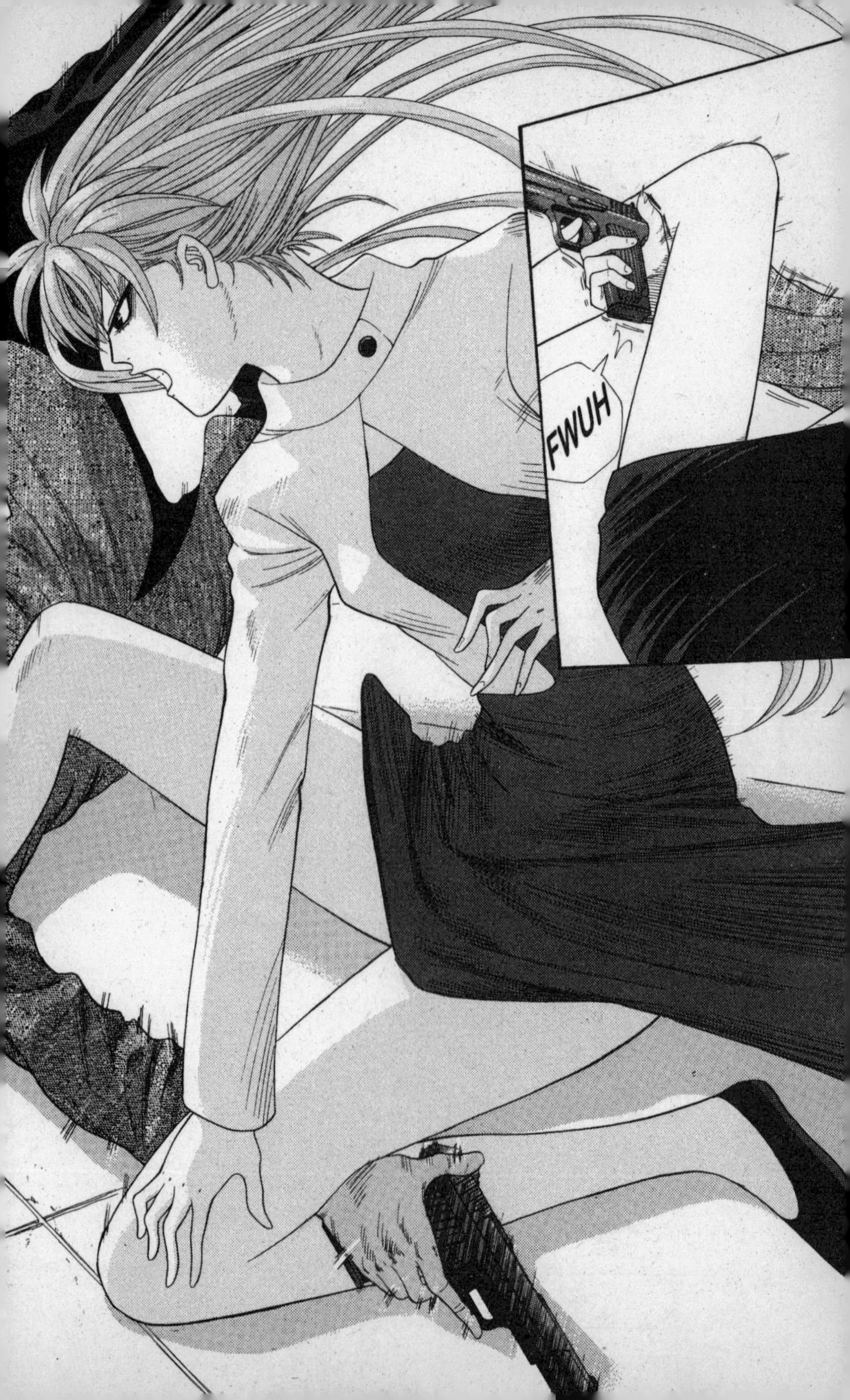
FWUH

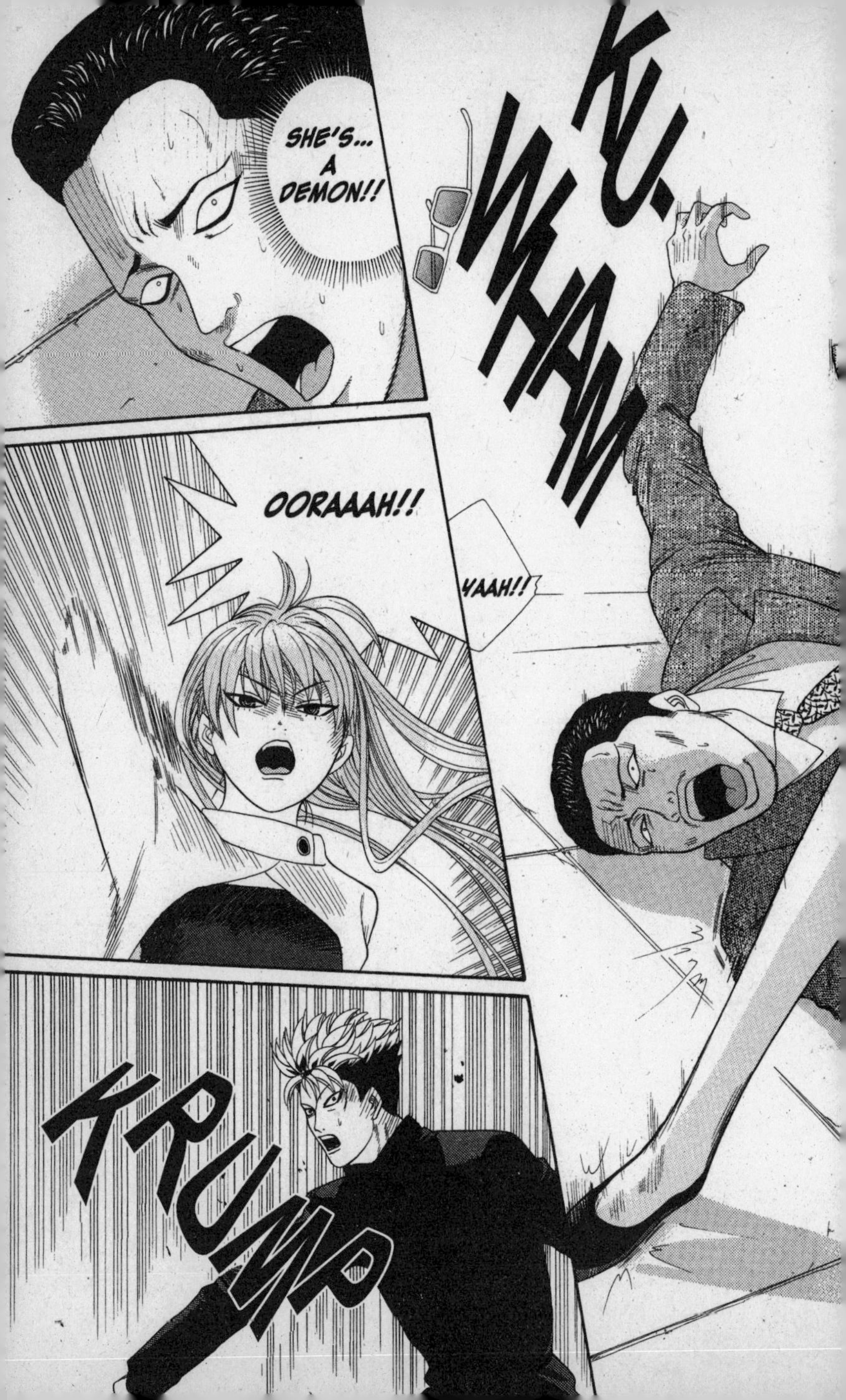
KU-WHAM
YAAH!!
SHE'S... A DEMON!!
OORAAAH!!
KRUMP

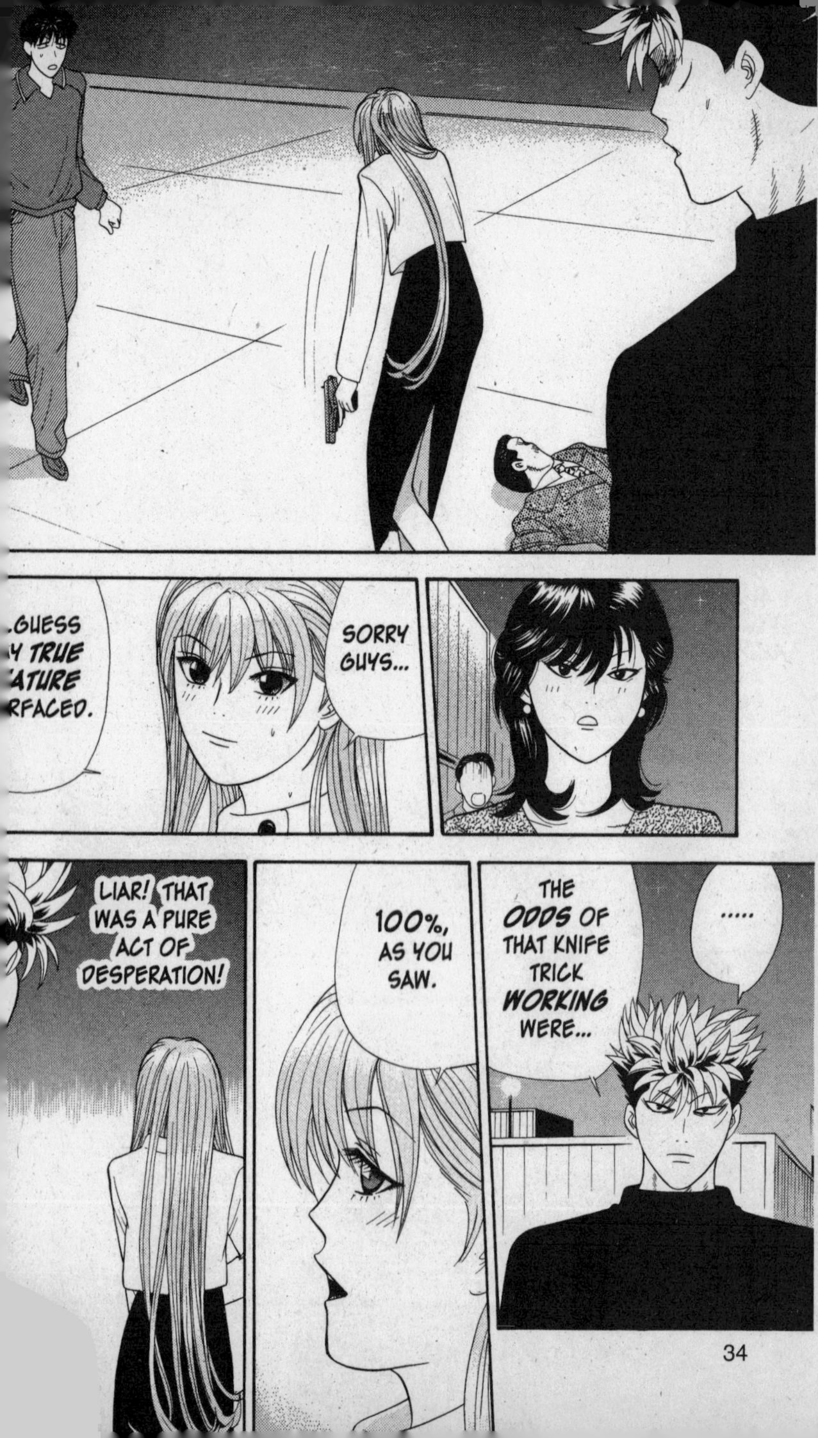
SORRY GUYS...
.GUESS Y TRUE ATURE RFACED.
.....
THE ODDS OF THAT KNIFE TRICK WORKING WERE...
100%, AS YOU SAW.
LIAR! THAT WAS A PURE ACT OF DESPERATION!

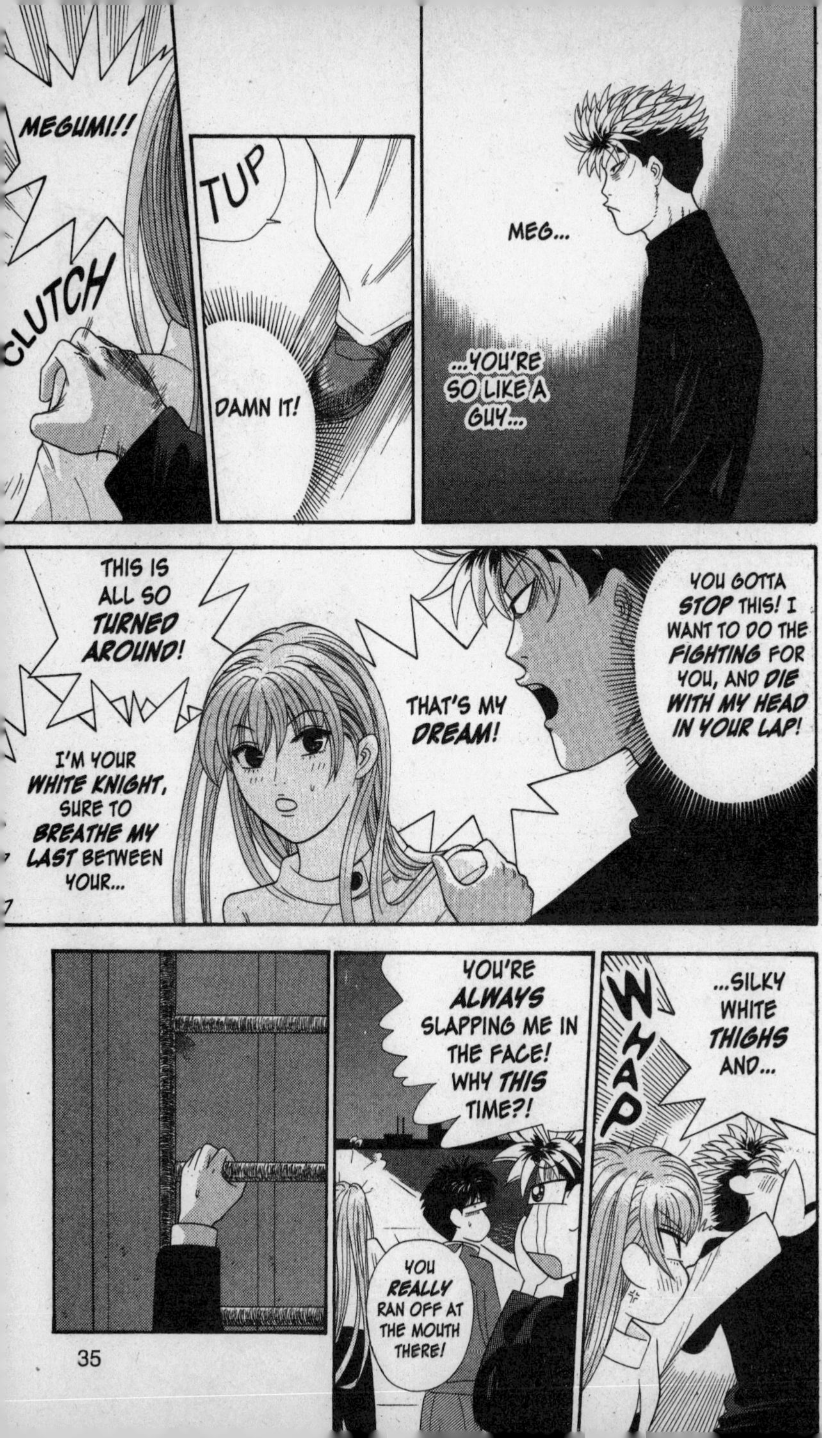
MEG...
...YOU'RE SO LIKE A GUY...
TUP
DAMN IT!
MEGUMI!!
CLUTCH
YOU GOTTA STOP THIS! I WANT TO DO THE FIGHTING FOR YOU, AND DIE WITH MY HEAD IN YOUR LAP!
THAT'S MY DREAM!
THIS IS ALL SO TURNED AROUND!
I'M YOUR WHITE KNIGHT, SURE TO BREATHE MY LAST BETWEEN YOUR...
WHAP
...SILKY WHITE THIGHS AND...
YOU'RE ALWAYS SLAPPING ME IN THE FACE! WHY THIS TIME?!
YOU REALLY RAN OFF AT THE MOUTH THERE!

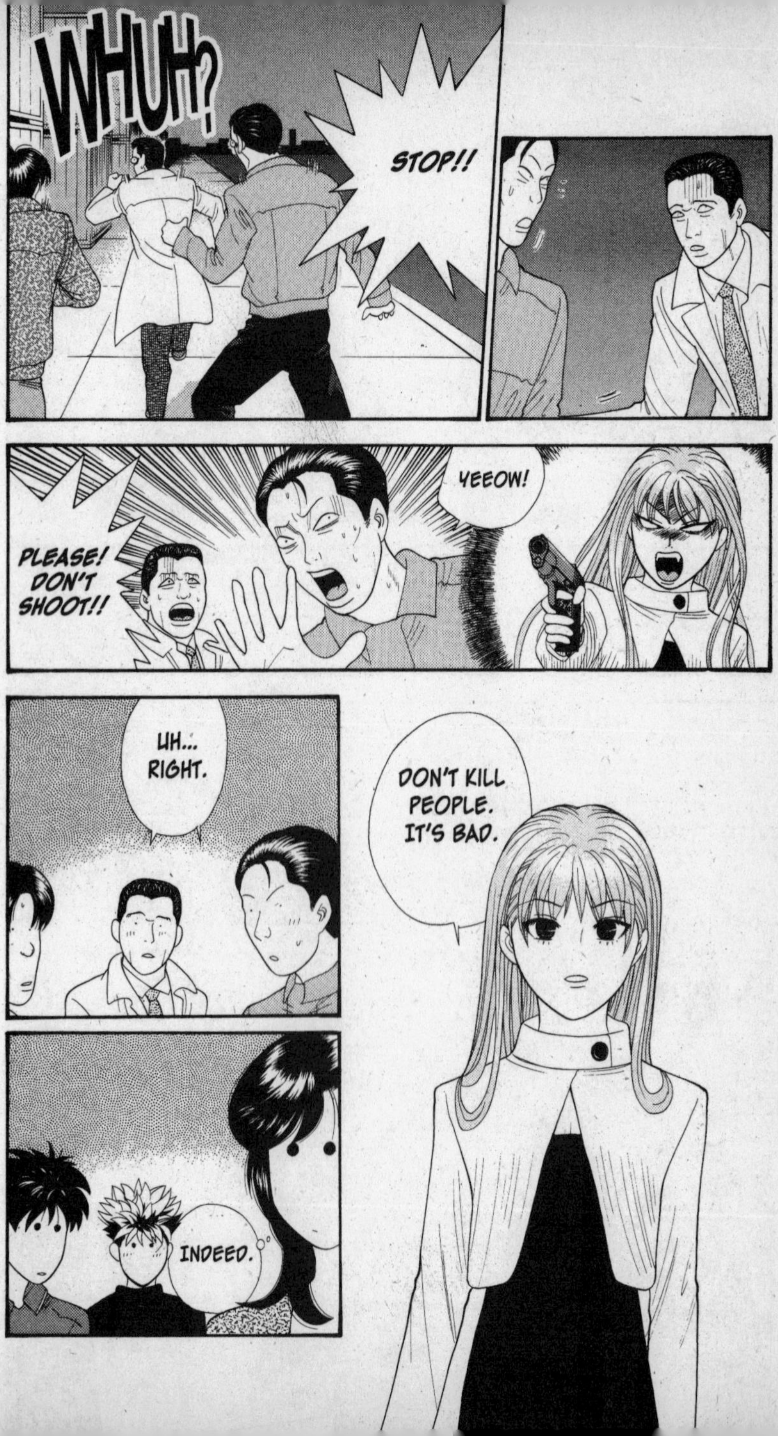
STOP!!
WHUH?
YEEOW!
PLEASE! DON'T SHOOT!!
DON'T KILL PEOPLE. IT'S BAD.
UH... RIGHT.
INDEED.

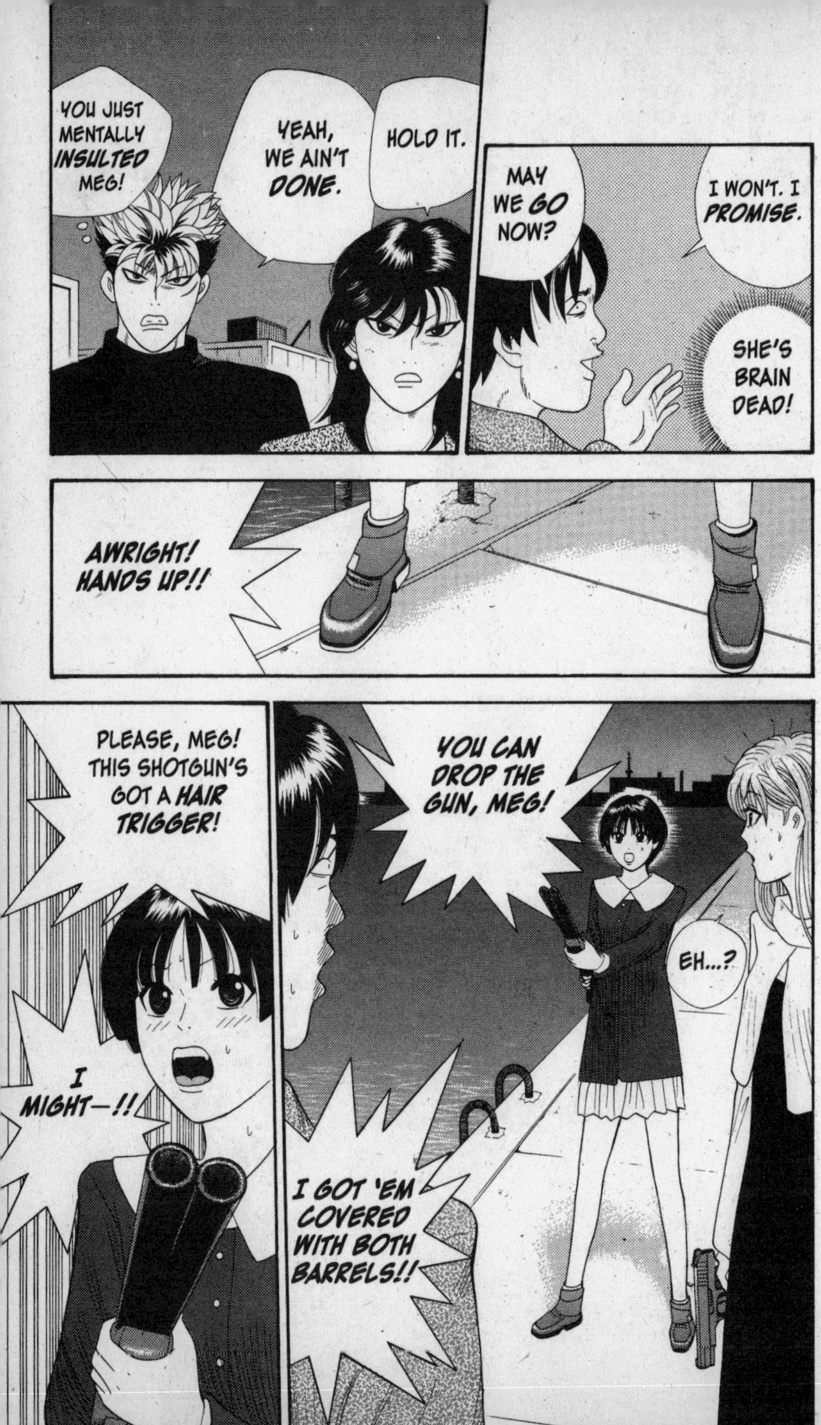
I WON'T. I PROMISE.
MAY WE GO NOW?
SHE'S BRAIN DEAD!
HOLD IT.
YEAH, WE AIN'T DONE.
YOU JUST MENTALLY INSULTED MEG!
AWRIGHT! HANDS UP!!
YOU CAN DROP THE GUN, MEG!
EH...?
I GOT 'EM COVERED WITH BOTH BARRELS!!
PLEASE, MEG! THIS SHOTGUN'S GOT A HAIR TRIGGER!
I MIGHT—!!

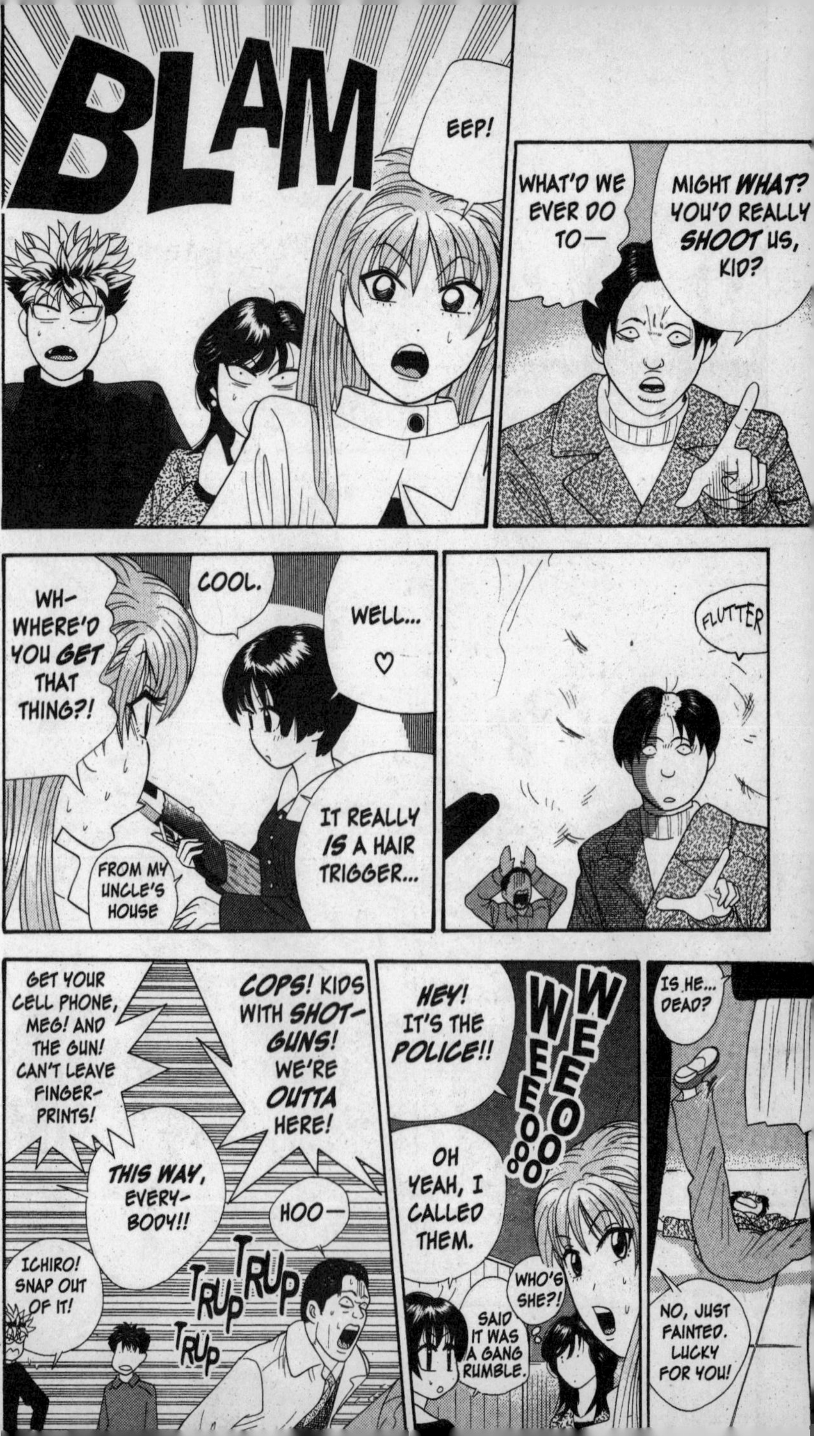
MIGHT WHAT? YOU'D REALLY SHOOT US, KID?
WHAT'D WE EVER DO TO—
BLAM
EEP!
FLUTTER
WH-WHERE'D YOU GET THAT THING?!
FROM MY UNCLE'S HOUSE
COOL.
WELL... ♡
IT REALLY IS A HAIR TRIGGER...
IS HE... DEAD?
NO, JUST FAINTED. LUCKY FOR YOU!
WEEOOO WEEOOO
HEY! IT'S THE POLICE!!
OH YEAH, I CALLED THEM.
WHO'S SHE?!
SAID IT WAS A GANG RUMBLE.
COPS! KIDS WITH SHOT-GUNS! WE'RE OUTTA HERE!
GET YOUR CELL PHONE, MEG! AND THE GUN! CAN'T LEAVE FINGER-PRINTS!
THIS WAY, EVERY-BODY!!
HOO—
TRUP TRUP TRUP TRUP
ICHIRO! SNAP OUT OF IT!

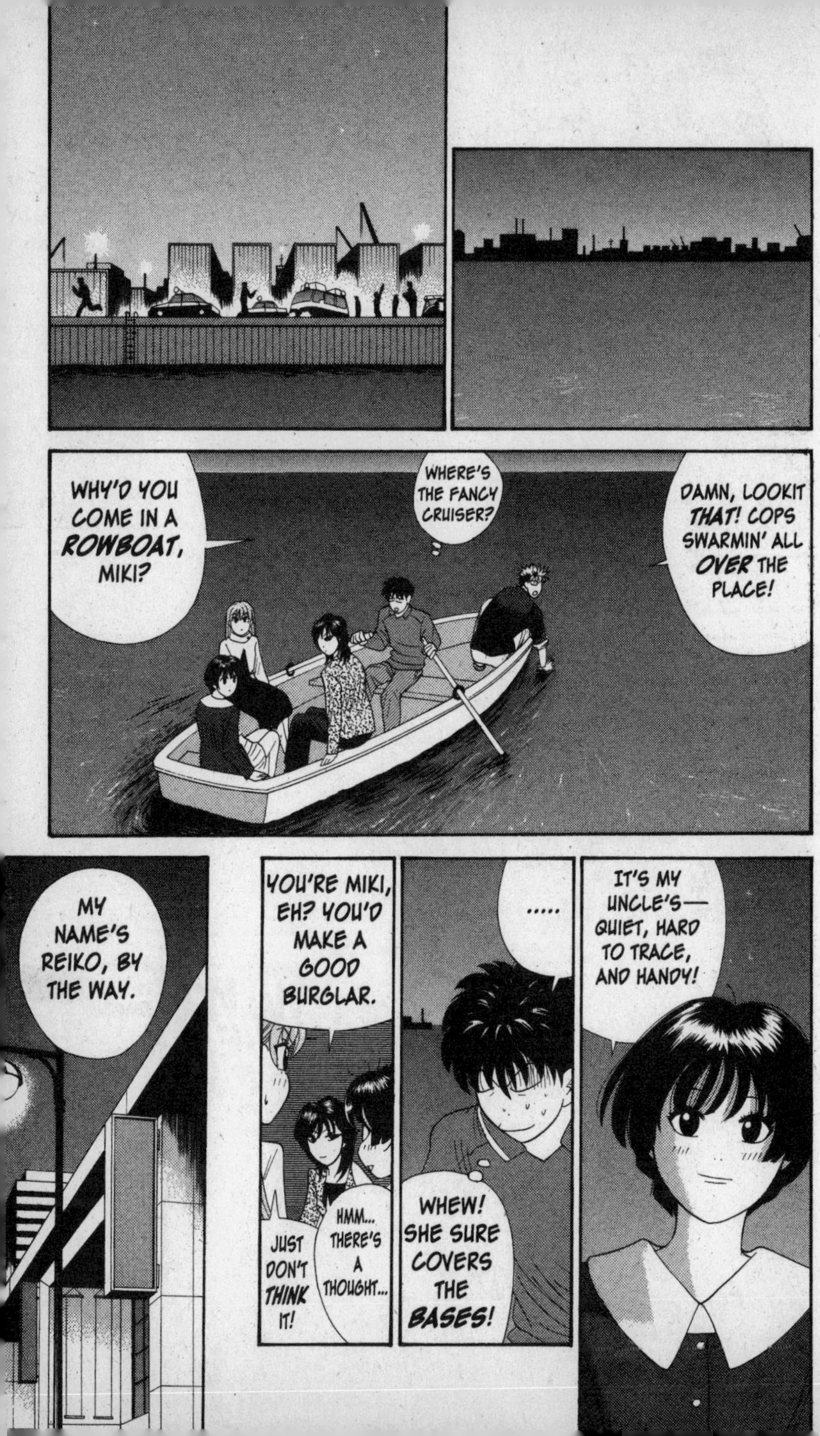
DAMN, LOOKIT THAT! COPS SWARMIN' ALL OVER THE PLACE!
WHERE'S THE FANCY CRUISER?
WHY'D YOU COME IN A ROWBOAT, MIKI?
IT'S MY UNCLE'S— QUIET, HARD TO TRACE, AND HANDY!
.....
WHEW! SHE SURE COVERS THE BASES!
YOU'RE MIKI, EH? YOU'D MAKE A GOOD BURGLAR.
HMM... THERE'S A THOUGHT...
JUST DON'T THINK IT!
MY NAME'S REIKO, BY THE WAY.

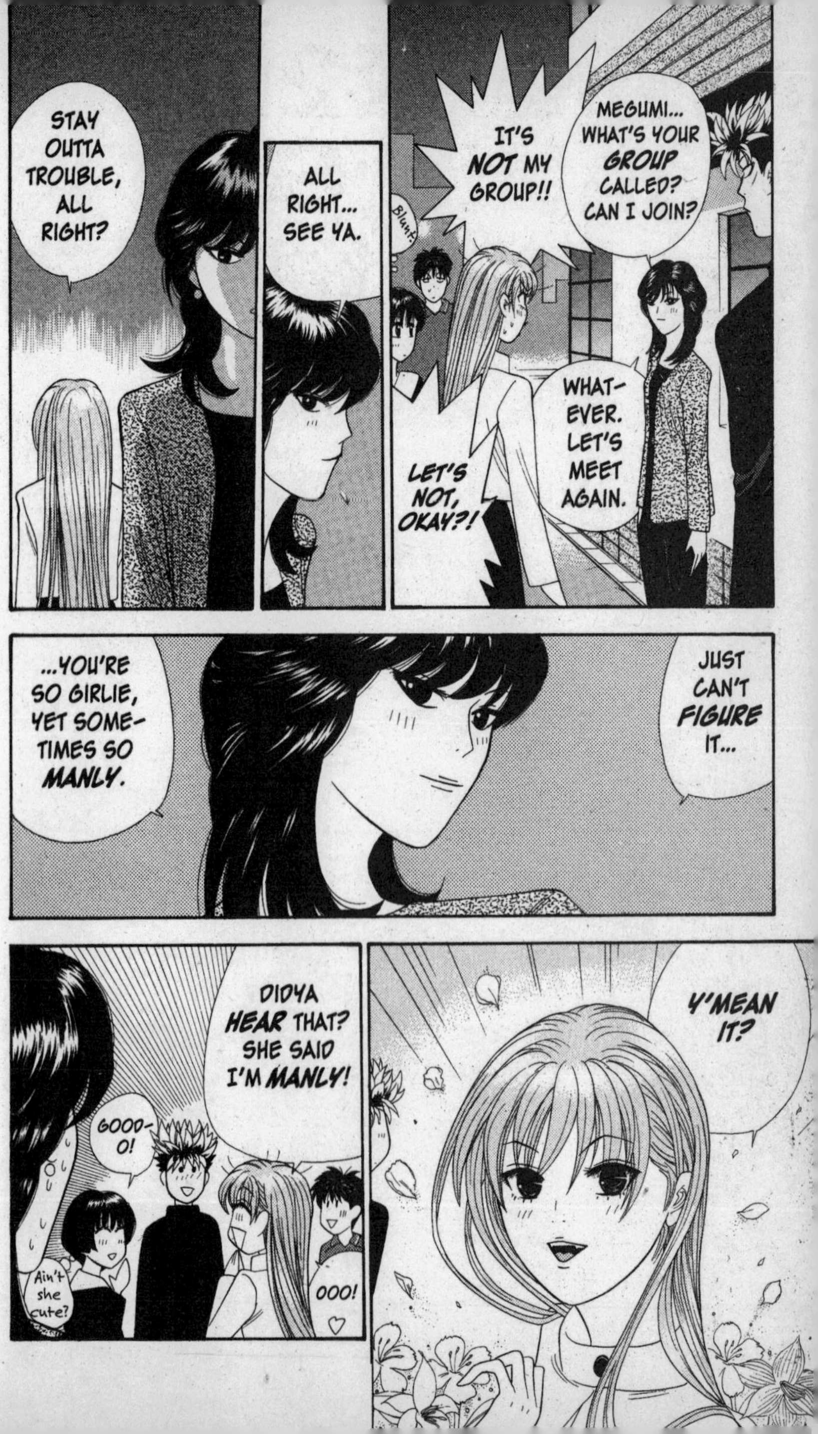
MEGUMI... WHAT'S YOUR GROUP CALLED? CAN I JOIN?
IT'S NOT MY GROUP!!
Blunt
WHAT-EVER. LET'S MEET AGAIN.
LET'S NOT, OKAY?!
ALL RIGHT... SEE YA.
STAY OUTTA TROUBLE, ALL RIGHT?
JUST CAN'T FIGURE IT...
...YOU'RE SO GIRLIE, YET SOME-TIMES SO MANLY.
Y'MEAN IT?
DIDYA HEAR THAT? SHE SAID I'M MANLY!
OOO!
GOOD-O!
Ain't she cute?

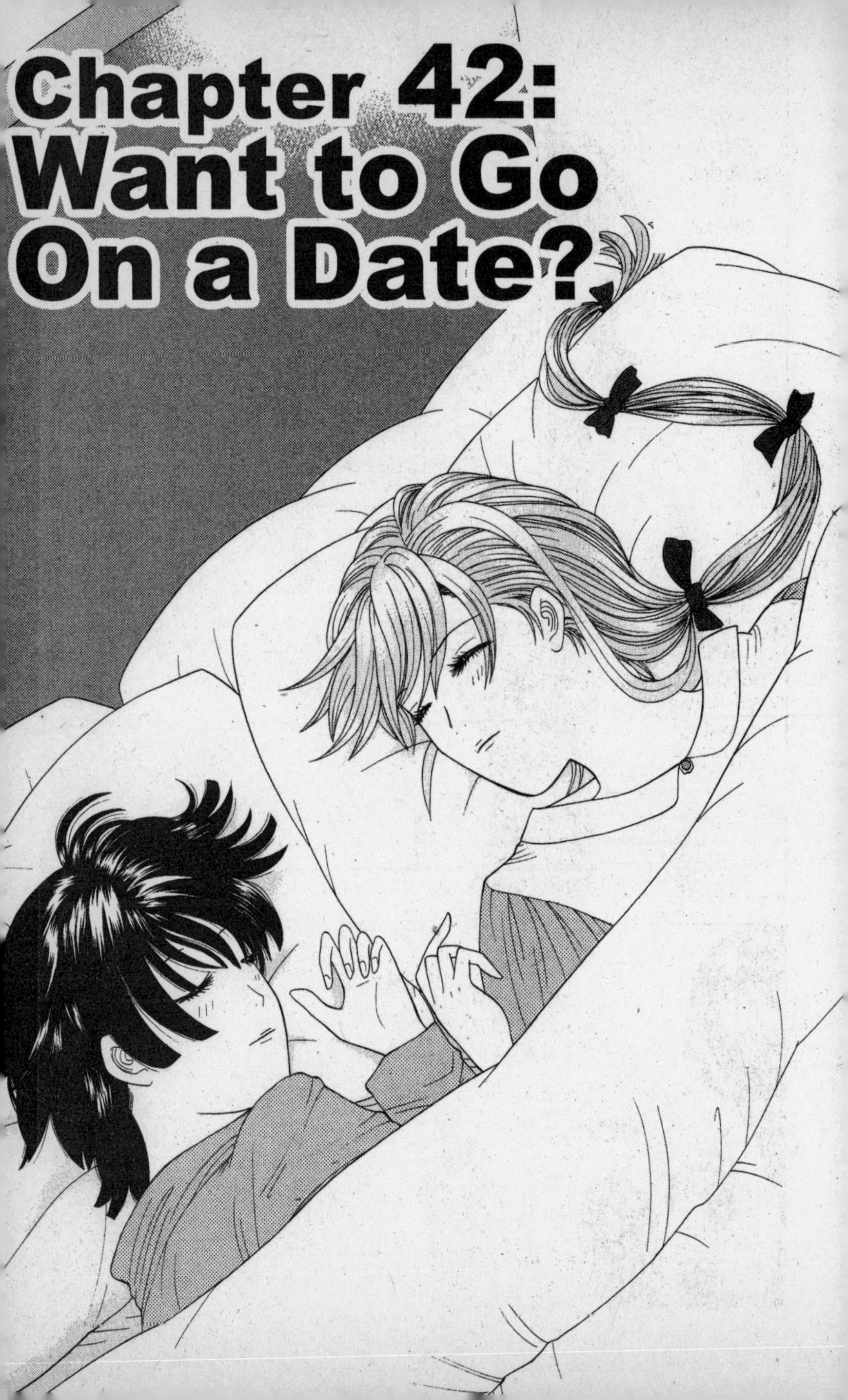
Chapter 42:
Want to Go
On a Date?

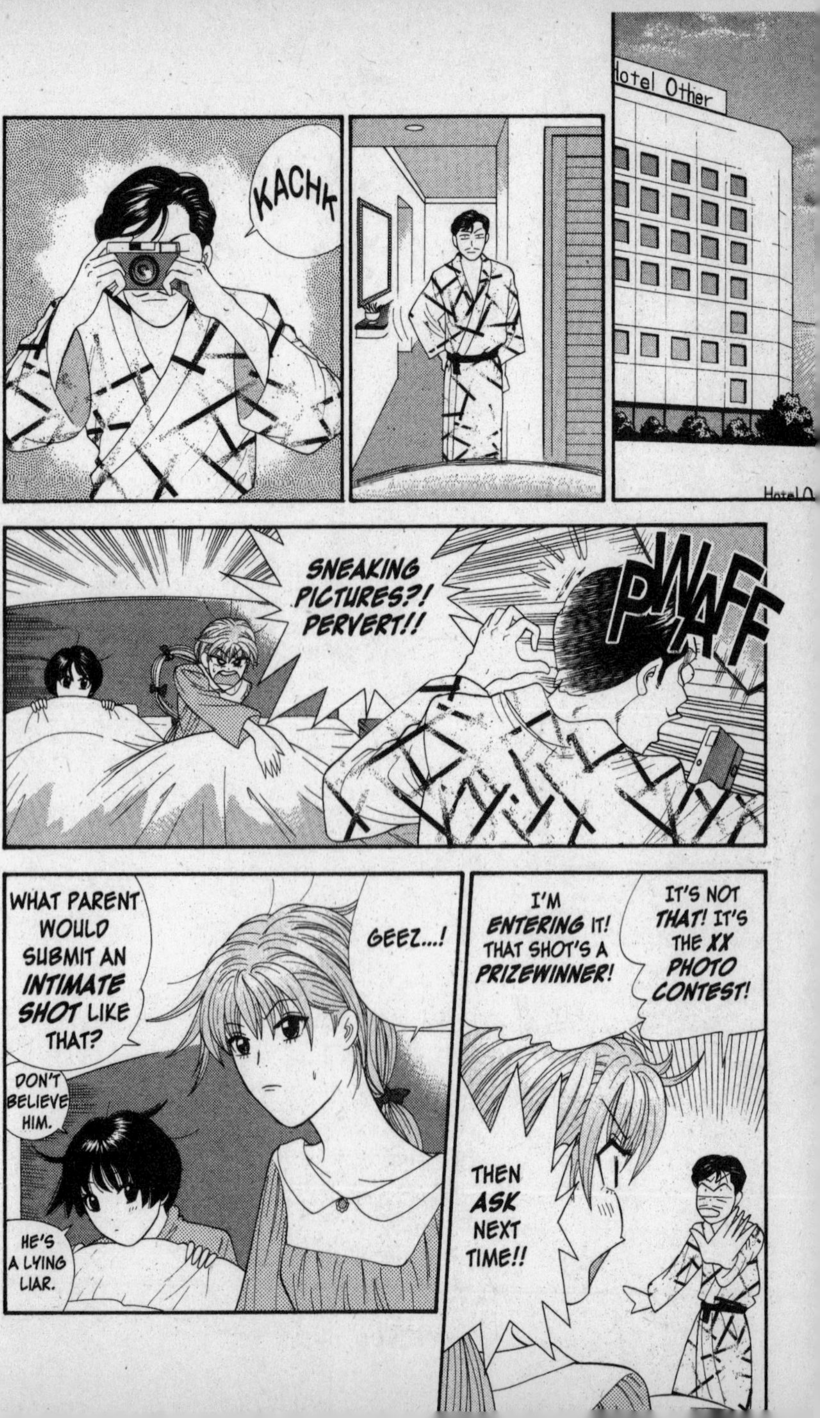
Hotel Other
KACHK
SNEAKING PICTURES?! PERVERT!!
PWAFF
IT'S NOT THAT! IT'S THE XX PHOTO CONTEST!
I'M ENTERING IT! THAT SHOT'S A PRIZEWINNER!
THEN ASK NEXT TIME!!
GEEZ...!
WHAT PARENT WOULD SUBMIT AN INTIMATE SHOT LIKE THAT?
DON'T BELIEVE HIM.
HE'S A LYING LIAR.

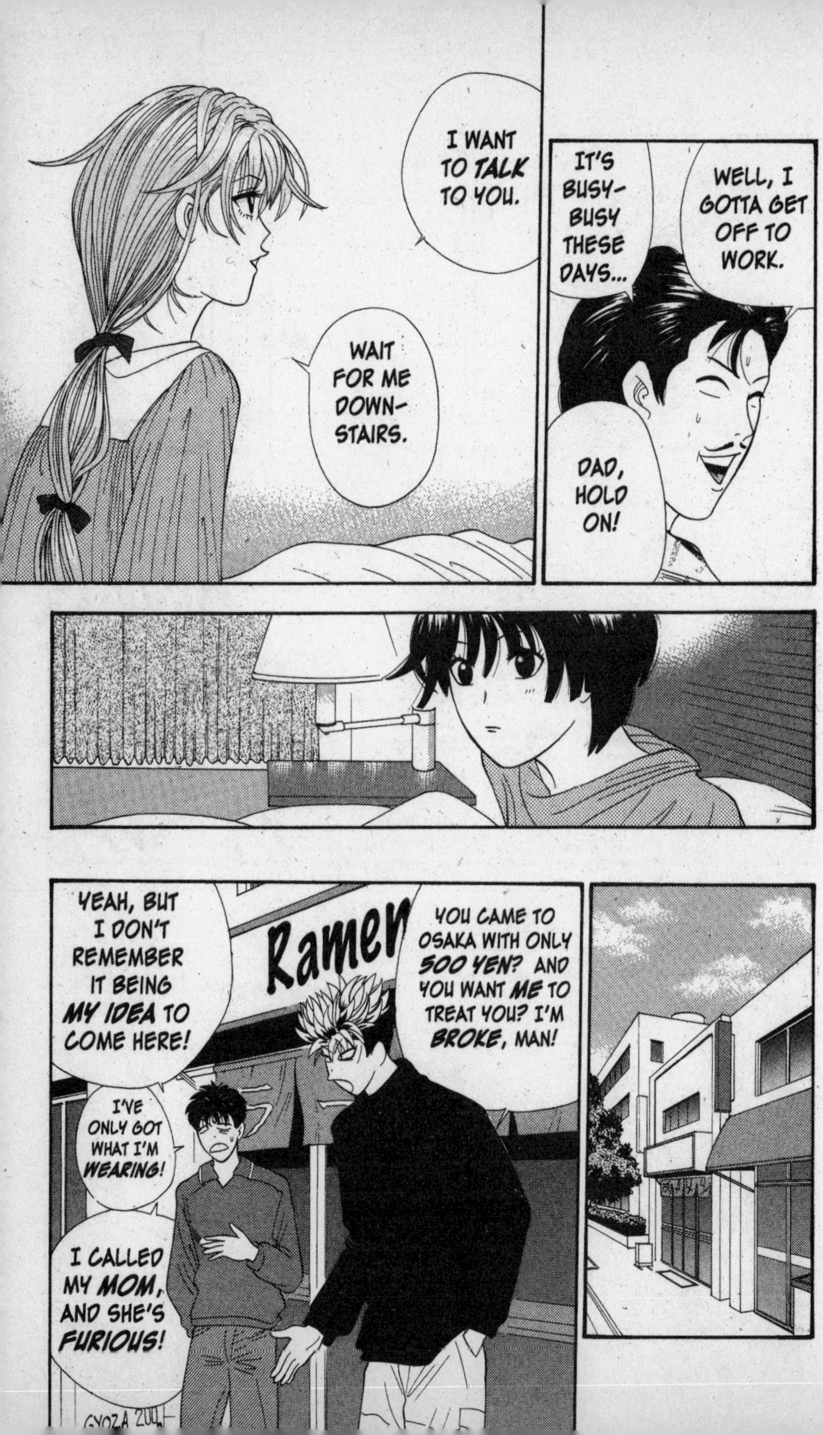
WELL, I GOTTA GET OFF TO WORK.
IT'S BUSY-BUSY THESE DAYS...
DAD, HOLD ON!
I WANT TO TALK TO YOU.
WAIT FOR ME DOWN-STAIRS.
YOU CAME TO OSAKA WITH ONLY 500 YEN? AND YOU WANT ME TO TREAT YOU? I'M BROKE, MAN!
Ramen
YEAH, BUT I DON'T REMEMBER IT BEING MY IDEA TO COME HERE!
I'VE ONLY GOT WHAT I'M WEARING!
I CALLED MY MOM, AND SHE'S FURIOUS!

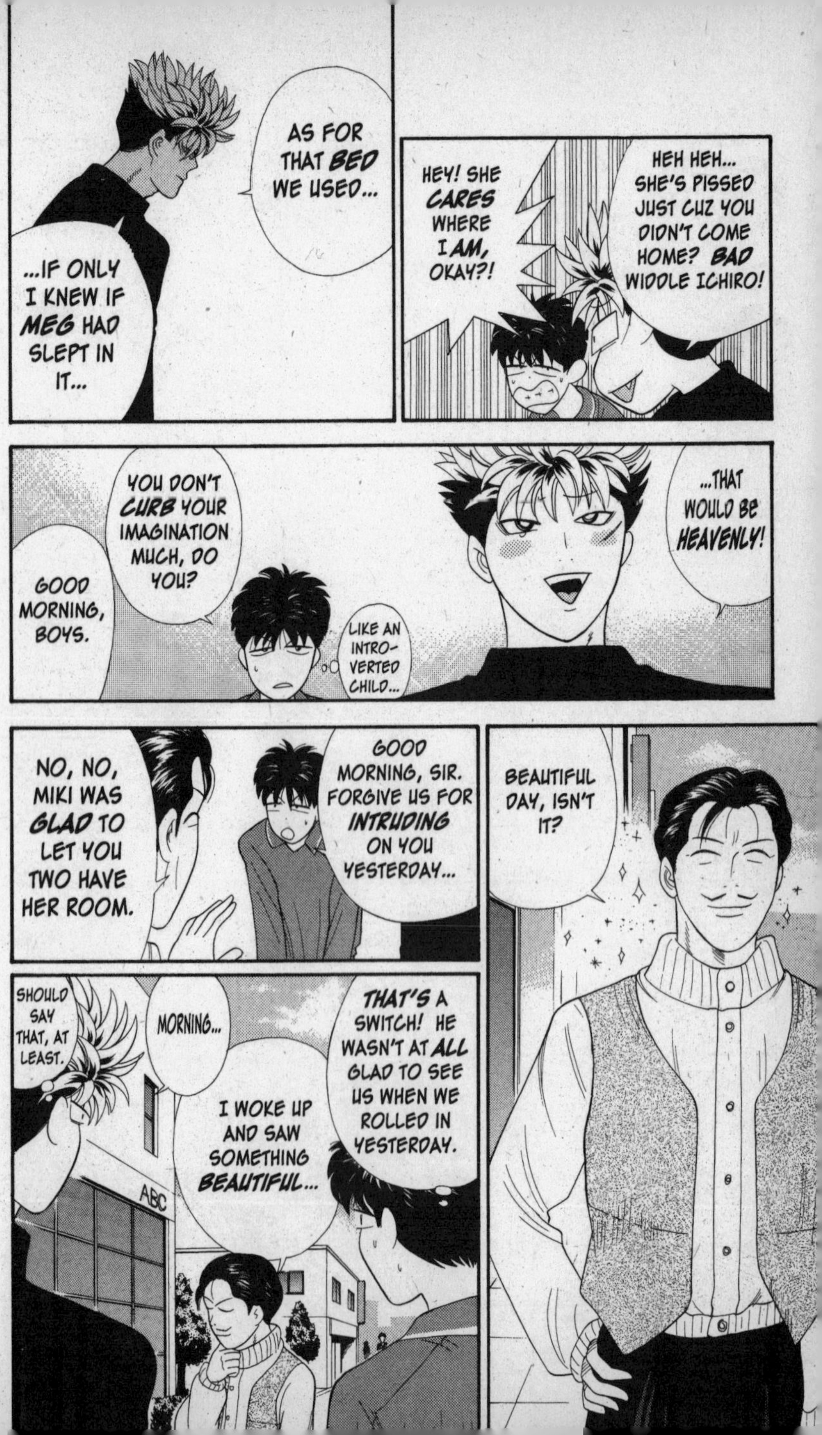
HEH HEH... SHE'S PISSED JUST CUZ YOU DIDN'T COME HOME? BAD WIDDLE ICHIRO!
HEY! SHE CARES WHERE I AM, OKAY?!
AS FOR THAT BED WE USED...
...IF ONLY I KNEW IF MEG HAD SLEPT IN IT...
...THAT WOULD BE HEAVENLY!
LIKE AN INTRO-VERTED CHILD...
YOU DON'T CURB YOUR IMAGINATION MUCH, DO YOU?
GOOD MORNING, BOYS.
BEAUTIFUL DAY, ISN'T IT?
GOOD MORNING, SIR. FORGIVE US FOR INTRUDING ON YOU YESTERDAY...
NO, NO, MIKI WAS GLAD TO LET YOU TWO HAVE HER ROOM.
THAT'S A SWITCH! HE WASN'T AT ALL GLAD TO SEE US WHEN WE ROLLED IN YESTERDAY.
MORNING...
SHOULD SAY THAT, AT LEAST.
I WOKE UP AND SAW SOMETHING BEAUTIFUL...
ABC

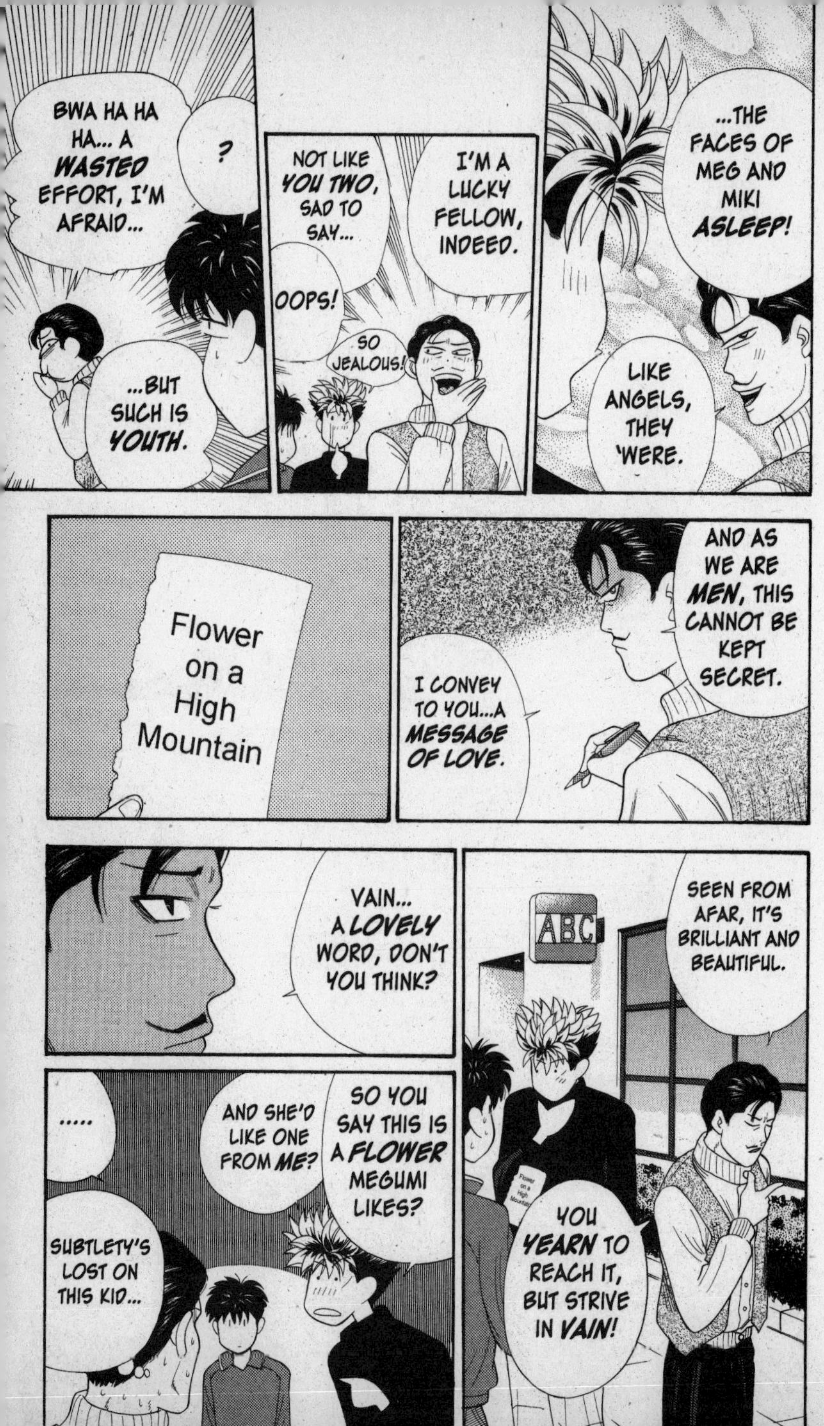
...THE FACES OF MEG AND MIKI ASLEEP!
LIKE ANGELS, THEY 'WERE.
I'M A LUCKY FELLOW, INDEED.
NOT LIKE YOU TWO, SAD TO SAY...
OOPS!
SO JEALOUS!
?
BWA HA HA HA... A WASTED EFFORT, I'M AFRAID...
...BUT SUCH IS YOUTH.
AND AS WE ARE MEN, THIS CANNOT BE KEPT SECRET.
I CONVEY TO YOU...A MESSAGE OF LOVE.
Flower on a High Mountain
SEEN FROM AFAR, IT'S BRILLIANT AND BEAUTIFUL.
YOU YEARN TO REACH IT, BUT STRIVE IN VAIN!
VAIN... A LOVELY WORD, DON'T YOU THINK?
SO YOU SAY THIS IS A FLOWER MEGUMI LIKES?
AND SHE'D LIKE ONE FROM ME?
.....
SUBTLETY'S LOST ON THIS KID...

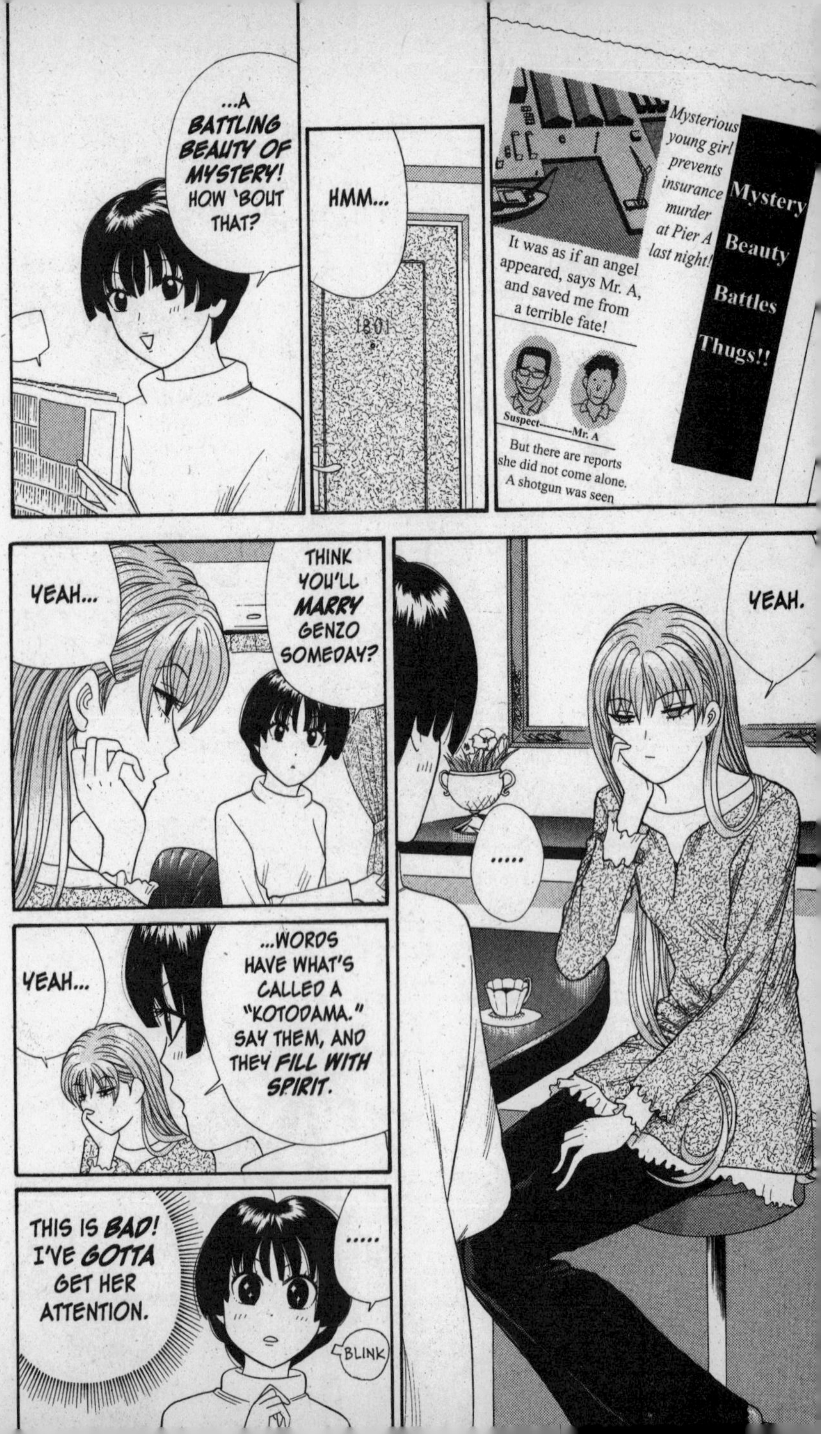

Mystery Beauty Battles Thugs!!
Mysterious young girl prevents insurance murder at Pier A last night!
It was as if an angel appeared, says Mr. A, and saved me from a terrible fate!
Suspect---------Mr. A
But there are reports she did not come alone. A shotgun was seen
HMM...
...A BATTLING BEAUTY OF MYSTERY! HOW 'BOUT THAT?
YEAH.
.....
THINK YOU'LL MARRY GENZO SOMEDAY?
YEAH...
...WORDS HAVE WHAT'S CALLED A "KOTODAMA." SAY THEM, AND THEY FILL WITH SPIRIT.
YEAH...
.....
THIS IS BAD! I'VE GOTTA GET HER ATTENTION.
BLINK

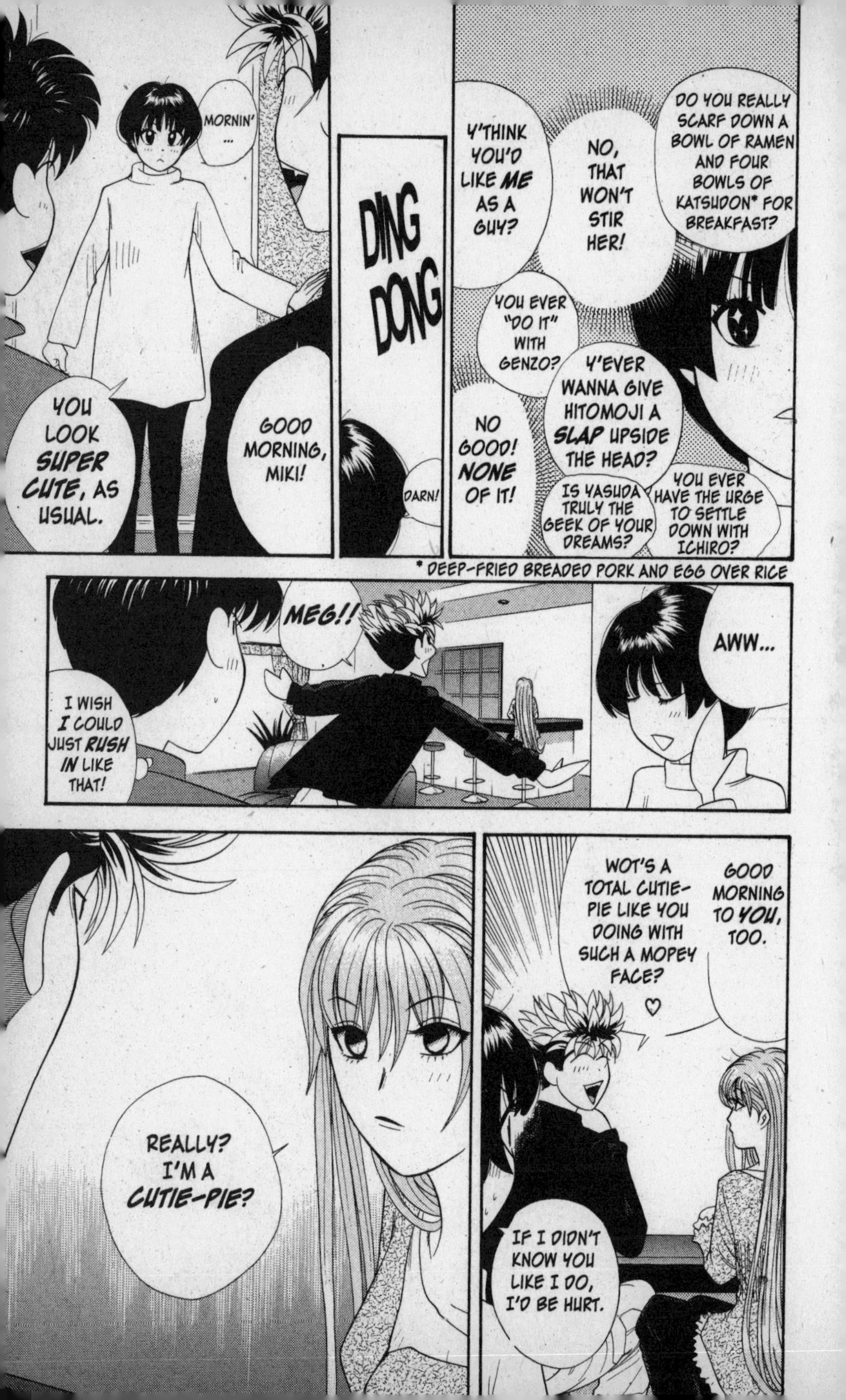
DO YOU REALLY SCARF DOWN A BOWL OF RAMEN AND FOUR BOWLS OF KATSUDON* FOR BREAKFAST?
NO, THAT WON'T STIR HER!
Y'THINK YOU'D LIKE ME AS A GUY?
Y'EVER WANNA GIVE HITOMOJI A SLAP UPSIDE THE HEAD?
YOU EVER "DO IT" WITH GENZO?
YOU EVER HAVE THE URGE TO SETTLE DOWN WITH ICHIRO?
IS YASUDA TRULY THE GEEK OF YOUR DREAMS?
NO GOOD! NONE OF IT!
* DEEP-FRIED BREADED PORK AND EGG OVER RICE
DING DONG
DARN!
MORNIN' ...
GOOD MORNING, MIKI!
YOU LOOK SUPER CUTE, AS USUAL.
AWW...
MEG!!
I WISH I COULD JUST RUSH IN LIKE THAT!
GOOD MORNING TO YOU, TOO.
WOT'S A TOTAL CUTIE-PIE LIKE YOU DOING WITH SUCH A MOPEY FACE? ♡
IF I DIDN'T KNOW YOU LIKE I DO, I'D BE HURT.
REALLY? I'M A CUTIE-PIE?

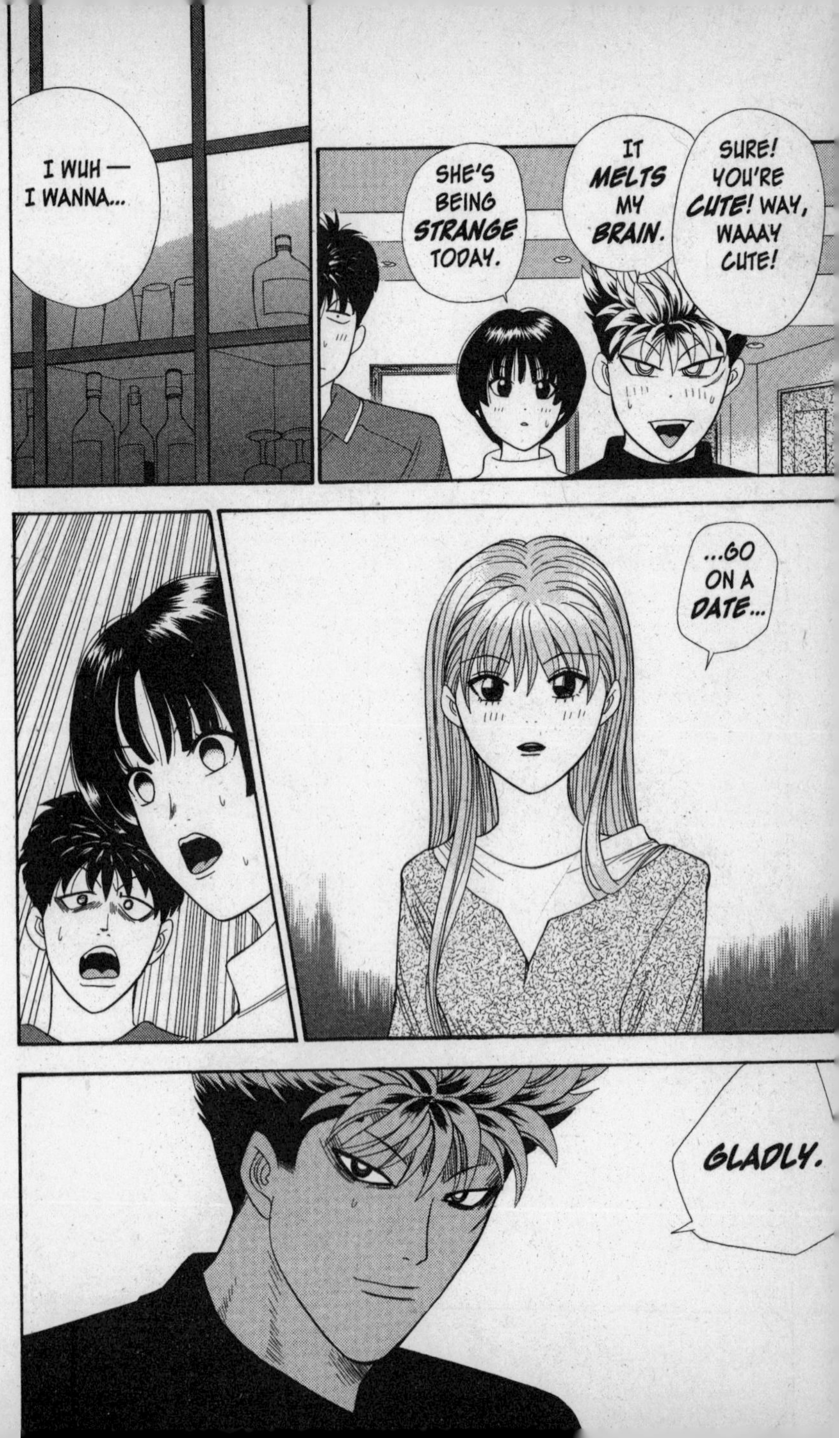
SURE! YOU'RE CUTE! WAY, WAAAY CUTE!
IT MELTS MY BRAIN.
SHE'S BEING STRANGE TODAY.
I WUH — I WANNA...
...GO ON A DATE...
GLADLY.

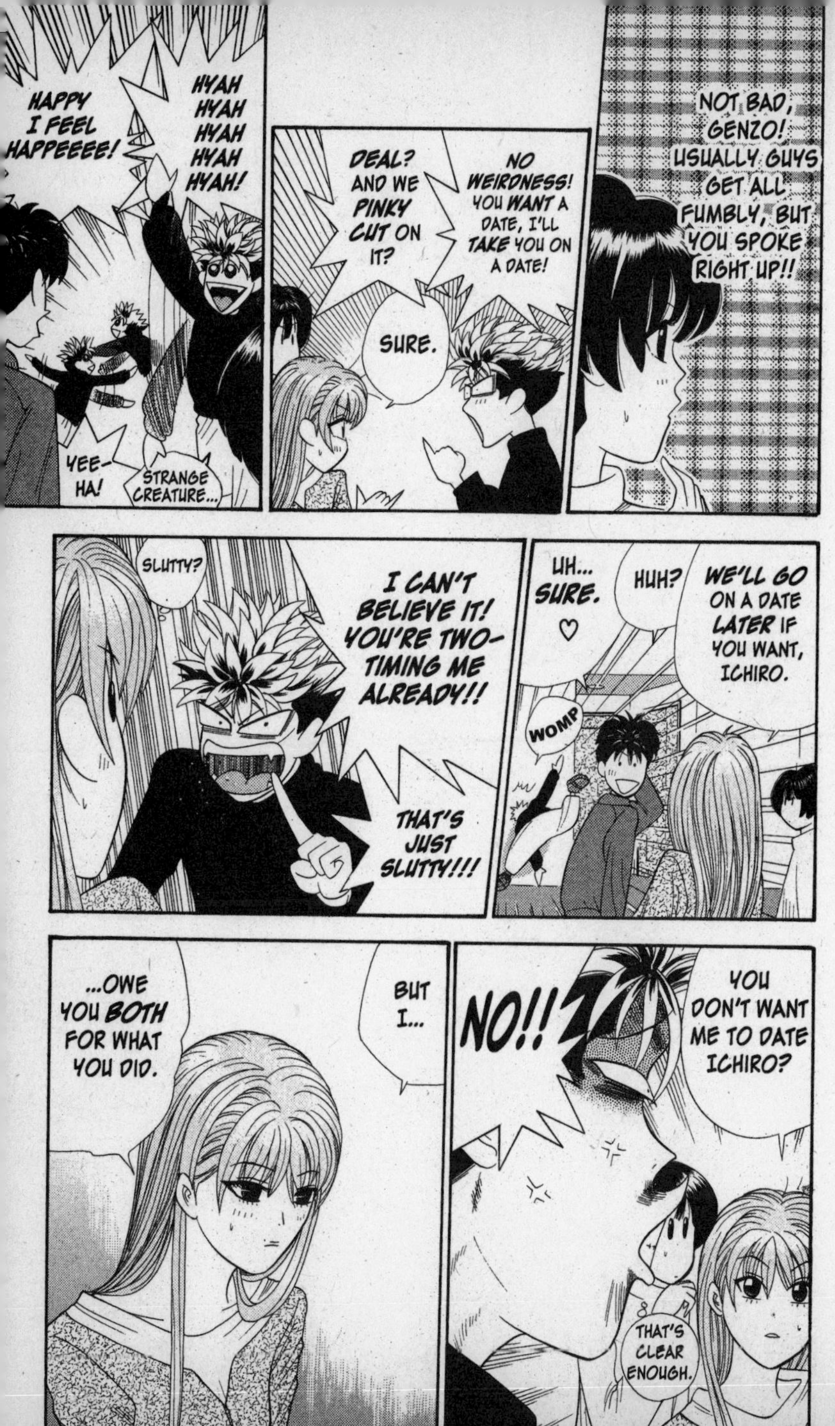
NOT BAD, GENZO! USUALLY GUYS GET ALL FUMBLY, BUT YOU SPOKE RIGHT UP!!
NO WEIRDNESS! YOU WANT A DATE, I'LL TAKE YOU ON A DATE!
DEAL? AND WE PINKY CUT ON IT?
SURE.
HYAH HYAH HYAH HYAH HYAH!
HAPPY I FEEL HAPPEEEEE!
YEE-HA!
STRANGE CREATURE...
WE'LL GO ON A DATE LATER IF YOU WANT, ICHIRO.
HUH?
UH... SURE. ♡
WOMP
I CAN'T BELIEVE IT! YOU'RE TWO-TIMING ME ALREADY!!
THAT'S JUST SLUTTY!!!
SLUTTY?
YOU DON'T WANT ME TO DATE ICHIRO?
NO!!
THAT'S CLEAR ENOUGH.
BUT I...
...OWE YOU BOTH FOR WHAT YOU DID.

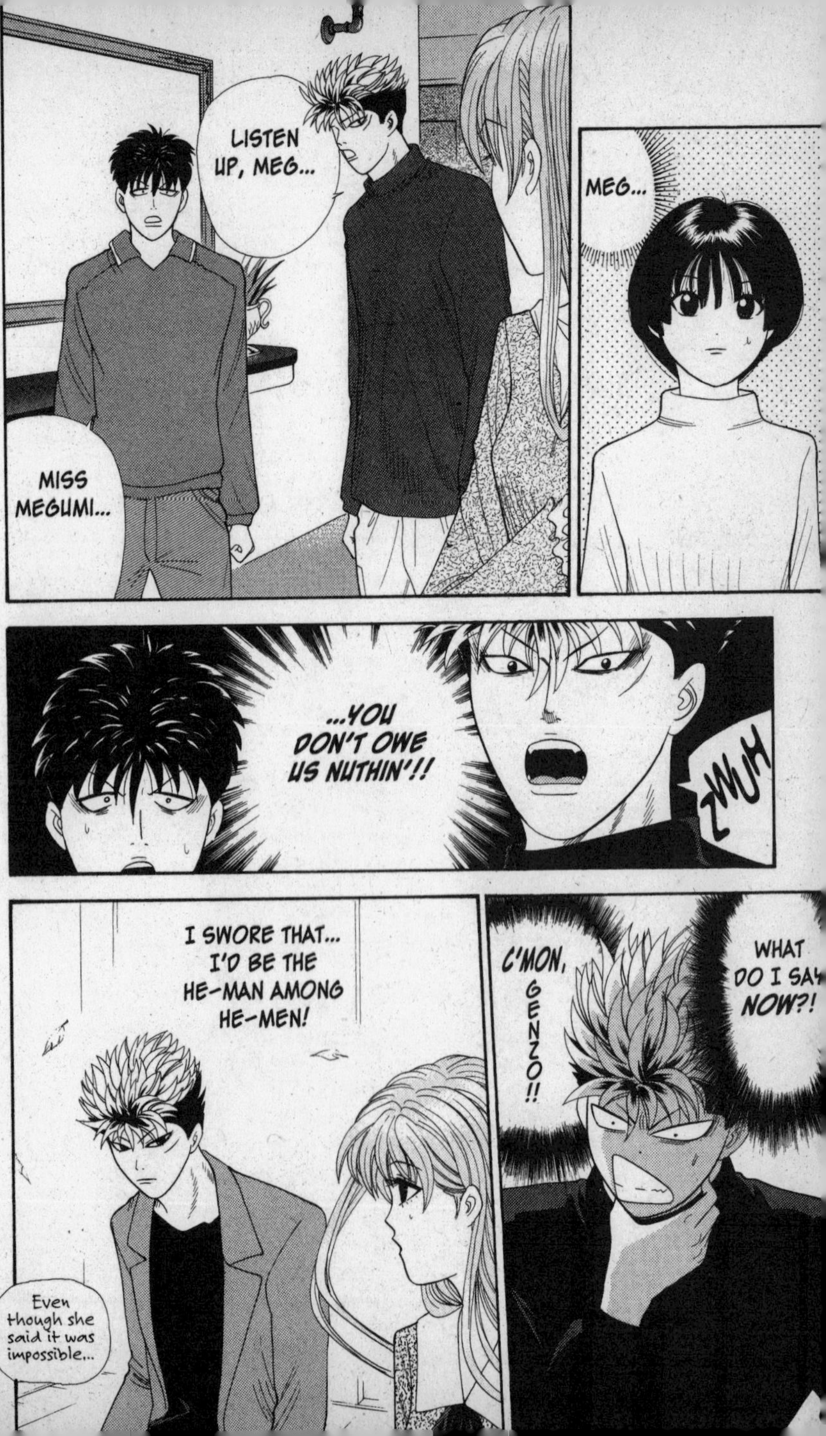
MEG...
LISTEN UP, MEG...
MISS MEGUMI...
HUH?
...YOU DON'T OWE US NUTHIN'!!
WHAT DO I SAY NOW?!
C'MON, GENZO!!
I SWORE THAT... I'D BE THE HE-MAN AMONG HE-MEN!
Even though she said it was impossible...

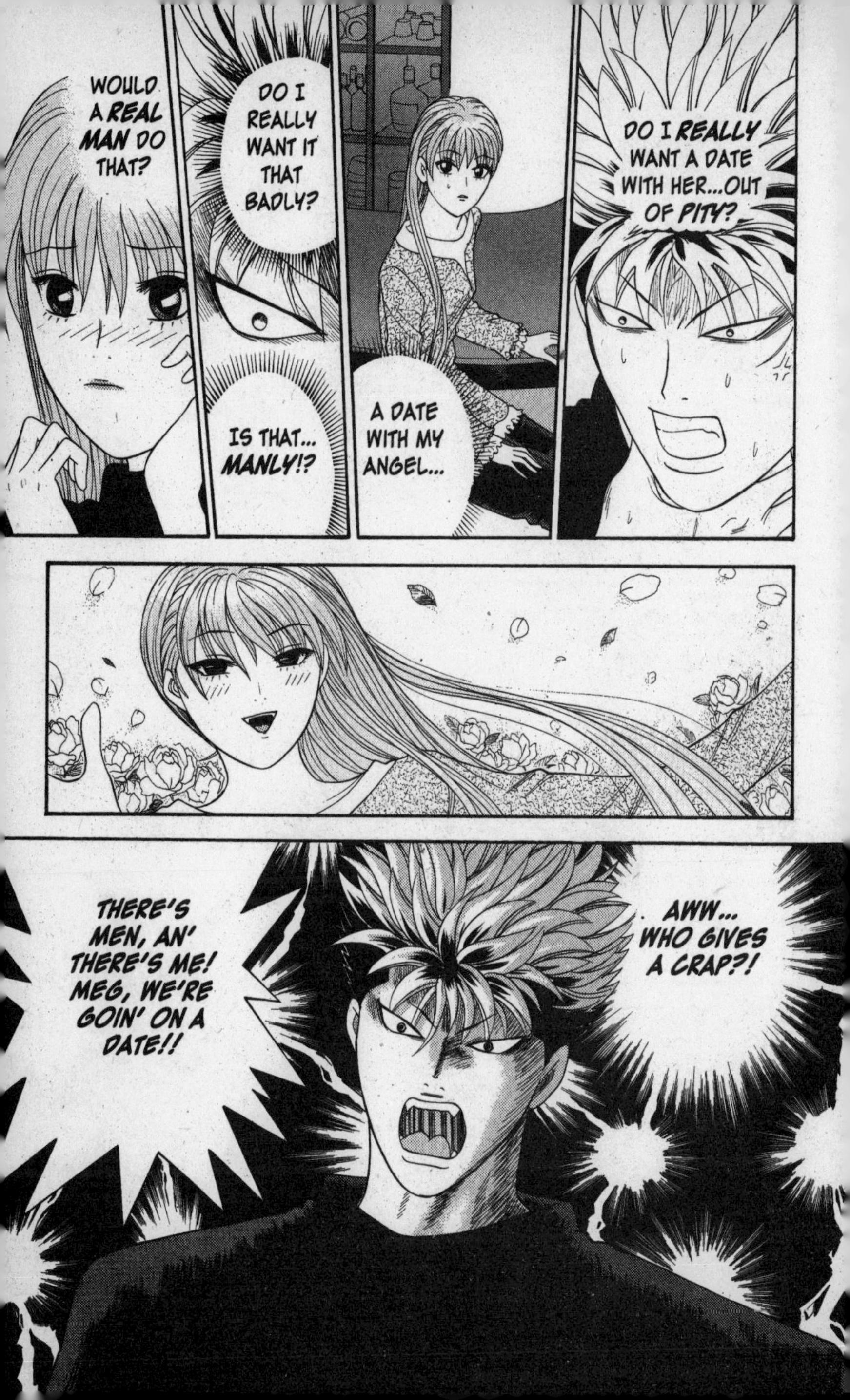
DO I REALLY WANT A DATE WITH HER...OUT OF PITY?
A DATE WITH MY ANGEL...
DO I REALLY WANT IT THAT BADLY?
IS THAT... MANLY!?
WOULD A REAL MAN DO THAT?
AWW... WHO GIVES A CRAP?!
THERE'S MEN, AN' THERE'S ME! MEG, WE'RE GOIN' ON A DATE!!

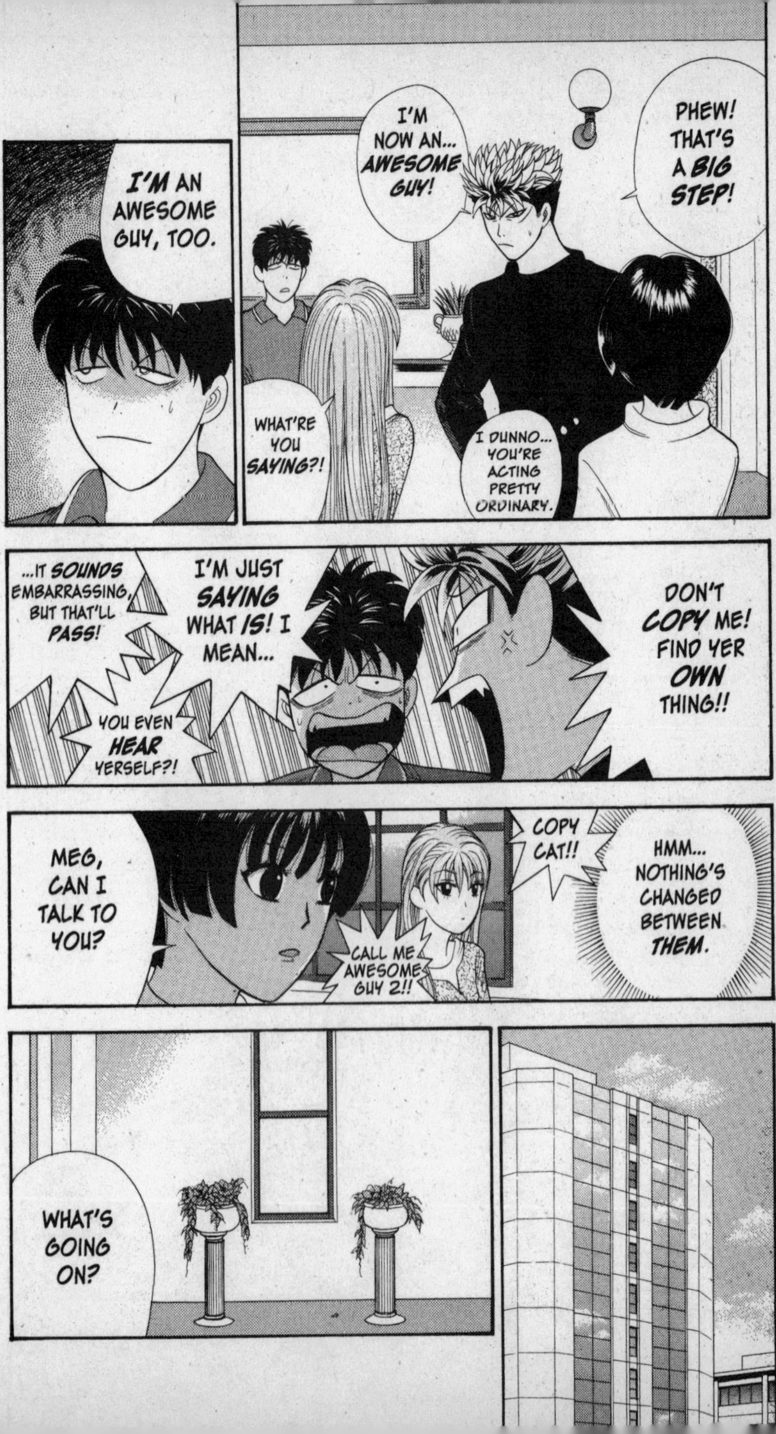
PHEW! THAT'S A BIG STEP!
I'M NOW AN... AWESOME GUY!
I DUNNO... YOU'RE ACTING PRETTY ORDINARY.
WHAT'RE YOU SAYING?!
I'M AN AWESOME GUY, TOO.
DON'T COPY ME! FIND YER OWN THING!!
I'M JUST SAYING WHAT IS! I MEAN...
...IT SOUNDS EMBARRASSING, BUT THAT'LL PASS!
YOU EVEN HEAR YERSELF?!
HMM... NOTHING'S CHANGED BETWEEN THEM.
COPY CAT!!
CALL ME AWESOME GUY 2!!
MEG, CAN I TALK TO YOU?
WHAT'S GOING ON?

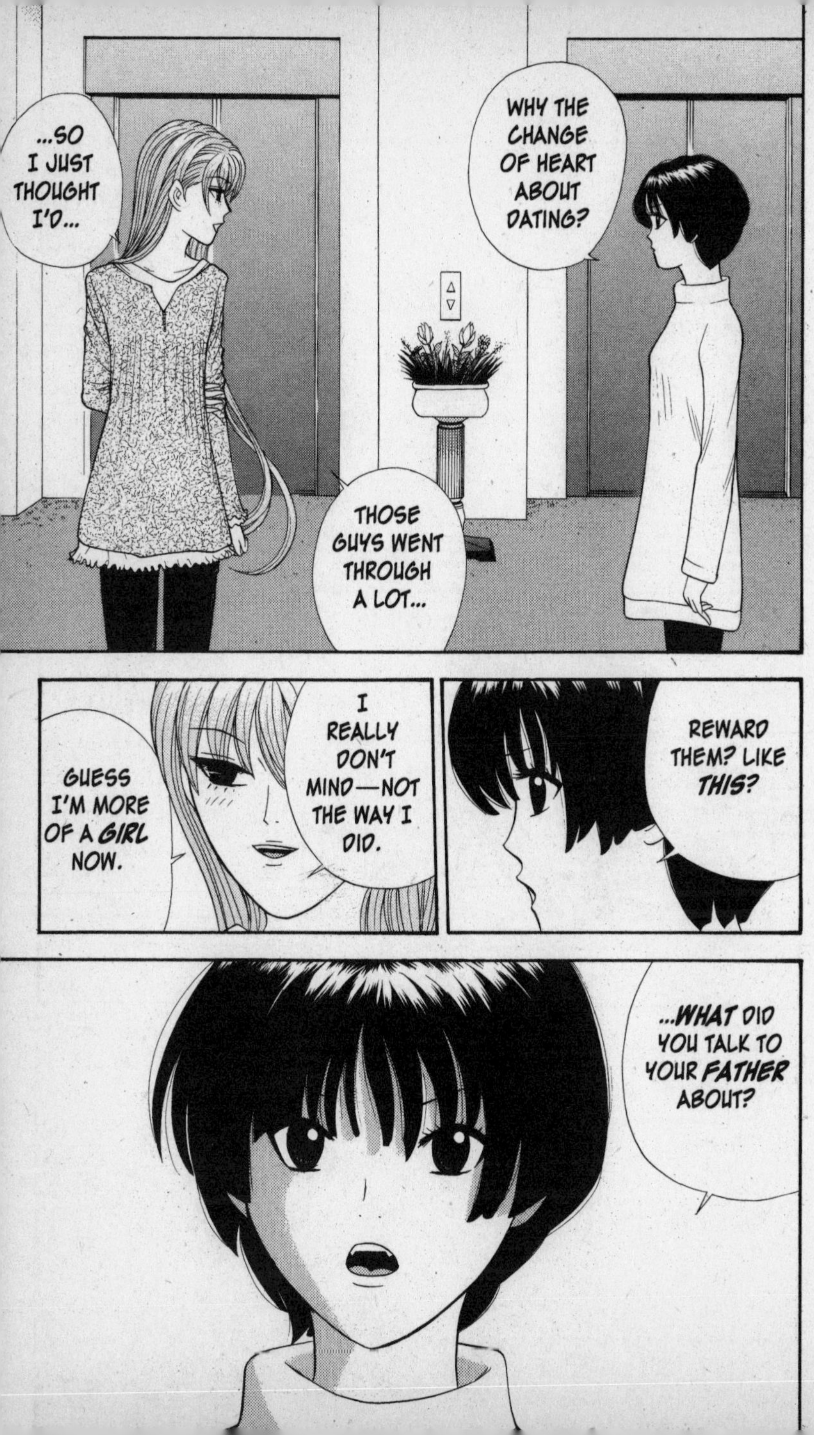
WHY THE CHANGE OF HEART ABOUT DATING?
...SO I JUST THOUGHT I'D...
THOSE GUYS WENT THROUGH A LOT...
REWARD THEM? LIKE *THIS?*
I REALLY DON'T MIND—NOT THE WAY I DID.
GUESS I'M MORE OF A *GIRL* NOW.
...*WHAT* DID YOU TALK TO YOUR *FATHER* ABOUT?

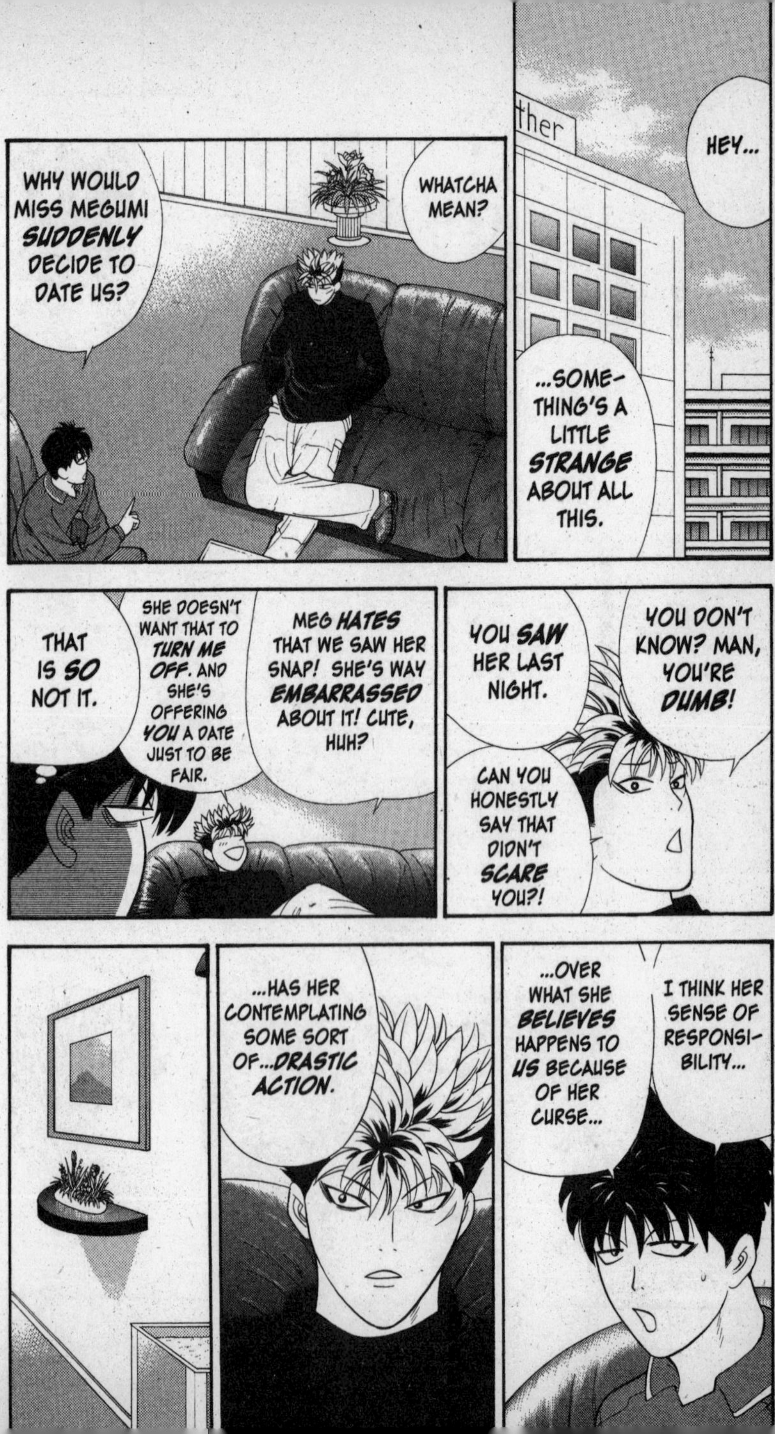
ther
HEY...
...SOMETHING'S A LITTLE STRANGE ABOUT ALL THIS.
WHATCHA MEAN?
WHY WOULD MISS MEGUMI SUDDENLY DECIDE TO DATE US?
YOU DON'T KNOW? MAN, YOU'RE DUMB!
YOU SAW HER LAST NIGHT.
CAN YOU HONESTLY SAY THAT DIDN'T SCARE YOU?!
MEG HATES THAT WE SAW HER SNAP! SHE'S WAY EMBARRASSED ABOUT IT! CUTE, HUH?
SHE DOESN'T WANT THAT TO TURN ME OFF. AND SHE'S OFFERING YOU A DATE JUST TO BE FAIR.
THAT IS SO NOT IT.
I THINK HER SENSE OF RESPONSIBILITY...
...OVER WHAT SHE BELIEVES HAPPENS TO US BECAUSE OF HER CURSE...
...HAS HER CONTEMPLATING SOME SORT OF...DRASTIC ACTION.

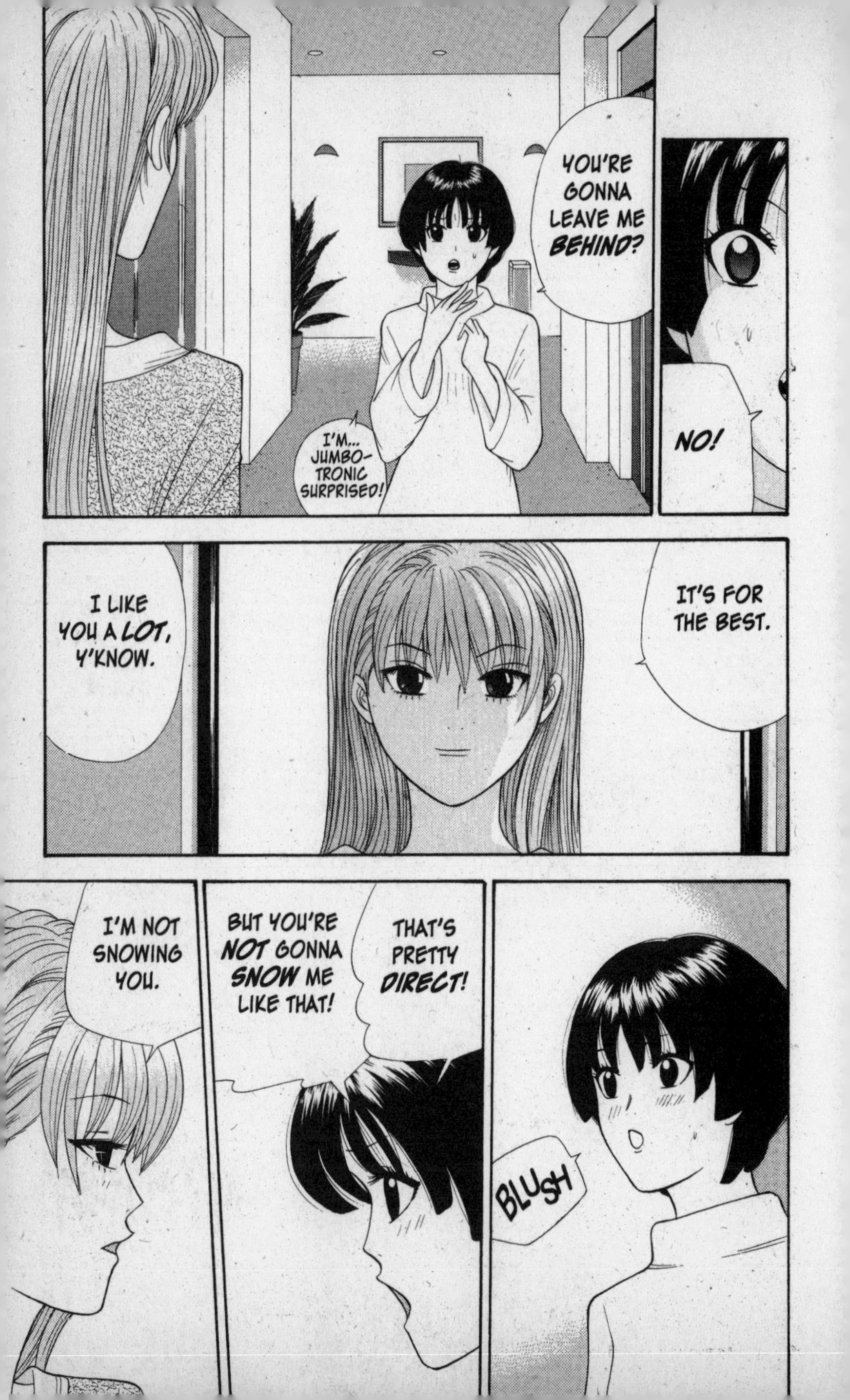
NO!
YOU'RE GONNA LEAVE ME BEHIND?
I'M... JUMBO-TRONIC SURPRISED!
IT'S FOR THE BEST.
I LIKE YOU A LOT, Y'KNOW.
BLUSH
THAT'S PRETTY DIRECT!
BUT YOU'RE NOT GONNA SNOW ME LIKE THAT!
I'M NOT SNOWING YOU.

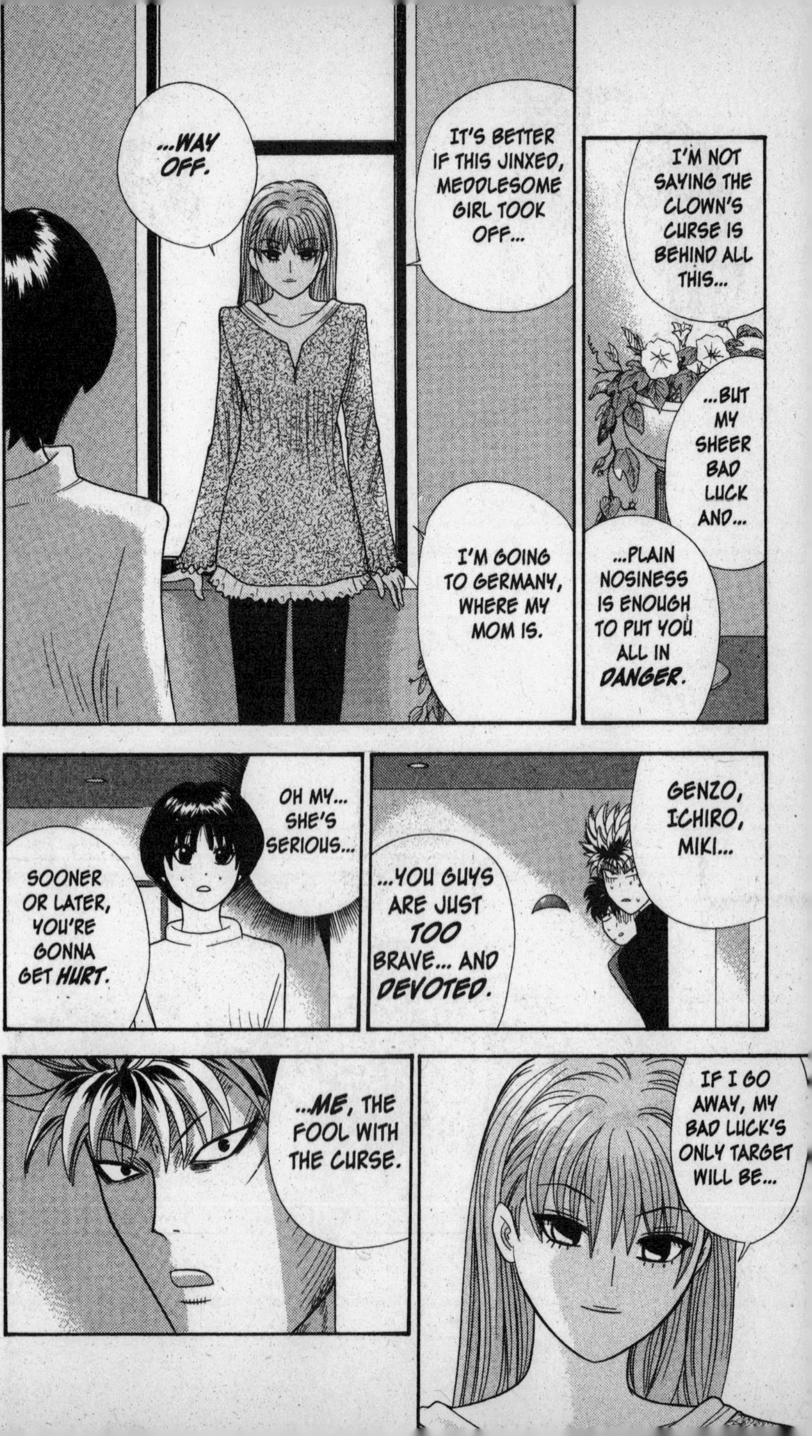
I'M NOT SAYING THE CLOWN'S CURSE IS BEHIND ALL THIS...
...BUT MY SHEER BAD LUCK AND...
...PLAIN NOSINESS IS ENOUGH TO PUT YOU ALL IN DANGER.
IT'S BETTER IF THIS JINXED, MEDDLESOME GIRL TOOK OFF...
...WAY OFF.
I'M GOING TO GERMANY, WHERE MY MOM IS.
GENZO, ICHIRO, MIKI...
...YOU GUYS ARE JUST TOO BRAVE... AND DEVOTED.
OH MY... SHE'S SERIOUS...
SOONER OR LATER, YOU'RE GONNA GET HURT.
IF I GO AWAY, MY BAD LUCK'S ONLY TARGET WILL BE...
...ME, THE FOOL WITH THE CURSE.

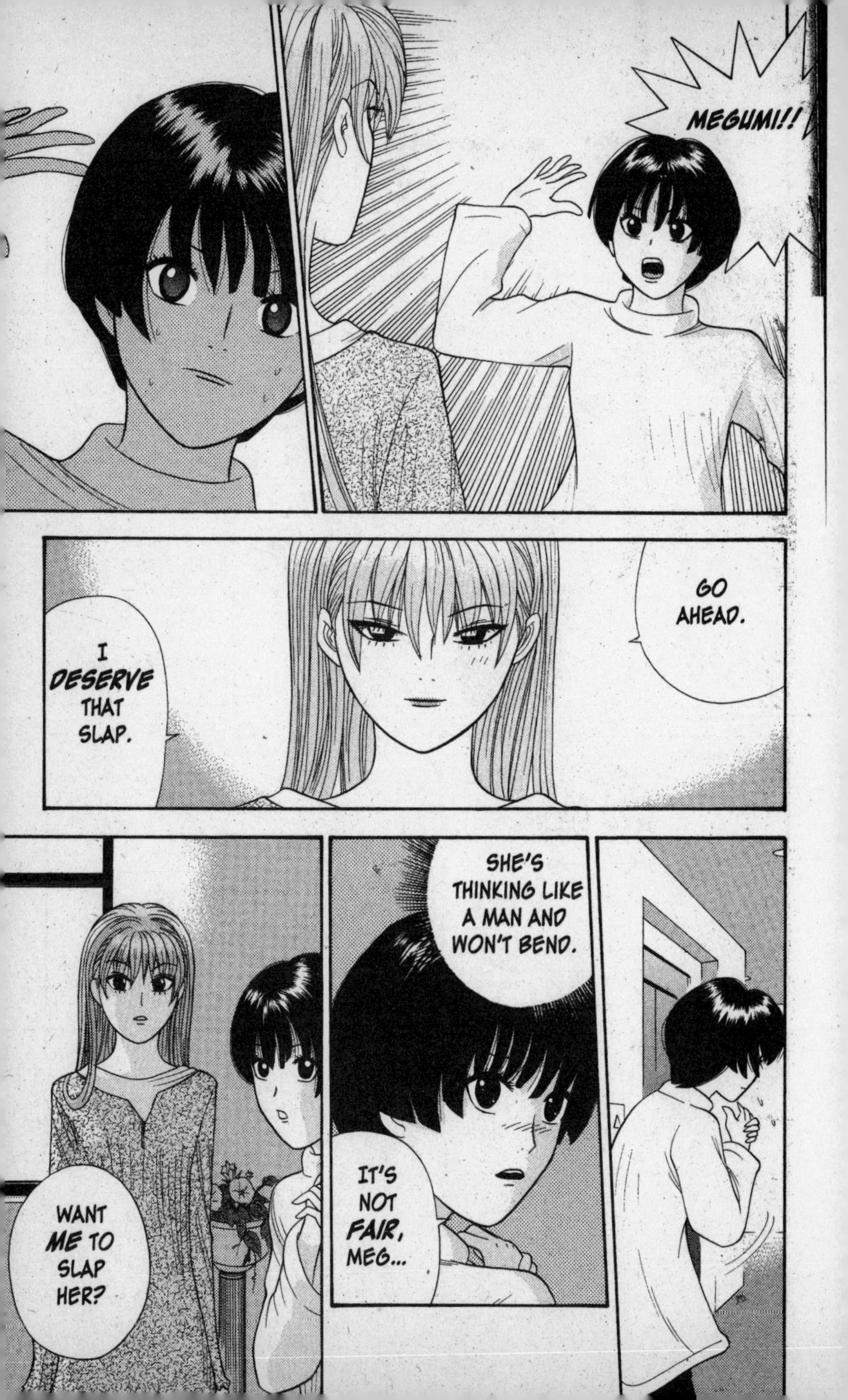
MEGUMI!!
GO AHEAD.
I DESERVE THAT SLAP.
SHE'S THINKING LIKE A MAN AND WON'T BEND.
IT'S NOT FAIR, MEG...
WANT ME TO SLAP HER?

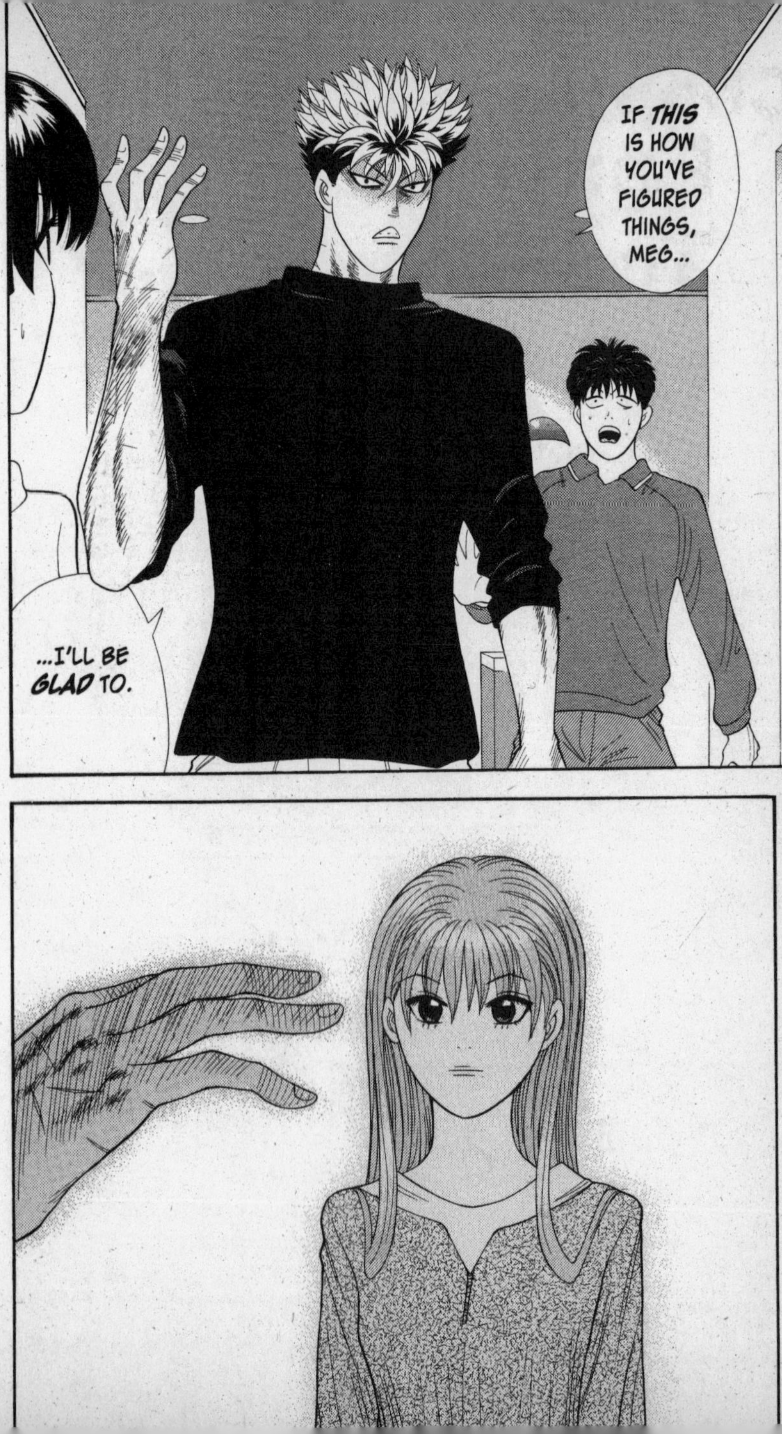
IF THIS IS HOW YOU'VE FIGURED THINGS, MEG...
...I'LL BE GLAD TO.

Chapter 43: Fantasize Together

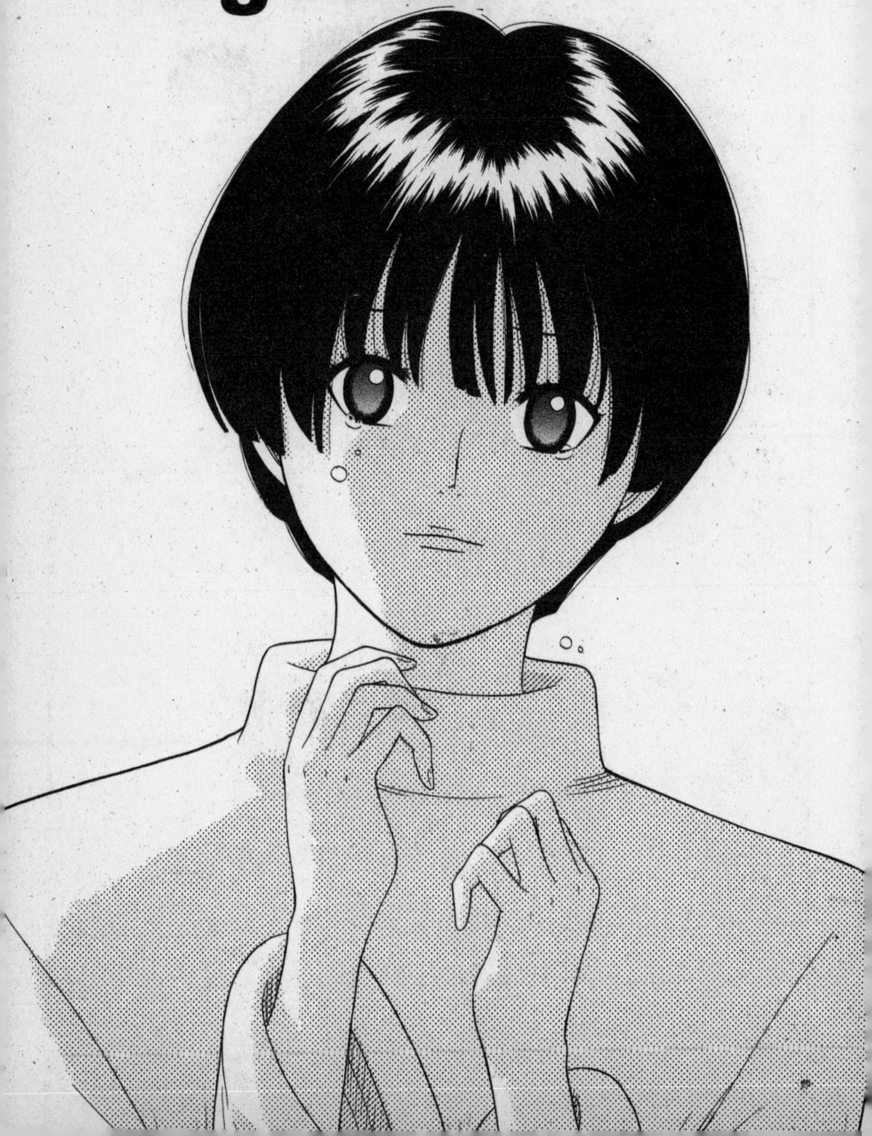

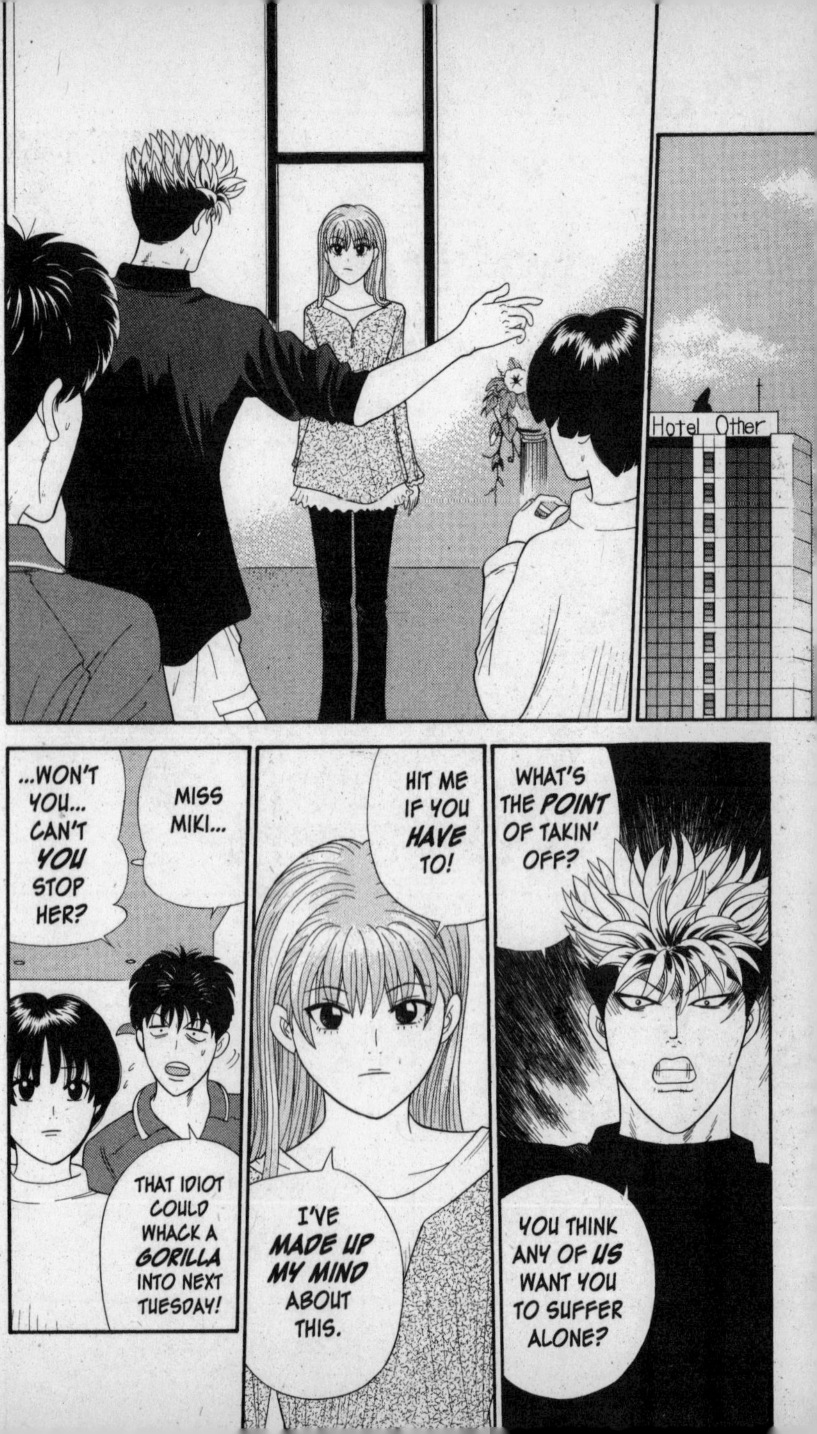
Hotel Other
WHAT'S THE POINT OF TAKIN' OFF?
YOU THINK ANY OF US WANT YOU TO SUFFER ALONE?
HIT ME IF YOU HAVE TO!
I'VE MADE UP MY MIND ABOUT THIS.
MISS MIKI...
...WON'T YOU... CAN'T YOU STOP HER?
THAT IDIOT COULD WHACK A GORILLA INTO NEXT TUESDAY!

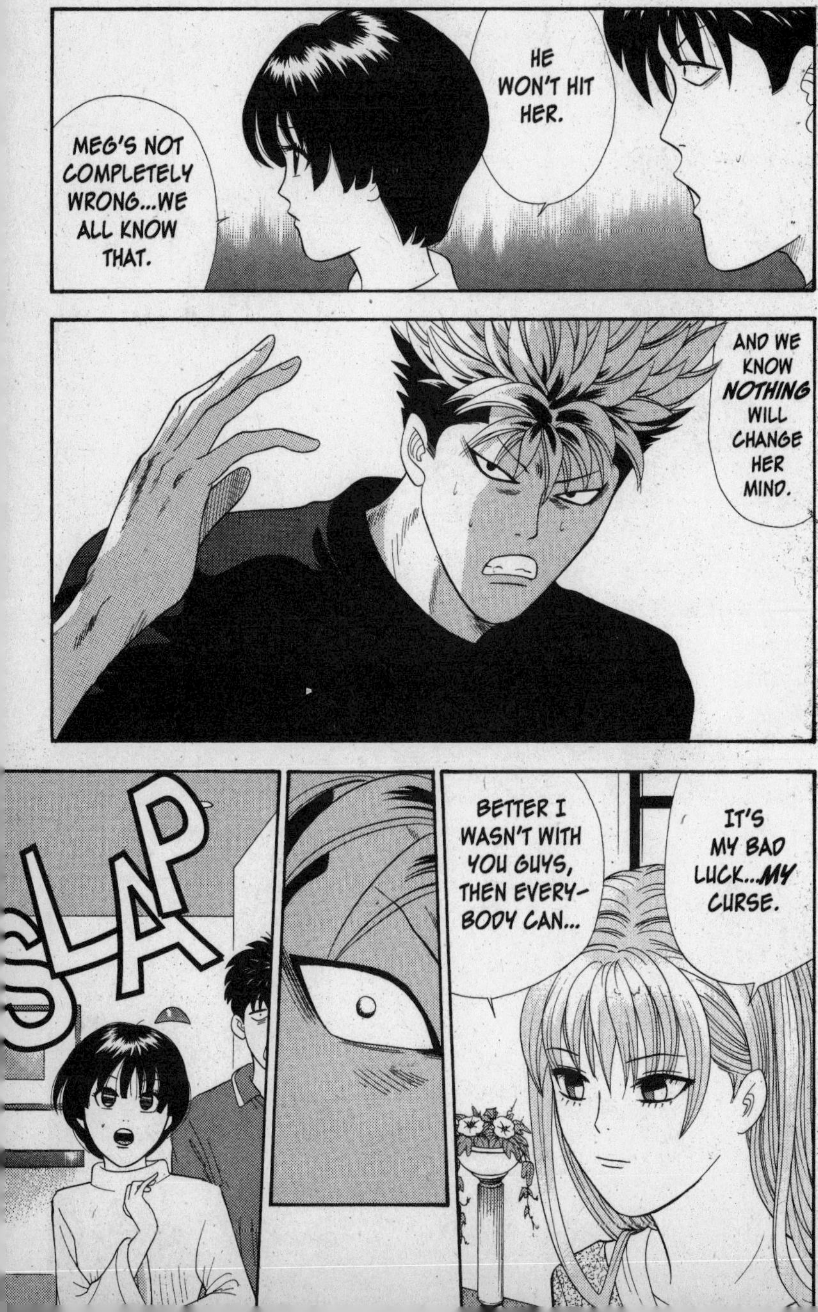
HE WON'T HIT HER.
MEG'S NOT COMPLETELY WRONG...WE ALL KNOW THAT.
AND WE KNOW NOTHING WILL CHANGE HER MIND.
IT'S MY BAD LUCK...MY CURSE.
BETTER I WASN'T WITH YOU GUYS, THEN EVERY-BODY CAN...
SLAP

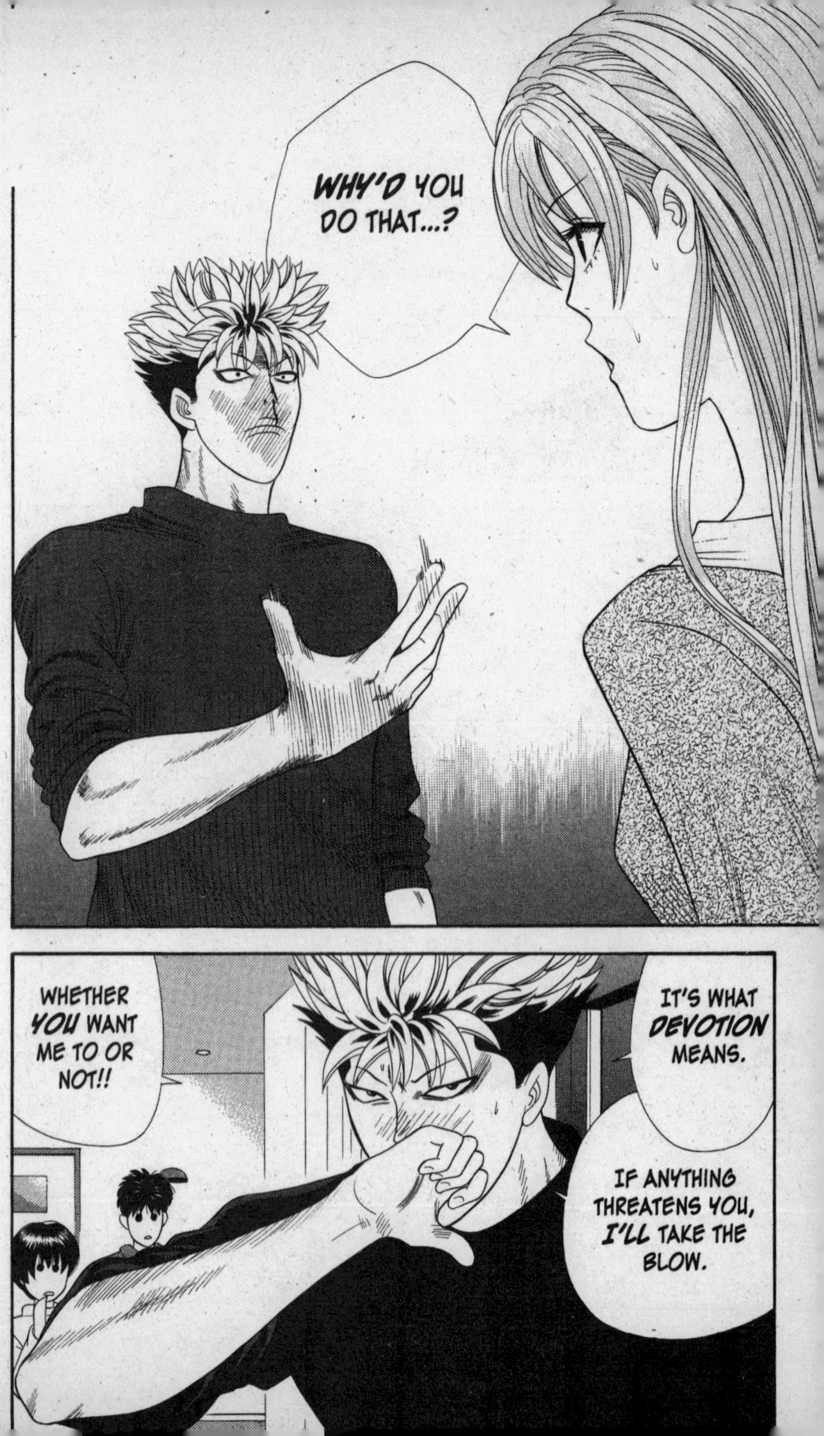
WHY'D YOU DO THAT...?
IT'S WHAT DEVOTION MEANS.
IF ANYTHING THREATENS YOU, I'LL TAKE THE BLOW.
WHETHER YOU WANT ME TO OR NOT!!

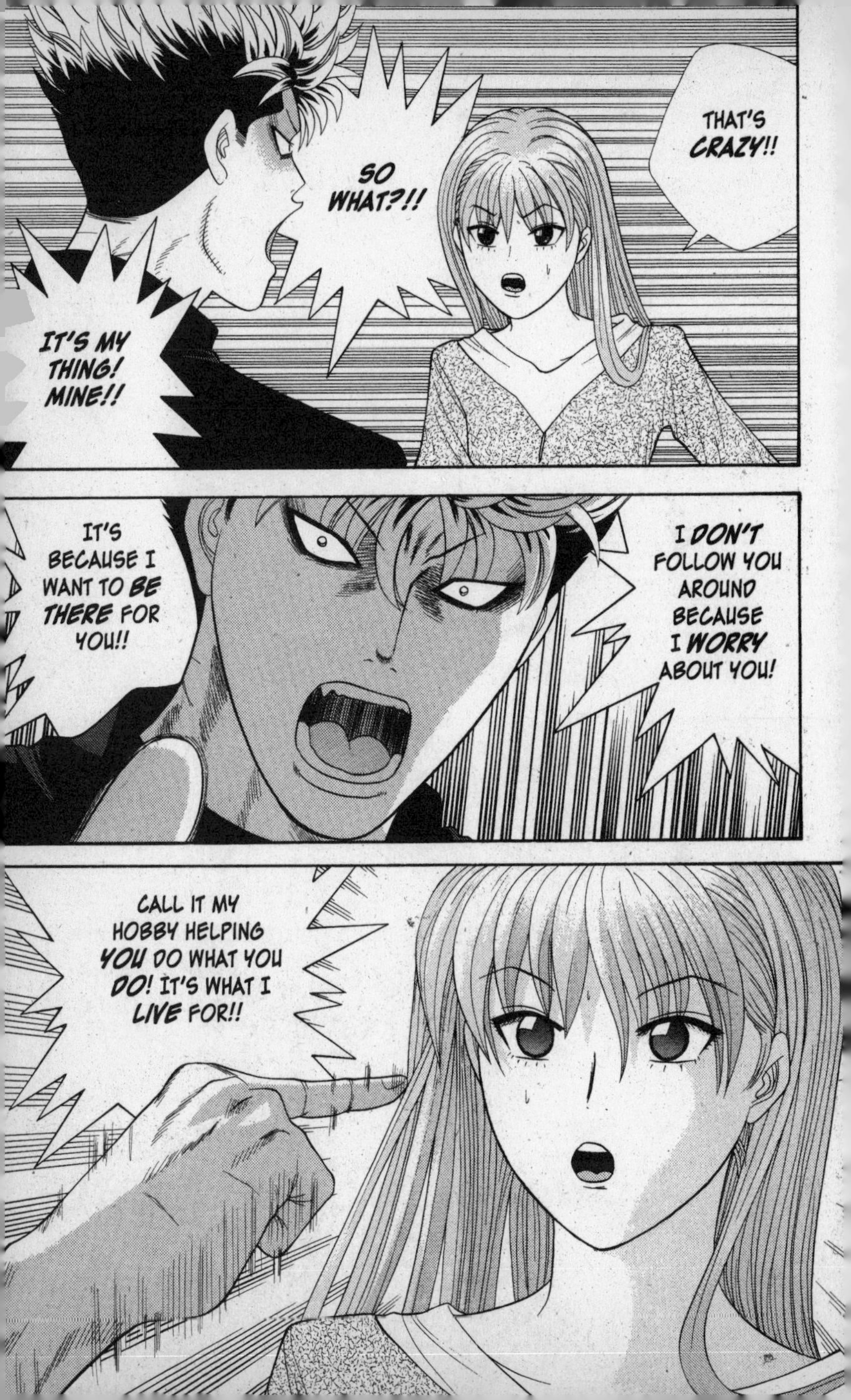
THAT'S *CRAZY*!!
SO WHAT?!!
IT'S MY THING! MINE!!
I *DON'T* FOLLOW YOU AROUND BECAUSE I *WORRY* ABOUT YOU!
IT'S BECAUSE I WANT TO *BE THERE* FOR YOU!!
CALL IT MY HOBBY HELPING *YOU* DO WHAT YOU *DO*! IT'S WHAT I *LIVE* FOR!!

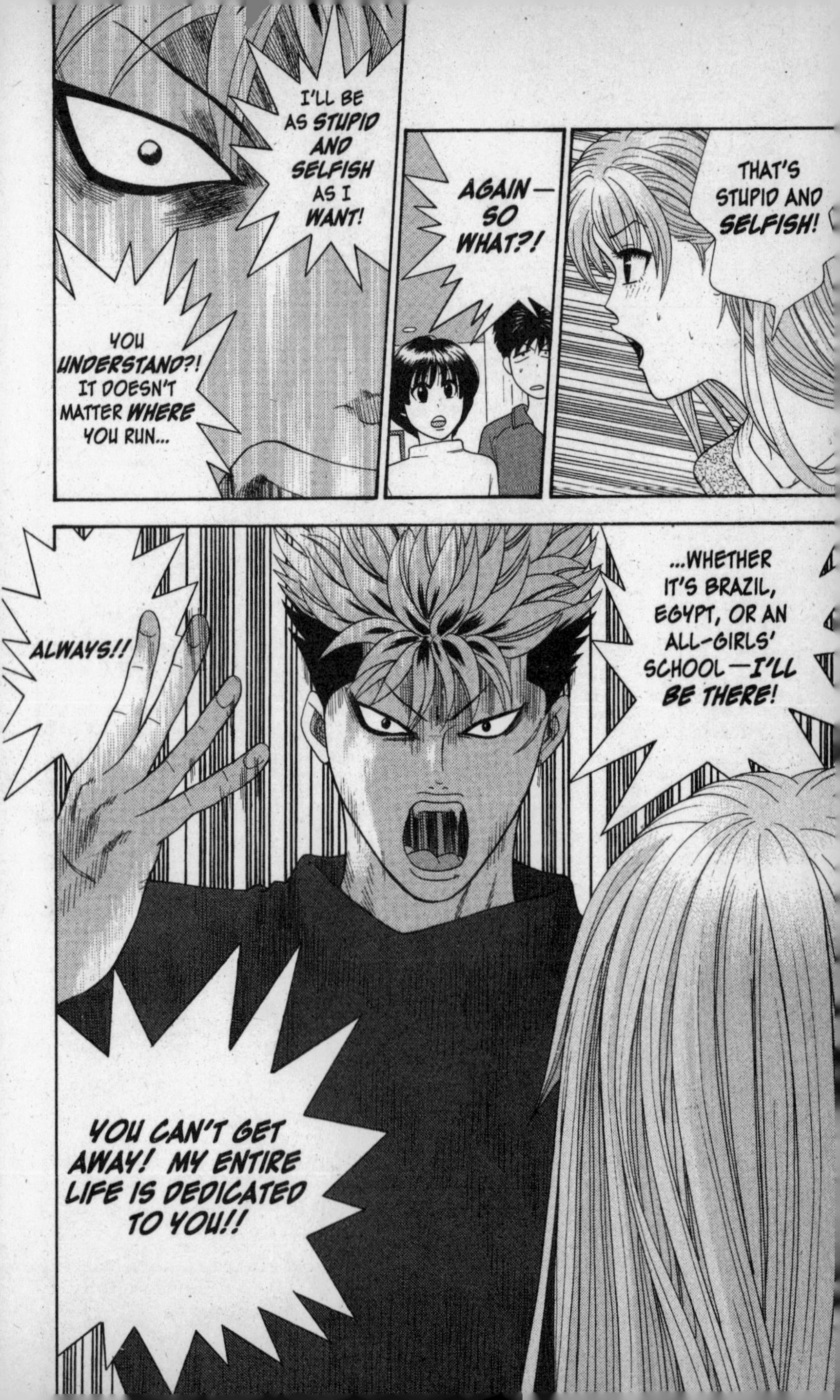
THAT'S STUPID AND SELFISH!
AGAIN—SO WHAT?!
I'LL BE AS STUPID AND SELFISH AS I WANT!
YOU UNDERSTAND?! IT DOESN'T MATTER WHERE YOU RUN...
...WHETHER IT'S BRAZIL, EGYPT, OR AN ALL-GIRLS' SCHOOL—I'LL BE THERE!
ALWAYS!!
YOU CAN'T GET AWAY! MY ENTIRE LIFE IS DEDICATED TO YOU!!

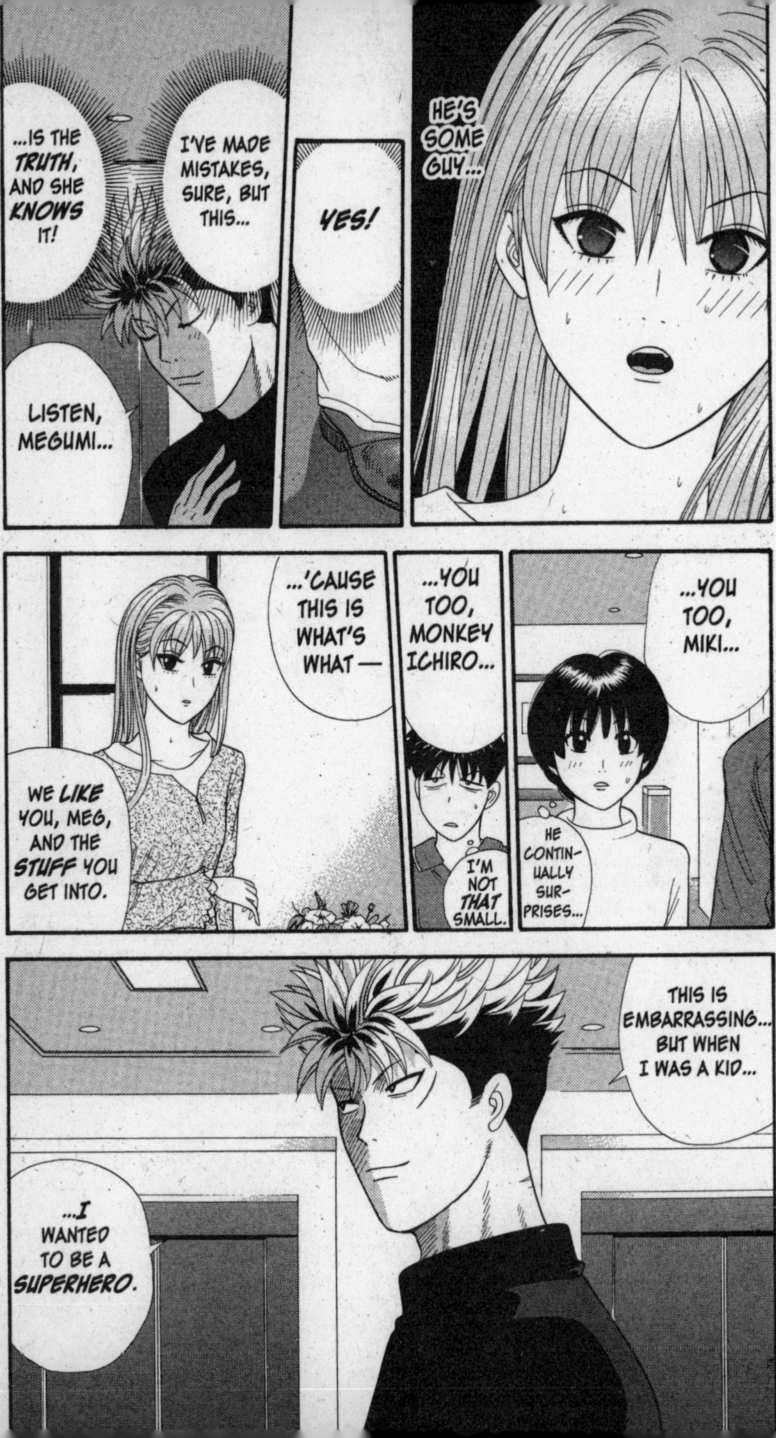
HE'S SOME GUY...
YES!
I'VE MADE MISTAKES, SURE, BUT THIS...
...IS THE TRUTH, AND SHE KNOWS IT!
LISTEN, MEGUMI...
...YOU TOO, MIKI...
HE CONTIN-UALLY SUR-PRISES...
...YOU TOO, MONKEY ICHIRO...
I'M NOT THAT SMALL.
...'CAUSE THIS IS WHAT'S WHAT —
WE LIKE YOU, MEG, AND THE STUFF YOU GET INTO.
THIS IS EMBARRASSING... BUT WHEN I WAS A KID...
...I WANTED TO BE A SUPERHERO.

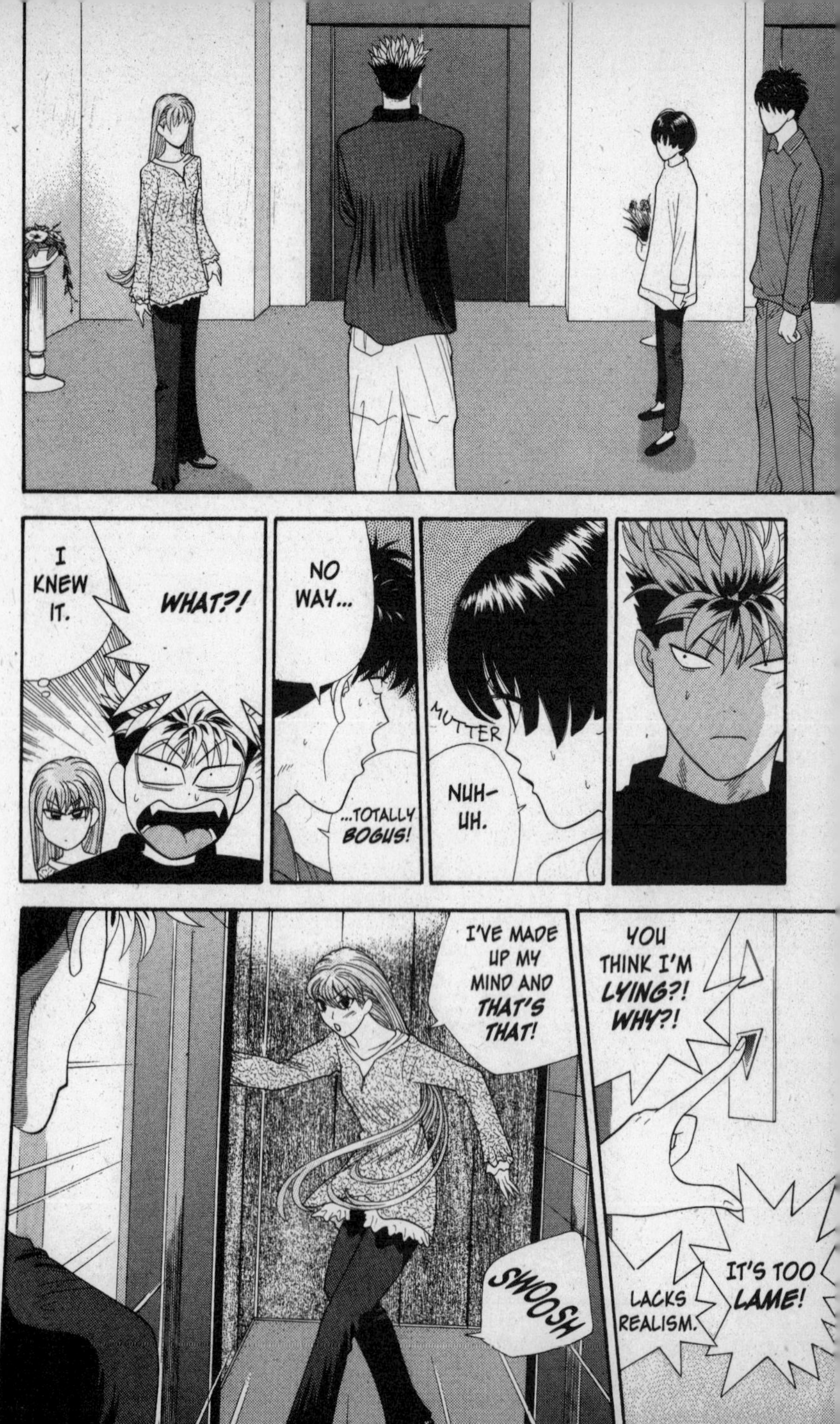
MUTTER
NUH-UH.
NO WAY...
...TOTALLY BOGUS!
WHAT?!
I KNEW IT.
YOU THINK I'M LYING?! WHY?!
IT'S TOO LAME!
LACKS REALISM.
I'VE MADE UP MY MIND AND THAT'S THAT!
SWOOSH

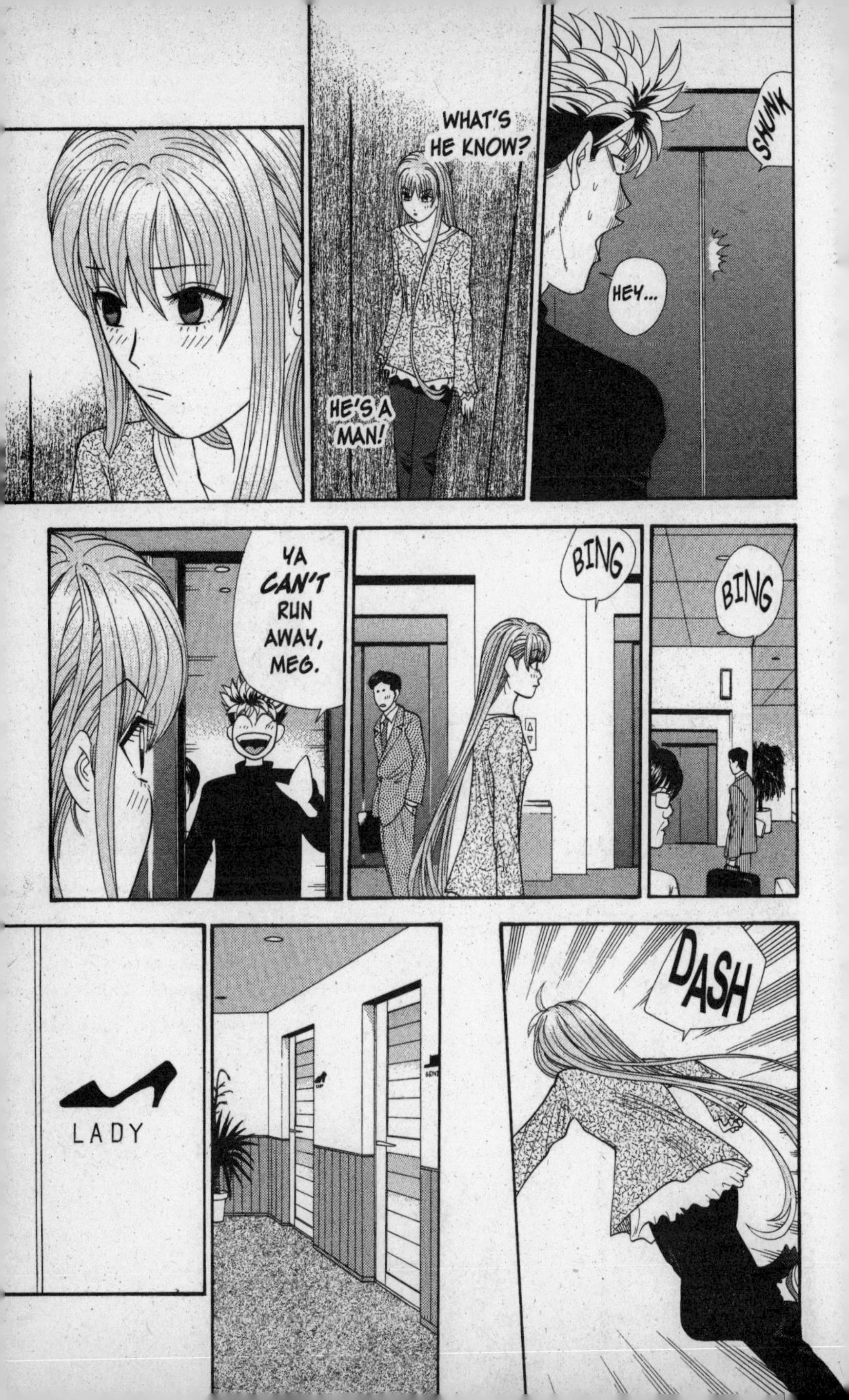
SHUNK
HEY...
WHAT'S HE KNOW?
HE'S A MAN!
BING
BING
YA CAN'T RUN AWAY, MEG.
DASH
LADY

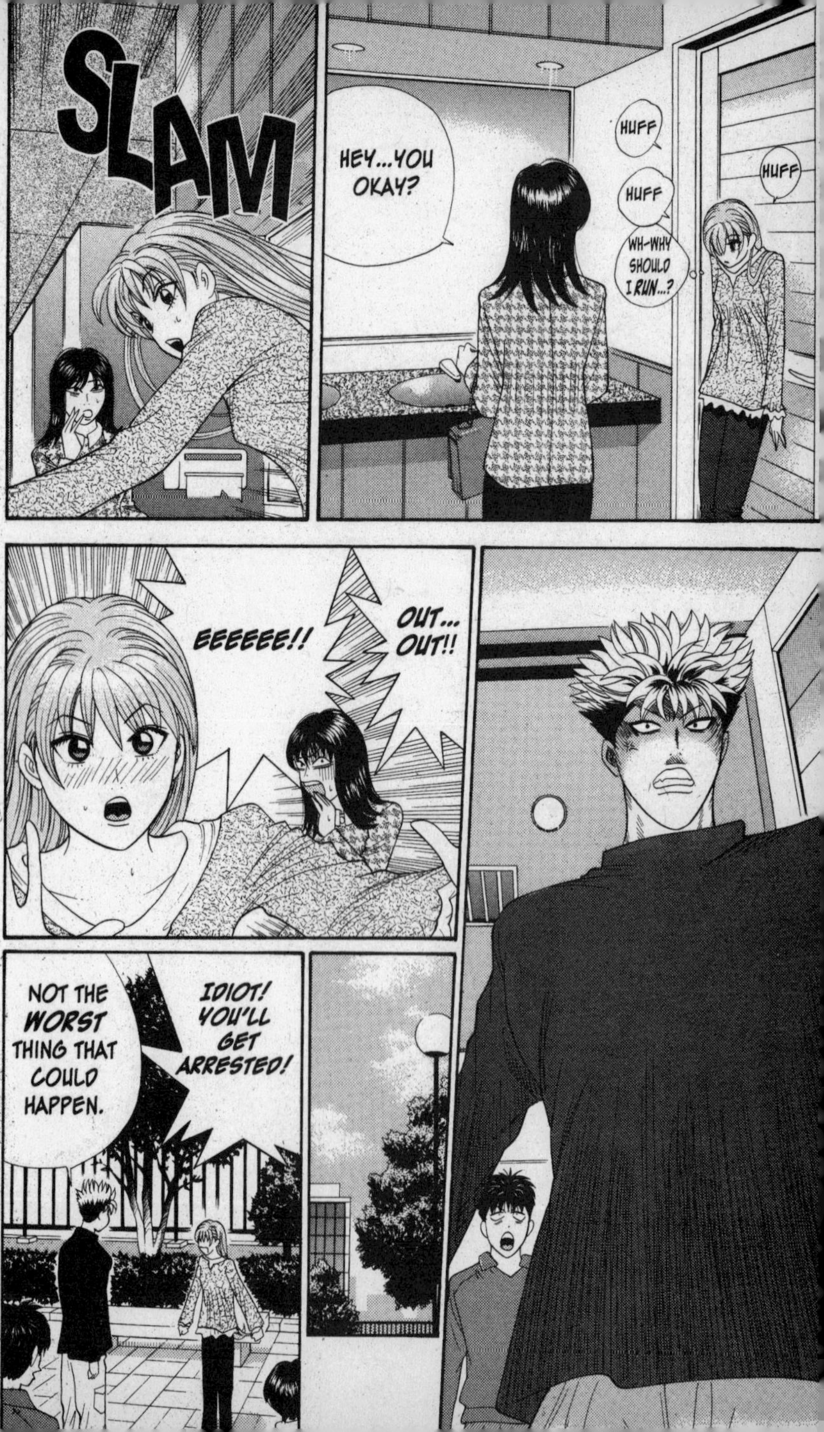
HUFF
HUFF
HUFF
WH-WHY SHOULD I RUN...?
HEY...YOU OKAY?
SLAM
OUT... OUT!!
EEEEEE!!
IDIOT! YOU'LL GET ARRESTED!
NOT THE WORST THING THAT COULD HAPPEN.

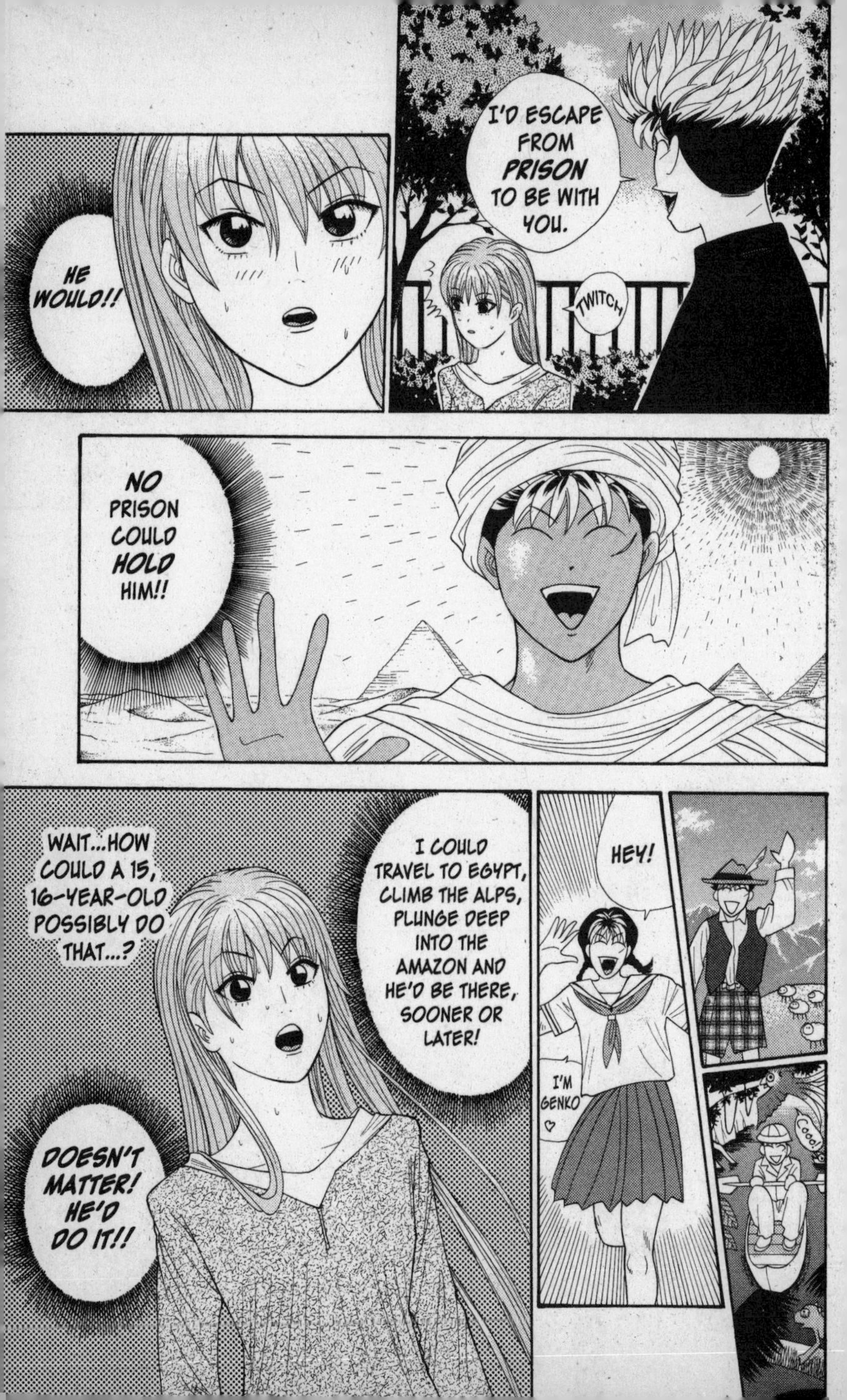

I'D ESCAPE FROM PRISON TO BE WITH YOU.
TWITCH
HE WOULD!!
NO PRISON COULD HOLD HIM!!
HEY!
I'M GENKO ♡
I COULD TRAVEL TO EGYPT, CLIMB THE ALPS, PLUNGE DEEP INTO THE AMAZON AND HE'D BE THERE, SOONER OR LATER!
WAIT...HOW COULD A 15, 16-YEAR-OLD POSSIBLY DO THAT...?
DOESN'T MATTER! HE'D DO IT!!

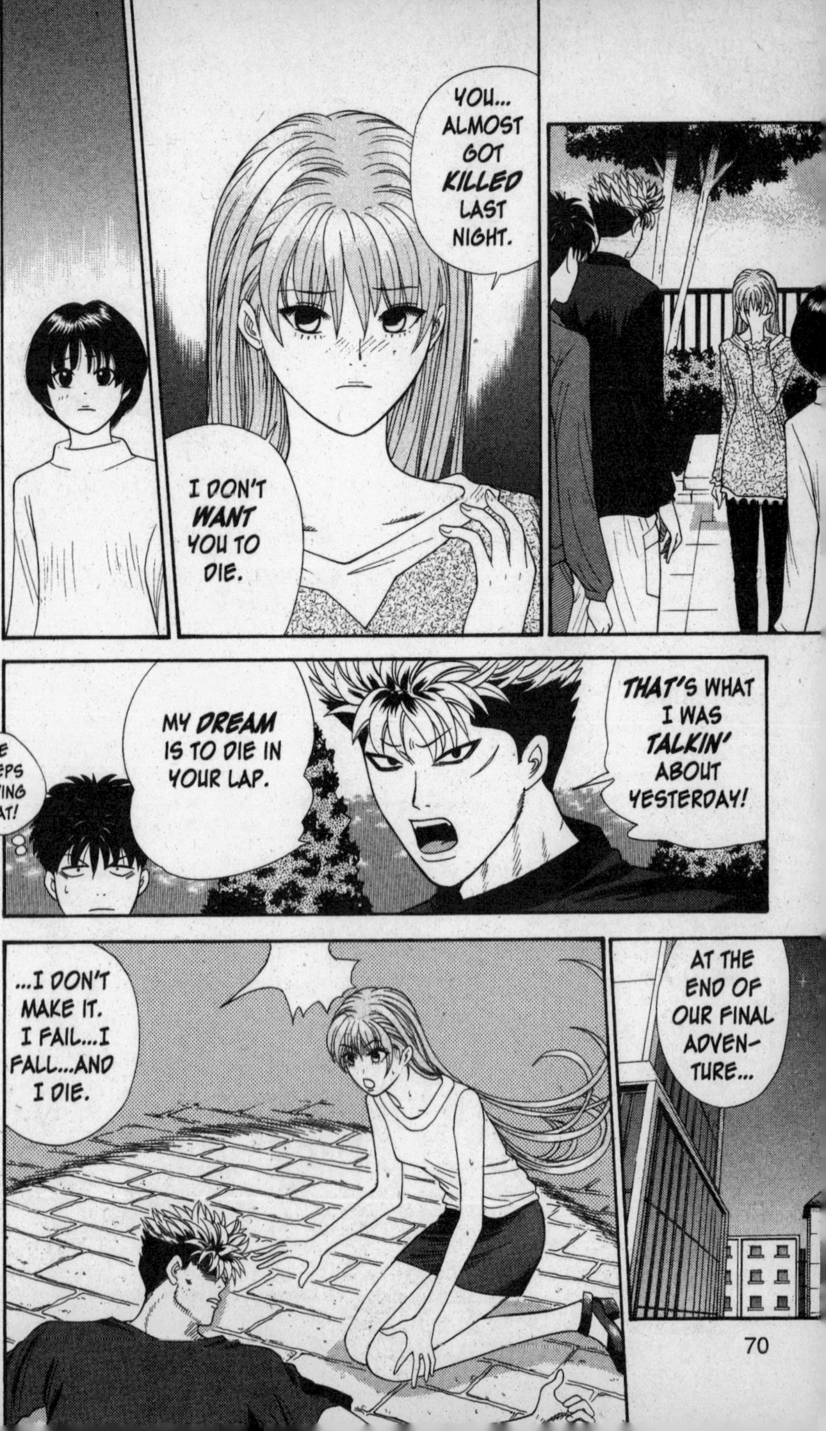
YOU... ALMOST GOT KILLED LAST NIGHT.
I DON'T WANT YOU TO DIE.
THAT'S WHAT I WAS TALKIN' ABOUT YESTERDAY!
MY DREAM IS TO DIE IN YOUR LAP.
HE KEEPS SAYING THAT!
AT THE END OF OUR FINAL ADVEN-TURE...
...I DON'T MAKE IT. I FAIL...I FALL...AND I DIE.

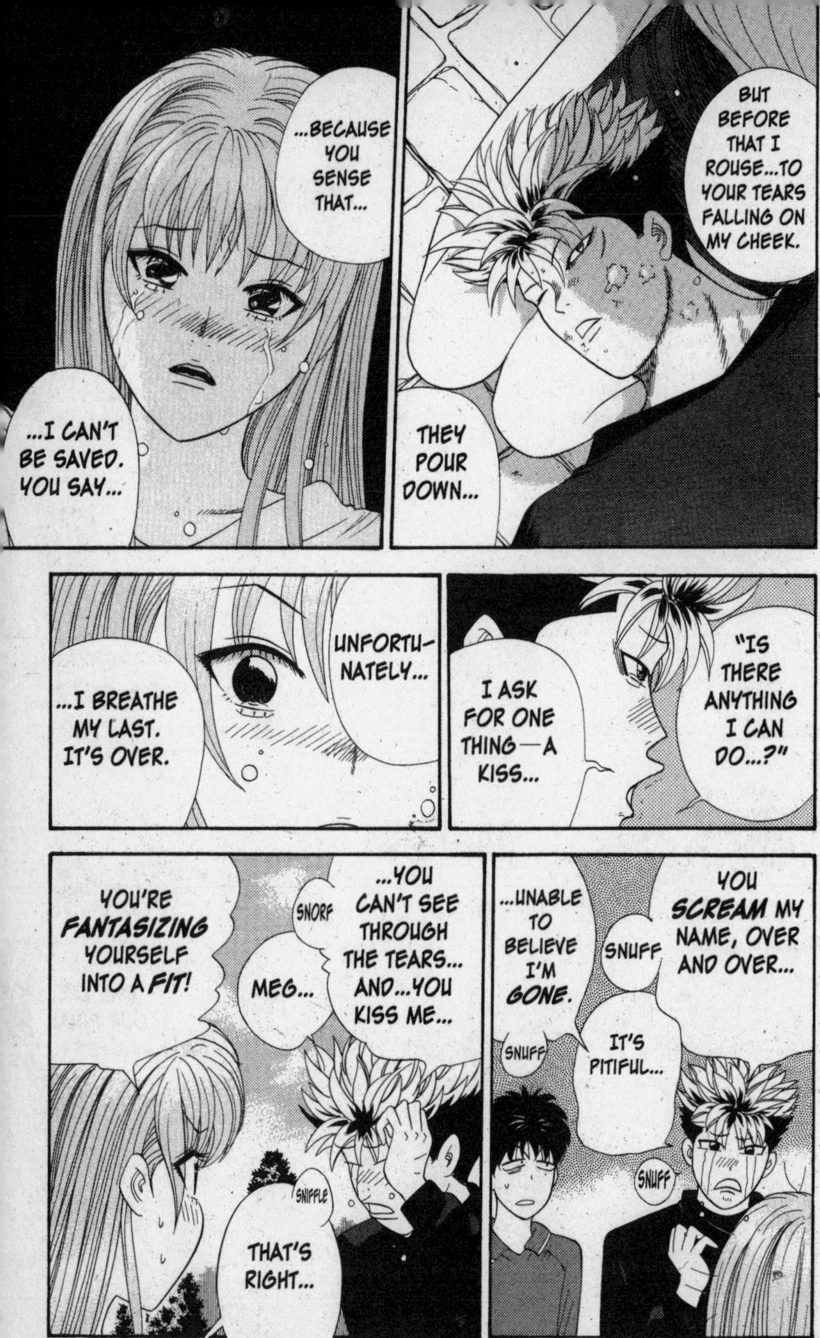
BUT BEFORE THAT I ROUSE...TO YOUR TEARS FALLING ON MY CHEEK.
THEY POUR DOWN...
...BECAUSE YOU SENSE THAT...
...I CAN'T BE SAVED. YOU SAY...
"IS THERE ANYTHING I CAN DO...?"
I ASK FOR ONE THING—A KISS...
UNFORTUNATELY...
...I BREATHE MY LAST. IT'S OVER.
YOU SCREAM MY NAME, OVER AND OVER...
SNUFF
...UNABLE TO BELIEVE I'M GONE.
IT'S PITIFUL...
SNUFF
SNUFF
...YOU CAN'T SEE THROUGH THE TEARS... AND...YOU KISS ME...
SNORF
MEG...
YOU'RE FANTASIZING YOURSELF INTO A FIT!
SNIFFLE
THAT'S RIGHT...

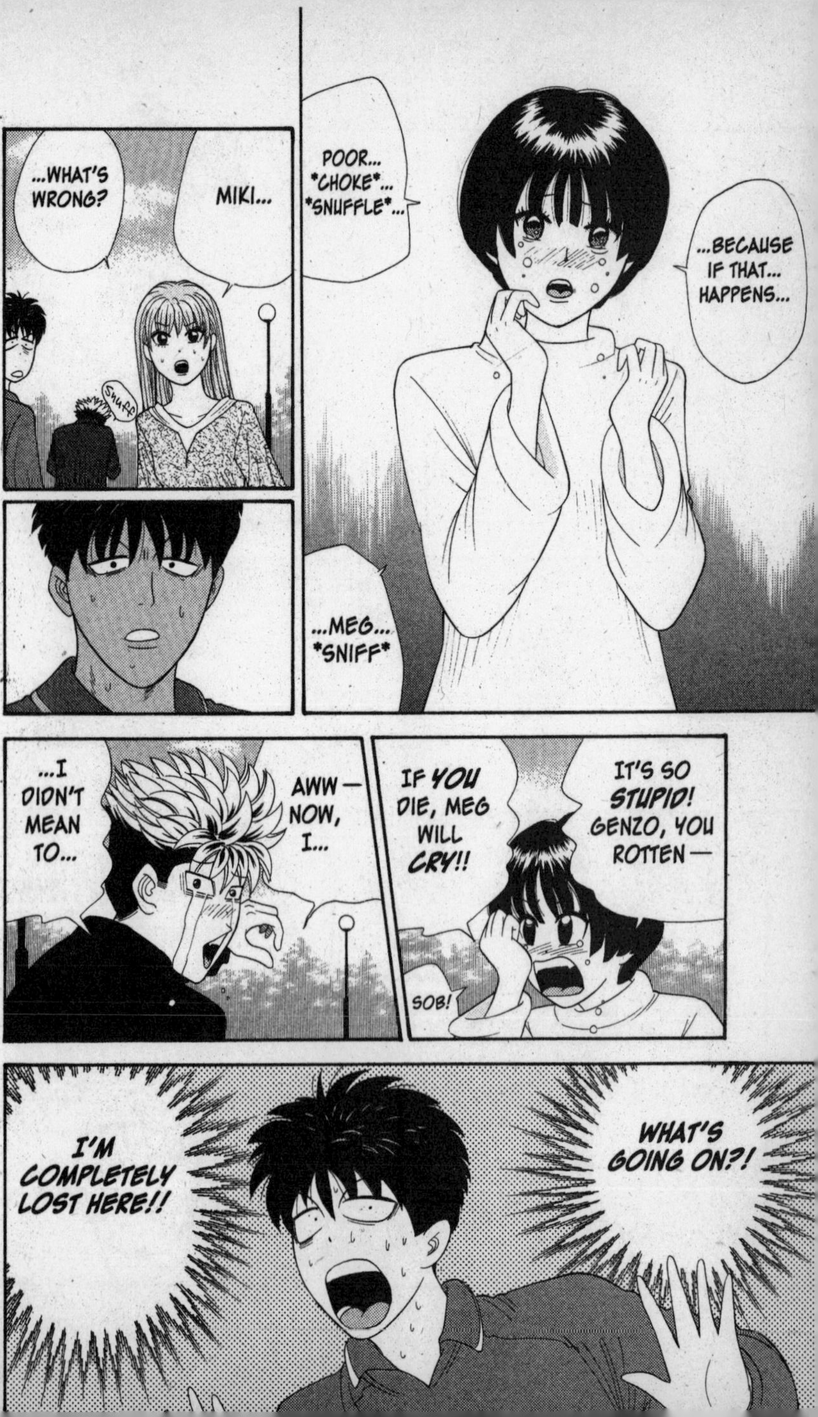
...BECAUSE IF THAT... HAPPENS...
POOR... *CHOKE*... *SNUFFLE*...
...MEG... *SNIFF*
MIKI...
...WHAT'S WRONG?
Snuff
IT'S SO STUPID! GENZO, YOU ROTTEN—
IF YOU DIE, MEG WILL CRY!!
SOB!
AWW— NOW, I...
...I DIDN'T MEAN TO...
WHAT'S GOING ON?!
I'M COMPLETELY LOST HERE!!

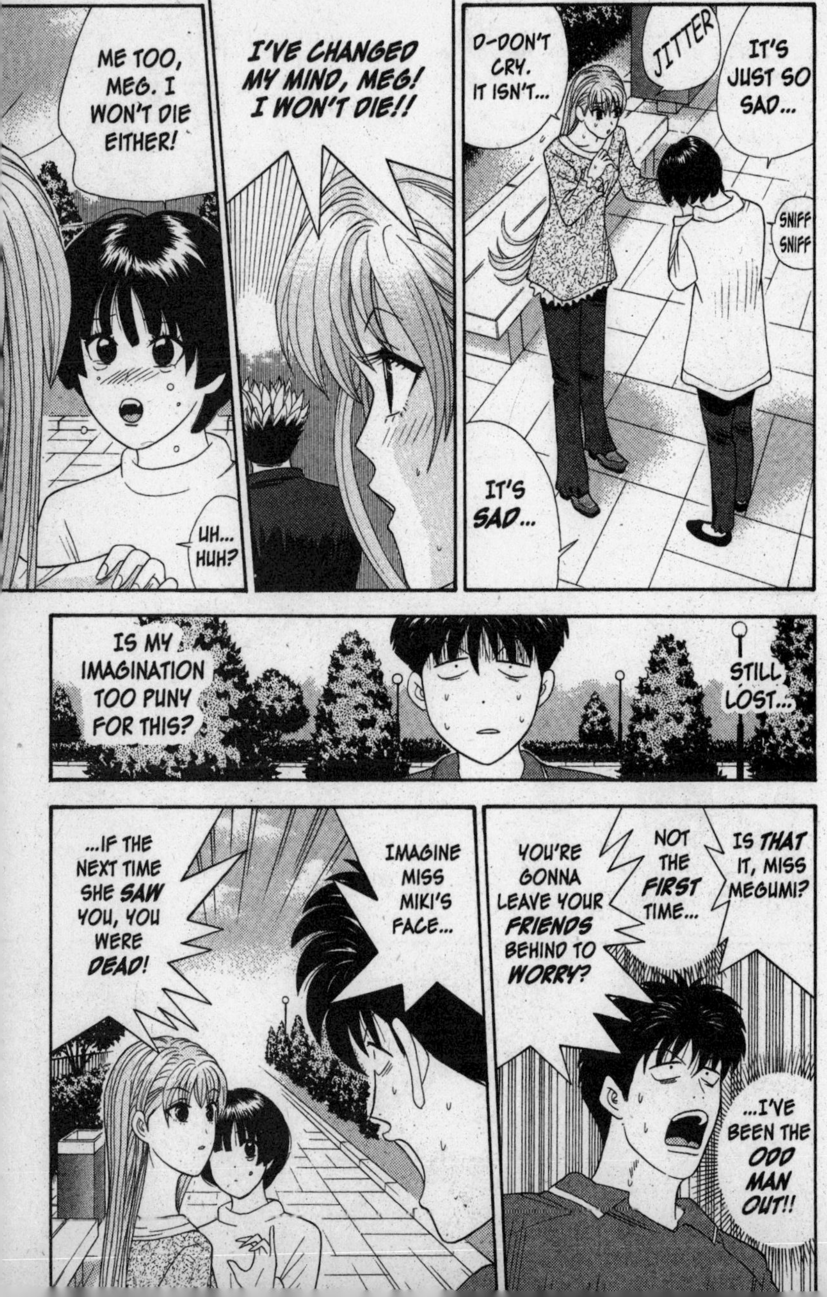
IT'S JUST SO SAD...
JITTER
D-DON'T CRY. IT ISN'T...
SNIFF SNIFF
IT'S SAD...
I'VE CHANGED MY MIND, MEG! I WON'T DIE!!
ME TOO, MEG. I WON'T DIE EITHER!
UH... HUH?
STILL LOST...
IS MY IMAGINATION TOO PUNY FOR THIS?
IS THAT IT, MISS MEGUMI?
NOT THE FIRST TIME...
YOU'RE GONNA LEAVE YOUR FRIENDS BEHIND TO WORRY?
...I'VE BEEN THE ODD MAN OUT!!
IMAGINE MISS MIKI'S FACE...
...IF THE NEXT TIME SHE SAW YOU, YOU WERE DEAD!

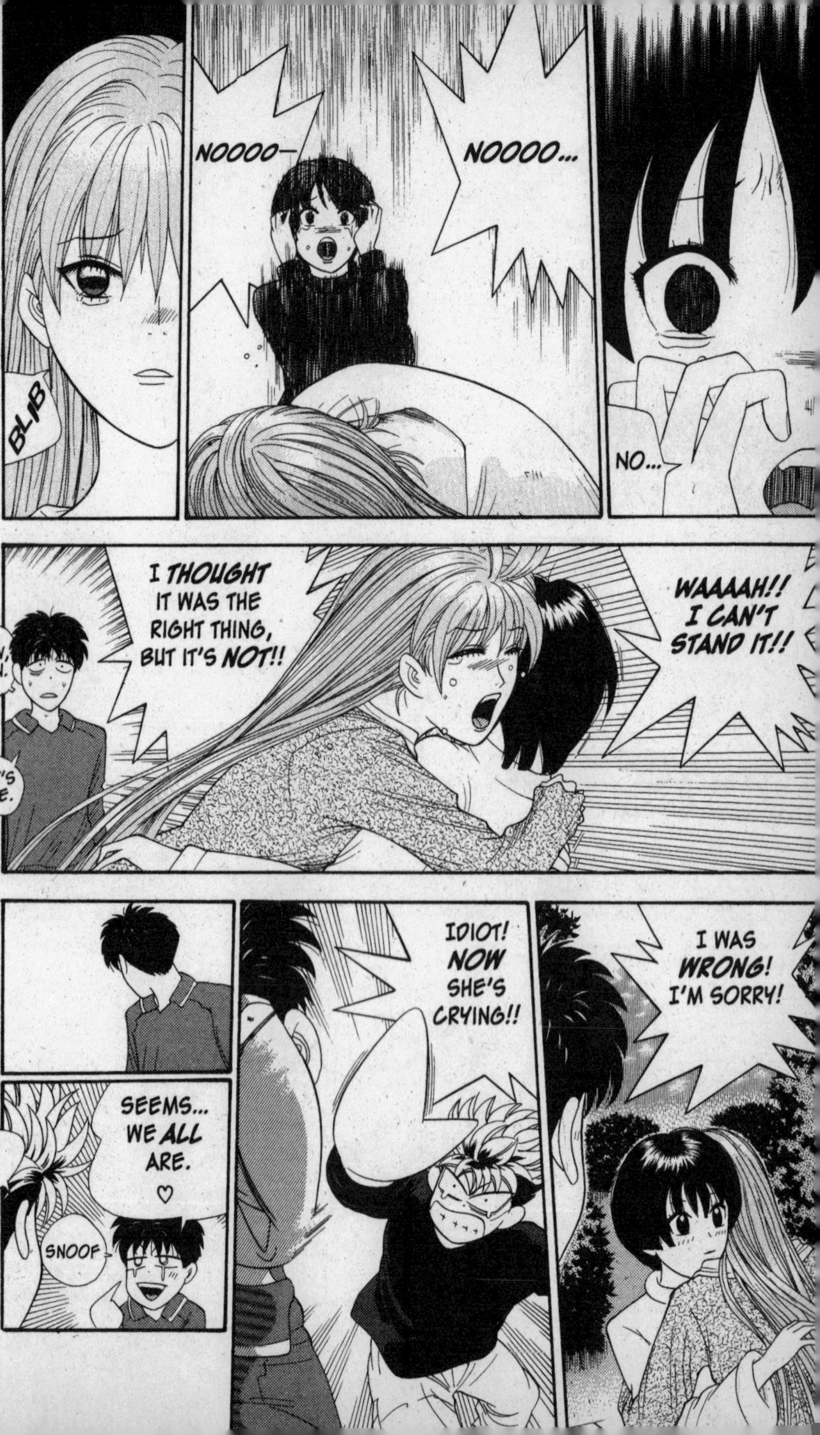
NO...
NOOOO...
NOOOO—
BLIB
WAAAAH!! I CAN'T STAND IT!!
I THOUGHT IT WAS THE RIGHT THING, BUT IT'S NOT!!
AWW, MAN.
IT'S ME.
I WAS WRONG! I'M SORRY!
IDIOT! NOW SHE'S CRYING!!
SEEMS... WE ALL ARE. ♡
?!
SNOOF

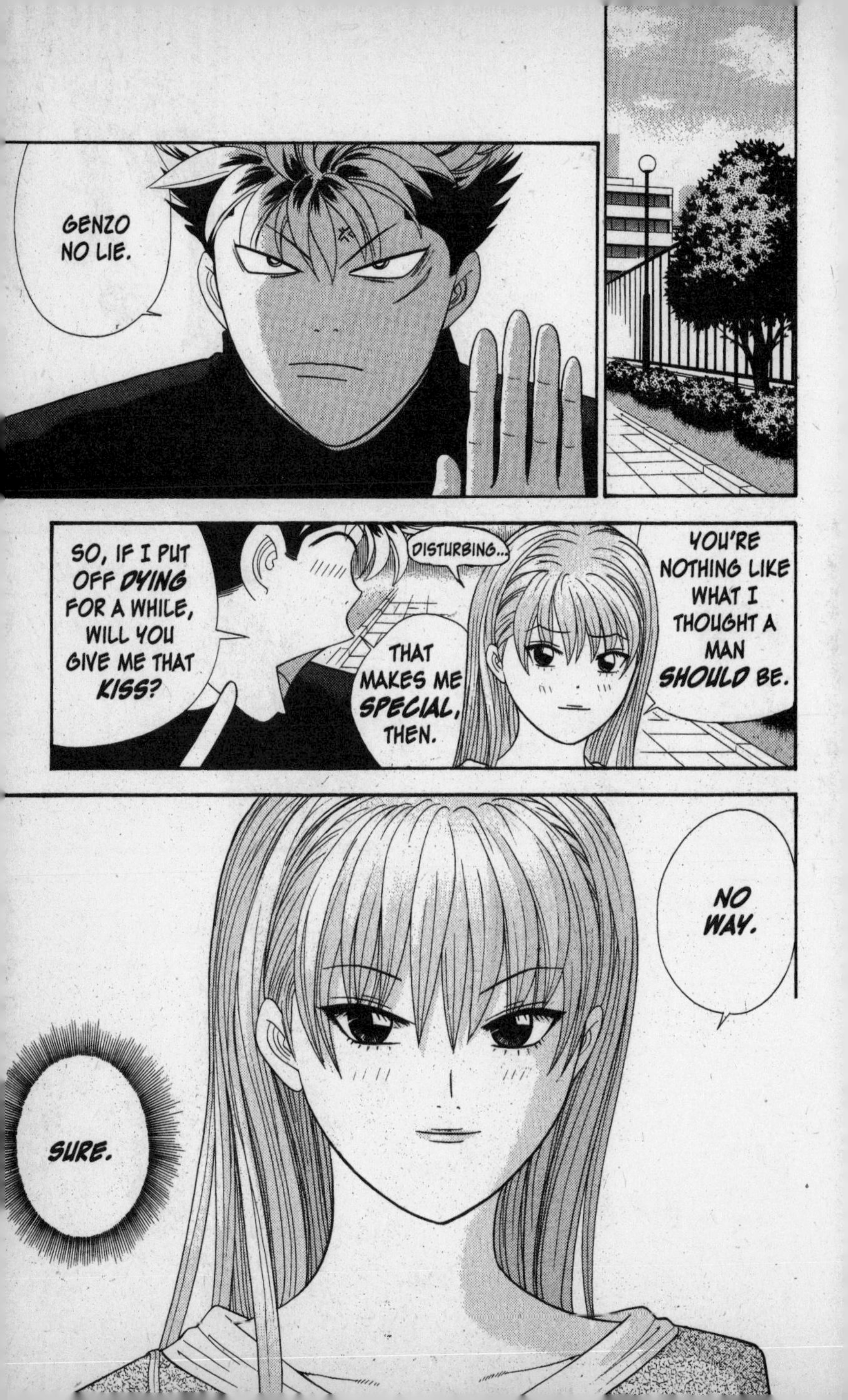
GENZO NO LIE.
YOU'RE NOTHING LIKE WHAT I THOUGHT A MAN SHOULD BE.
DISTURBING...
THAT MAKES ME SPECIAL, THEN.
SO, IF I PUT OFF DYING FOR A WHILE, WILL YOU GIVE ME THAT KISS?
NO WAY.
SURE.

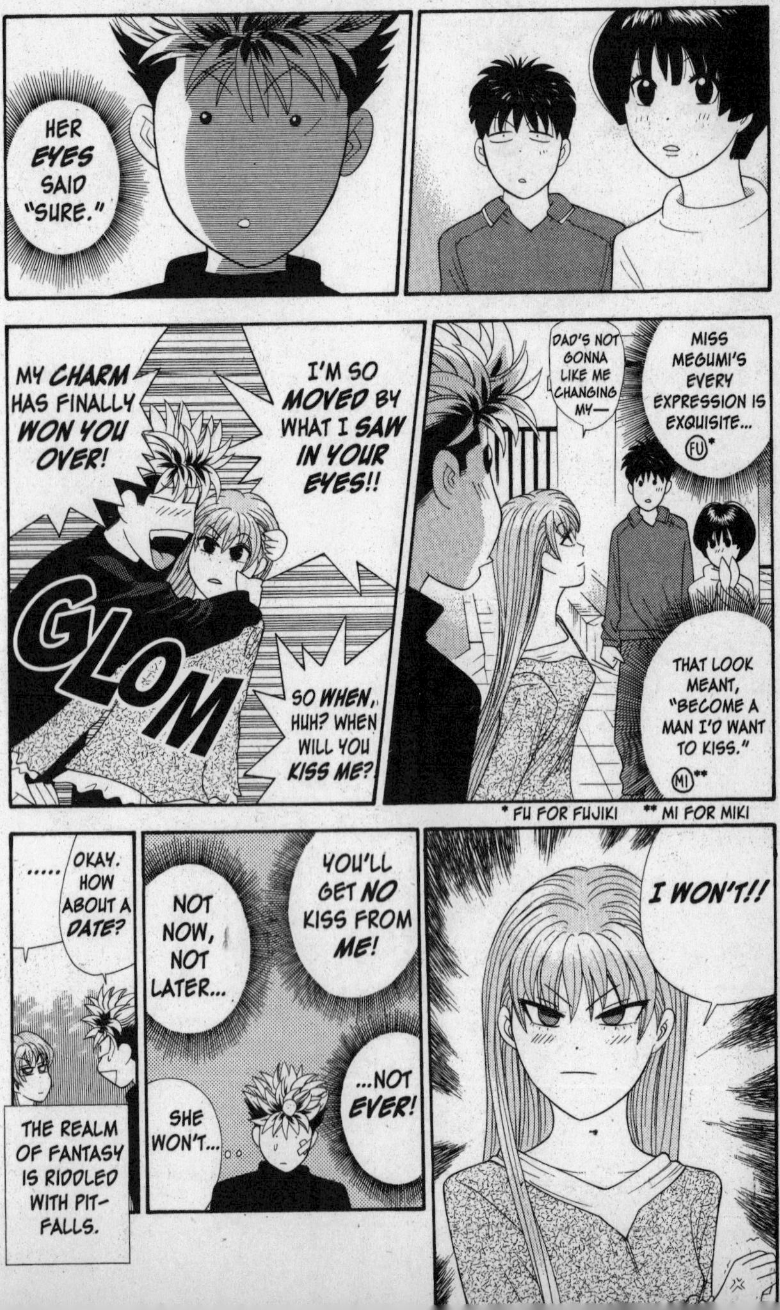
HER EYES SAID "SURE."
MISS MEGUMI'S EVERY EXPRESSION IS EXQUISITE... FU*
DAD'S NOT GONNA LIKE ME CHANGING MY—
THAT LOOK MEANT, "BECOME A MAN I'D WANT TO KISS." MI**
I'M SO MOVED BY WHAT I SAW IN YOUR EYES!!
MY CHARM HAS FINALLY WON YOU OVER!
GLOM
SO WHEN, HUH? WHEN WILL YOU KISS ME?
* FU FOR FUJIKI ** MI FOR MIKI
I WON'T!!
YOU'LL GET NO KISS FROM ME!
NOT NOW, NOT LATER...
...NOT EVER!
SHE WON'T...
OKAY. HOW ABOUT A DATE?
.....
THE REALM OF FANTASY IS RIDDLED WITH PIT-FALLS.

Chapter 44: Let's Go With Group Meg!

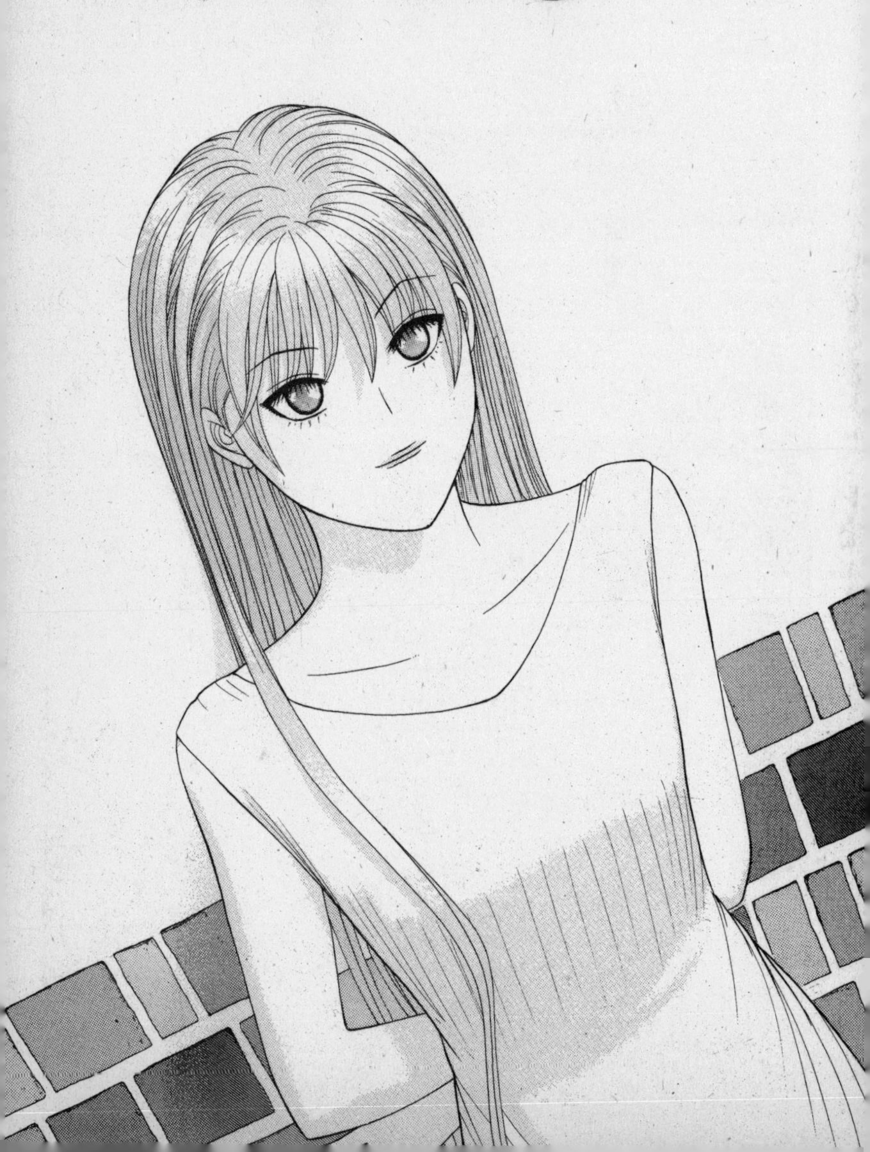

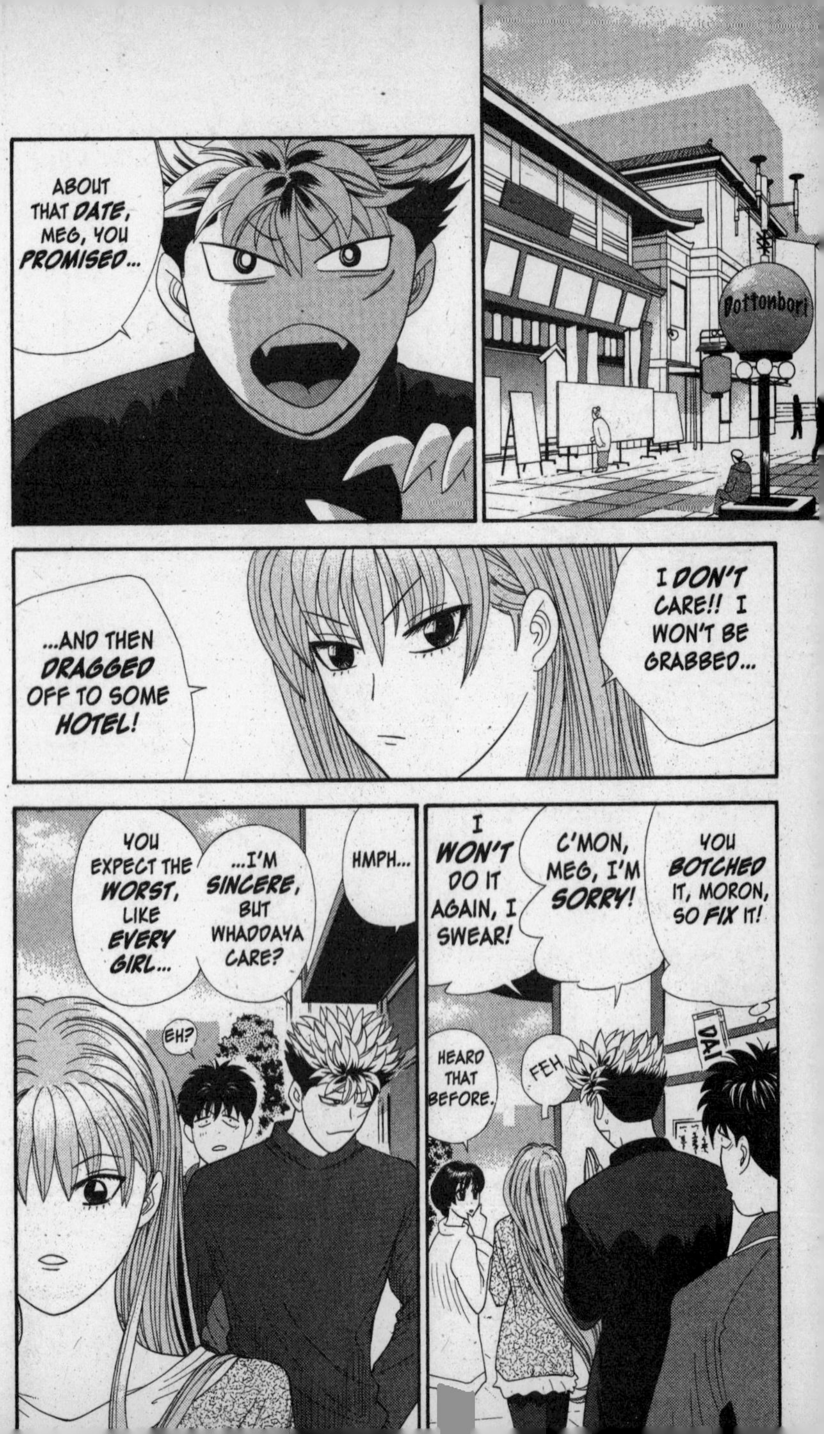
Dottonbori
ABOUT THAT DATE, MEG, YOU PROMISED...
I DON'T CARE!! I WON'T BE GRABBED...
...AND THEN DRAGGED OFF TO SOME HOTEL!
YOU BOTCHED IT, MORON, SO FIX IT!
C'MON, MEG, I'M SORRY!
I WON'T DO IT AGAIN, I SWEAR!
FEH
HEARD THAT BEFORE.
HMPH...
...I'M SINCERE, BUT WHADDAYA CARE?
YOU EXPECT THE WORST, LIKE EVERY GIRL...
EH?

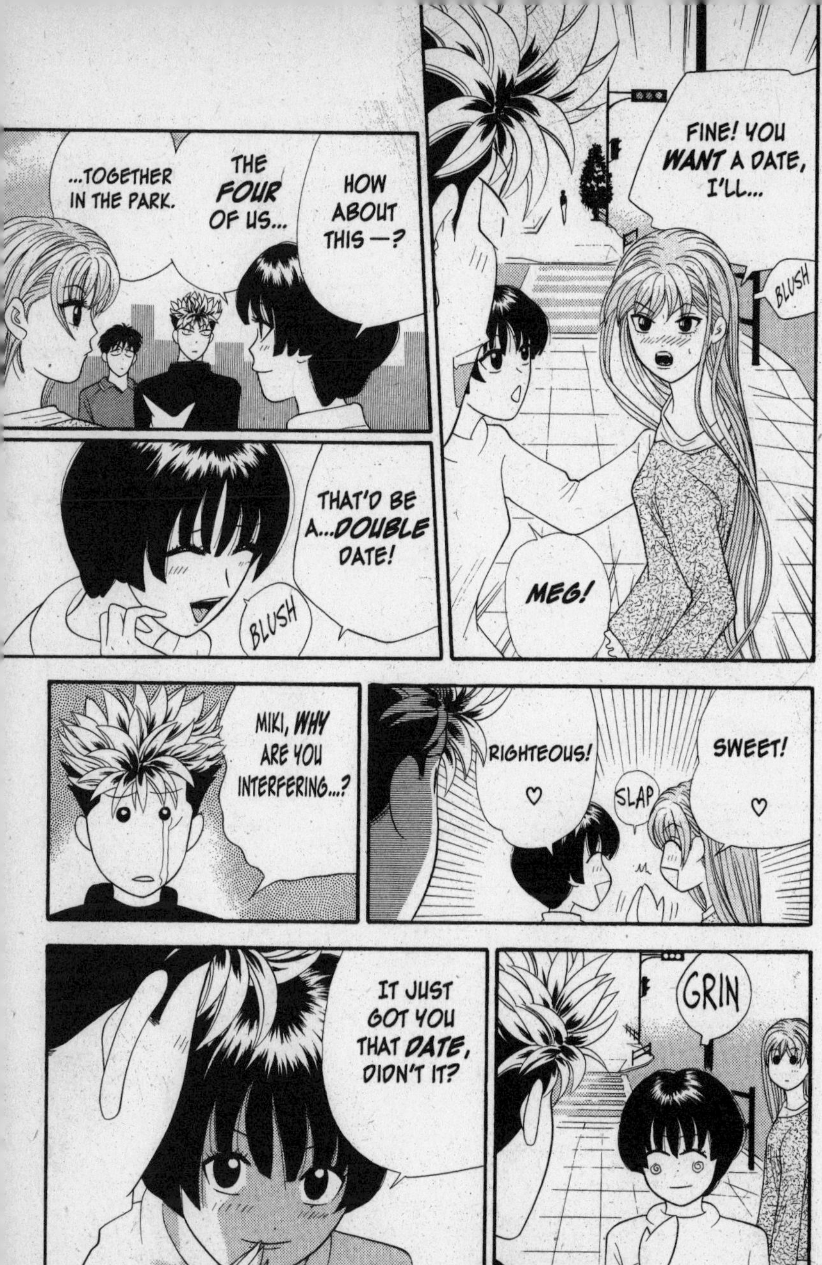
FINE! YOU WANT A DATE, I'LL...
BLUSH
MEG!
HOW ABOUT THIS—?
THE FOUR OF US...
...TOGETHER IN THE PARK.
THAT'D BE A...DOUBLE DATE!
BLUSH
SWEET! ♡
SLAP
RIGHTEOUS! ♡
MIKI, WHY ARE YOU INTERFERING...?
GRIN
IT JUST GOT YOU THAT DATE, DIDN'T IT?

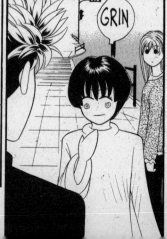

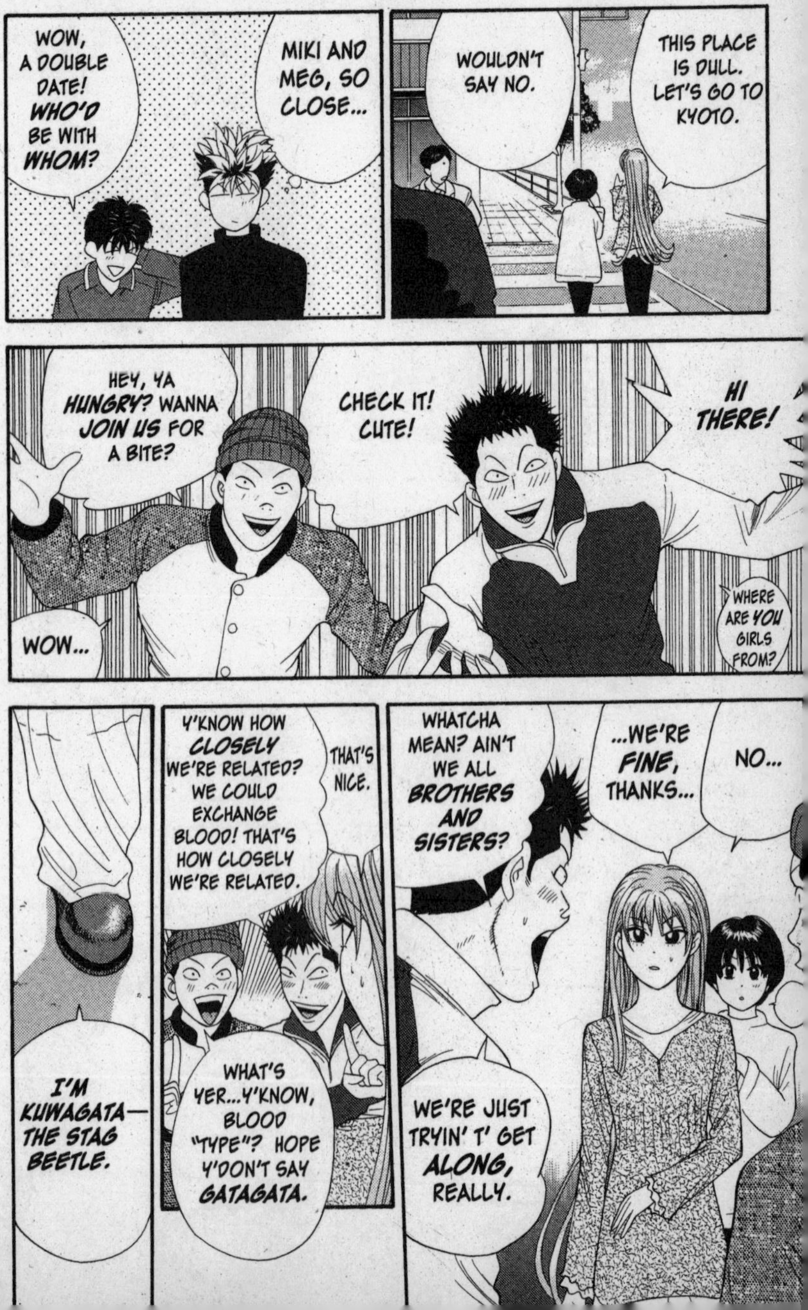

THIS PLACE IS DULL. LET'S GO TO KYOTO.
WOULDN'T SAY NO.
MIKI AND MEG, SO CLOSE...
WOW, A DOUBLE DATE! WHO'D BE WITH WHOM?
HI THERE!
CHECK IT! CUTE!
HEY, YA HUNGRY? WANNA JOIN US FOR A BITE?
WHERE ARE YOU GIRLS FROM?
WOW...
NO...
...WE'RE FINE, THANKS...
WHATCHA MEAN? AIN'T WE ALL BROTHERS AND SISTERS?
WE'RE JUST TRYIN' T' GET ALONG, REALLY.
THAT'S NICE.
Y'KNOW HOW CLOSELY WE'RE RELATED? WE COULD EXCHANGE BLOOD! THAT'S HOW CLOSELY WE'RE RELATED.
WHAT'S YER...Y'KNOW, BLOOD "TYPE"? HOPE Y'DON'T SAY GATAGATA.
I'M KUWAGATA—THE STAG BEETLE.

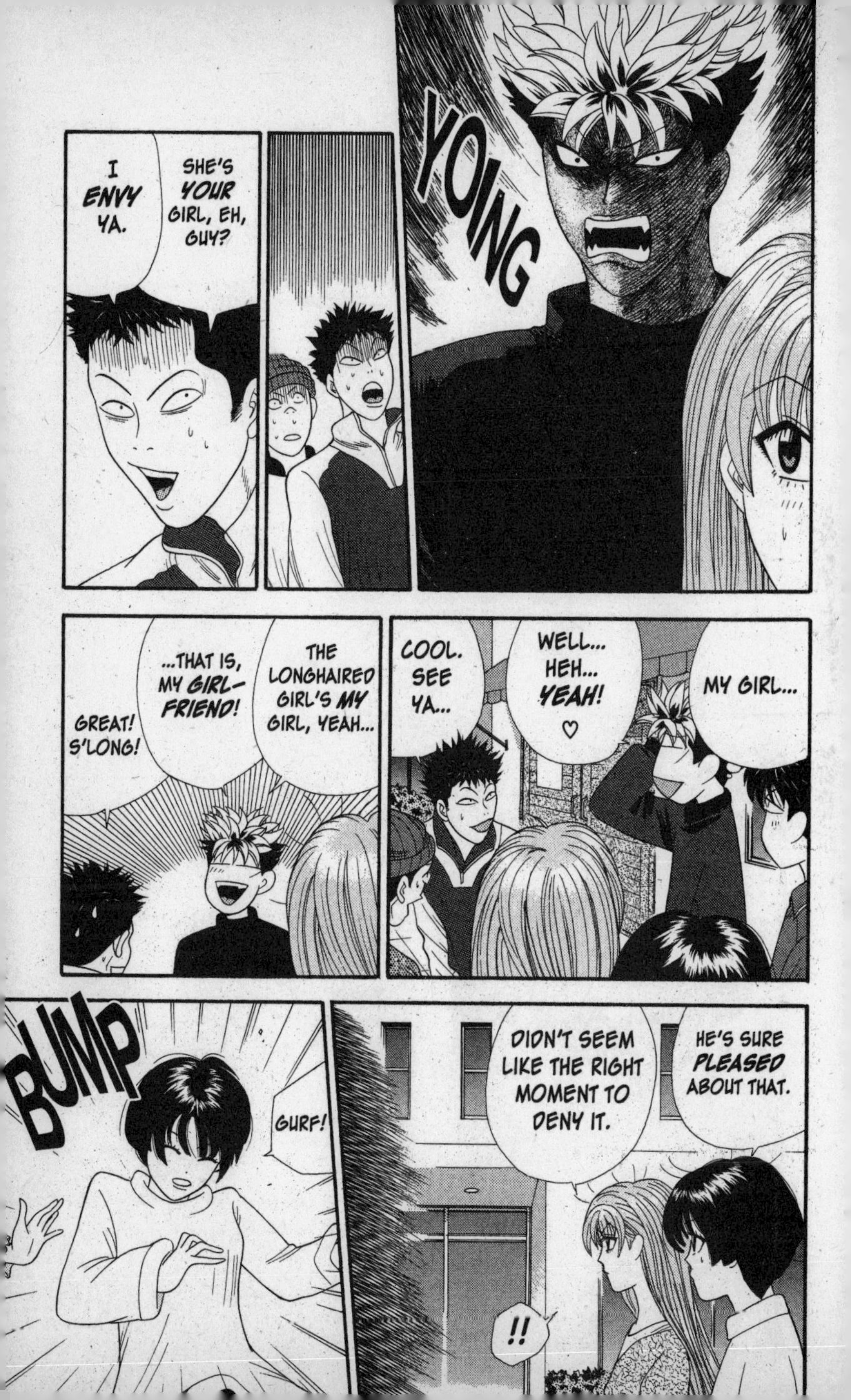
YOING
SHE'S YOUR GIRL, EH, GUY?
I ENVY YA.
MY GIRL...
WELL... HEH... YEAH! ♡
COOL. SEE YA...
THE LONGHAIRED GIRL'S MY GIRL, YEAH...
...THAT IS, MY GIRLFRIEND!
GREAT! S'LONG!
HE'S SURE PLEASED ABOUT THAT.
DIDN'T SEEM LIKE THE RIGHT MOMENT TO DENY IT.
!!
BUMP
GURF!

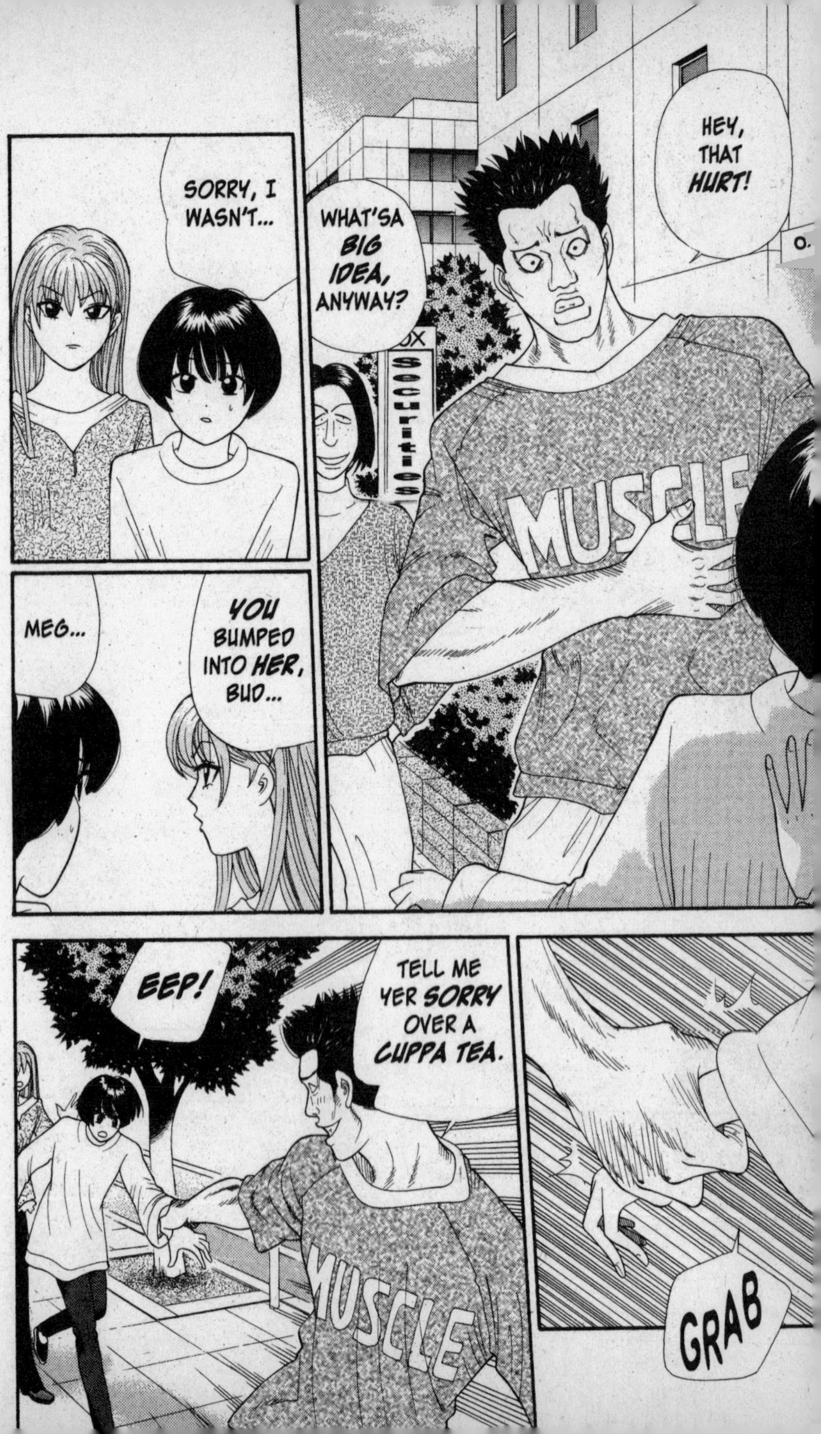
HEY, THAT HURT!
WHAT'SA BIG IDEA, ANYWAY?
Securities
MUSCLE
SORRY, I WASN'T...
YOU BUMPED INTO HER, BUD...
MEG...
GRAB
TELL ME YER SORRY OVER A CUPPA TEA.
EEP!
MUSCLE

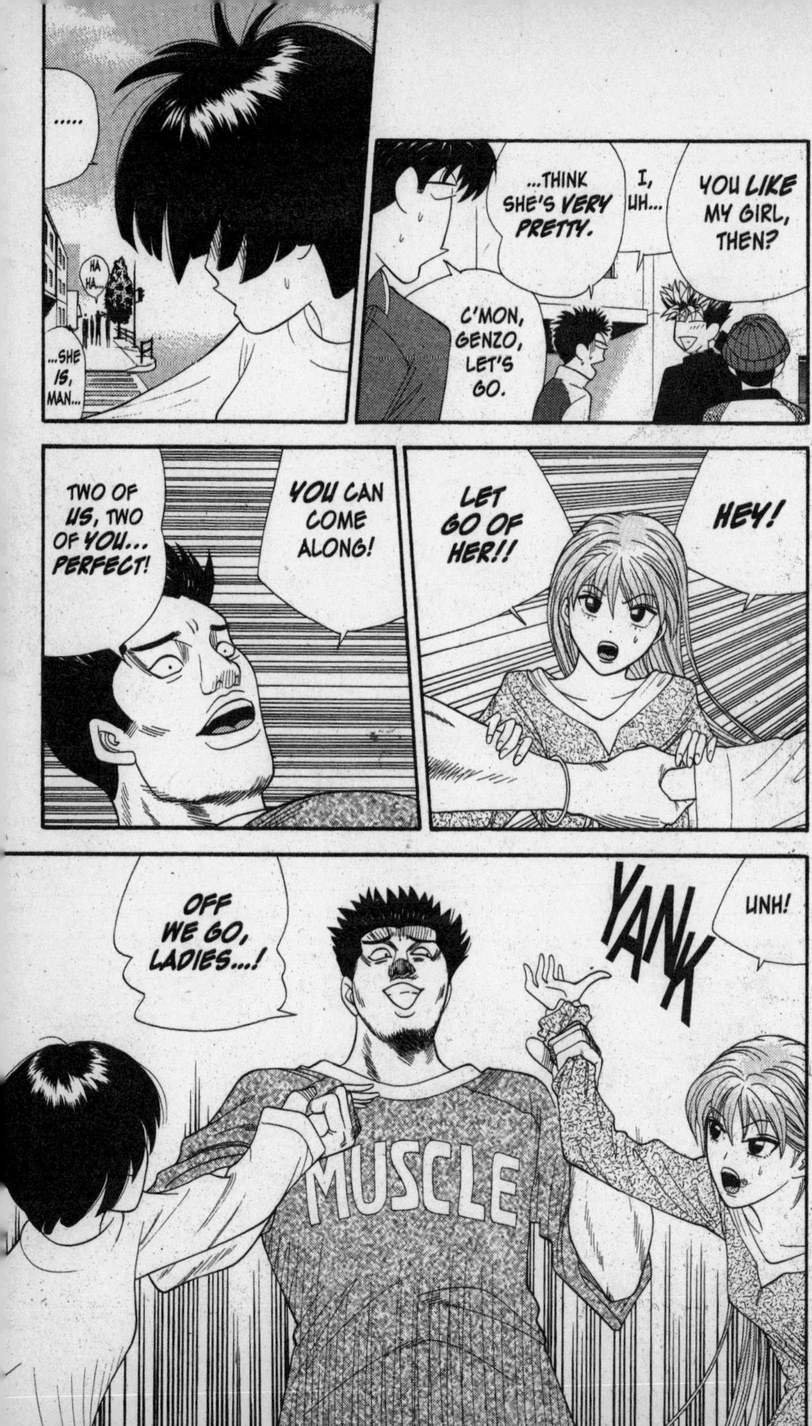
YOU LIKE MY GIRL, THEN?
I, UH...
...THINK SHE'S VERY PRETTY.
C'MON, GENZO, LET'S GO.
.....
HA HA...
...SHE IS, MAN...
HEY!
LET GO OF HER!!
YOU CAN COME ALONG!
TWO OF US, TWO OF YOU... PERFECT!
UNH!
YANK
OFF WE GO, LADIES...!
MUSCLE

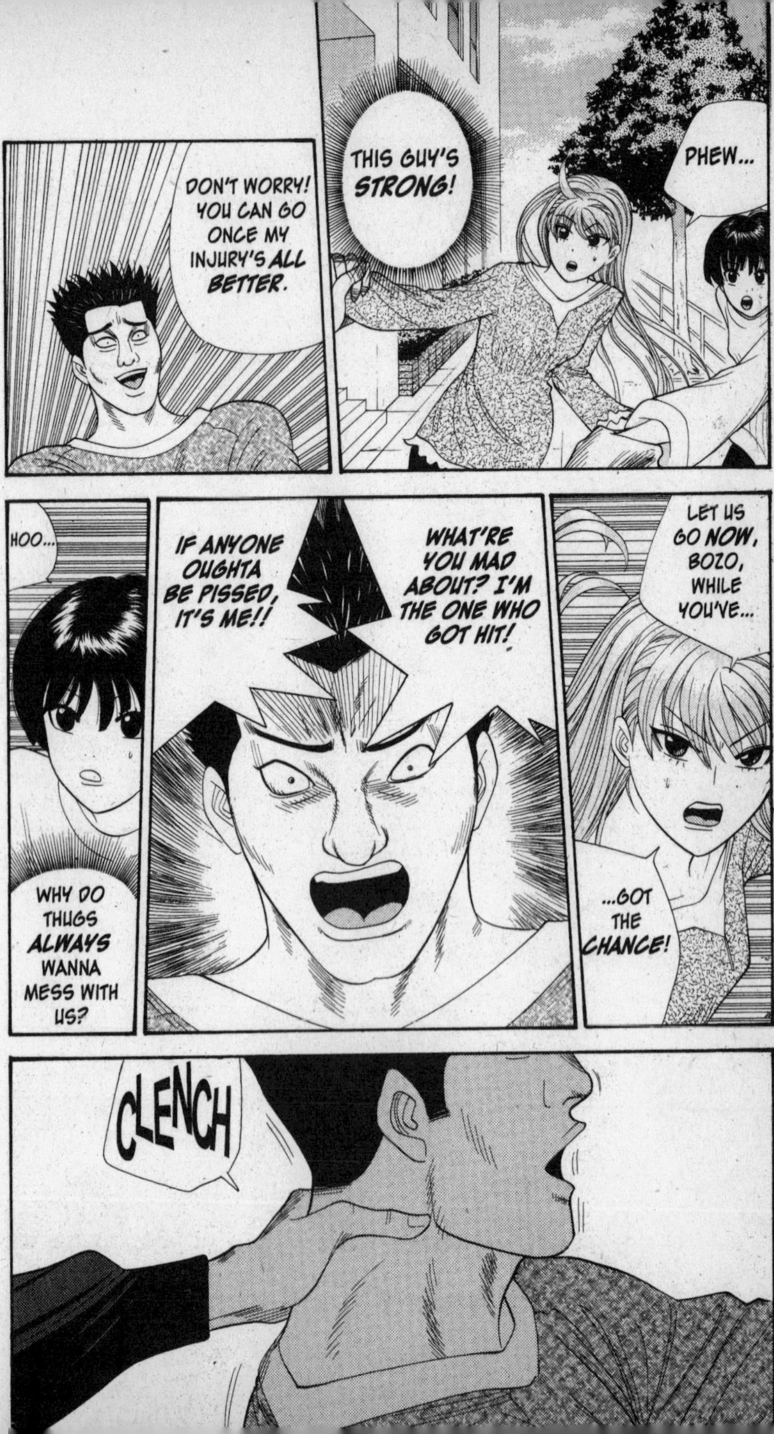
PHEW...
THIS GUY'S STRONG!
DON'T WORRY! YOU CAN GO ONCE MY INJURY'S ALL BETTER.
LET US GO NOW, BOZO, WHILE YOU'VE...
...GOT THE CHANCE!
WHAT'RE YOU MAD ABOUT? I'M THE ONE WHO GOT HIT!
IF ANYONE OUGHTA BE PISSED, IT'S ME!!
HOO...
WHY DO THUGS ALWAYS WANNA MESS WITH US?
CLENCH

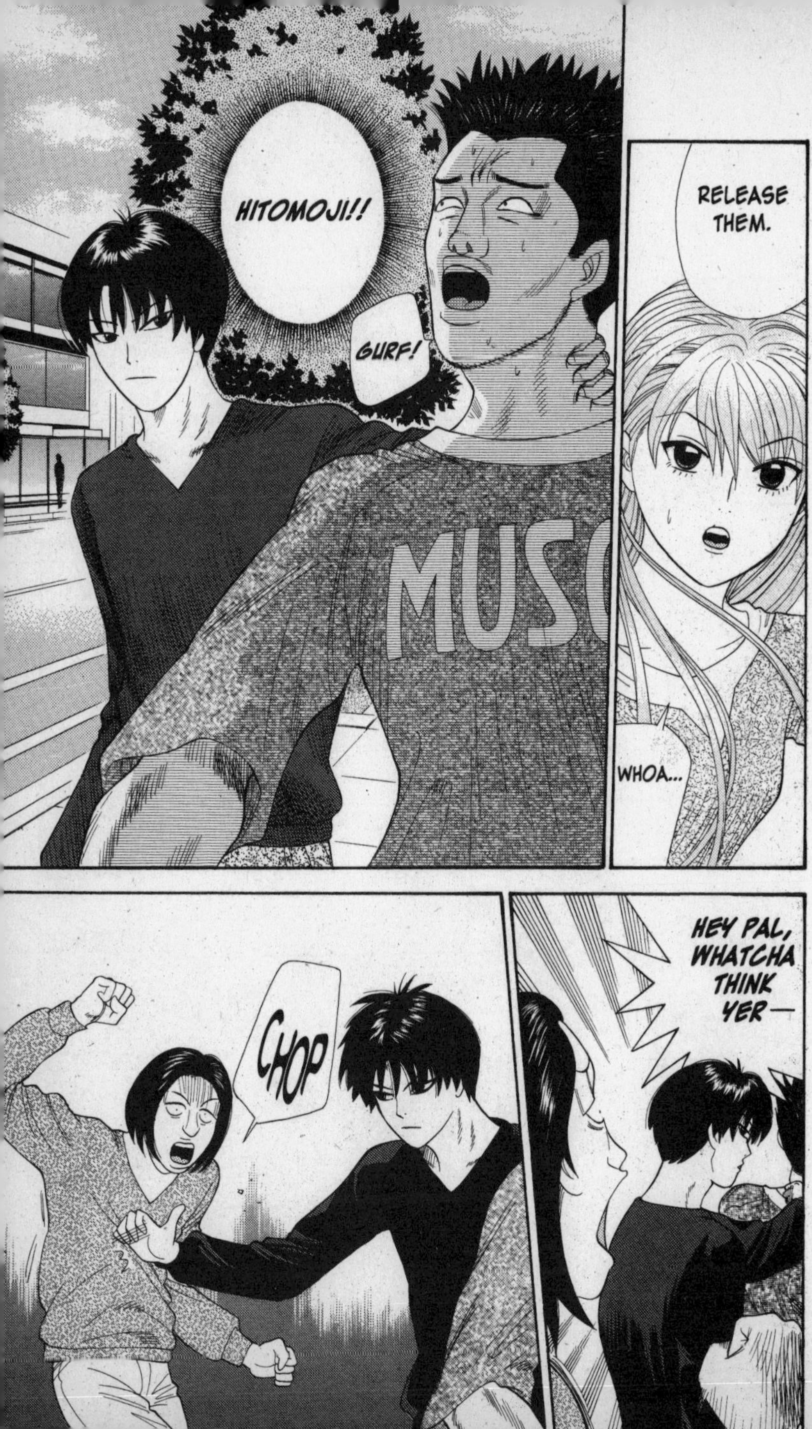
RELEASE THEM.
WHOA...
HITOMOJI!!
GURF!
MUSC
HEY PAL, WHATCHA THINK YER—
CHOP

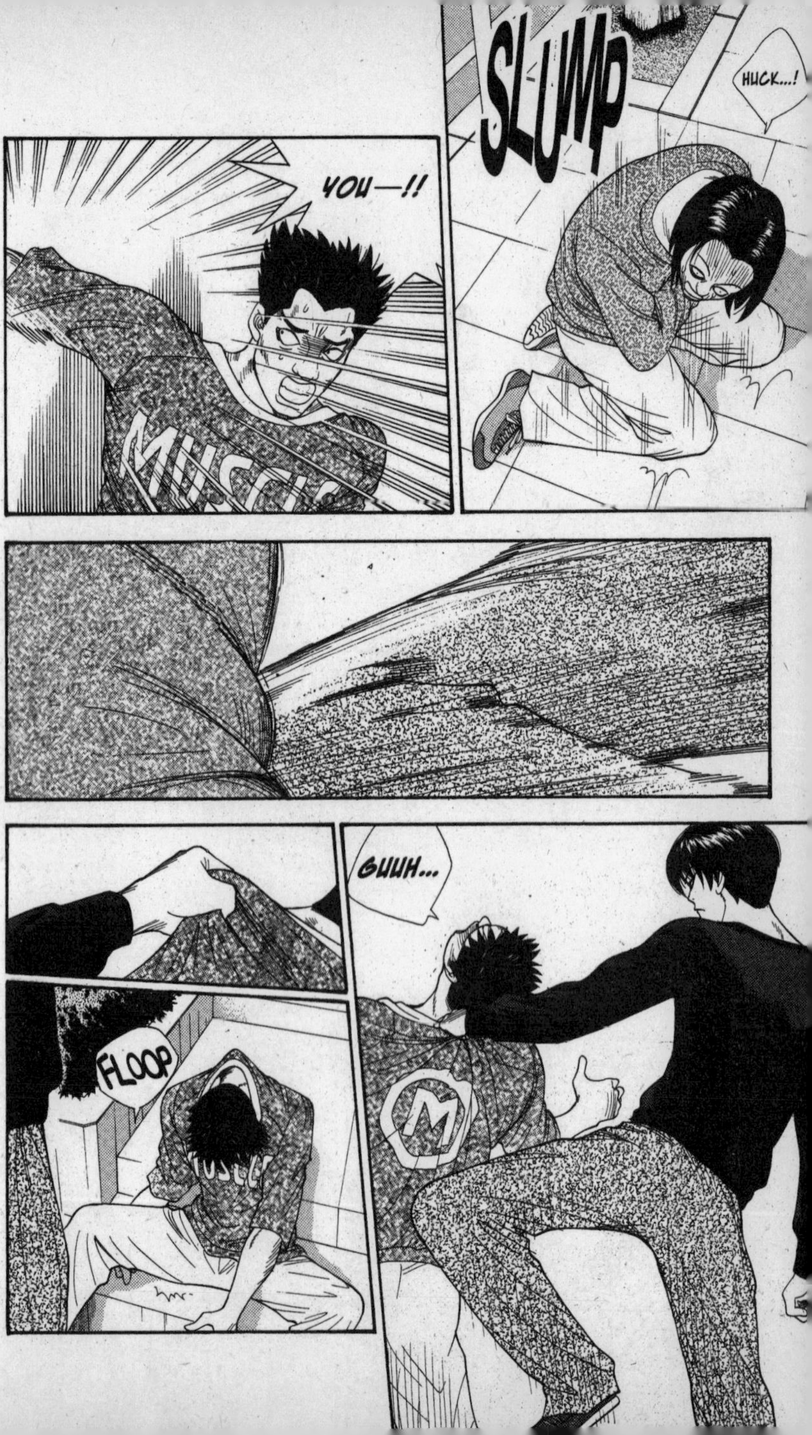
SLUMP
HUCK...!
YOU—!!
MUSCLE
GUUH...
FLOOP

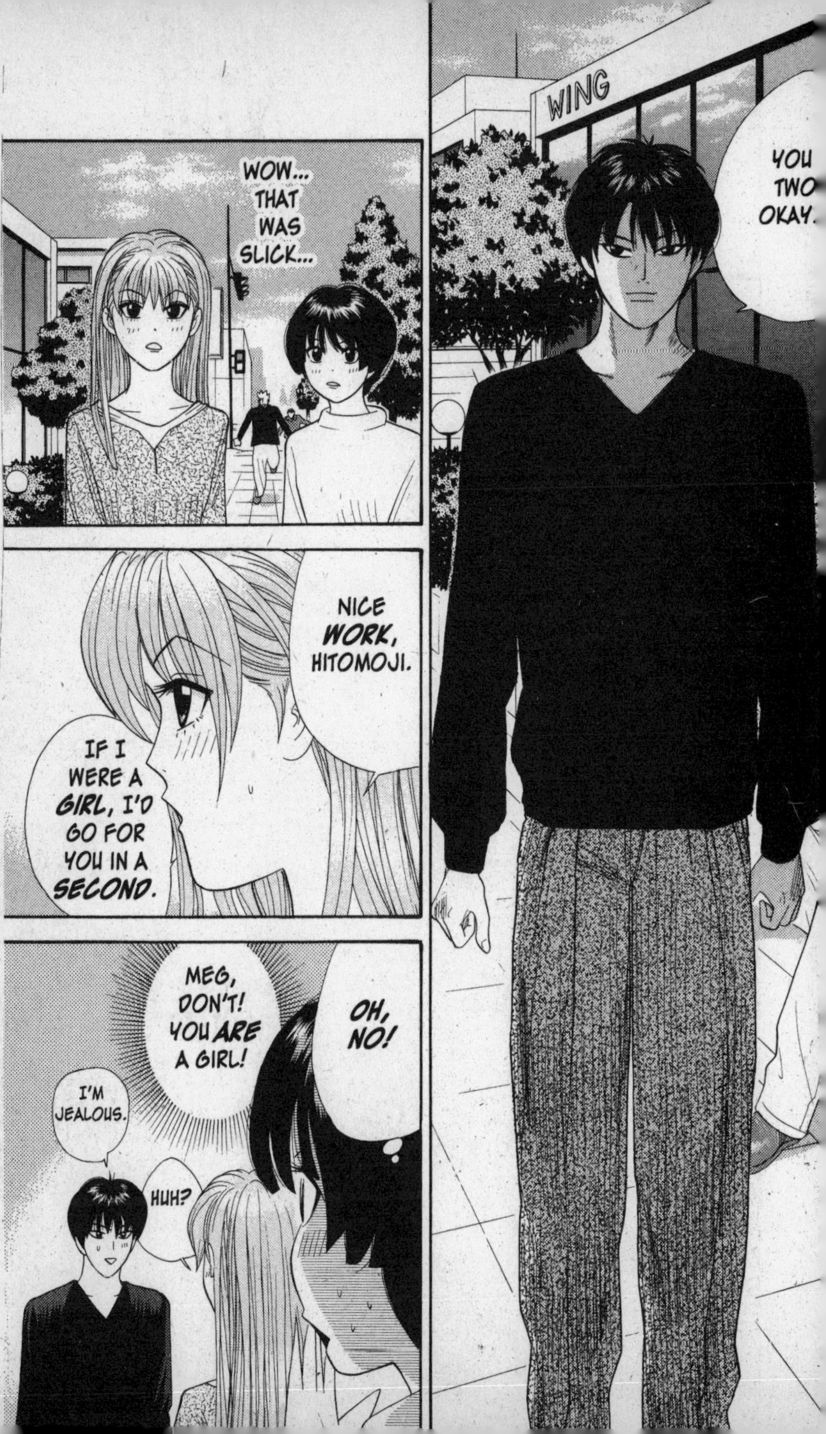
YOU TWO OKAY.
WOW... THAT WAS SLICK...
NICE WORK, HITOMOJI.
IF I WERE A GIRL, I'D GO FOR YOU IN A SECOND.
OH, NO!
MEG, DON'T! YOU ARE A GIRL!
I'M JEALOUS.
HUH?

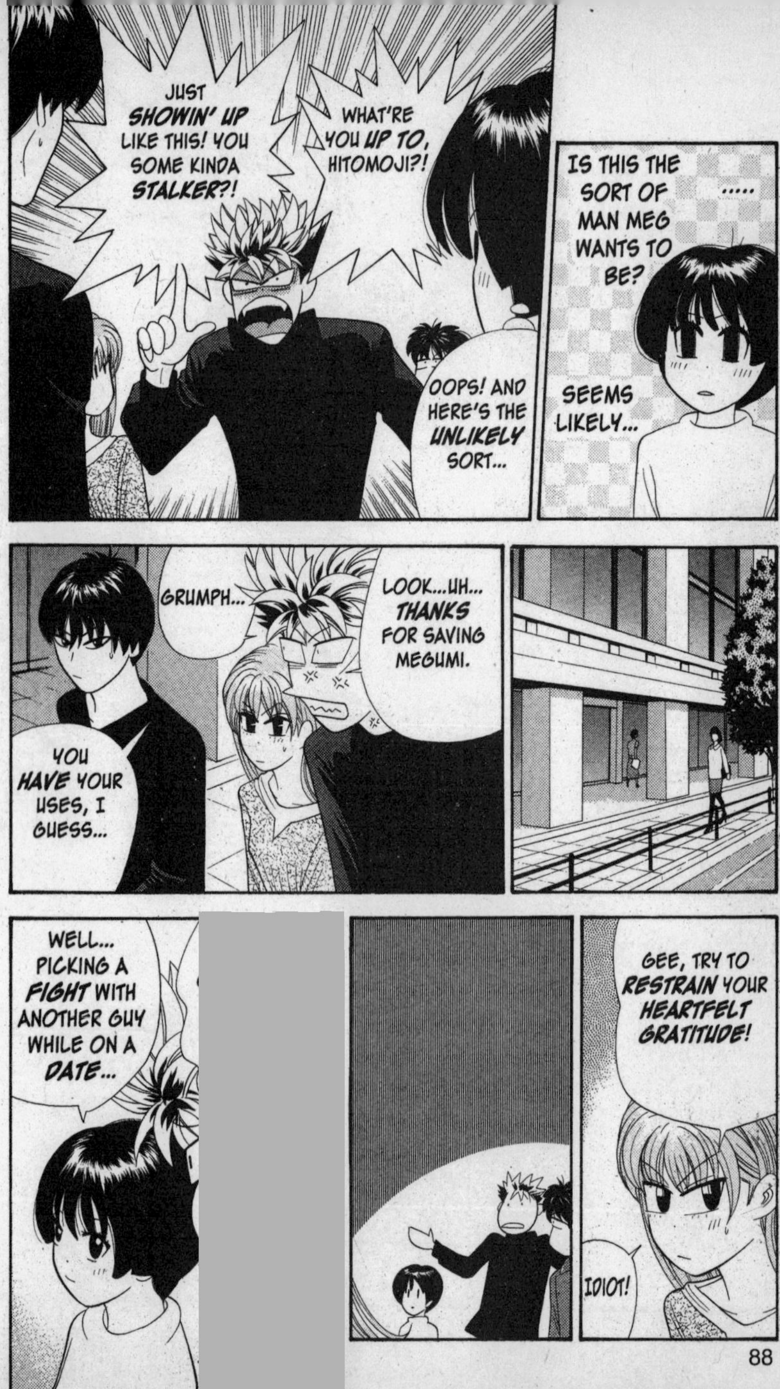
IS THIS THE SORT OF MAN MEG WANTS TO BE?
.....
SEEMS LIKELY...
WHAT'RE YOU UP TO, HITOMOJI?!
JUST SHOWIN' UP LIKE THIS! YOU SOME KINDA STALKER?!
OOPS! AND HERE'S THE UNLIKELY SORT...
LOOK...UH... THANKS FOR SAVING MEGUMI.
GRUMPH...
YOU HAVE YOUR USES, I GUESS...
GEE, TRY TO RESTRAIN YOUR HEARTFELT GRATITUDE!
IDIOT!
WELL... PICKING A FIGHT WITH ANOTHER GUY WHILE ON A DATE...

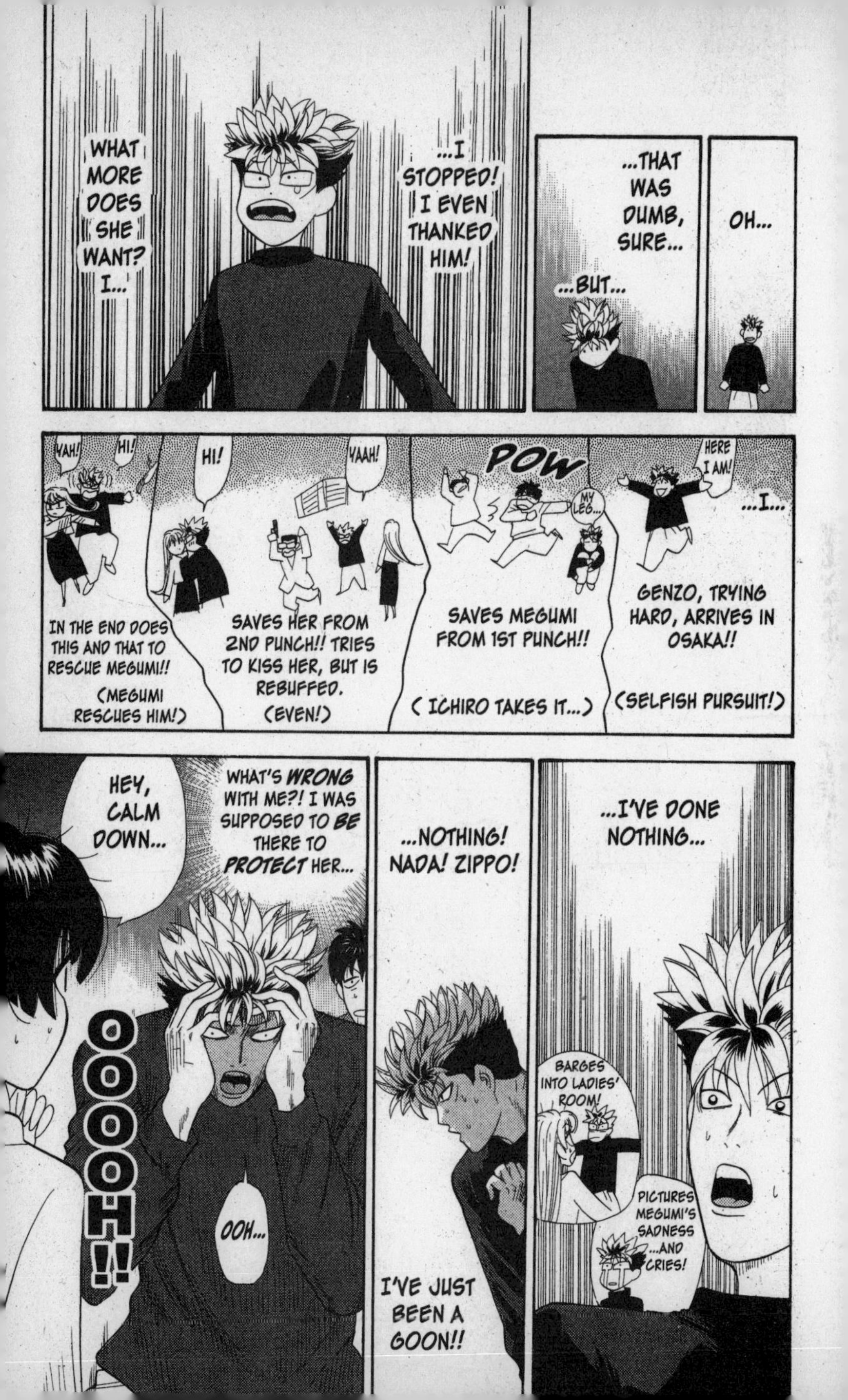
OH...
...THAT WAS DUMB, SURE...
...BUT...
...I STOPPED! I EVEN THANKED HIM!
WHAT MORE DOES SHE WANT? I...
HERE I AM!
...I...
GENZO, TRYING HARD, ARRIVES IN OSAKA!!
(SELFISH PURSUIT!)
POW
MY LEG...
SAVES MEGUMI FROM 1ST PUNCH!!
(ICHIRO TAKES IT...)
YAAH!
HI!
SAVES HER FROM 2ND PUNCH!! TRIES TO KISS HER, BUT IS REBUFFED.
(EVEN!)
HI!
YAH!
IN THE END DOES THIS AND THAT TO RESCUE MEGUMI!!
(MEGUMI RESCUES HIM!)
...I'VE DONE NOTHING...
BARGES INTO LADIES' ROOM!
PICTURES MEGUMI'S SADNESS ...AND CRIES!
...NOTHING! NADA! ZIPPO!
I'VE JUST BEEN A GOON!!
WHAT'S WRONG WITH ME?! I WAS SUPPOSED TO BE THERE TO PROTECT HER...
HEY, CALM DOWN...
OOOOOOH!!
OOH...

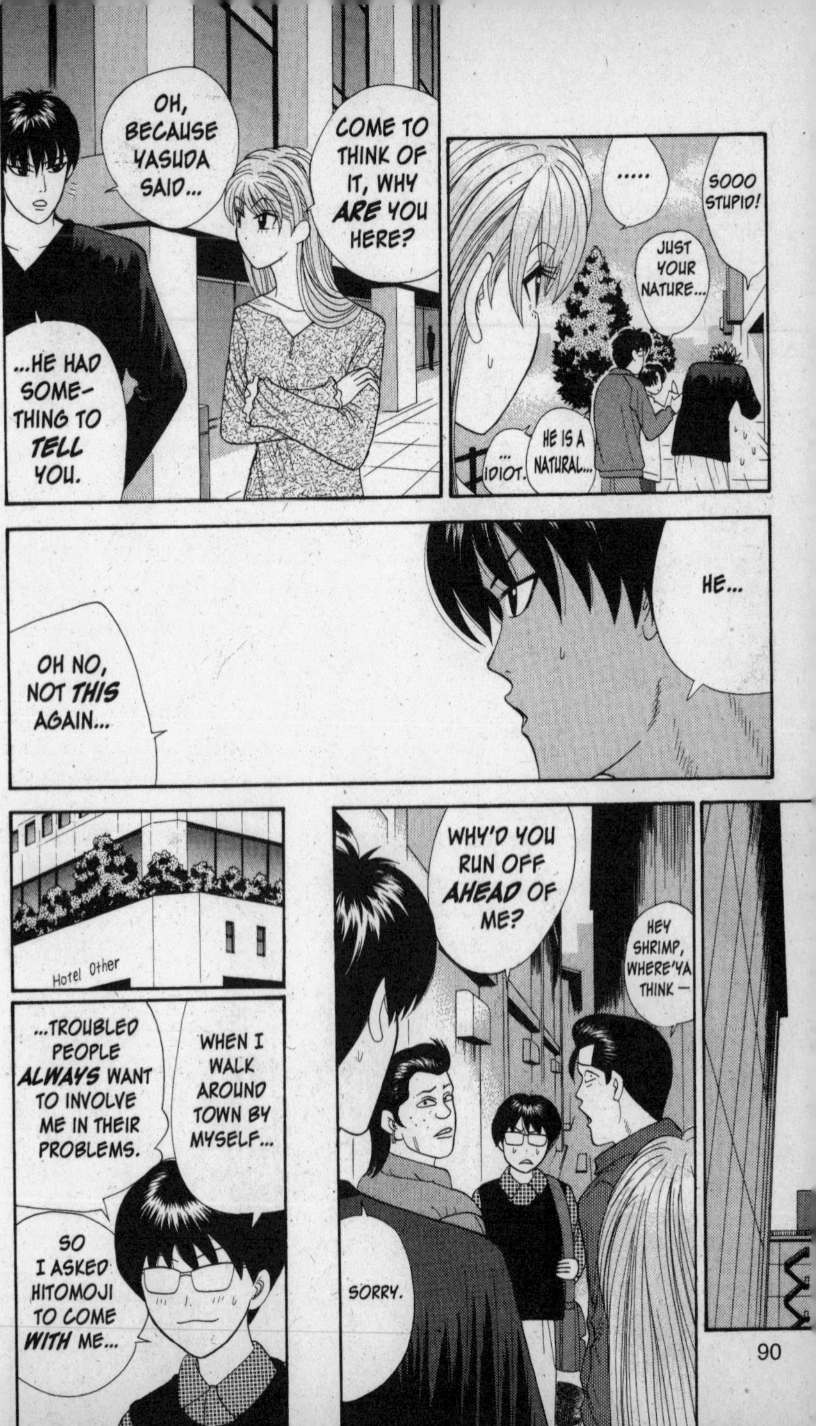
SOOO STUPID!
.....
JUST YOUR NATURE...
HE IS A NATURAL...
... IDIOT.
COME TO THINK OF IT, WHY ARE YOU HERE?
OH, BECAUSE YASUDA SAID...
...HE HAD SOME-THING TO TELL YOU.
HE...
OH NO, NOT THIS AGAIN...
HEY SHRIMP, WHERE'YA THINK —
WHY'D YOU RUN OFF AHEAD OF ME?
SORRY.
Hotel Other
WHEN I WALK AROUND TOWN BY MYSELF...
...TROUBLED PEOPLE ALWAYS WANT TO INVOLVE ME IN THEIR PROBLEMS.
SO I ASKED HITOMOJI TO COME WITH ME...

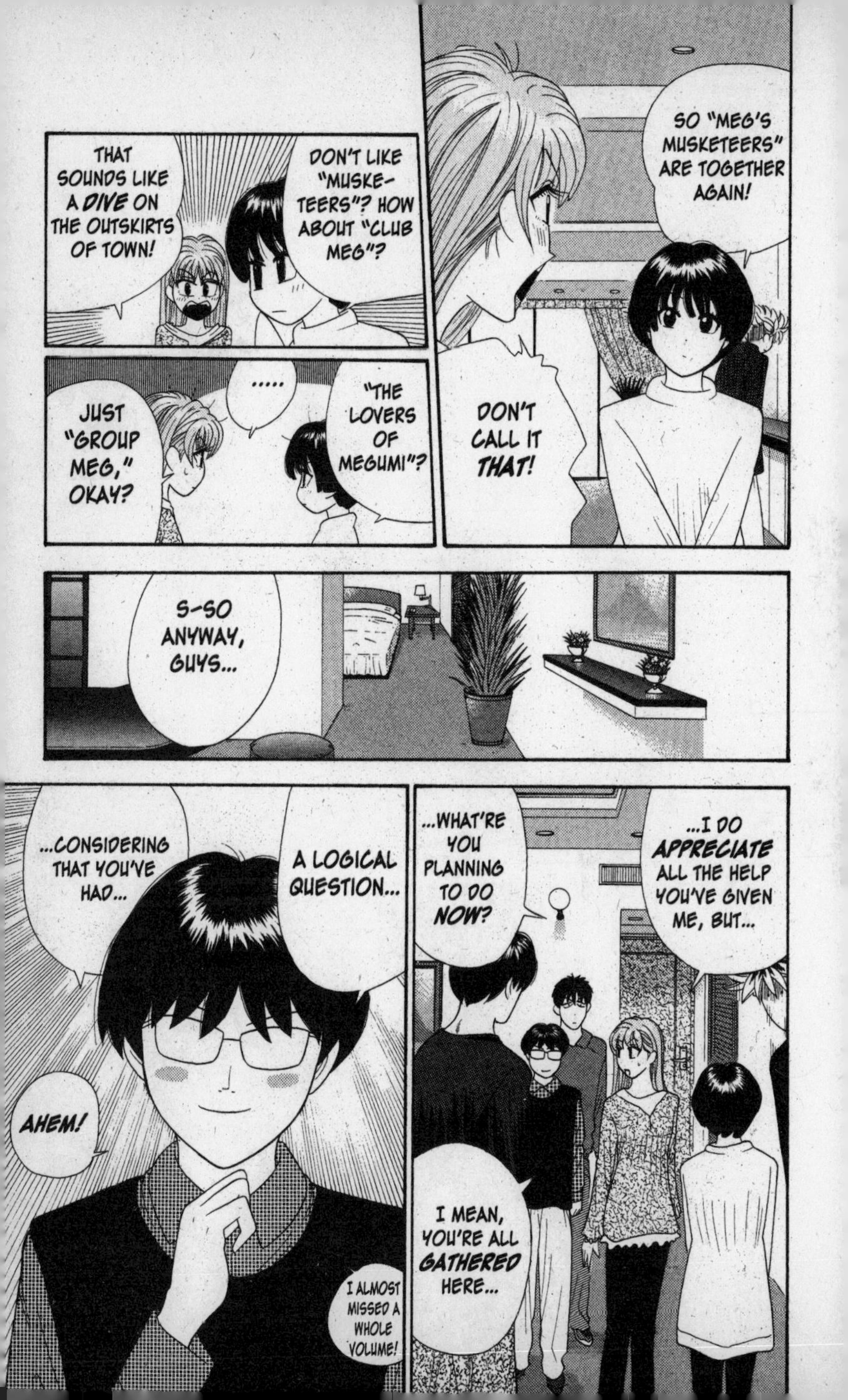
SO "MEG'S MUSKETEERS" ARE TOGETHER AGAIN!
DON'T CALL IT *THAT!*
DON'T LIKE "MUSKE-TEERS"? HOW ABOUT "CLUB MEG"?
THAT SOUNDS LIKE A *DIVE* ON THE OUTSKIRTS OF TOWN!
"THE LOVERS OF MEGUMI"?
.....
JUST "GROUP MEG," OKAY?
S-SO ANYWAY, GUYS...
...I DO *APPRECIATE* ALL THE HELP YOU'VE GIVEN ME, BUT...
...WHAT'RE YOU PLANNING TO DO *NOW?*
I MEAN, YOU'RE ALL *GATHERED* HERE...
A LOGICAL QUESTION...
...CONSIDERING THAT YOU'VE HAD...
I ALMOST MISSED A WHOLE VOLUME!
AHEM!

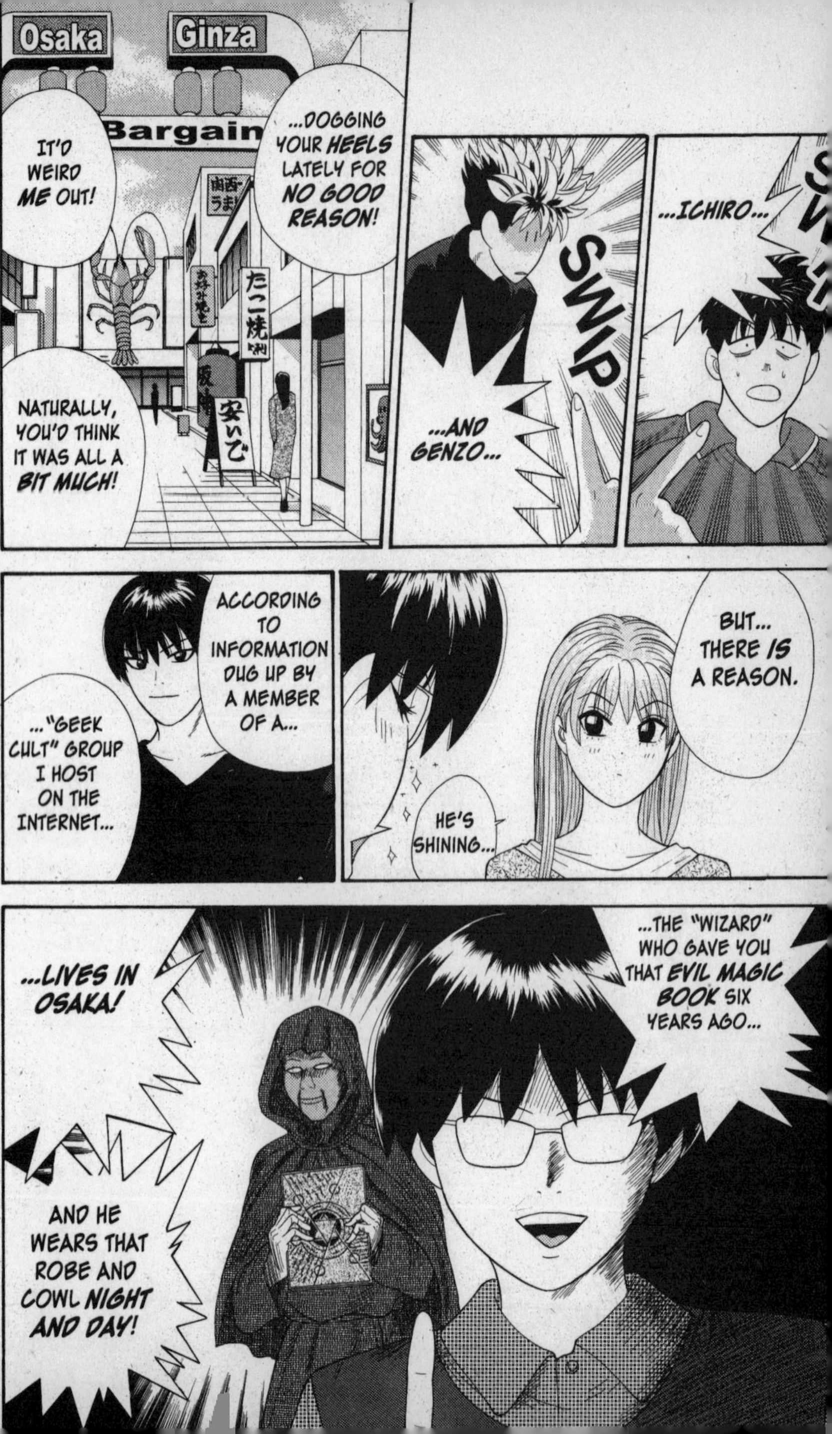
...ICHIRO...
SWIP
...AND GENZO...
...DOGGING YOUR HEELS LATELY FOR NO GOOD REASON!
Osaka
Ginza
Bargain
たこ焼
安いで
IT'D WEIRD ME OUT!
NATURALLY, YOU'D THINK IT WAS ALL A BIT MUCH!
BUT... THERE IS A REASON.
HE'S SHINING...
ACCORDING TO INFORMATION DUG UP BY A MEMBER OF A...
..."GEEK CULT" GROUP I HOST ON THE INTERNET...
...THE "WIZARD" WHO GAVE YOU THAT EVIL MAGIC BOOK SIX YEARS AGO...
...LIVES IN OSAKA!
AND HE WEARS THAT ROBE AND COWL NIGHT AND DAY!

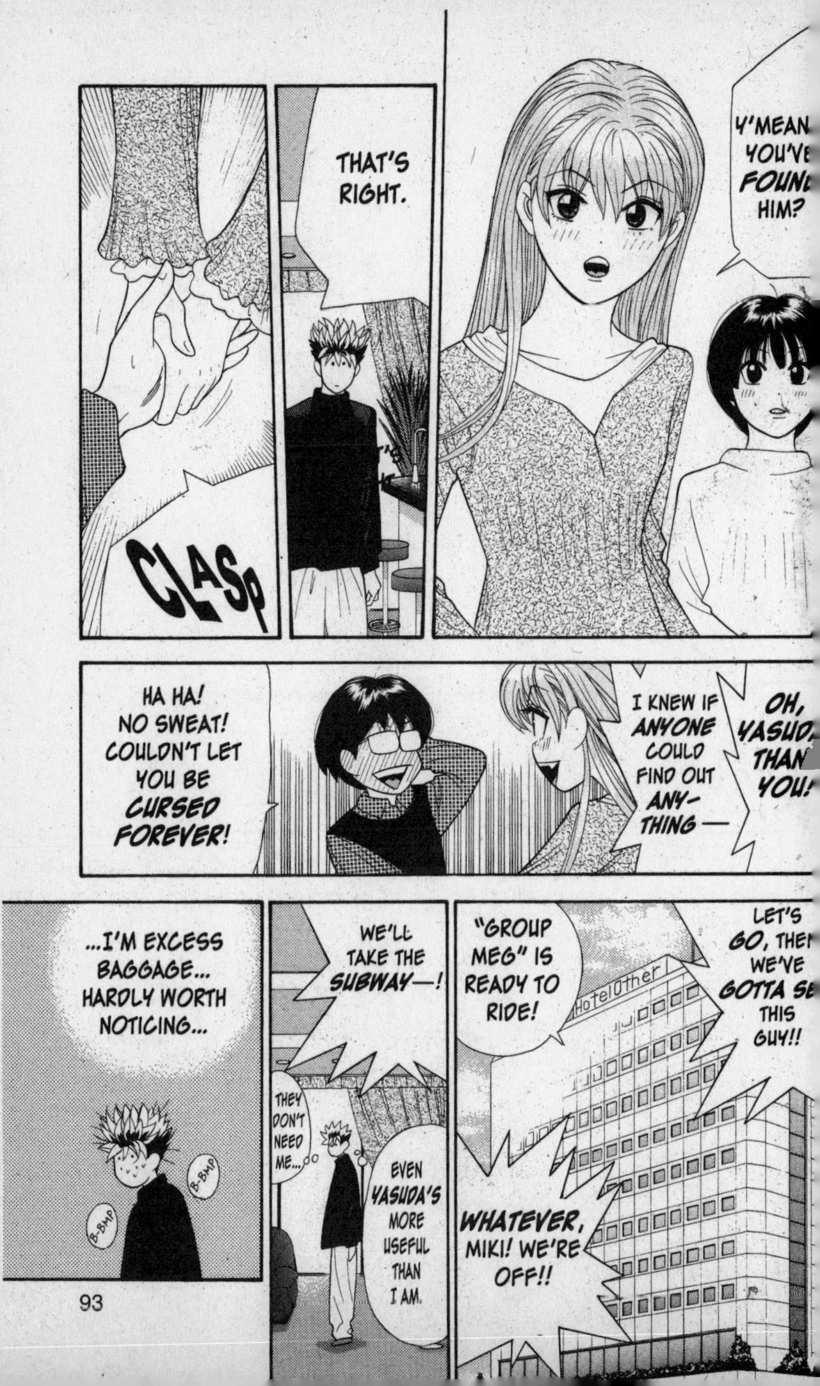
Y'MEAN YOU'VE FOUN HIM?
THAT'S RIGHT.
CLASP
OH, YASUDA THAN YOU!
I KNEW IF ANYONE COULD FIND OUT ANYTHING —
HA HA! NO SWEAT! COULDN'T LET YOU BE CURSED FOREVER!
LET'S GO, THEN WE'VE GOTTA SE THIS GUY!!
Hotel Other
"GROUP MEG" IS READY TO RIDE!
WHATEVER, MIKI! WE'RE OFF!!
WE'LL TAKE THE SUBWAY—!
THEY DON'T NEED ME...
EVEN YASUDA'S MORE USEFUL THAN I AM.
...I'M EXCESS BAGGAGE... HARDLY WORTH NOTICING...
B-BMP
B-BMP

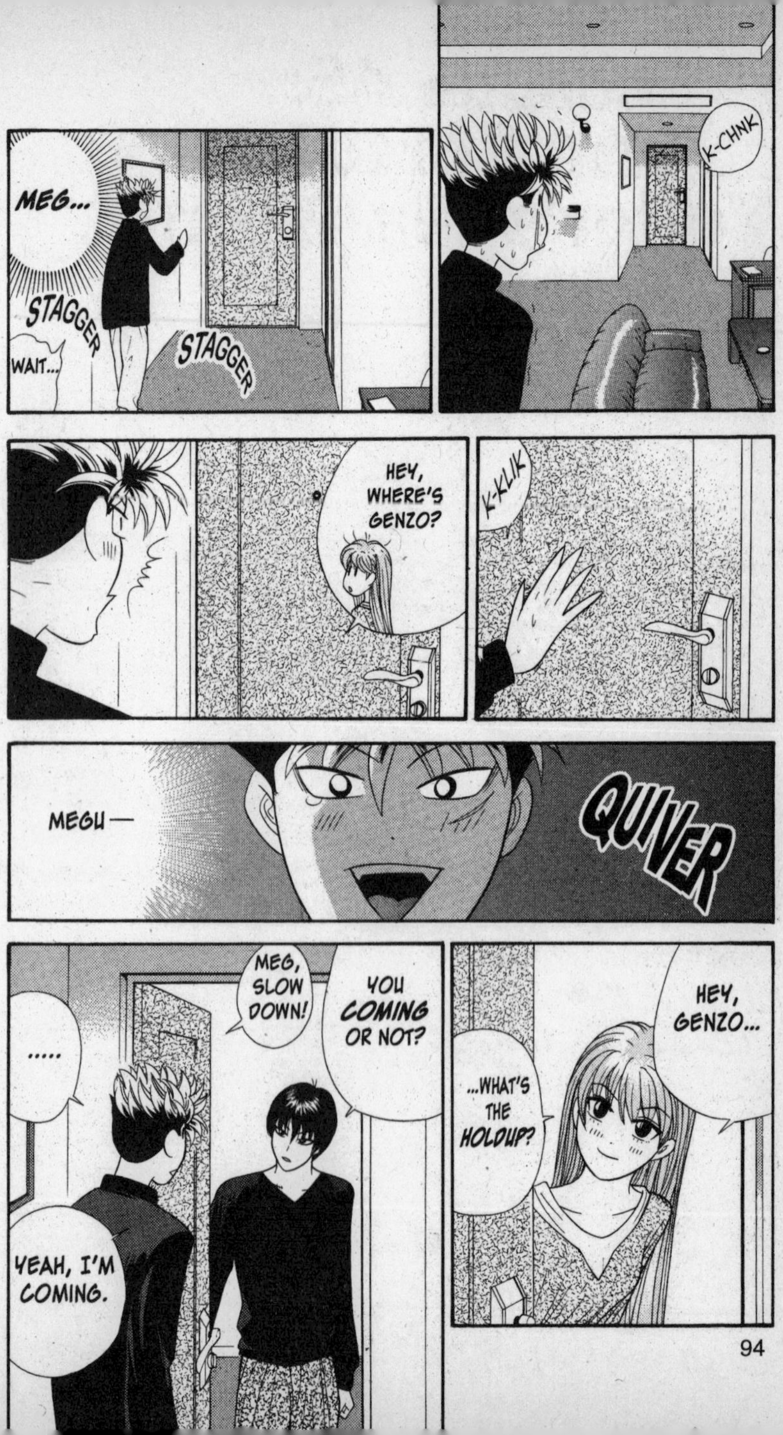
K-CHNK
MEG...
STAGGER
STAGGER
WAIT...
K-KLIK
HEY, WHERE'S GENZO?
QUIVER
MEGU—
HEY, GENZO...
...WHAT'S THE HOLDUP?
YOU COMING OR NOT?
MEG, SLOW DOWN!
.....
YEAH, I'M COMING.

Chapter 45: The Fortune Teller's Mansion

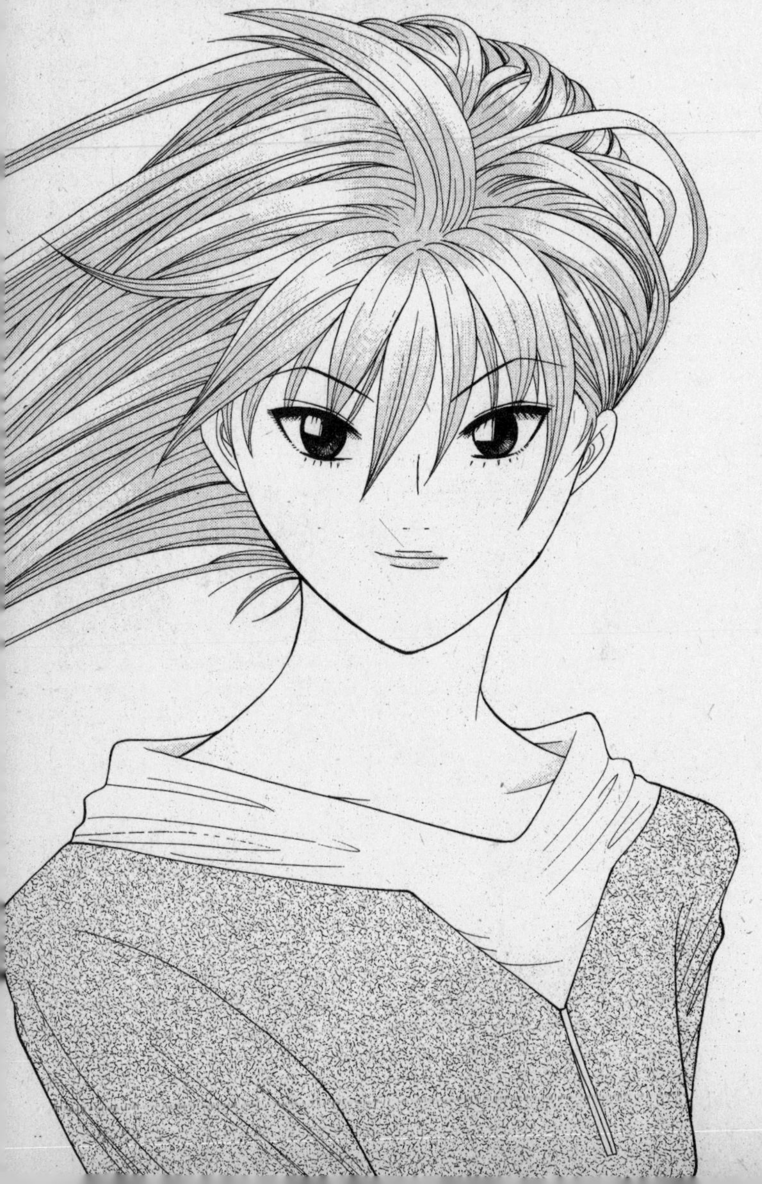

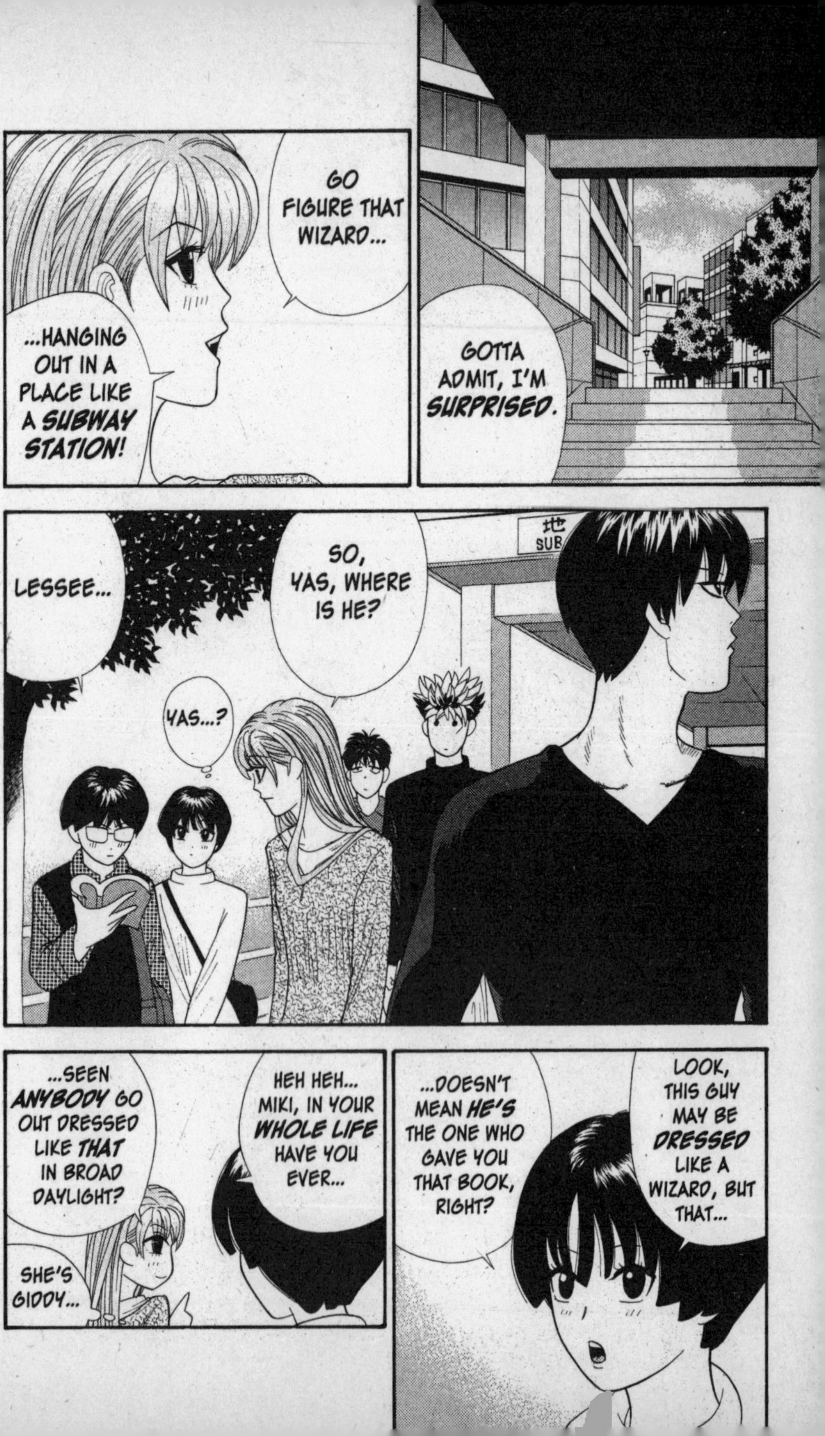
GOTTA ADMIT, I'M SURPRISED.
GO FIGURE THAT WIZARD...
...HANGING OUT IN A PLACE LIKE A SUBWAY STATION!
SO, YAS, WHERE IS HE?
LESSEE...
YAS...?
LOOK, THIS GUY MAY BE DRESSED LIKE A WIZARD, BUT THAT...
...DOESN'T MEAN HE'S THE ONE WHO GAVE YOU THAT BOOK, RIGHT?
HEH HEH... MIKI, IN YOUR WHOLE LIFE HAVE YOU EVER...
...SEEN ANYBODY GO OUT DRESSED LIKE THAT IN BROAD DAYLIGHT?
SHE'S GIDDY...

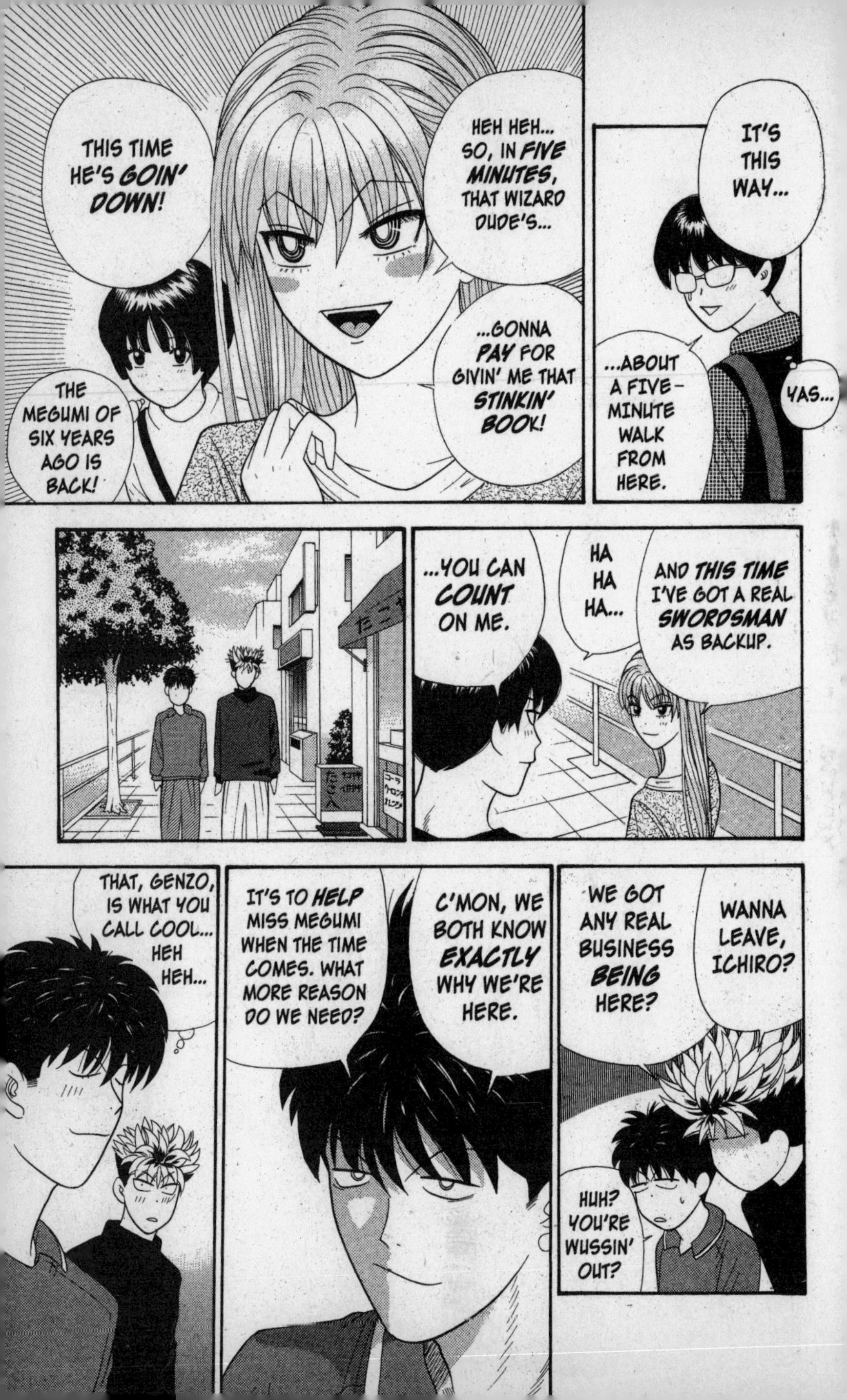
IT'S THIS WAY...
...ABOUT A FIVE-MINUTE WALK FROM HERE.
YAS...
HEH HEH... SO, IN FIVE MINUTES, THAT WIZARD DUDE'S...
...GONNA PAY FOR GIVIN' ME THAT STINKIN' BOOK!
THIS TIME HE'S GOIN' DOWN!
THE MEGUMI OF SIX YEARS AGO IS BACK!
AND THIS TIME I'VE GOT A REAL SWORDSMAN AS BACKUP.
HA HA HA...
...YOU CAN COUNT ON ME.
WANNA LEAVE, ICHIRO?
WE GOT ANY REAL BUSINESS BEING HERE?
HUH? YOU'RE WUSSIN' OUT?
C'MON, WE BOTH KNOW EXACTLY WHY WE'RE HERE.
IT'S TO HELP MISS MEGUMI WHEN THE TIME COMES. WHAT MORE REASON DO WE NEED?
THAT, GENZO, IS WHAT YOU CALL COOL... HEH HEH...

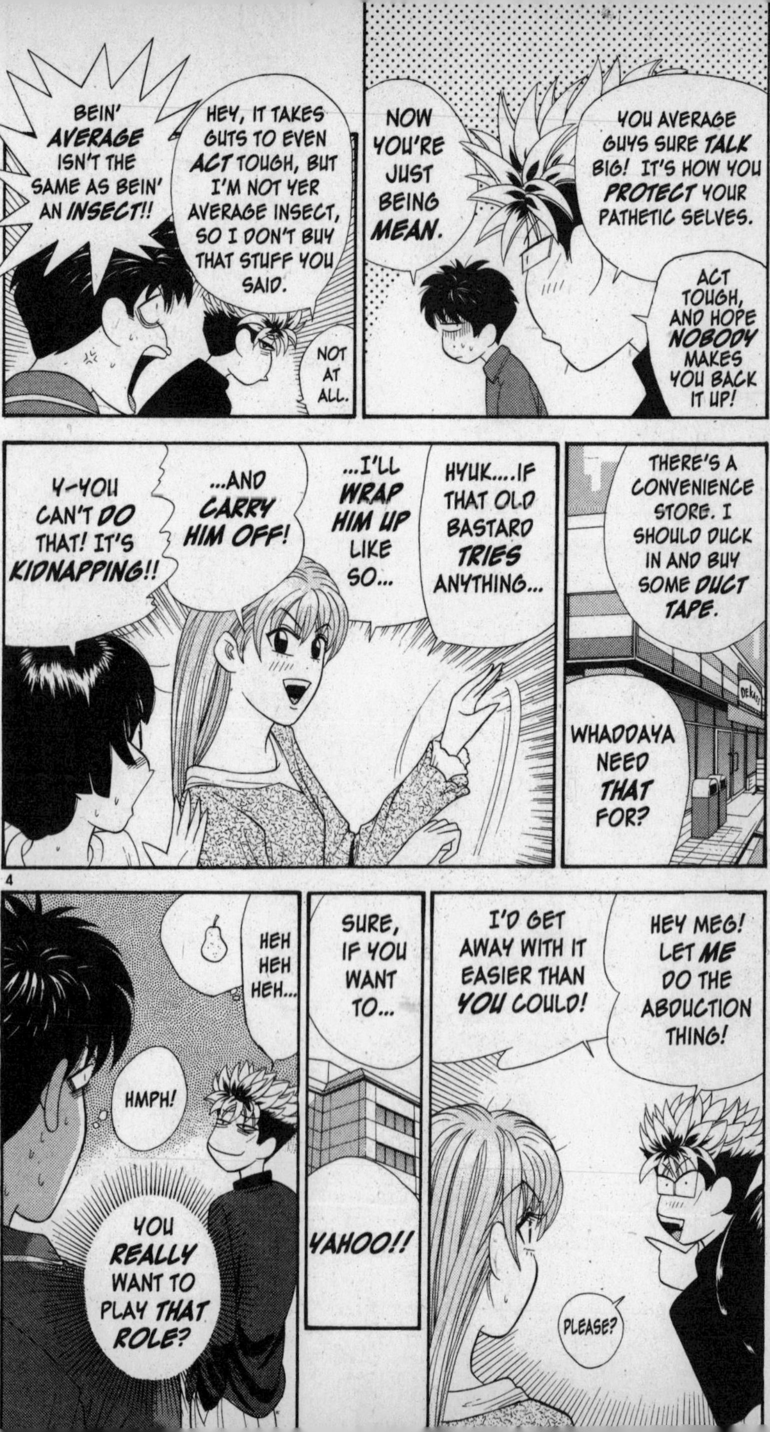
YOU AVERAGE GUYS SURE TALK BIG! IT'S HOW YOU PROTECT YOUR PATHETIC SELVES.
ACT TOUGH, AND HOPE NOBODY MAKES YOU BACK IT UP!
NOW YOU'RE JUST BEING MEAN.
HEY, IT TAKES GUTS TO EVEN ACT TOUGH, BUT I'M NOT YER AVERAGE INSECT, SO I DON'T BUY THAT STUFF YOU SAID.
BEIN' AVERAGE ISN'T THE SAME AS BEIN' AN INSECT!!
NOT AT ALL.
THERE'S A CONVENIENCE STORE. I SHOULD DUCK IN AND BUY SOME DUCT TAPE.
WHADDAYA NEED THAT FOR?
HYUK....IF THAT OLD BASTARD TRIES ANYTHING...
...I'LL WRAP HIM UP LIKE SO...
...AND CARRY HIM OFF!
Y-YOU CAN'T DO THAT! IT'S KIDNAPPING!!
HEY MEG! LET ME DO THE ABDUCTION THING!
I'D GET AWAY WITH IT EASIER THAN YOU COULD!
PLEASE?
SURE, IF YOU WANT TO...
YAHOO!!
HEH HEH HEH...
HMPH!
YOU REALLY WANT TO PLAY THAT ROLE?

4

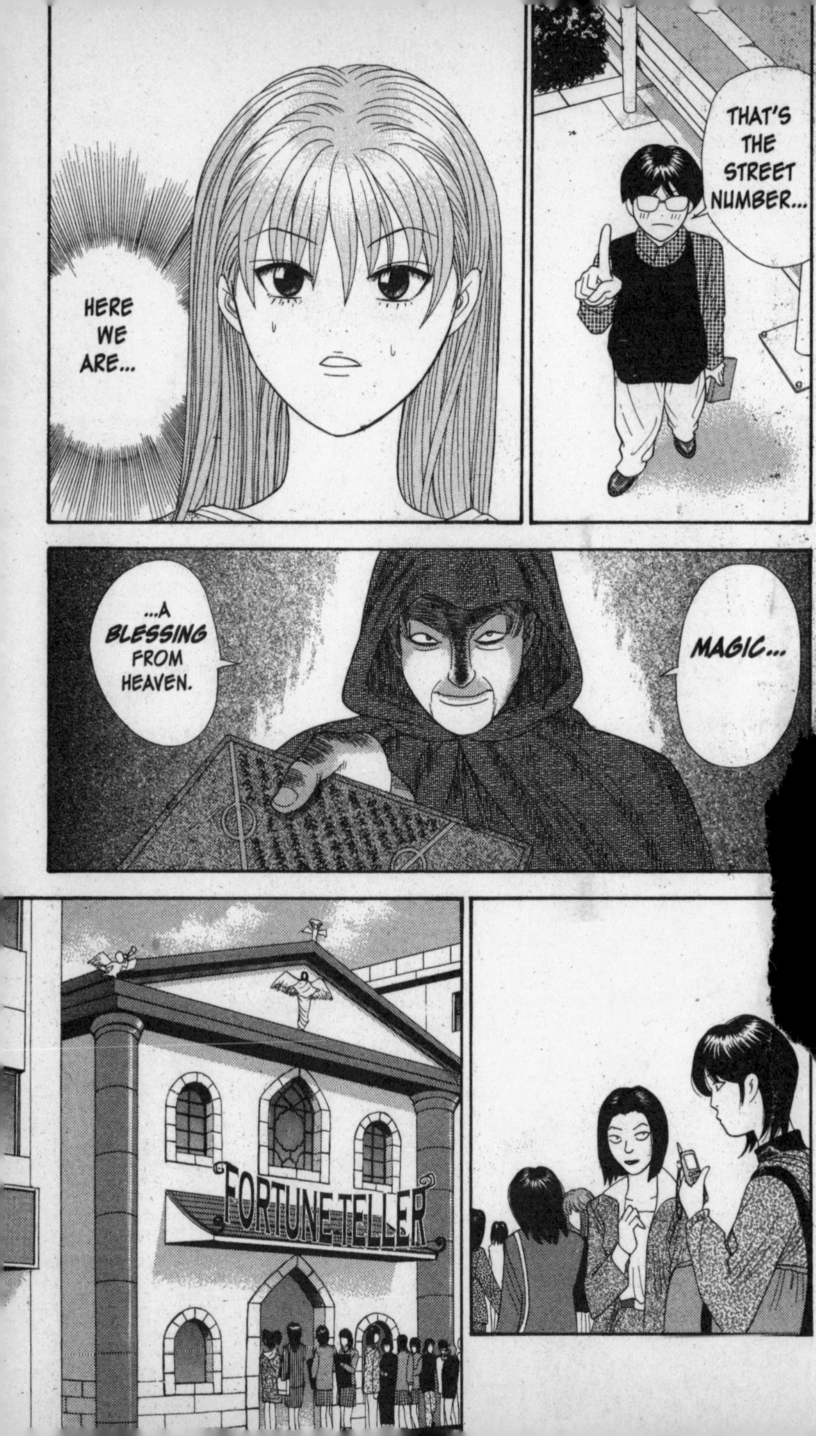
THAT'S THE STREET NUMBER...
HERE WE ARE...
MAGIC...
...A BLESSING FROM HEAVEN.
FORTUNE TELLER

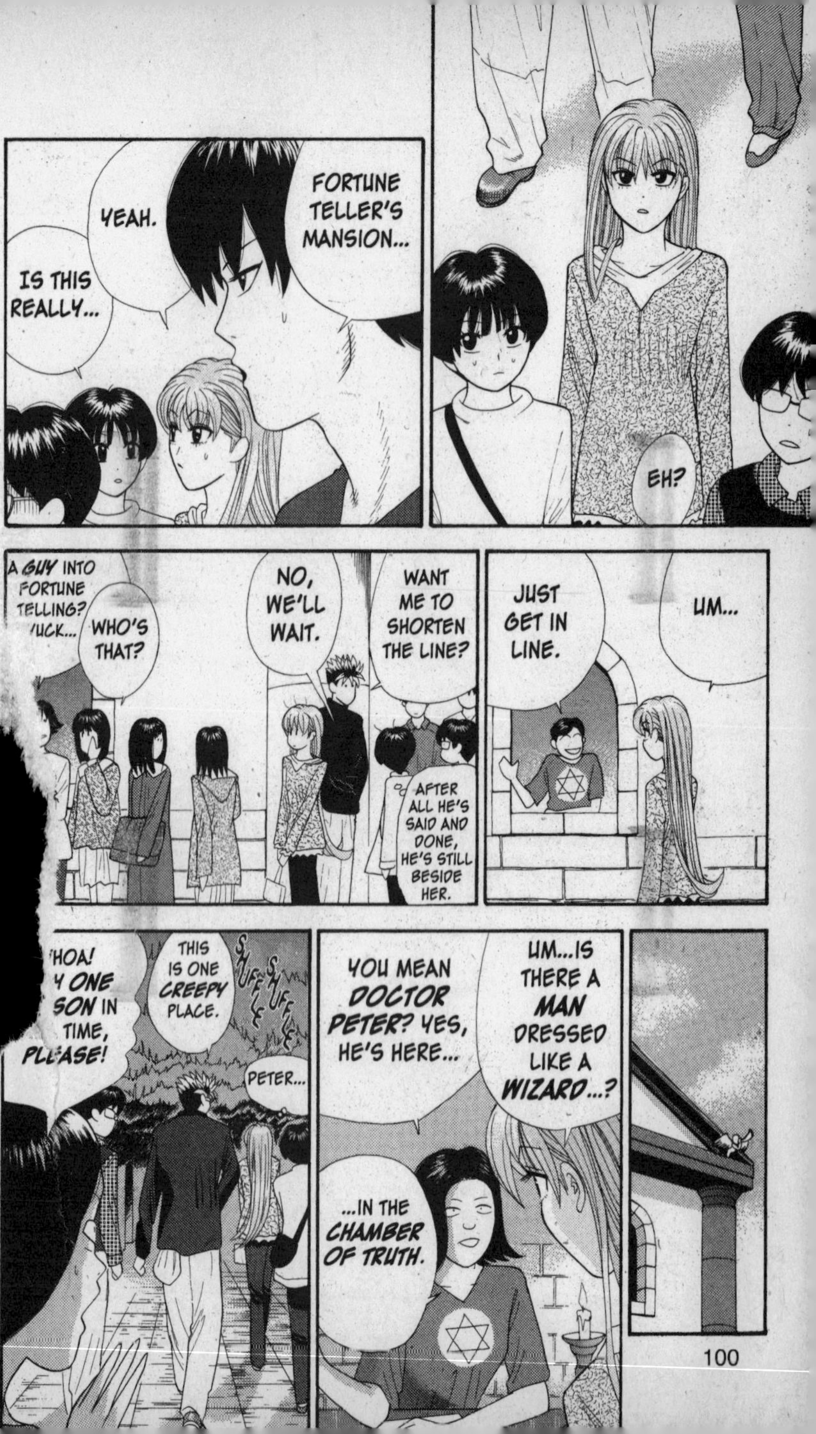
EH?
FORTUNE TELLER'S MANSION...
YEAH.
IS THIS REALLY...
UM...
JUST GET IN LINE.
WANT ME TO SHORTEN THE LINE?
NO, WE'LL WAIT.
AFTER ALL HE'S SAID AND DONE, HE'S STILL BESIDE HER.
WHO'S THAT?
A GUY INTO FORTUNE TELLING? YUCK...
UM...IS THERE A MAN DRESSED LIKE A WIZARD...?
YOU MEAN DOCTOR PETER? YES, HE'S HERE...
...IN THE CHAMBER OF TRUTH.
THIS IS ONE CREEPY PLACE.
SHUFFLE
SHUFFLE
PETER...
HOA! Y ONE SON IN TIME, PLEASE!

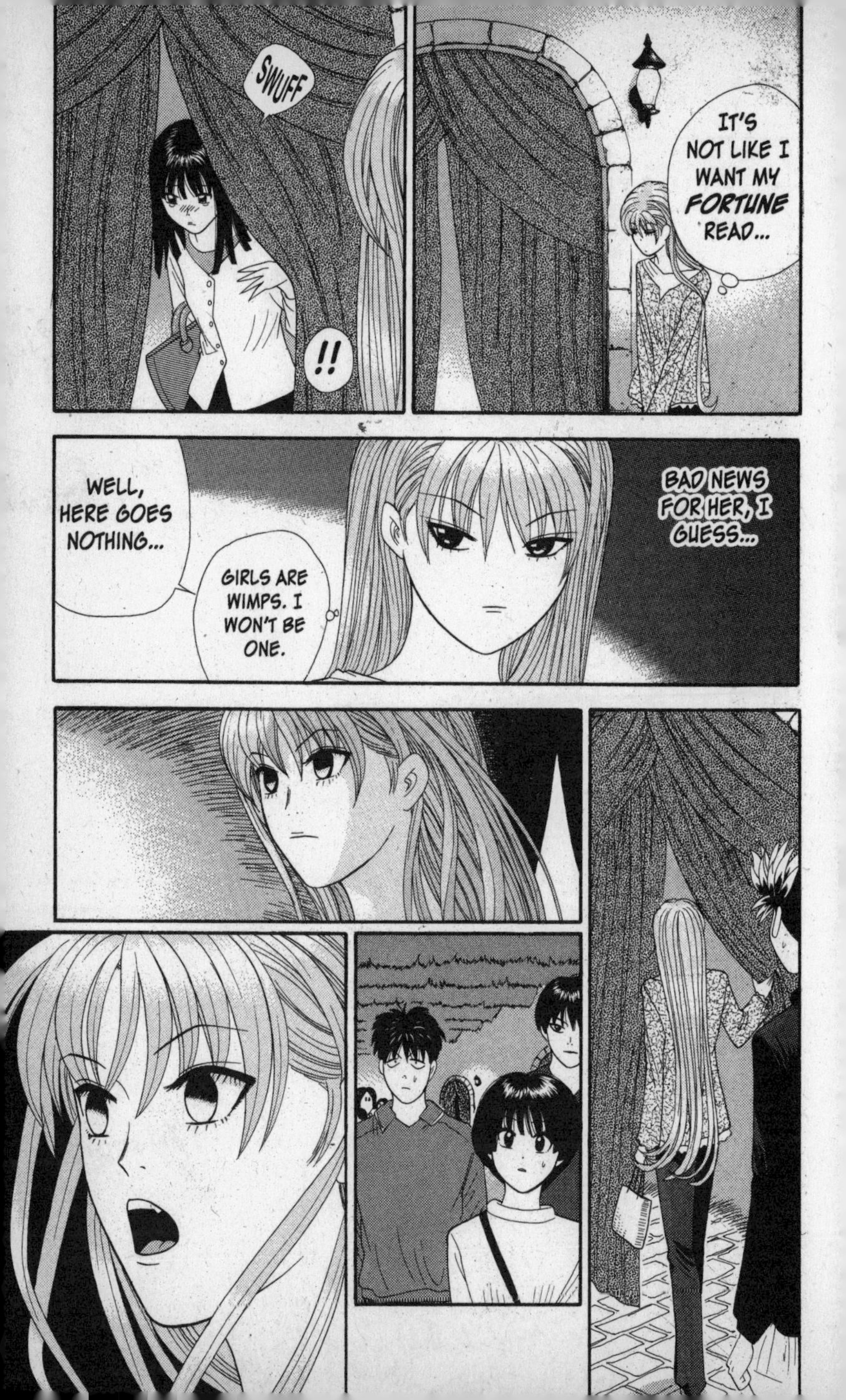
IT'S NOT LIKE I WANT MY FORTUNE READ...
SWUFF
!!
BAD NEWS FOR HER, I GUESS...
WELL, HERE GOES NOTHING...
GIRLS ARE WIMPS. I WON'T BE ONE.

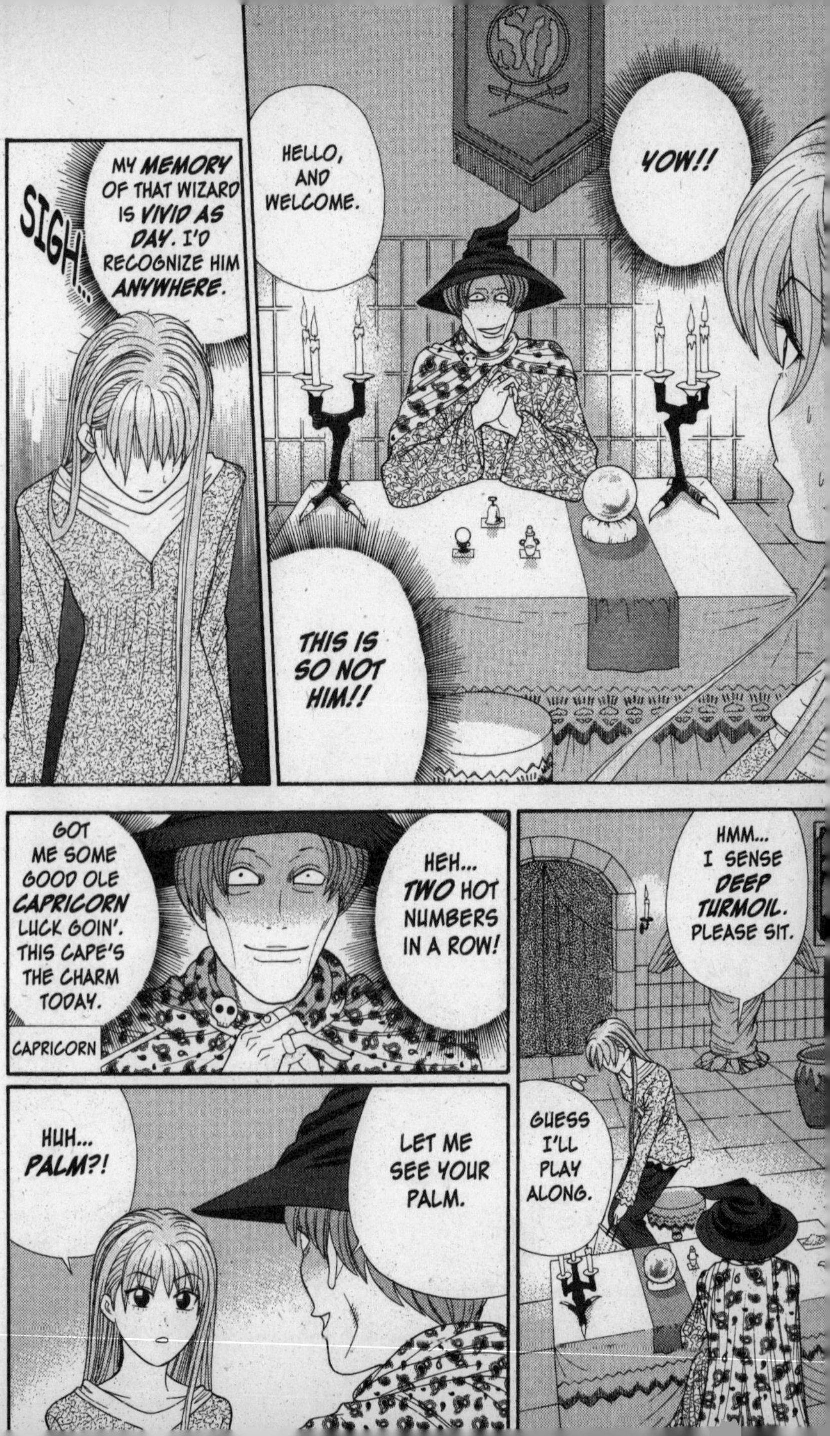
YOW!!
HELLO, AND WELCOME.
THIS IS SO NOT HIM!!
MY MEMORY OF THAT WIZARD IS VIVID AS DAY. I'D RECOGNIZE HIM ANYWHERE.
SIGH...
HMM... I SENSE DEEP TURMOIL. PLEASE SIT.
GUESS I'LL PLAY ALONG.
HEH... TWO HOT NUMBERS IN A ROW!
GOT ME SOME GOOD OLE CAPRICORN LUCK GOIN'. THIS CAPE'S THE CHARM TODAY.
CAPRICORN
LET ME SEE YOUR PALM.
HUH... PALM?!

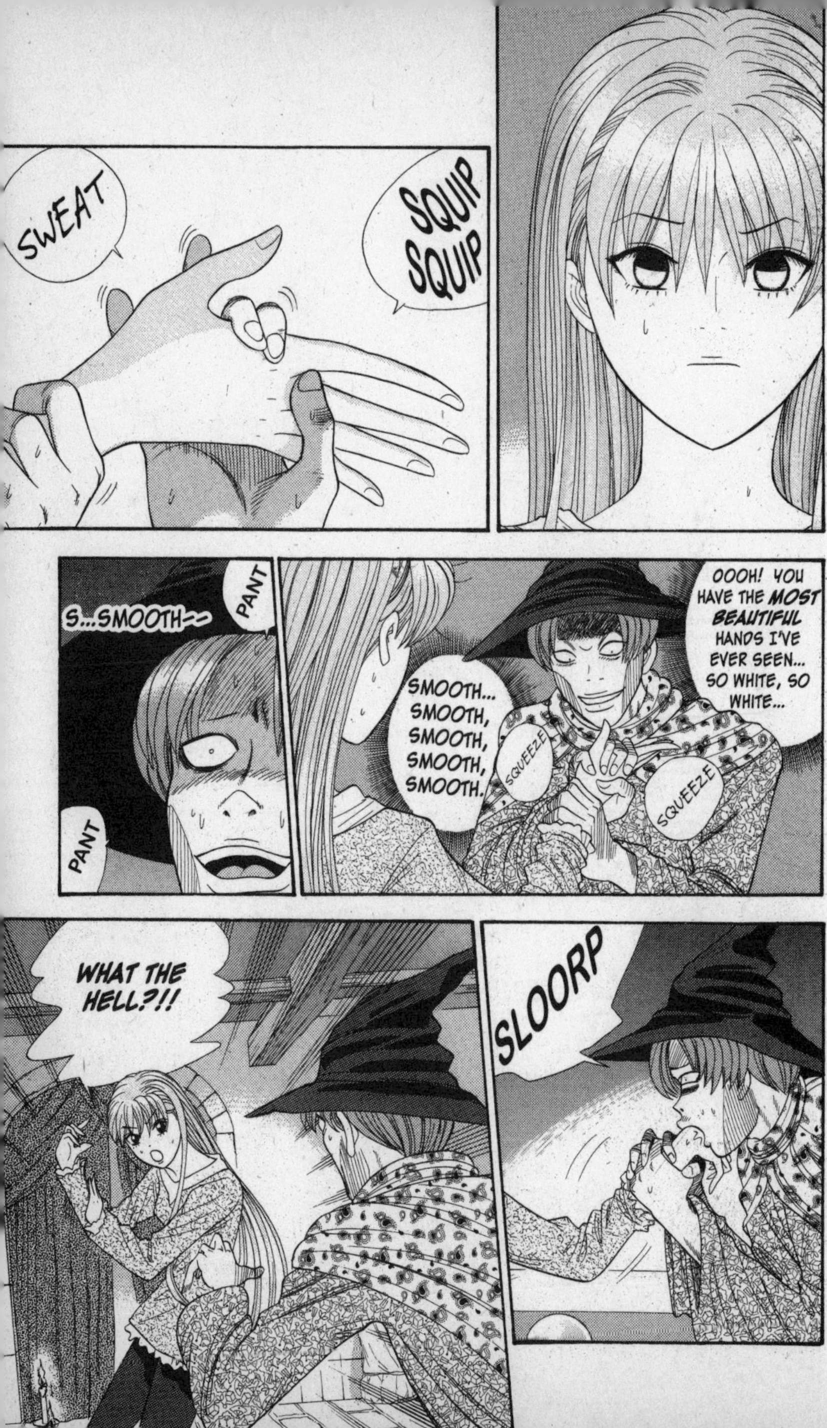
SQUIP SQUIP
SWEAT
OOOH! YOU HAVE THE MOST BEAUTIFUL HANDS I'VE EVER SEEN... SO WHITE, SO WHITE...
SQUEEZE
SMOOTH... SMOOTH, SMOOTH, SMOOTH, SMOOTH.
SQUEEZE
PANT
S...SMOOTH~~
PANT
SLOORP
WHAT THE HELL?!!

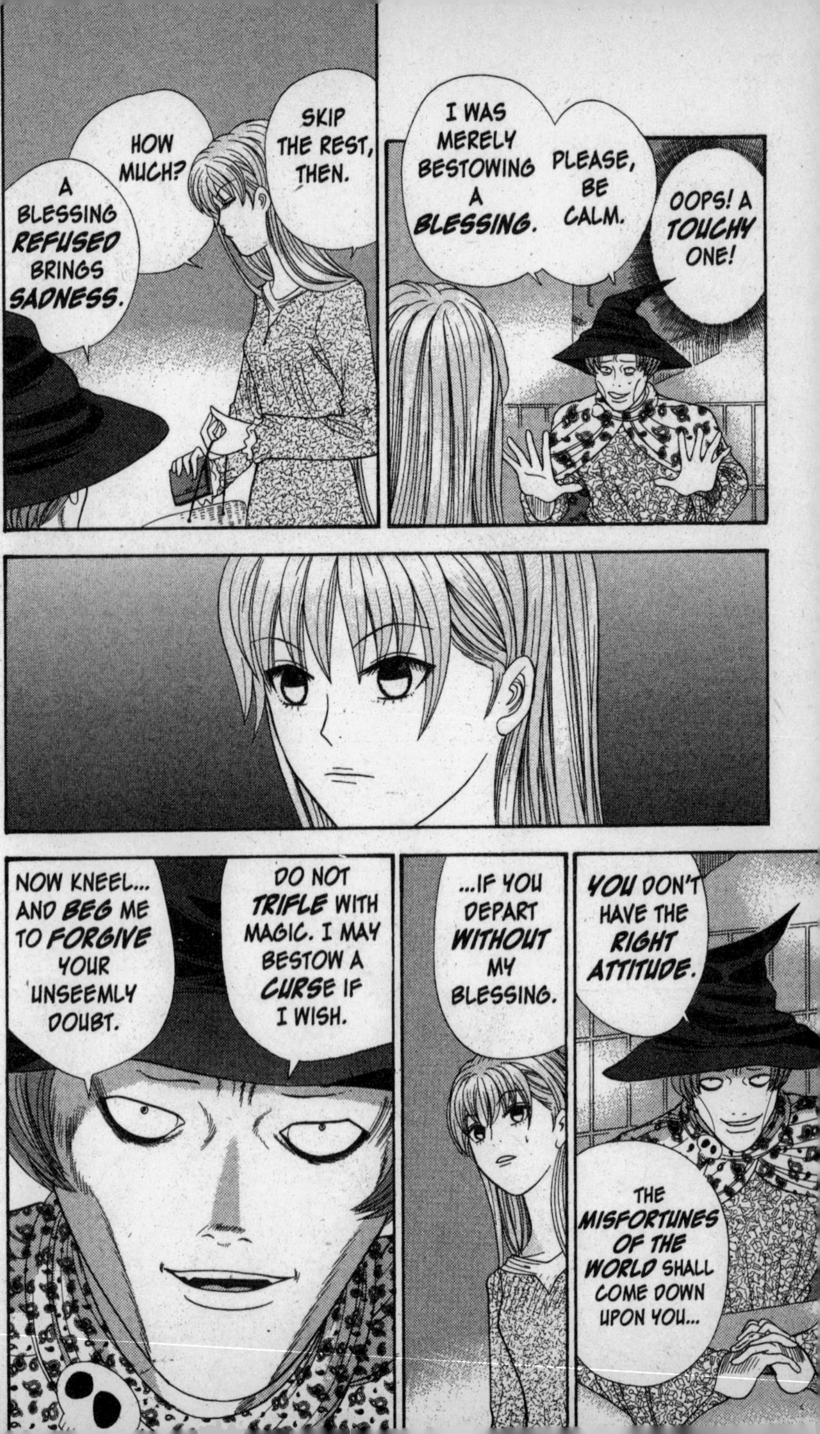
OOPS! A TOUCHY ONE!
PLEASE, BE CALM.
I WAS MERELY BESTOWING A BLESSING.
SKIP THE REST, THEN.
HOW MUCH?
A BLESSING REFUSED BRINGS SADNESS.
YOU DON'T HAVE THE RIGHT ATTITUDE.
THE MISFORTUNES OF THE WORLD SHALL COME DOWN UPON YOU...
...IF YOU DEPART WITHOUT MY BLESSING.
DO NOT TRIFLE WITH MAGIC. I MAY BESTOW A CURSE IF I WISH.
NOW KNEEL... AND BEG ME TO FORGIVE YOUR UNSEEMLY DOUBT.

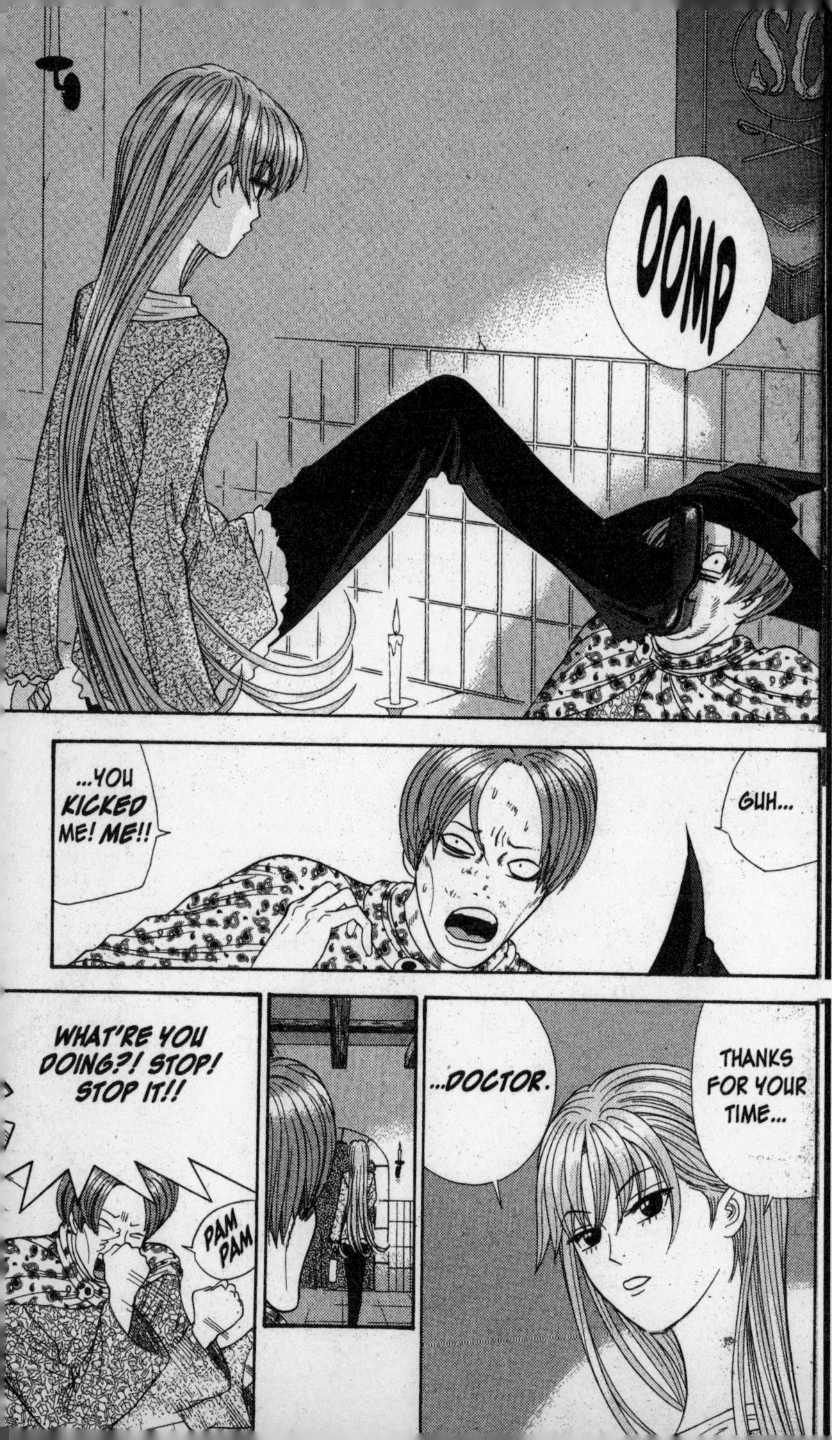
OOMP
GUH...
...YOU KICKED ME! ME!!
THANKS FOR YOUR TIME...
...DOCTOR.
WHAT'RE YOU DOING?! STOP! STOP IT!!
PAM PAM

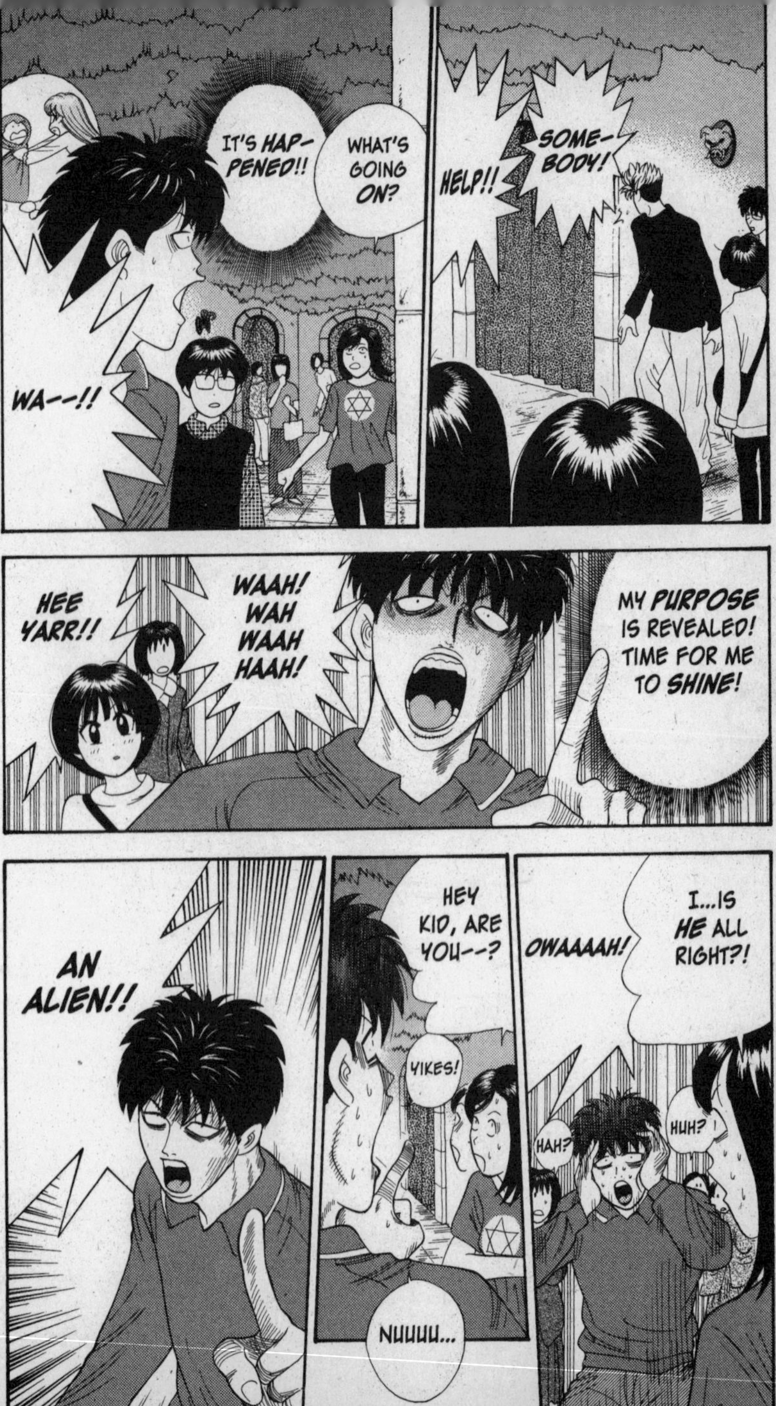
SOME-BODY!
HELP!!
WHAT'S GOING ON?
IT'S HAP-PENED!!
WA--!!
MY PURPOSE IS REVEALED! TIME FOR ME TO SHINE!
WAAH! WAH WAAH HAAH!
HEE YARR!!
I...IS HE ALL RIGHT?!
OWAAAAH!
HUH?
HAH?
HEY KID, ARE YOU--?
YIKES!
NUUUU...
AN ALIEN!!

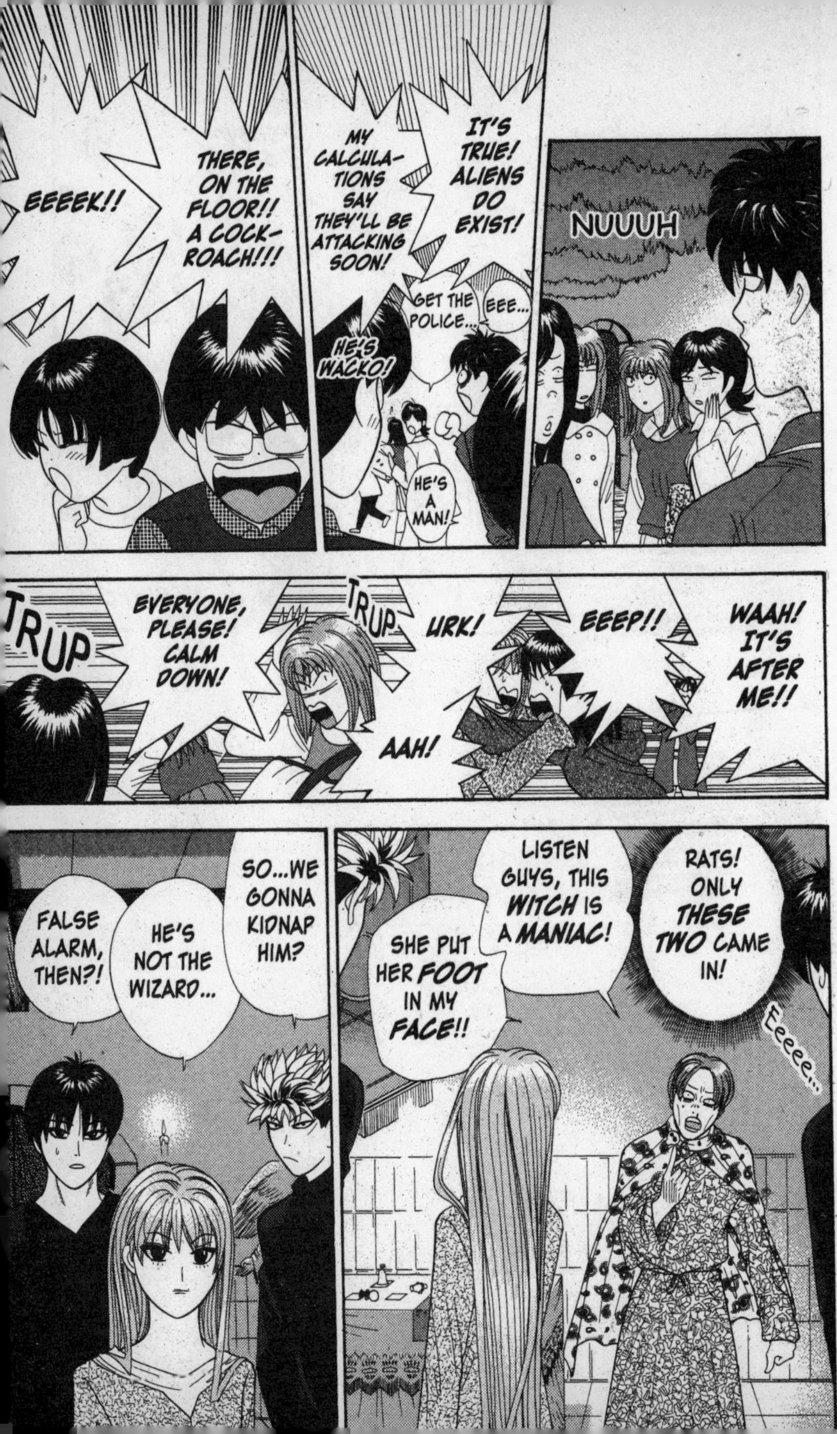
NUUUH
IT'S TRUE! ALIENS DO EXIST!
MY CALCULATIONS SAY THEY'LL BE ATTACKING SOON!
EEE...
GET THE POLICE...
HE'S WACKO!
HE'S A MAN!
THERE, ON THE FLOOR!! A COCKROACH!!!
EEEEK!!
WAAH! IT'S AFTER ME!!
EEEP!!
URK!
TRUP
AAH!
EVERYONE, PLEASE! CALM DOWN!
TRUP
RATS! ONLY THESE TWO CAME IN!
Eeeee...
LISTEN GUYS, THIS WITCH IS A MANIAC!
SHE PUT HER FOOT IN MY FACE!!
SO...WE GONNA KIDNAP HIM?
HE'S NOT THE WIZARD...
FALSE ALARM, THEN?!

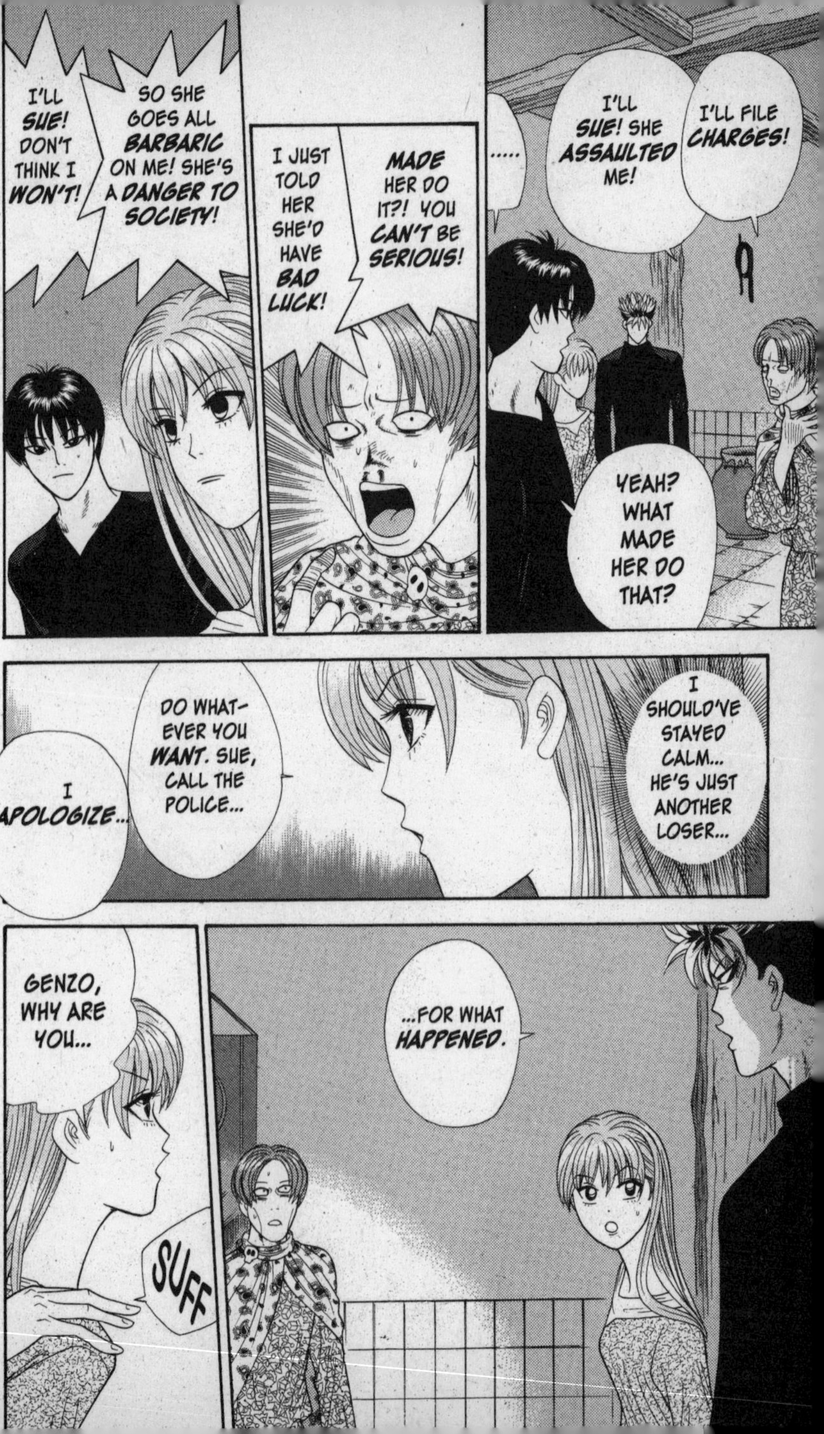
I'LL FILE CHARGES!
I'LL SUE! SHE ASSAULTED ME!
.....
YEAH? WHAT MADE HER DO THAT?
MADE HER DO IT?! YOU CAN'T BE SERIOUS!
I JUST TOLD HER SHE'D HAVE BAD LUCK!
SO SHE GOES ALL BARBARIC ON ME! SHE'S A DANGER TO SOCIETY!
I'LL SUE! DON'T THINK I WON'T!
I SHOULD'VE STAYED CALM... HE'S JUST ANOTHER LOSER...
DO WHATEVER YOU WANT. SUE, CALL THE POLICE...
I APOLOGIZE...
...FOR WHAT HAPPENED.
GENZO, WHY ARE YOU...
SUFF

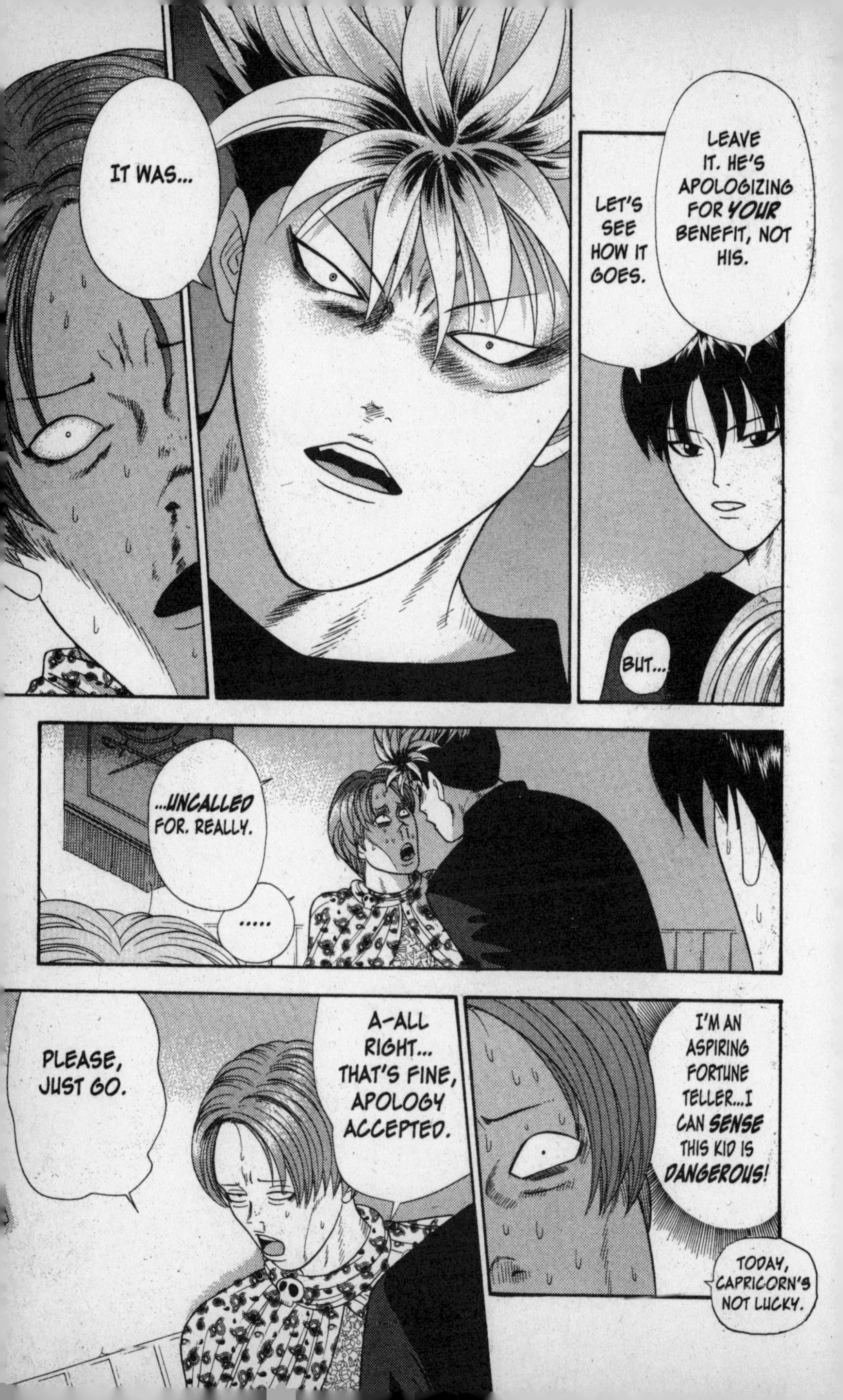
LEAVE IT. HE'S APOLOGIZING FOR YOUR BENEFIT, NOT HIS.
LET'S SEE HOW IT GOES.
BUT...
IT WAS...
...UNCALLED FOR. REALLY.
.....
I'M AN ASPIRING FORTUNE TELLER...I CAN SENSE THIS KID IS DANGEROUS!
TODAY, CAPRICORN'S NOT LUCKY.
A-ALL RIGHT... THAT'S FINE, APOLOGY ACCEPTED.
PLEASE, JUST GO.

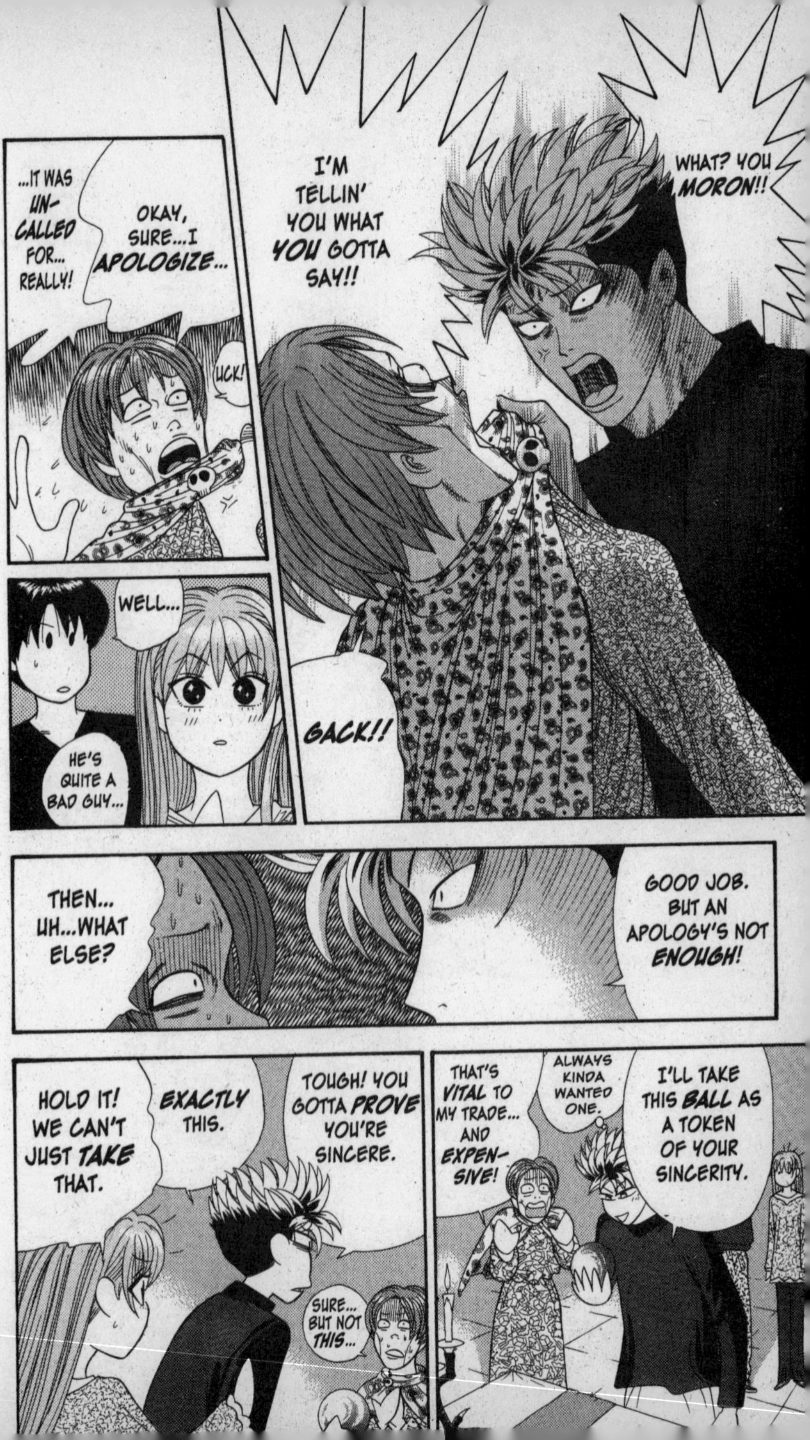
WHAT? YOU MORON!!
I'M TELLIN' YOU WHAT YOU GOTTA SAY!!
GACK!!
OKAY, SURE...I APOLOGIZE...
...IT WAS UN-CALLED FOR... REALLY!
UCK!
WELL...
HE'S QUITE A BAD GUY...
GOOD JOB. BUT AN APOLOGY'S NOT ENOUGH!
THEN... UH...WHAT ELSE?
I'LL TAKE THIS BALL AS A TOKEN OF YOUR SINCERITY.
ALWAYS KINDA WANTED ONE.
THAT'S VITAL TO MY TRADE... AND EXPEN-SIVE!
TOUGH! YOU GOTTA PROVE YOU'RE SINCERE.
EXACTLY THIS.
HOLD IT! WE CAN'T JUST TAKE THAT.
SURE... BUT NOT THIS...

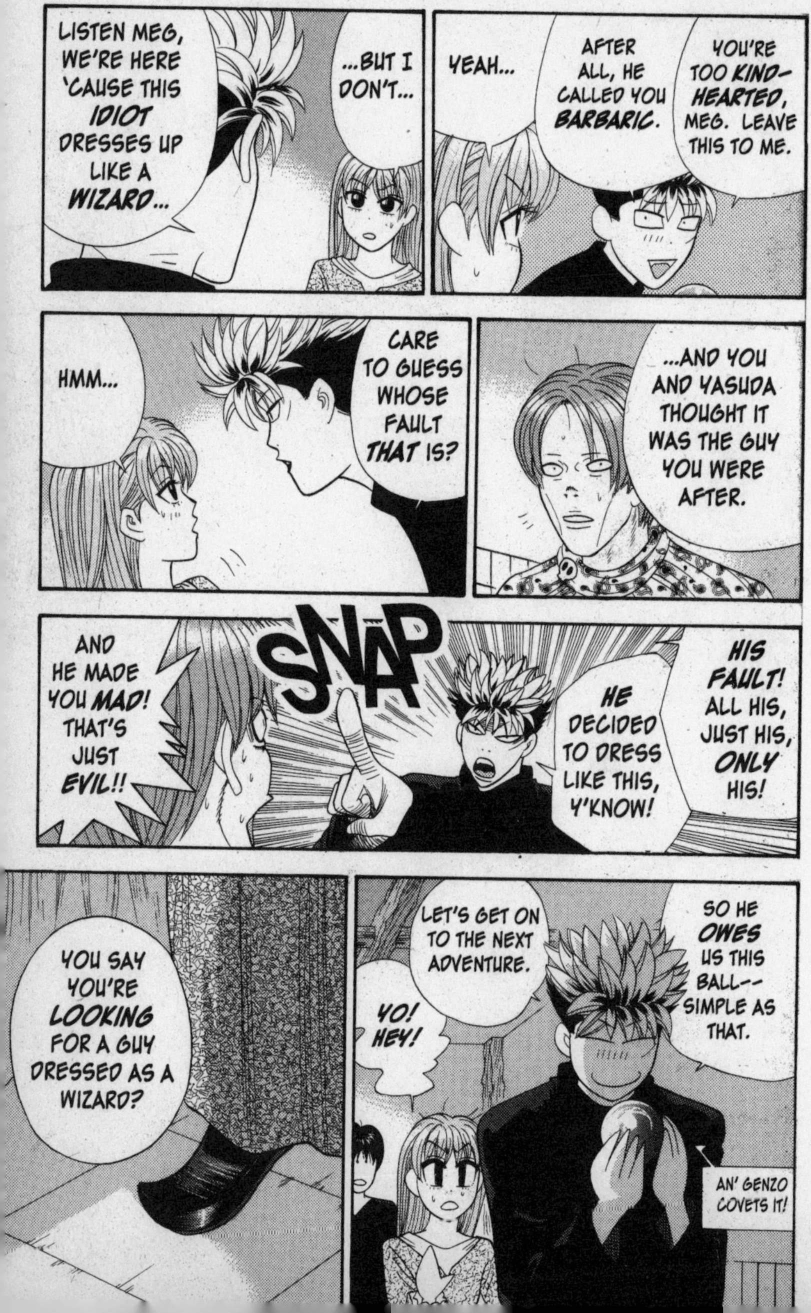
YOU'RE TOO KIND-HEARTED, MEG. LEAVE THIS TO ME.
AFTER ALL, HE CALLED YOU BARBARIC.
YEAH...
...BUT I DON'T...
LISTEN MEG, WE'RE HERE 'CAUSE THIS IDIOT DRESSES UP LIKE A WIZARD...
...AND YOU AND YASUDA THOUGHT IT WAS THE GUY YOU WERE AFTER.
CARE TO GUESS WHOSE FAULT THAT IS?
HMM...
HIS FAULT! ALL HIS, JUST HIS, ONLY HIS!
HE DECIDED TO DRESS LIKE THIS, Y'KNOW!
SNAP
AND HE MADE YOU MAD! THAT'S JUST EVIL!!
SO HE OWES US THIS BALL-- SIMPLE AS THAT.
LET'S GET ON TO THE NEXT ADVENTURE.
YO! HEY!
AN' GENZO COVETS IT!
YOU SAY YOU'RE LOOKING FOR A GUY DRESSED AS A WIZARD?

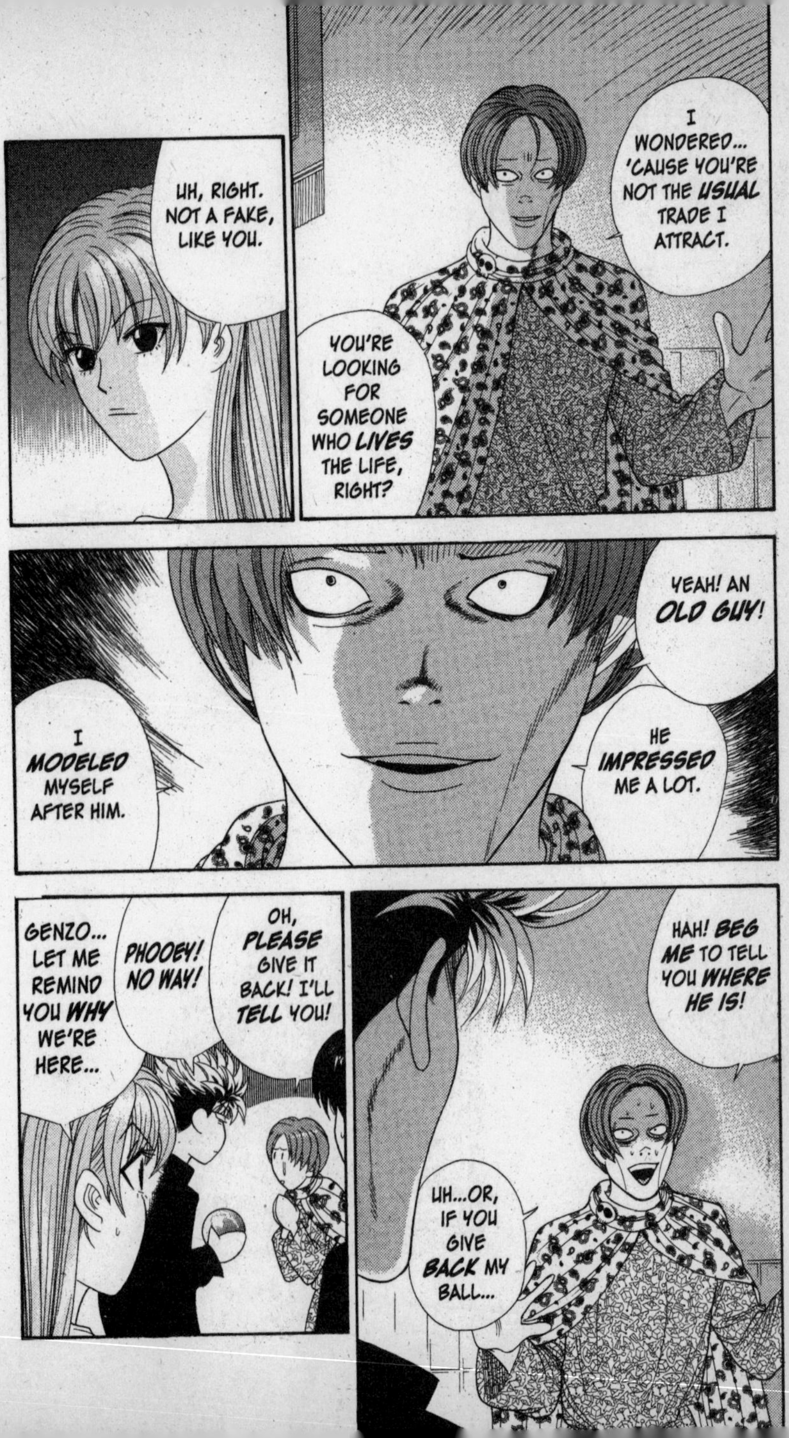

I WONDERED... 'CAUSE YOU'RE NOT THE USUAL TRADE I ATTRACT.
YOU'RE LOOKING FOR SOMEONE WHO LIVES THE LIFE, RIGHT?
UH, RIGHT. NOT A FAKE, LIKE YOU.
YEAH! AN OLD GUY!
HE IMPRESSED ME A LOT.
I MODELED MYSELF AFTER HIM.
HAH! BEG ME TO TELL YOU WHERE HE IS!
UH...OR, IF YOU GIVE BACK MY BALL...
OH, PLEASE GIVE IT BACK! I'LL TELL YOU!
PHOOEY! NO WAY!
GENZO... LET ME REMIND YOU WHY WE'RE HERE...

Chapter 46: Wizard

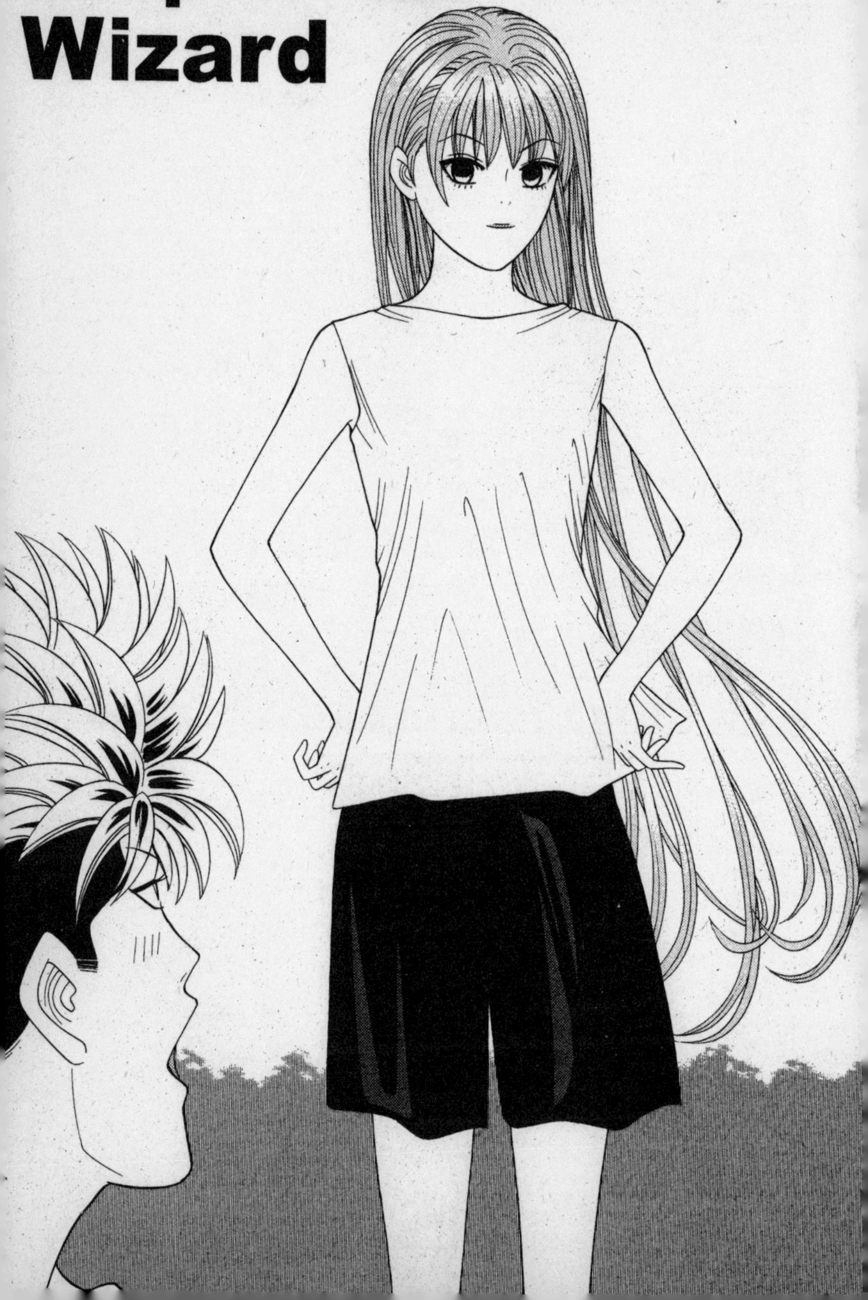

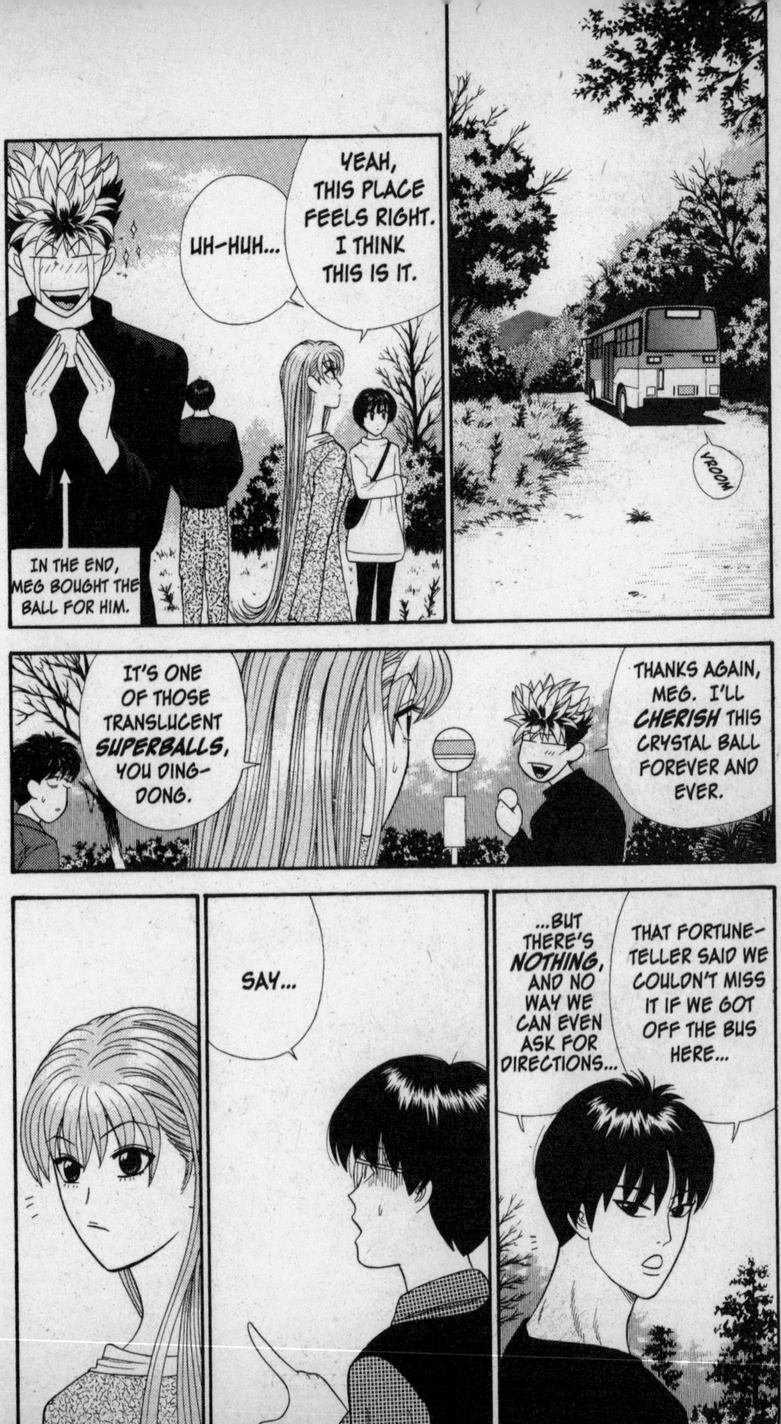
VROOM
YEAH, THIS PLACE FEELS RIGHT. I THINK THIS IS IT.
UH-HUH...
IN THE END, MEG BOUGHT THE BALL FOR HIM.
THANKS AGAIN, MEG. I'LL CHERISH THIS CRYSTAL BALL FOREVER AND EVER.
IT'S ONE OF THOSE TRANSLUCENT SUPERBALLS, YOU DING-DONG.
THAT FORTUNE-TELLER SAID WE COULDN'T MISS IT IF WE GOT OFF THE BUS HERE...
...BUT THERE'S NOTHING, AND NO WAY WE CAN EVEN ASK FOR DIRECTIONS...
SAY...

...CHECK *THAT* OUT...

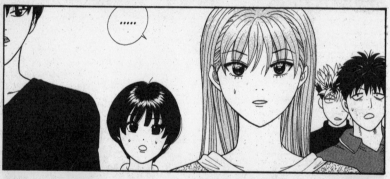

.....

WHEW! CREEPY PLACE!

THE WEAK OF HEART SHOULD NOT VENTURE THERE...

CAW

CAW

CAW

115

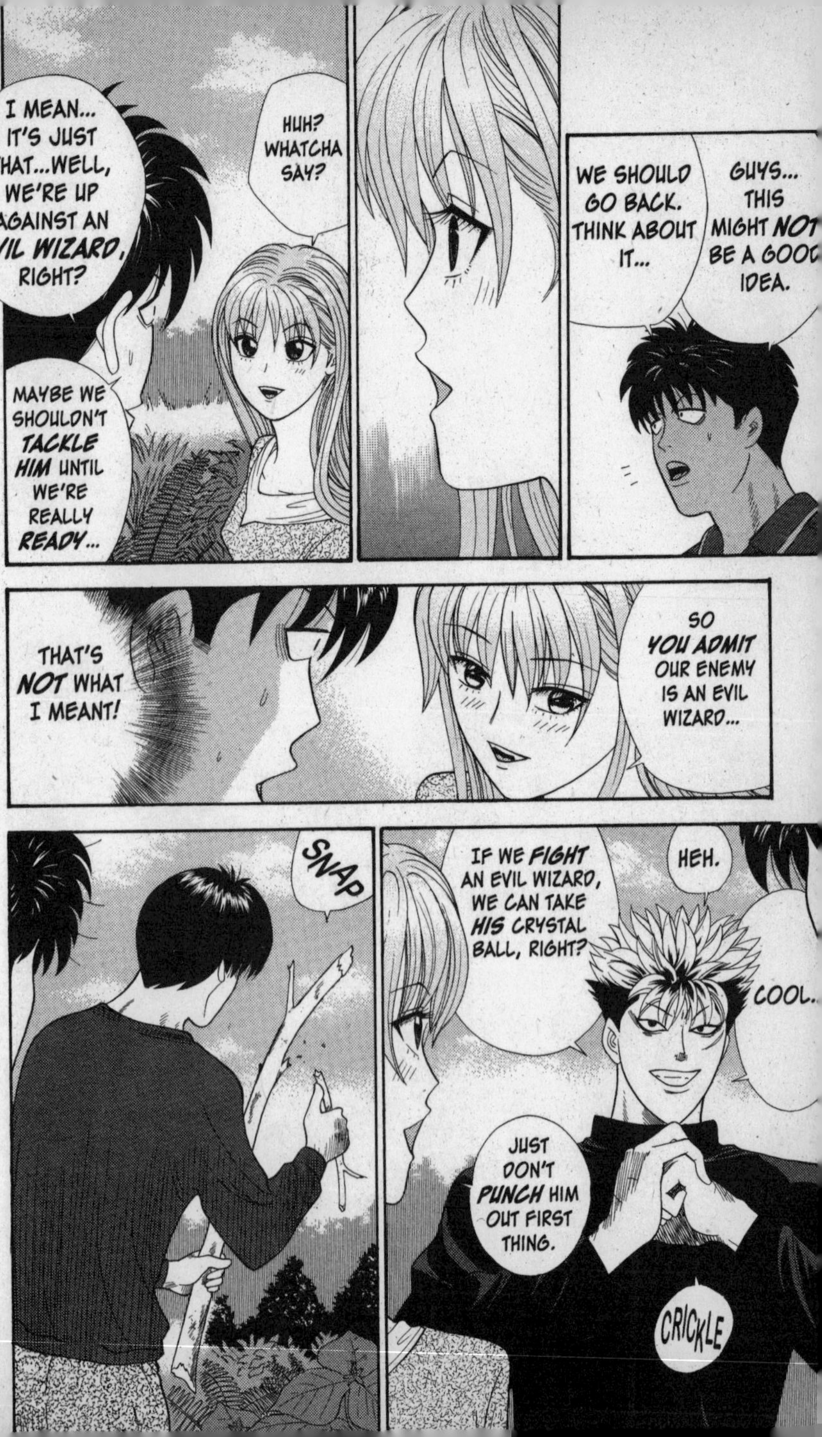
GUYS... THIS MIGHT NOT BE A GOOD IDEA.
WE SHOULD GO BACK. THINK ABOUT IT...
HUH? WHATCHA SAY?
I MEAN... IT'S JUST THAT...WELL, WE'RE UP AGAINST AN EVIL WIZARD, RIGHT?
MAYBE WE SHOULDN'T TACKLE HIM UNTIL WE'RE REALLY READY...
SO YOU ADMIT OUR ENEMY IS AN EVIL WIZARD...
THAT'S NOT WHAT I MEANT!
HEH.
COOL...
IF WE FIGHT AN EVIL WIZARD, WE CAN TAKE HIS CRYSTAL BALL, RIGHT?
JUST DON'T PUNCH HIM OUT FIRST THING.
CRICKLE
SNAP

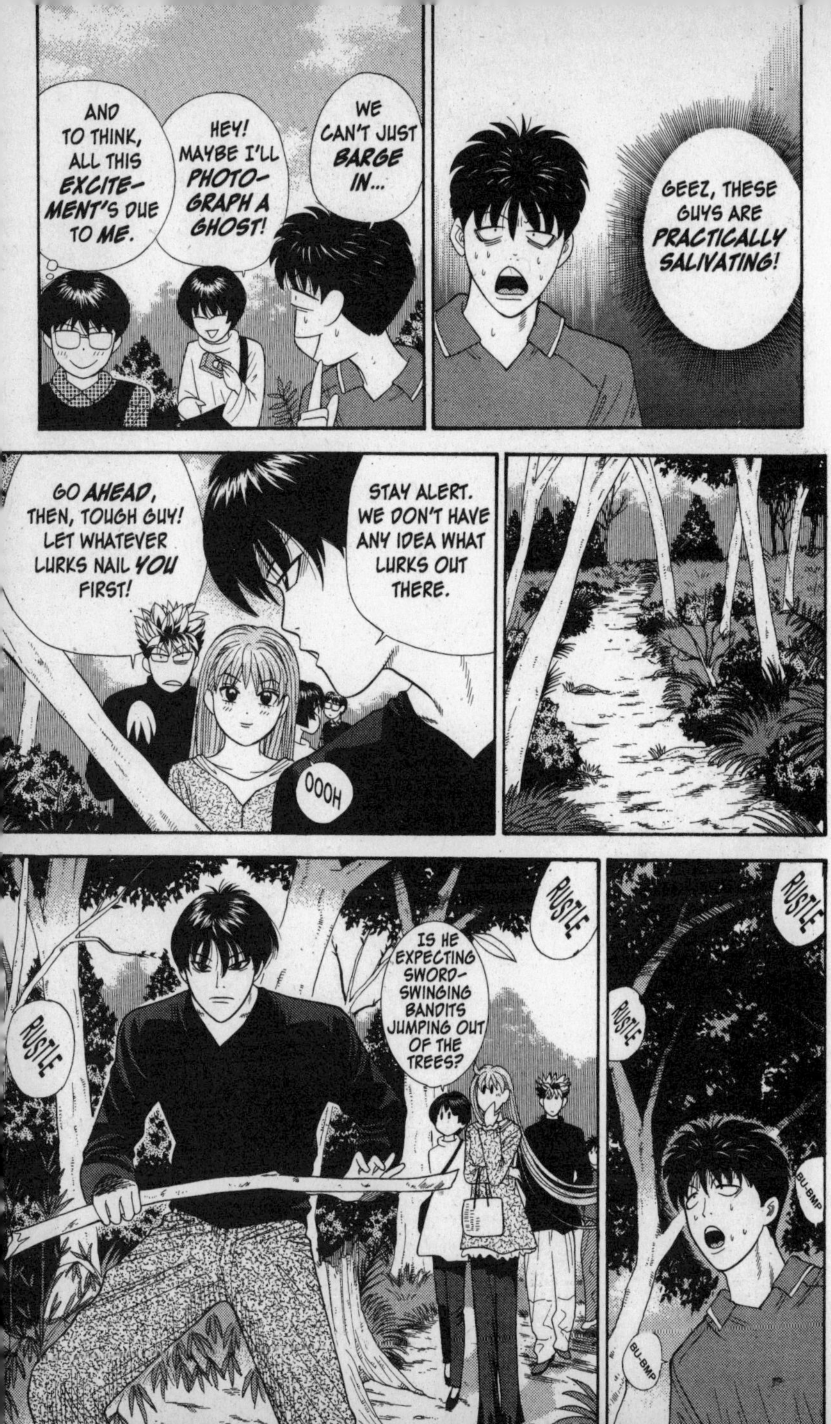

GEEZ, THESE GUYS ARE PRACTICALLY SALIVATING!
WE CAN'T JUST BARGE IN...
HEY! MAYBE I'LL PHOTOGRAPH A GHOST!
AND TO THINK, ALL THIS EXCITEMENT'S DUE TO ME.
STAY ALERT. WE DON'T HAVE ANY IDEA WHAT LURKS OUT THERE.
GO AHEAD, THEN, TOUGH GUY! LET WHATEVER LURKS NAIL YOU FIRST!
OOOH
RUSTLE
RUSTLE
BU-BMP
BU-BMP
RUSTLE
IS HE EXPECTING SWORD-SWINGING BANDITS JUMPING OUT OF THE TREES?
RUSTLE

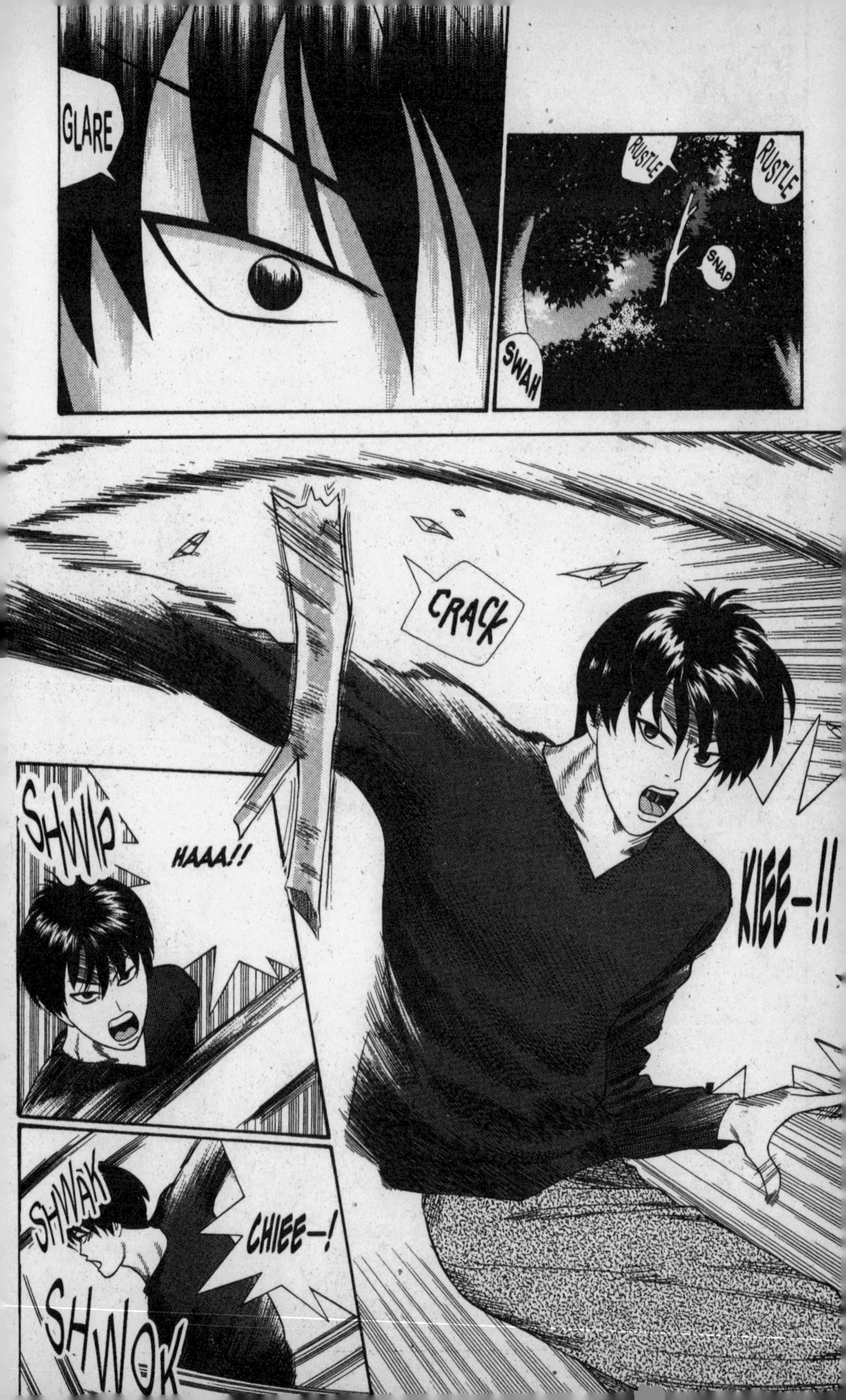
RUSTLE
RUSTLE
SNAP
SWAH
GLARE
CRACK
KIEE-!!
SHWIP
HAAA!!
SHWAK
CHIEE-!
SHWOK

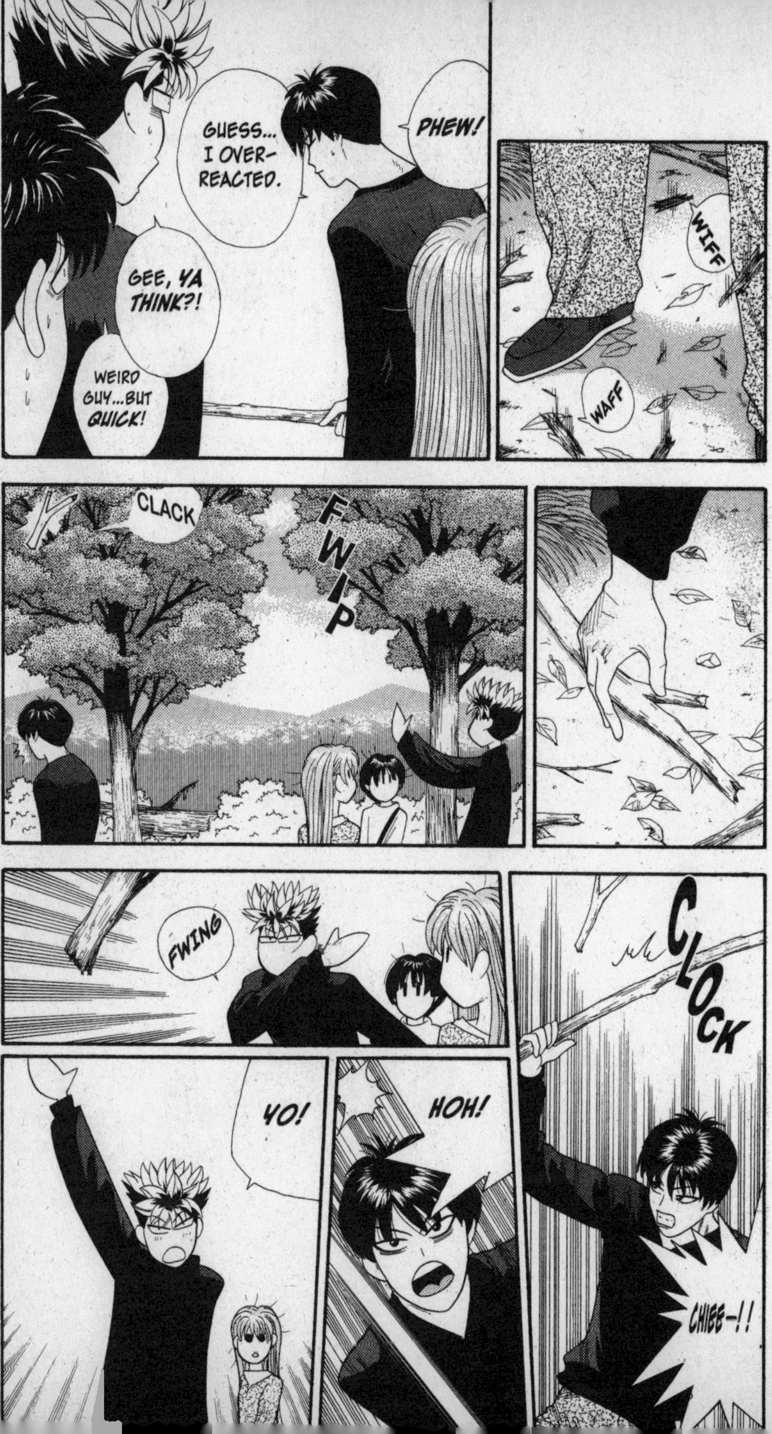
WIFF
WAFF
PHEW!
GUESS... I OVER-REACTED.
GEE, YA THINK?!
WEIRD GUY...BUT QUICK!
FWIP
CLACK
CLOCK
CHIBB–!!
FWING
HOH!
YO!

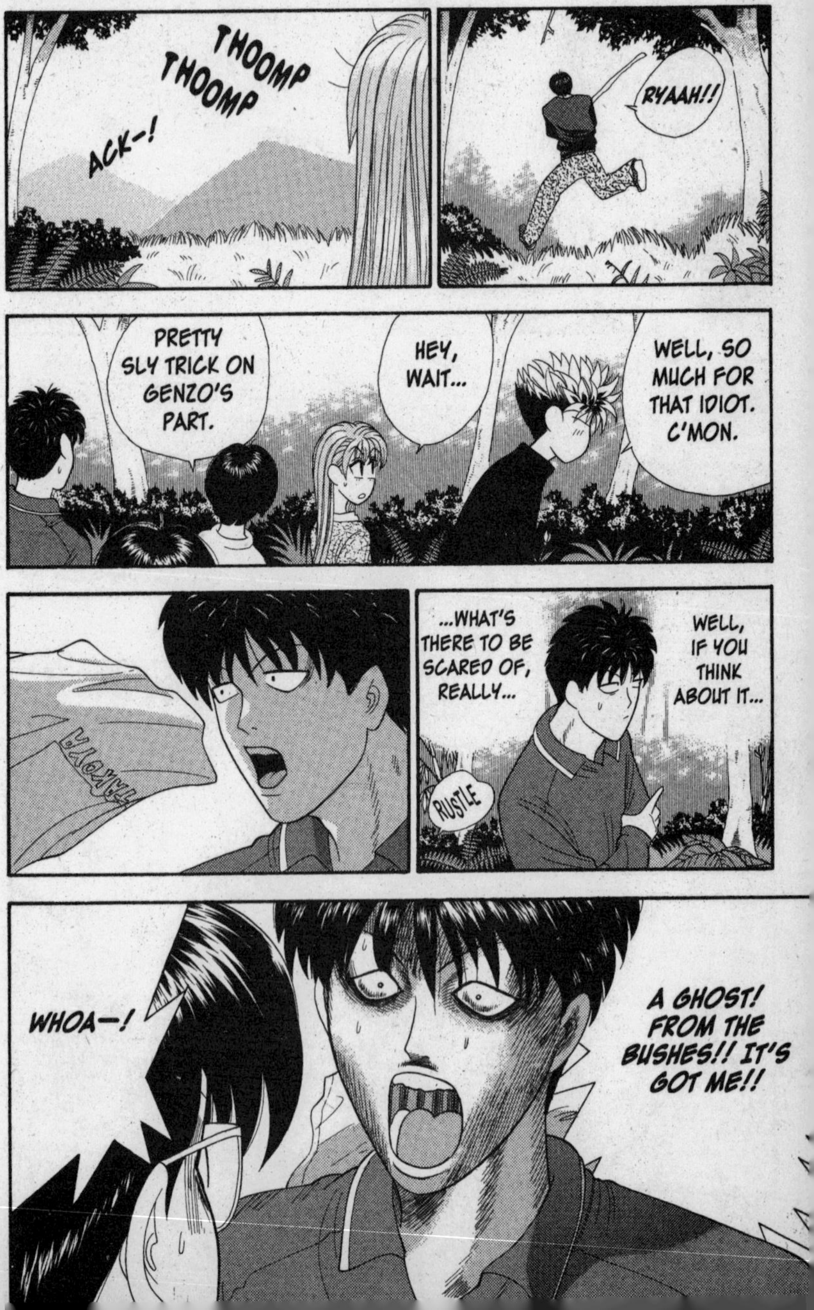
RYAAH!!
THOOMP
THOOMP
ACK-!
WELL, SO MUCH FOR THAT IDIOT. C'MON.
HEY, WAIT...
PRETTY SLY TRICK ON GENZO'S PART.
WELL, IF YOU THINK ABOUT IT...
...WHAT'S THERE TO BE SCARED OF, REALLY...
RUSTLE
A GHOST! FROM THE BUSHES!! IT'S GOT ME!!
WHOA-!

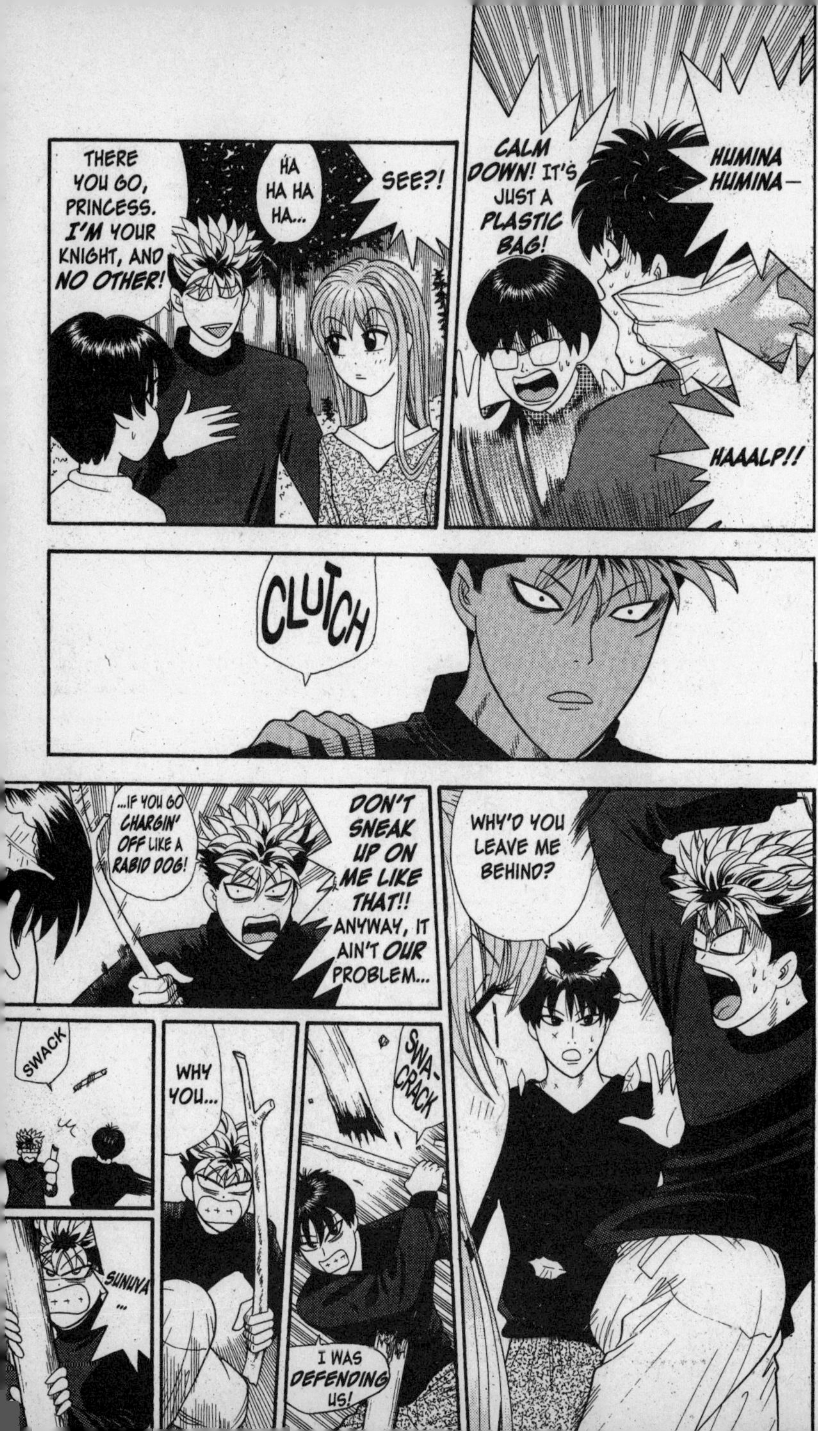
HUMINA HUMINA—
CALM DOWN! IT'S JUST A PLASTIC BAG!
HAAALP!!
SEE?!
HA HA HA HA...
THERE YOU GO, PRINCESS. I'M YOUR KNIGHT, AND NO OTHER!
CLUTCH
WHY'D YOU LEAVE ME BEHIND?
DON'T SNEAK UP ON ME LIKE THAT!! ANYWAY, IT AIN'T OUR PROBLEM...
...IF YOU GO CHARGIN' OFF LIKE A RABID DOG!
SNA-CRACK
WHY YOU...
SWACK
I WAS DEFENDING US!
SUNUVA ...

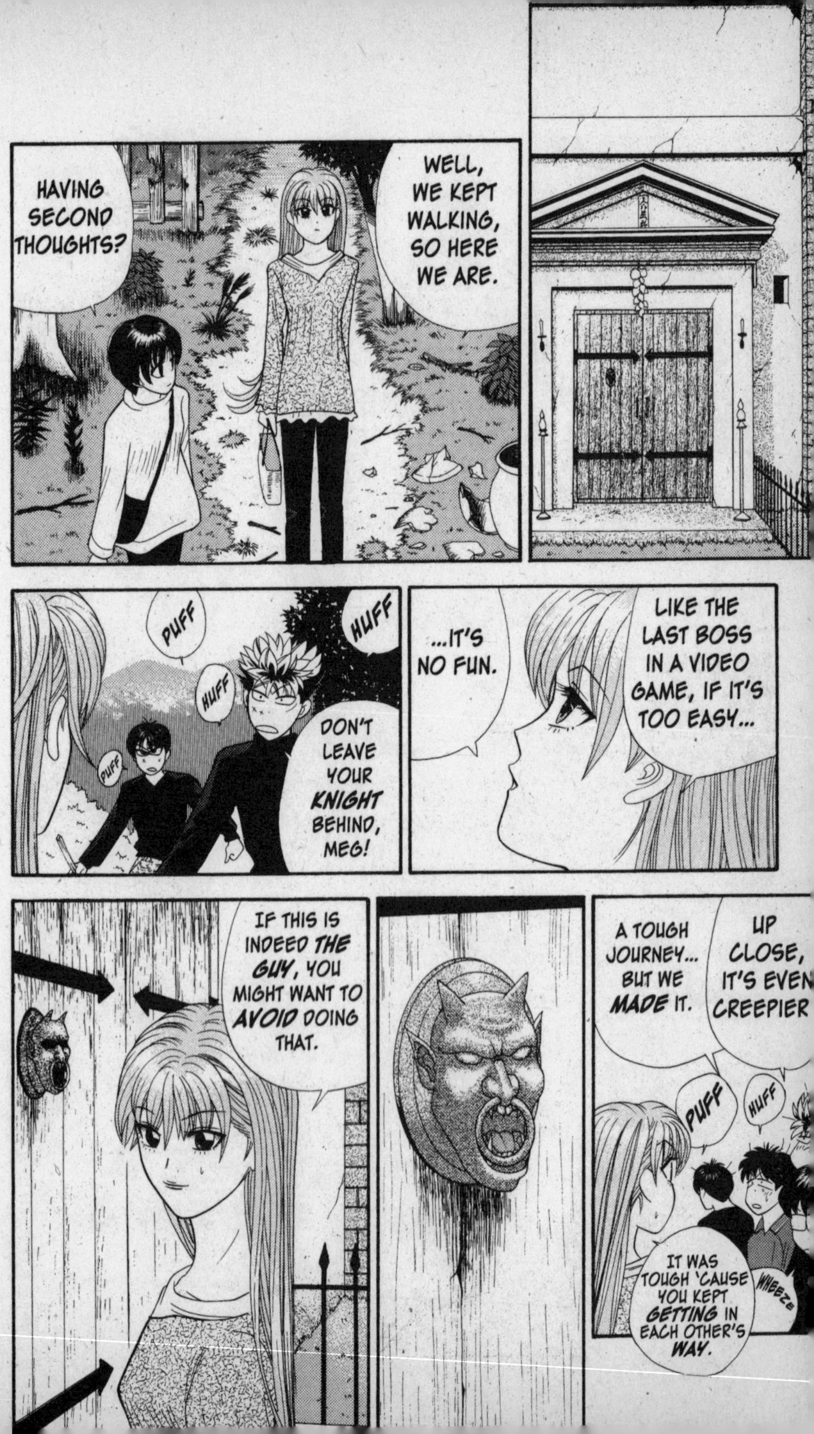
WELL, WE KEPT WALKING, SO HERE WE ARE.
HAVING SECOND THOUGHTS?
LIKE THE LAST BOSS IN A VIDEO GAME, IF IT'S TOO EASY...
...IT'S NO FUN.
HUFF
PUFF
HUFF
DON'T LEAVE YOUR KNIGHT BEHIND, MEG!
PUFF
UP CLOSE, IT'S EVEN CREEPIER
A TOUGH JOURNEY... BUT WE MADE IT.
HUFF
PUFF
WHEEZE
IT WAS TOUGH 'CAUSE YOU KEPT GETTING IN EACH OTHER'S WAY.
IF THIS IS INDEED THE GUY, YOU MIGHT WANT TO AVOID DOING THAT.

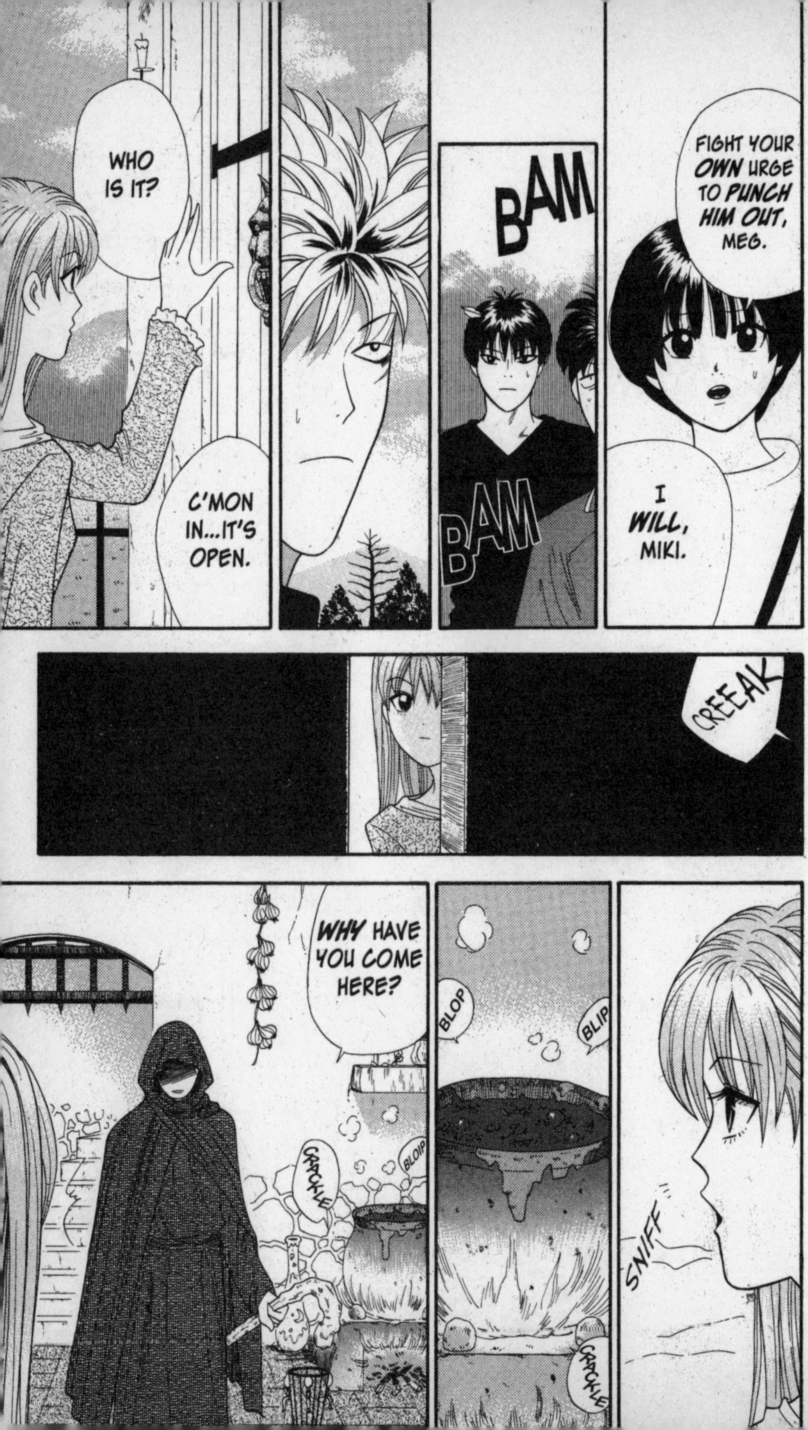
FIGHT YOUR OWN URGE TO PUNCH HIM OUT, MEG.
I WILL, MIKI.
BAM
BAM
WHO IS IT?
C'MON IN...IT'S OPEN.
CREEAK
SNIFF
BLIP
BLOP
CRACKLE
WHY HAVE YOU COME HERE?
BLOIP
CRACKLE

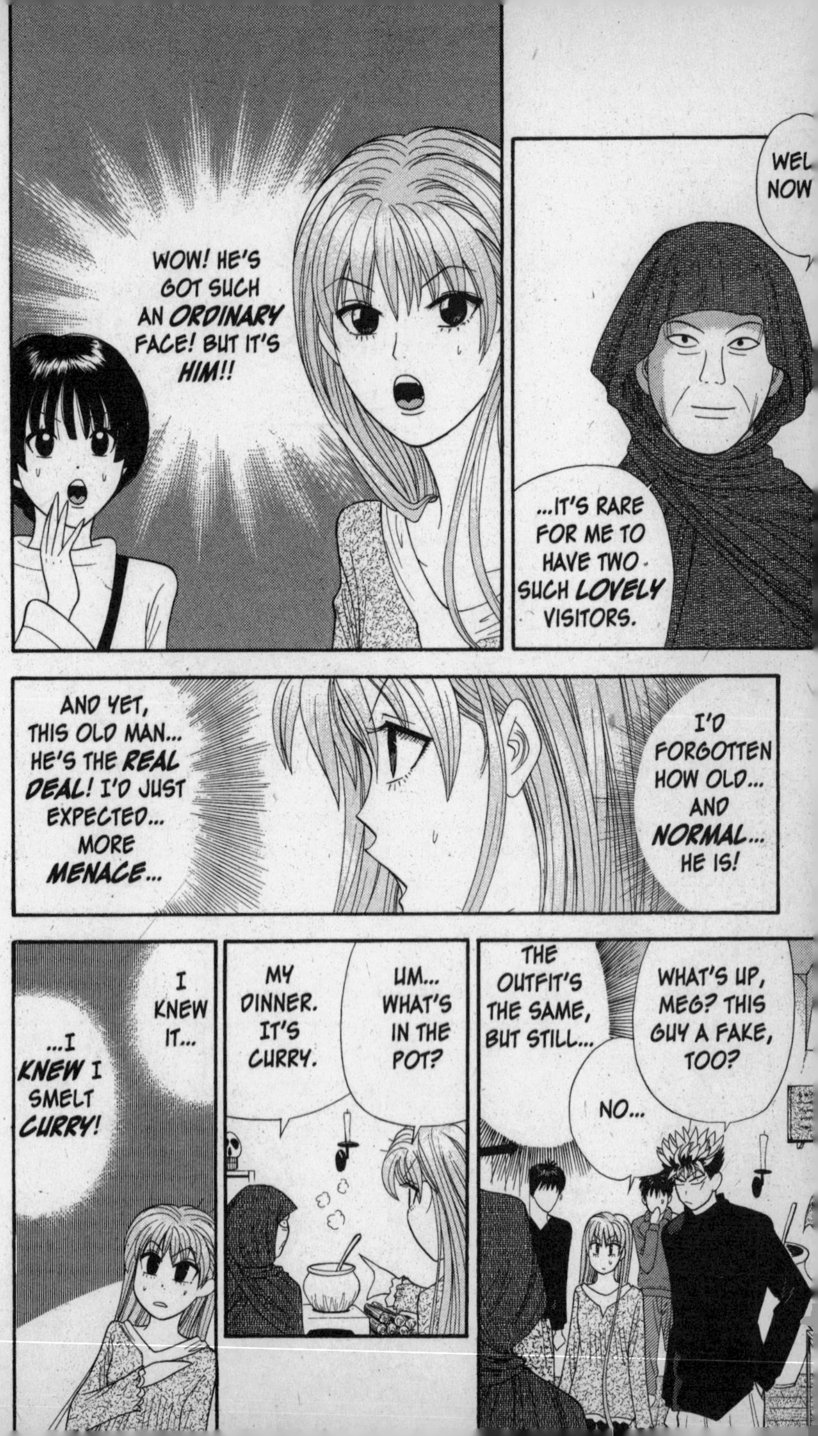
WEL NOW
...IT'S RARE FOR ME TO HAVE TWO SUCH LOVELY VISITORS.
WOW! HE'S GOT SUCH AN ORDINARY FACE! BUT IT'S HIM!!
I'D FORGOTTEN HOW OLD... AND NORMAL... HE IS!
AND YET, THIS OLD MAN... HE'S THE REAL DEAL! I'D JUST EXPECTED... MORE MENACE...
WHAT'S UP, MEG? THIS GUY A FAKE, TOO?
NO...
THE OUTFIT'S THE SAME, BUT STILL...
UM... WHAT'S IN THE POT?
MY DINNER. IT'S CURRY.
I KNEW IT...
...I KNEW I SMELT CURRY!

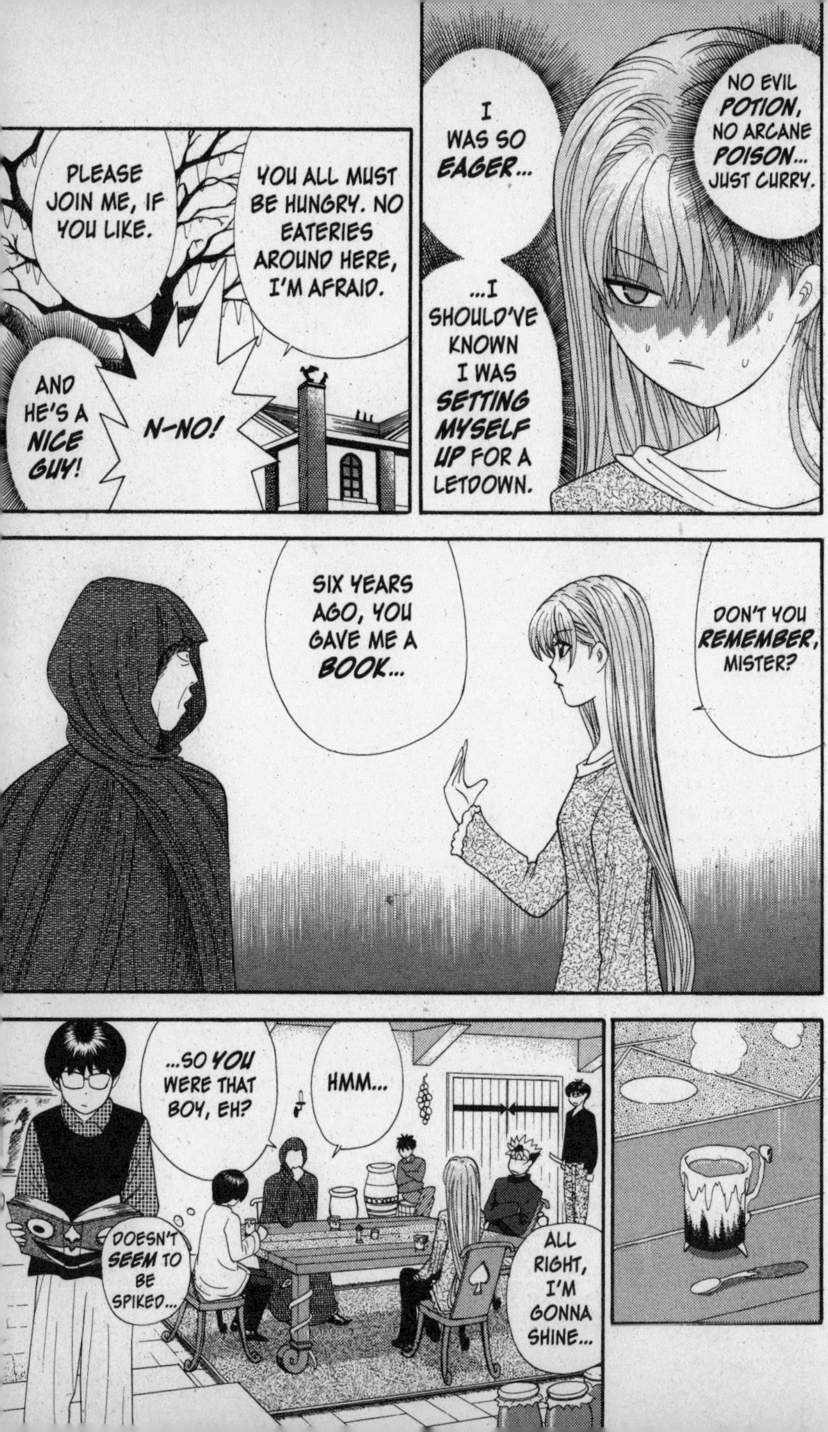
NO EVIL POTION, NO ARCANE POISON... JUST CURRY.
I WAS SO EAGER...
...I SHOULD'VE KNOWN I WAS SETTING MYSELF UP FOR A LETDOWN.
YOU ALL MUST BE HUNGRY. NO EATERIES AROUND HERE, I'M AFRAID.
PLEASE JOIN ME, IF YOU LIKE.
N-NO!
AND HE'S A NICE GUY!
DON'T YOU REMEMBER, MISTER?
SIX YEARS AGO, YOU GAVE ME A BOOK...
HMM...
...SO YOU WERE THAT BOY, EH?
ALL RIGHT, I'M GONNA SHINE...
DOESN'T SEEM TO BE SPIKED...

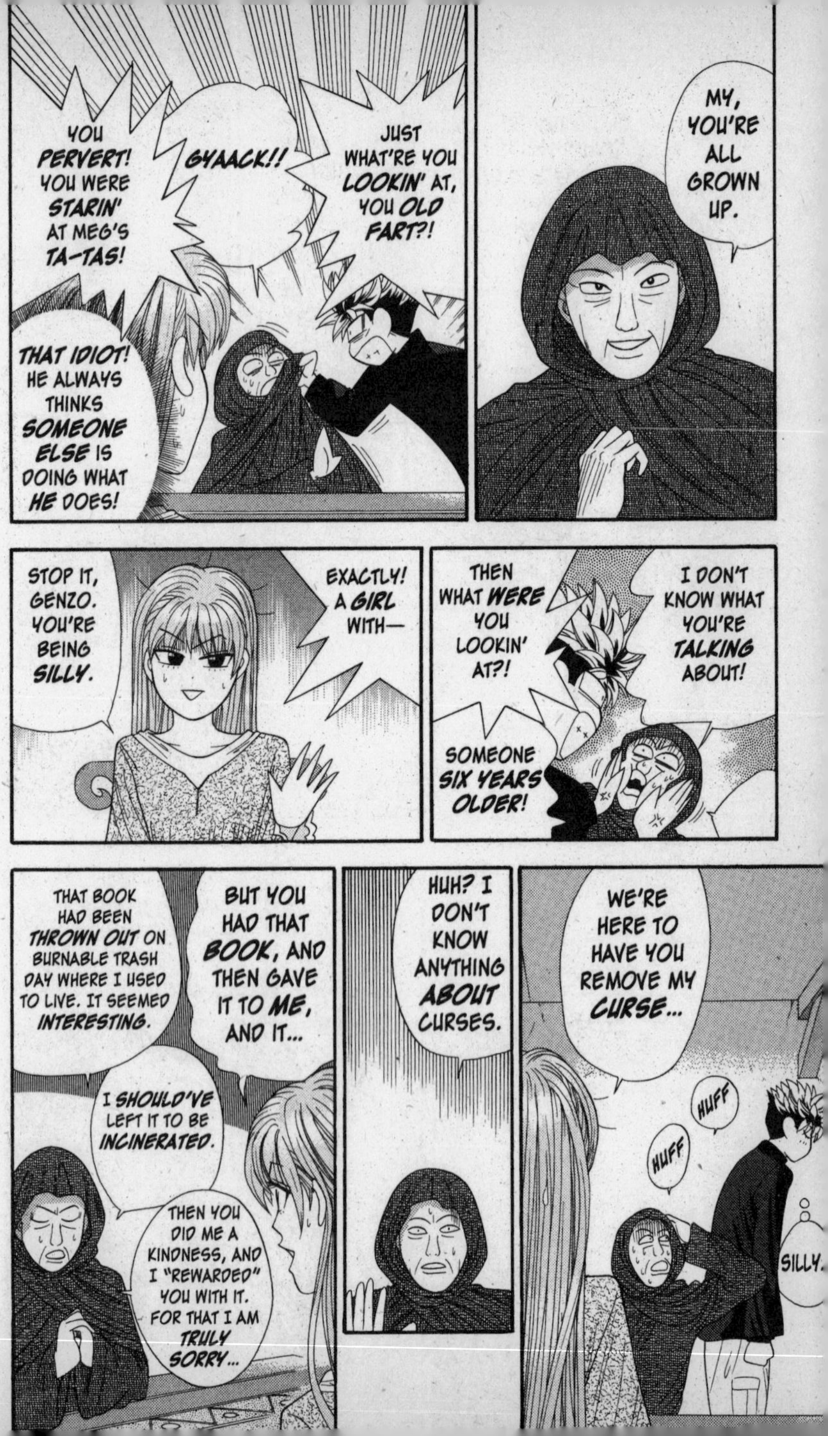
MY, YOU'RE ALL GROWN UP.
JUST WHAT'RE YOU LOOKIN' AT, YOU OLD FART?!
GYAACK!!
YOU PERVERT! YOU WERE STARIN' AT MEG'S TA-TAS!
THAT IDIOT! HE ALWAYS THINKS SOMEONE ELSE IS DOING WHAT HE DOES!
I DON'T KNOW WHAT YOU'RE TALKING ABOUT!
THEN WHAT WERE YOU LOOKIN' AT?!
SOMEONE SIX YEARS OLDER!
EXACTLY! A GIRL WITH—
STOP IT, GENZO. YOU'RE BEING SILLY.
WE'RE HERE TO HAVE YOU REMOVE MY CURSE...
HUFF
HUFF
SILLY.
HUH? I DON'T KNOW ANYTHING ABOUT CURSES.
BUT YOU HAD THAT BOOK, AND THEN GAVE IT TO ME, AND IT...
THAT BOOK HAD BEEN THROWN OUT ON BURNABLE TRASH DAY WHERE I USED TO LIVE. IT SEEMED INTERESTING.
I SHOULD'VE LEFT IT TO BE INCINERATED.
THEN YOU DID ME A KINDNESS, AND I "REWARDED" YOU WITH IT. FOR THAT I AM TRULY SORRY...

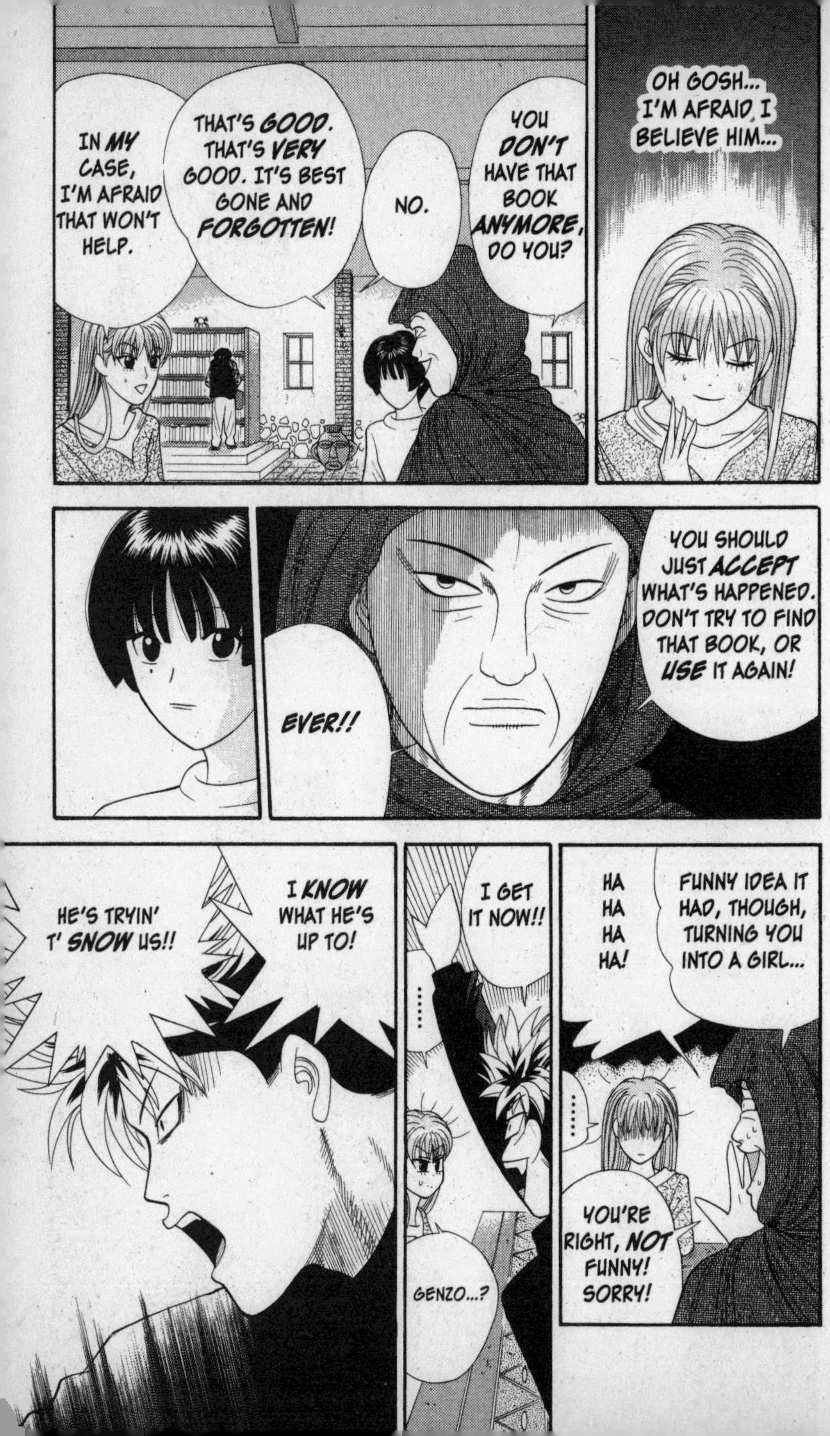
OH GOSH... I'M AFRAID I BELIEVE HIM...
YOU DON'T HAVE THAT BOOK ANYMORE, DO YOU?
NO.
THAT'S GOOD. THAT'S VERY GOOD. IT'S BEST GONE AND FORGOTTEN!
IN MY CASE, I'M AFRAID THAT WON'T HELP.
YOU SHOULD JUST ACCEPT WHAT'S HAPPENED. DON'T TRY TO FIND THAT BOOK, OR USE IT AGAIN!
EVER!!
FUNNY IDEA IT HAD, THOUGH, TURNING YOU INTO A GIRL...
HA HA HA HA!
......
YOU'RE RIGHT, NOT FUNNY! SORRY!
I GET IT NOW!!
......
GENZO...?
I KNOW WHAT HE'S UP TO!
HE'S TRYIN' T' SNOW US!!

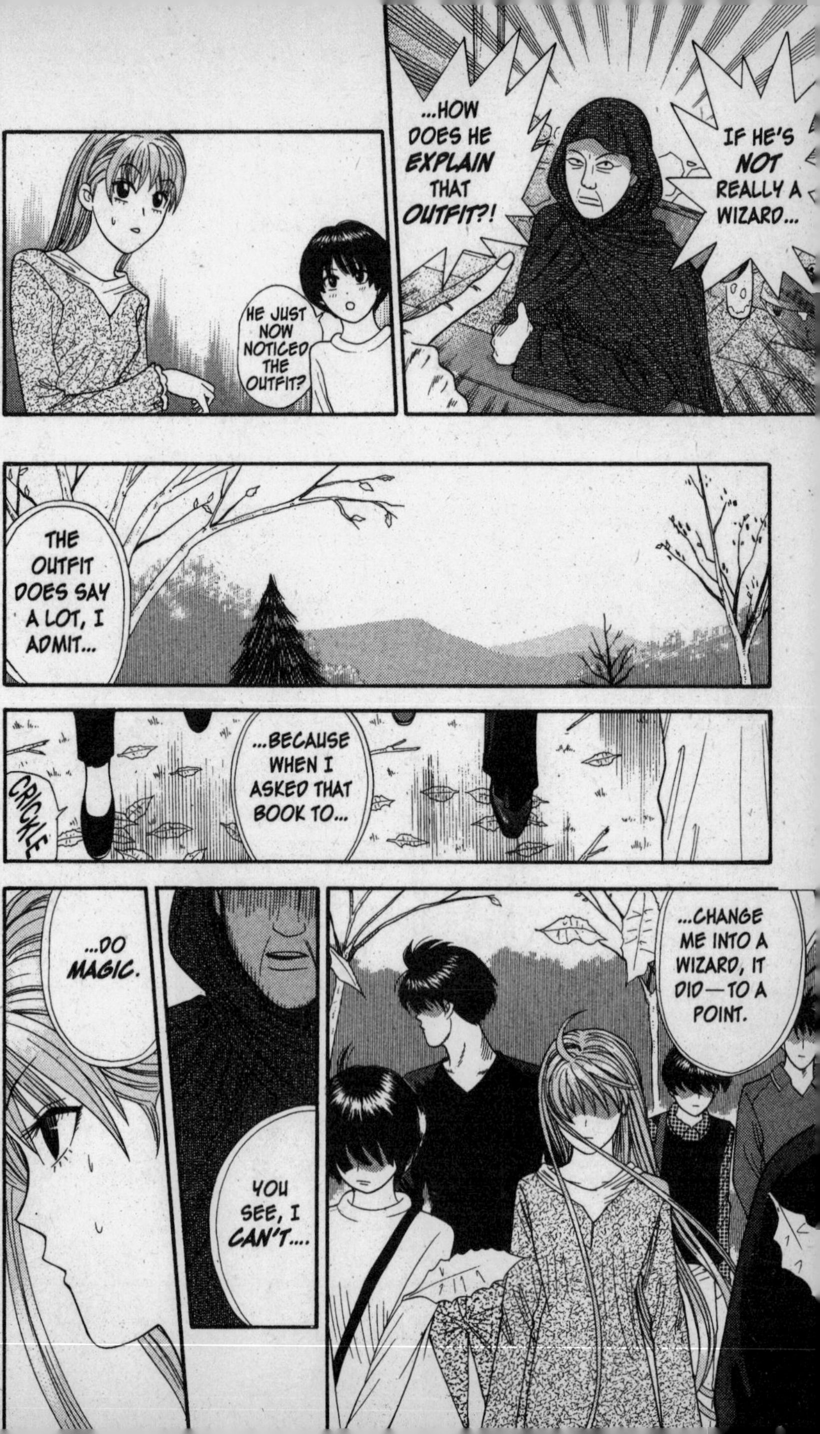
IF HE'S NOT REALLY A WIZARD...
...HOW DOES HE EXPLAIN THAT OUTFIT?!
HE JUST NOW NOTICED THE OUTFIT?
THE OUTFIT DOES SAY A LOT, I ADMIT...
...BECAUSE WHEN I ASKED THAT BOOK TO...
CRICKLE
...CHANGE ME INTO A WIZARD, IT DID—TO A POINT.
YOU SEE, I CAN'T....
...DO MAGIC.

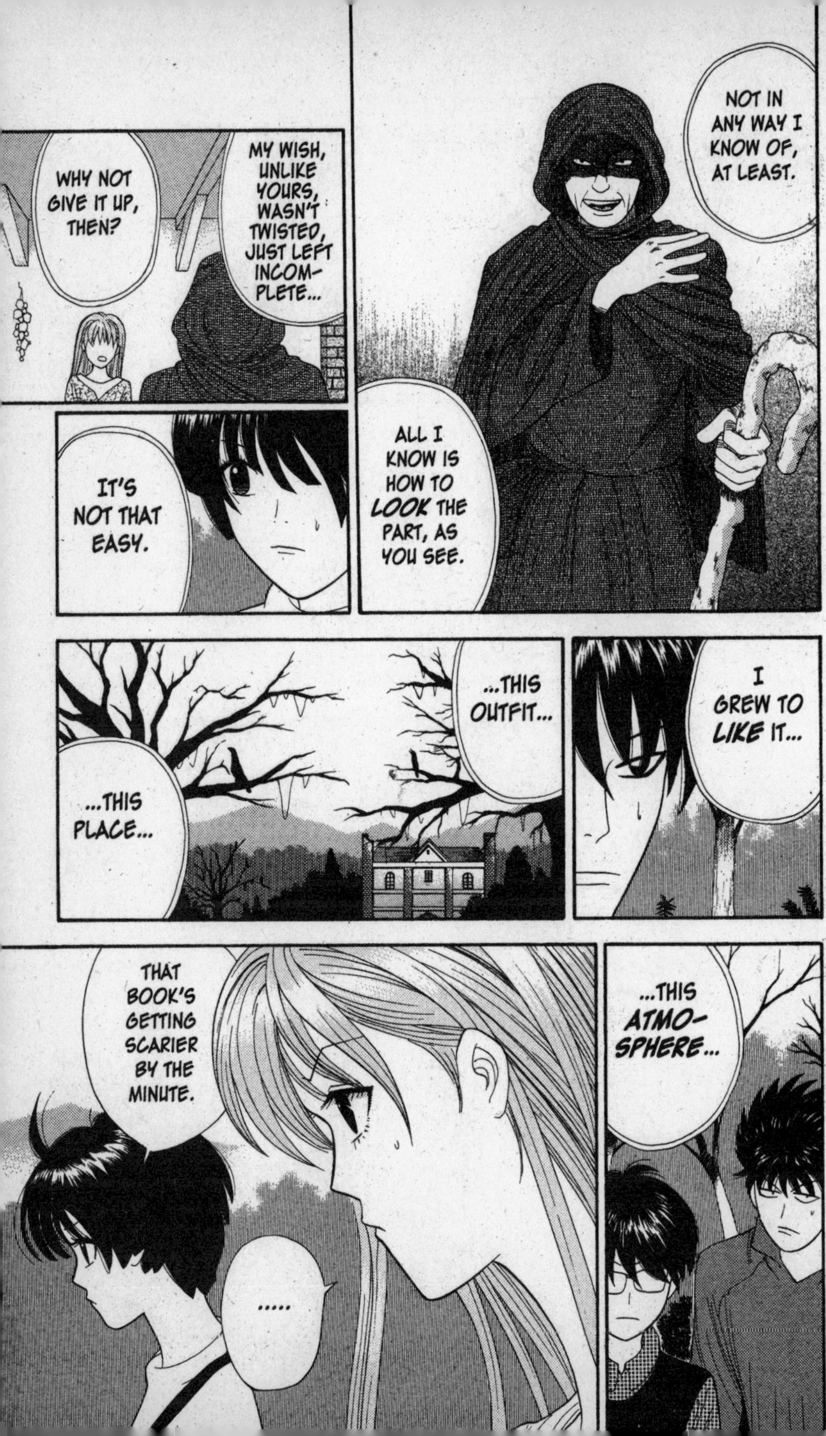
NOT IN ANY WAY I KNOW OF, AT LEAST.
ALL I KNOW IS HOW TO LOOK THE PART, AS YOU SEE.
MY WISH, UNLIKE YOURS, WASN'T TWISTED, JUST LEFT INCOMPLETE...
WHY NOT GIVE IT UP, THEN?
IT'S NOT THAT EASY.
I GREW TO LIKE IT...
...THIS OUTFIT...
...THIS PLACE...
...THIS ATMOSPHERE...
THAT BOOK'S GETTING SCARIER BY THE MINUTE.
.....

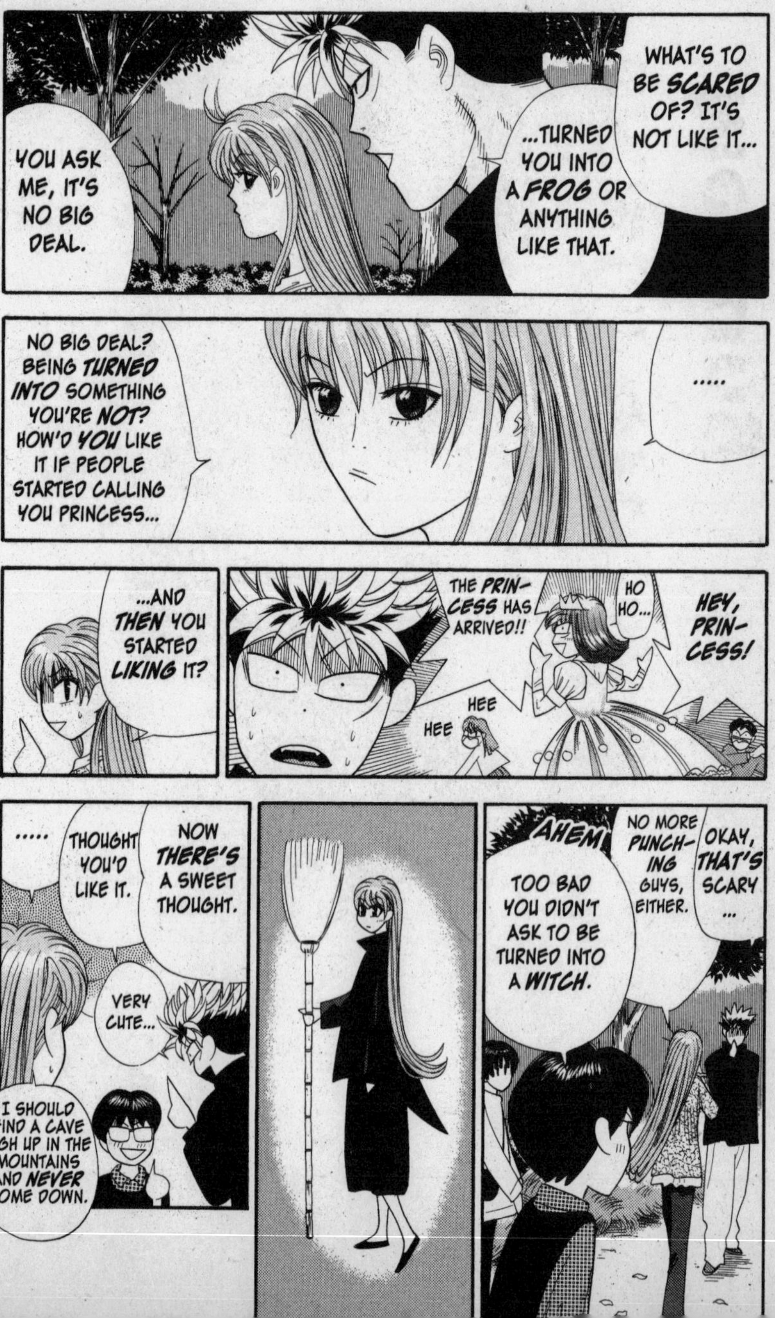
WHAT'S TO BE SCARED OF? IT'S NOT LIKE IT...
...TURNED YOU INTO A FROG OR ANYTHING LIKE THAT.
YOU ASK ME, IT'S NO BIG DEAL.
.....
NO BIG DEAL? BEING TURNED INTO SOMETHING YOU'RE NOT? HOW'D YOU LIKE IT IF PEOPLE STARTED CALLING YOU PRINCESS...
HEY, PRINCESS!
HO HO...
THE PRINCESS HAS ARRIVED!!
HEE HEE
...AND THEN YOU STARTED LIKING IT?
OKAY, THAT'S SCARY ...
NO MORE PUNCHING GUYS, EITHER.
AHEM
TOO BAD YOU DIDN'T ASK TO BE TURNED INTO A WITCH.
NOW THERE'S A SWEET THOUGHT.
THOUGHT YOU'D LIKE IT.
.....
VERY CUTE...
I SHOULD FIND A CAVE HIGH UP IN THE MOUNTAINS AND NEVER COME DOWN.

Chapter 47: Meeting

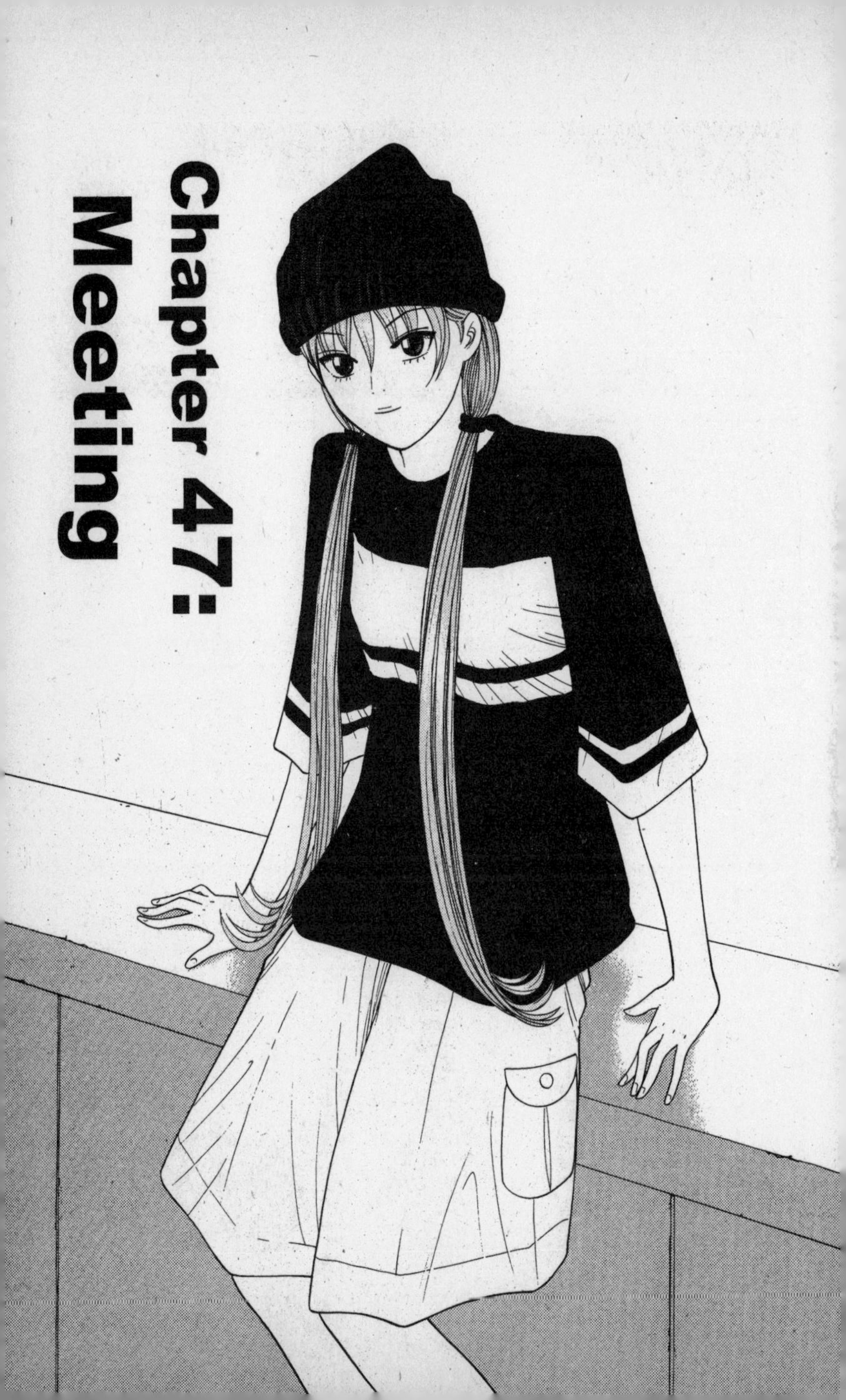

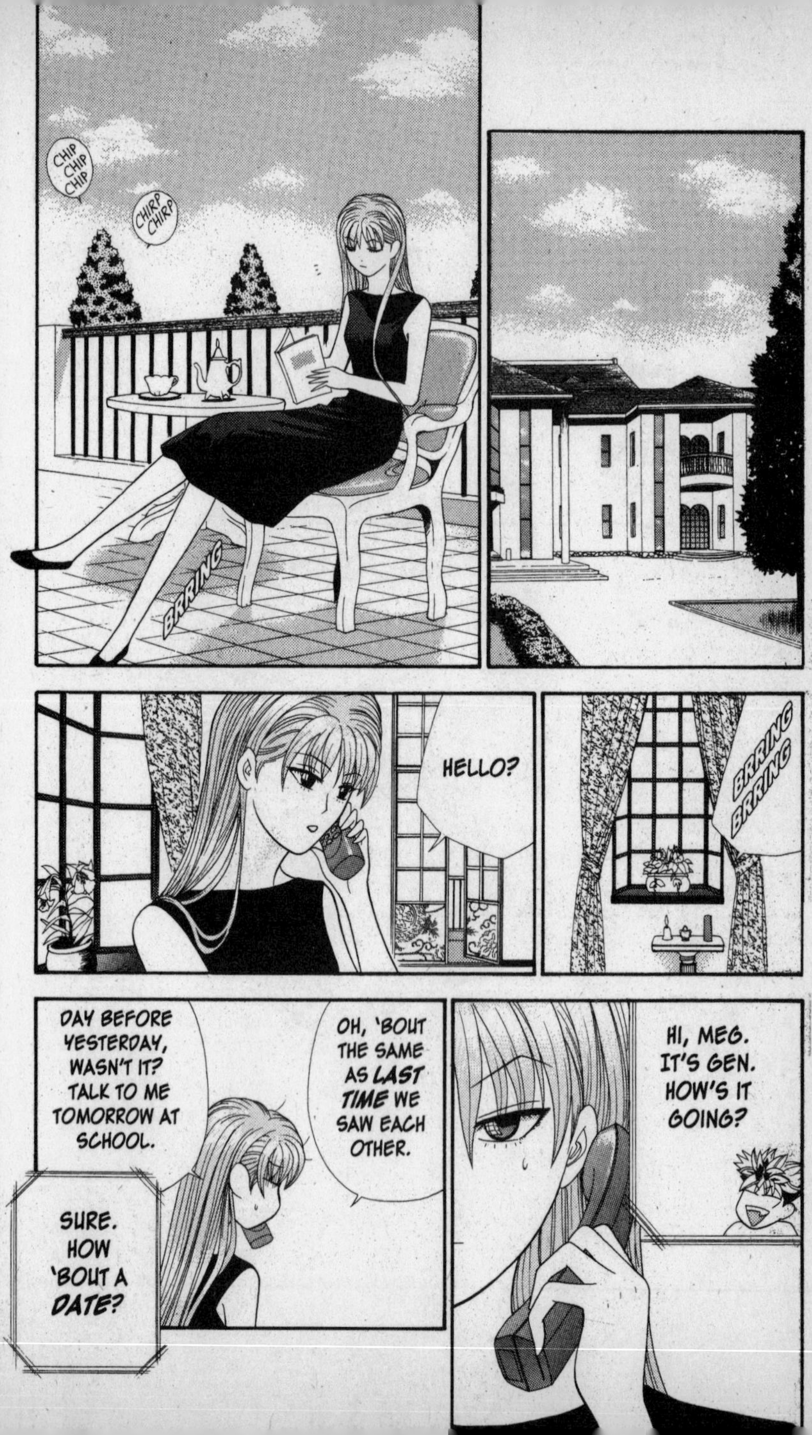
CHIRP CHIRP
CHIP CHIP CHIP
BRRING
BRRING BRRING
HELLO?
HI, MEG. IT'S GEN. HOW'S IT GOING?
OH, 'BOUT THE SAME AS **LAST TIME** WE SAW EACH OTHER.
DAY BEFORE YESTERDAY, WASN'T IT? TALK TO ME TOMORROW AT SCHOOL.
SURE. HOW 'BOUT A **DATE?**

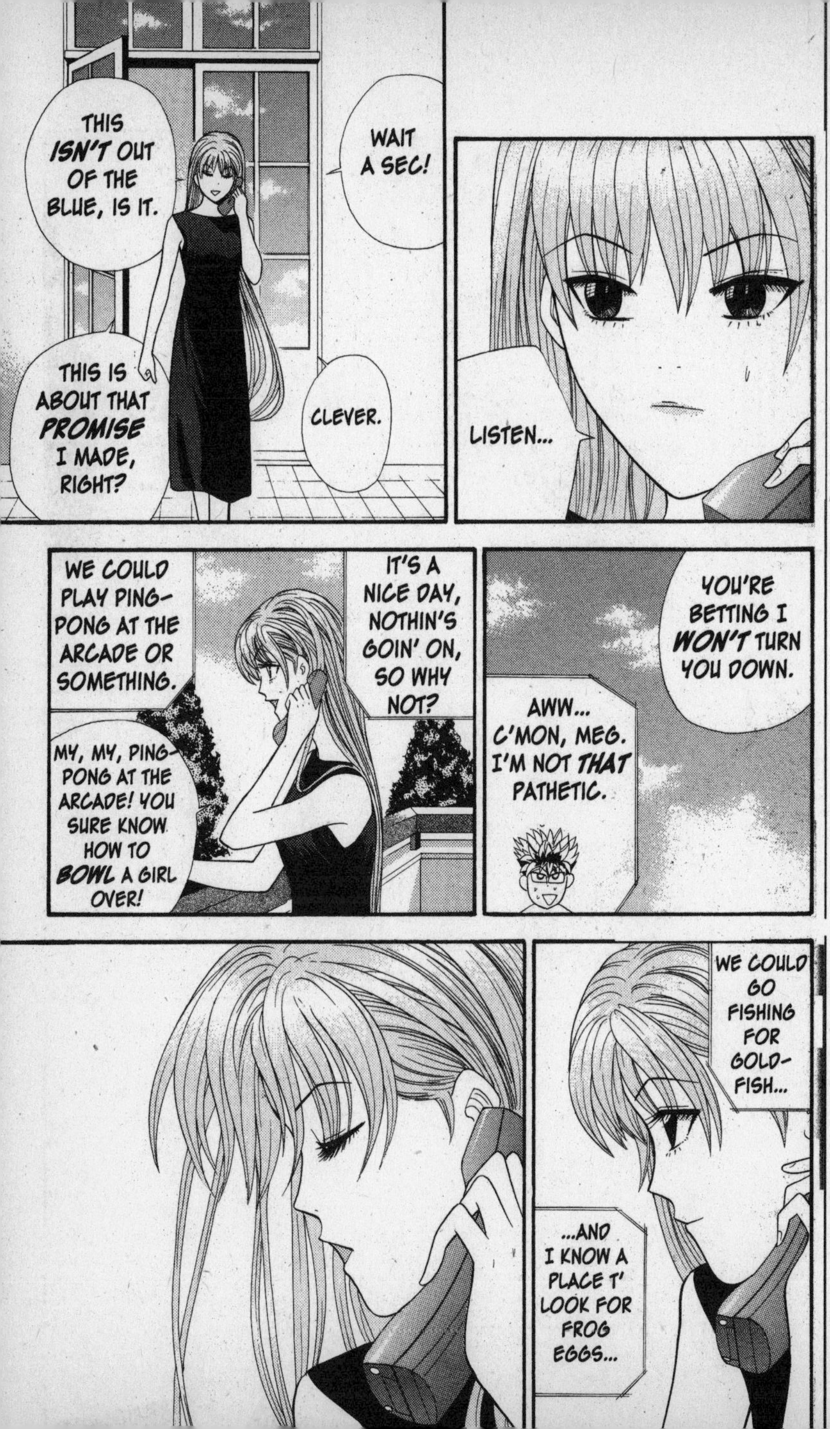
LISTEN...
WAIT A SEC!
THIS ISN'T OUT OF THE BLUE, IS IT.
CLEVER.
THIS IS ABOUT THAT PROMISE I MADE, RIGHT?
YOU'RE BETTING I WON'T TURN YOU DOWN.
AWW... C'MON, MEG. I'M NOT THAT PATHETIC.
IT'S A NICE DAY, NOTHIN'S GOIN' ON, SO WHY NOT?
WE COULD PLAY PING-PONG AT THE ARCADE OR SOMETHING.
MY, MY, PING-PONG AT THE ARCADE! YOU SURE KNOW HOW TO BOWL A GIRL OVER!
WE COULD GO FISHING FOR GOLD-FISH...
...AND I KNOW A PLACE T' LOOK FOR FROG EGGS...

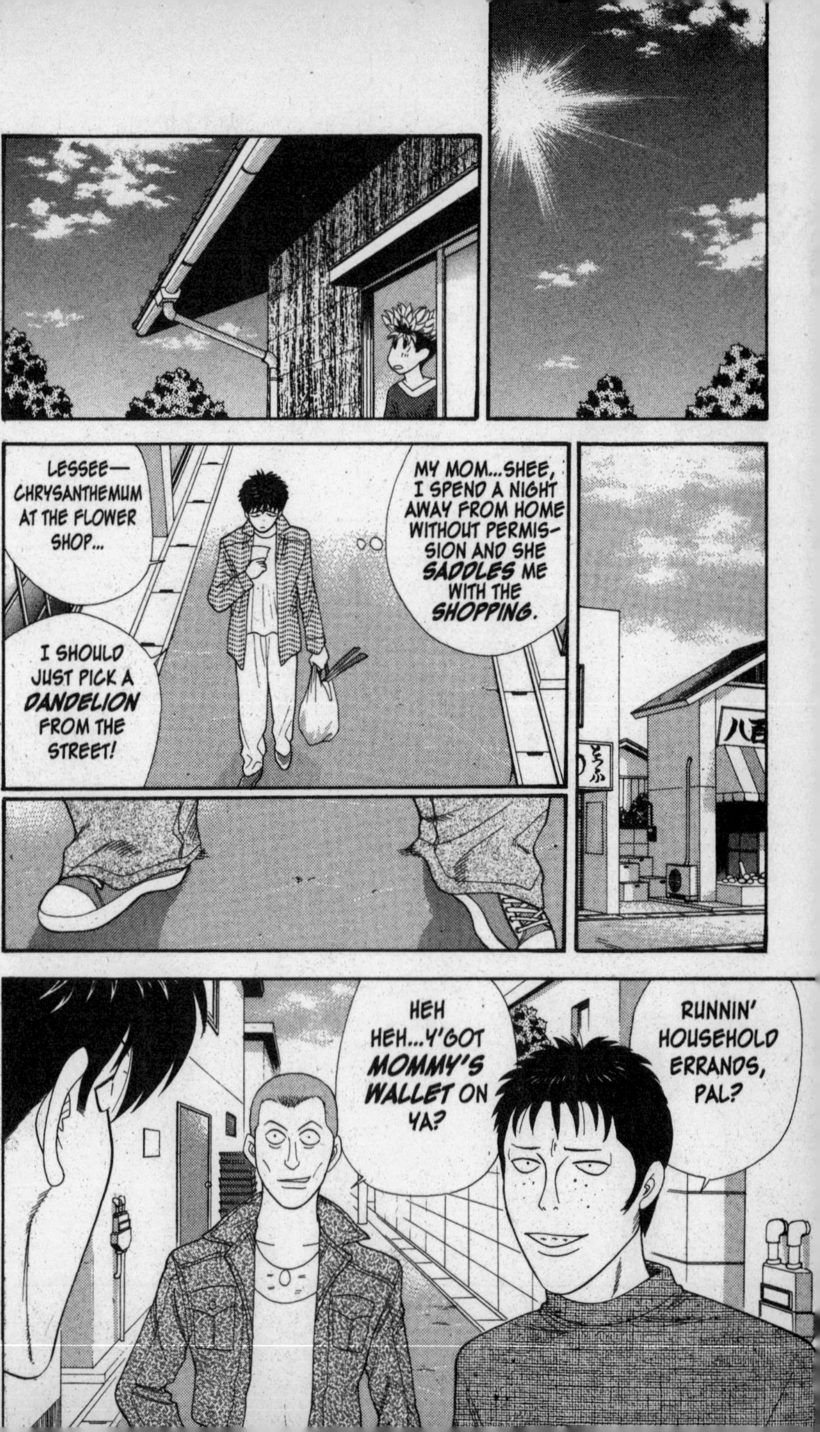
MY MOM...SHEE, I SPEND A NIGHT AWAY FROM HOME WITHOUT PERMISSION AND SHE SADDLES ME WITH THE SHOPPING.
LESSEE— CHRYSANTHEMUM AT THE FLOWER SHOP...
I SHOULD JUST PICK A DANDELION FROM THE STREET!
RUNNIN' HOUSEHOLD ERRANDS, PAL?
HEH HEH...Y'GOT MOMMY'S WALLET ON YA?

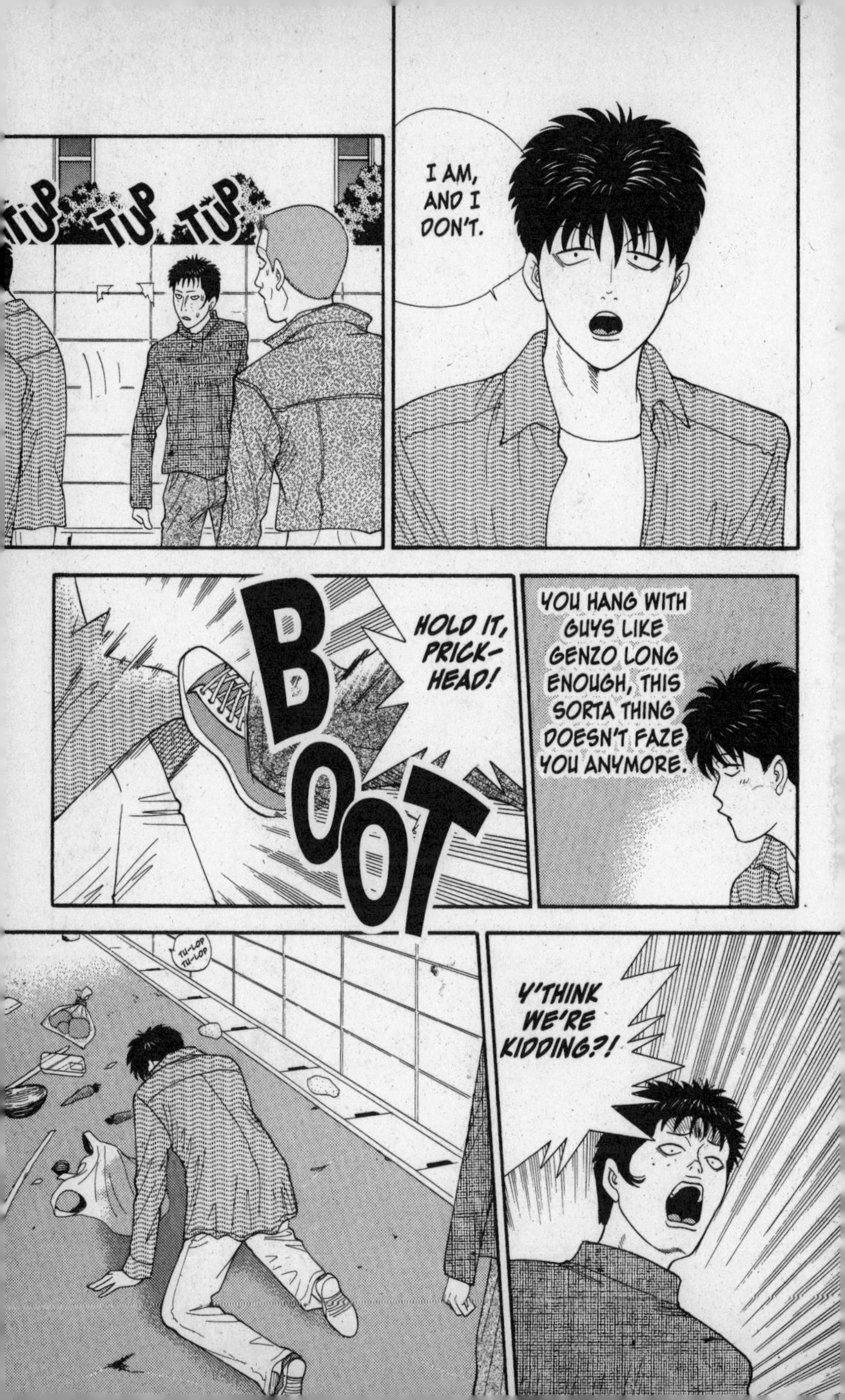
I AM, AND I DON'T.
TUP TUP TUP
YOU HANG WITH GUYS LIKE GENZO LONG ENOUGH, THIS SORTA THING DOESN'T FAZE YOU ANYMORE.
HOLD IT, PRICK-HEAD!
BOOT
Y'THINK WE'RE KIDDING?!
TU-LOP TU-LOP

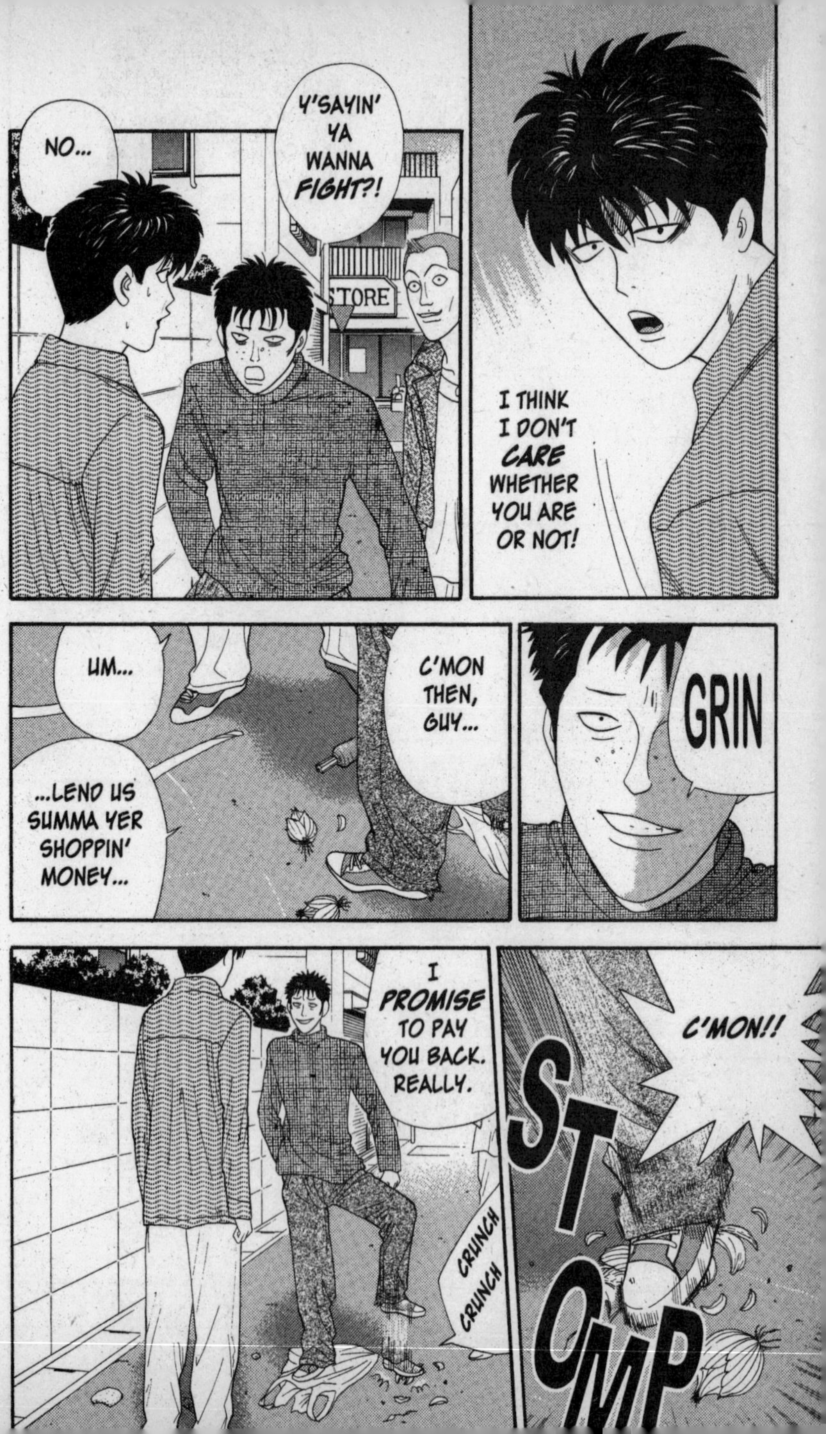
I THINK I DON'T CARE WHETHER YOU ARE OR NOT!
Y'SAYIN' YA WANNA FIGHT?!
NO...
GRIN
C'MON THEN, GUY...
UM...
...LEND US SUMMA YER SHOPPIN' MONEY...
C'MON!!
STOMP
I PROMISE TO PAY YOU BACK. REALLY.
CRUNCH
CRUNCH

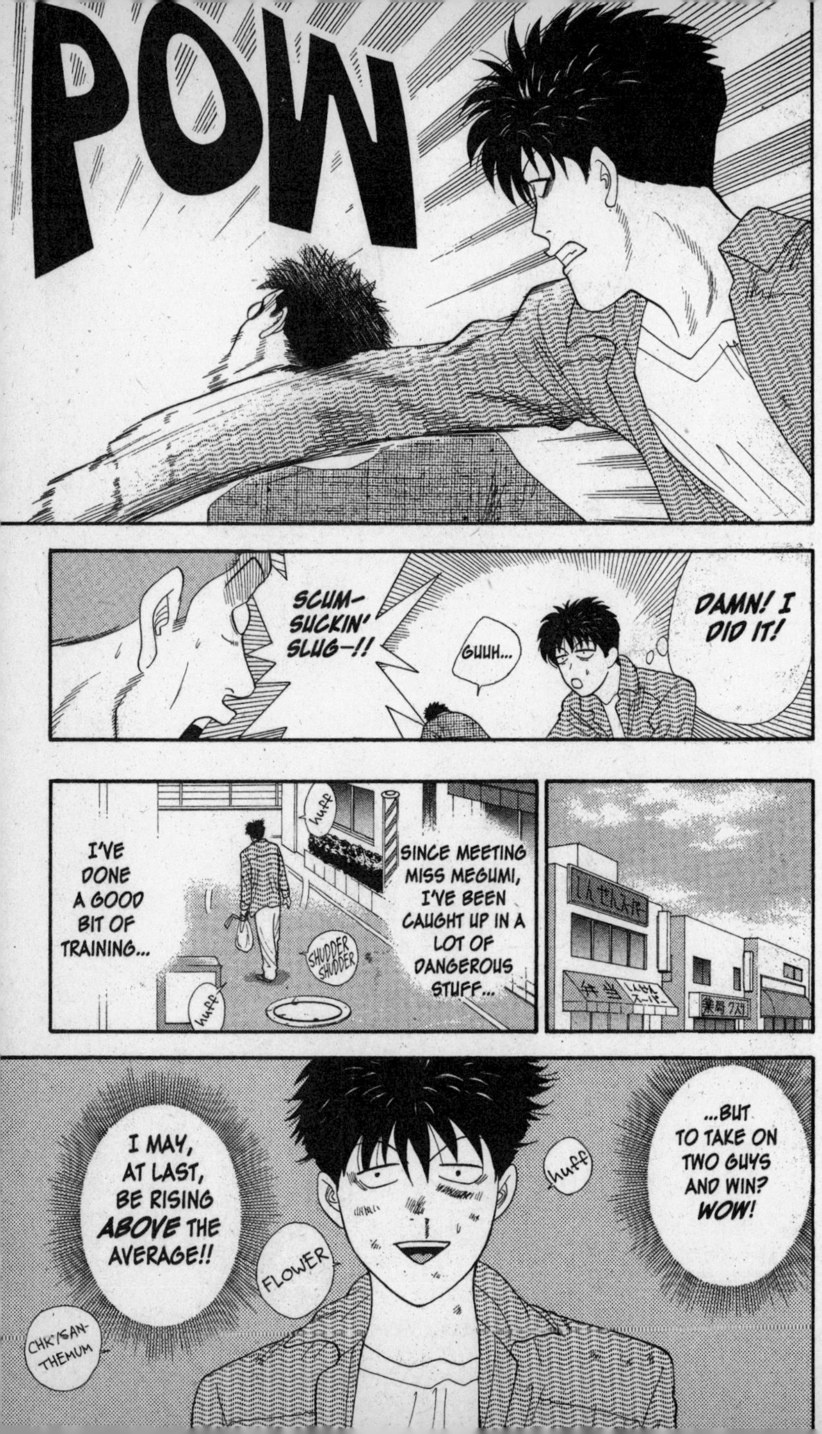
POW
DAMN! I DID IT!
GUUH...
SCUM-SUCKIN' SLUG-!!
huff
SINCE MEETING MISS MEGUMI, I'VE BEEN CAUGHT UP IN A LOT OF DANGEROUS STUFF...
I'VE DONE A GOOD BIT OF TRAINING...
SHUDDER SHUDDER
huff
...BUT TO TAKE ON TWO GUYS AND WIN? WOW!
huff
I MAY, AT LAST, BE RISING ABOVE THE AVERAGE!!
FLOWER
CHK'SAN-THEMUM

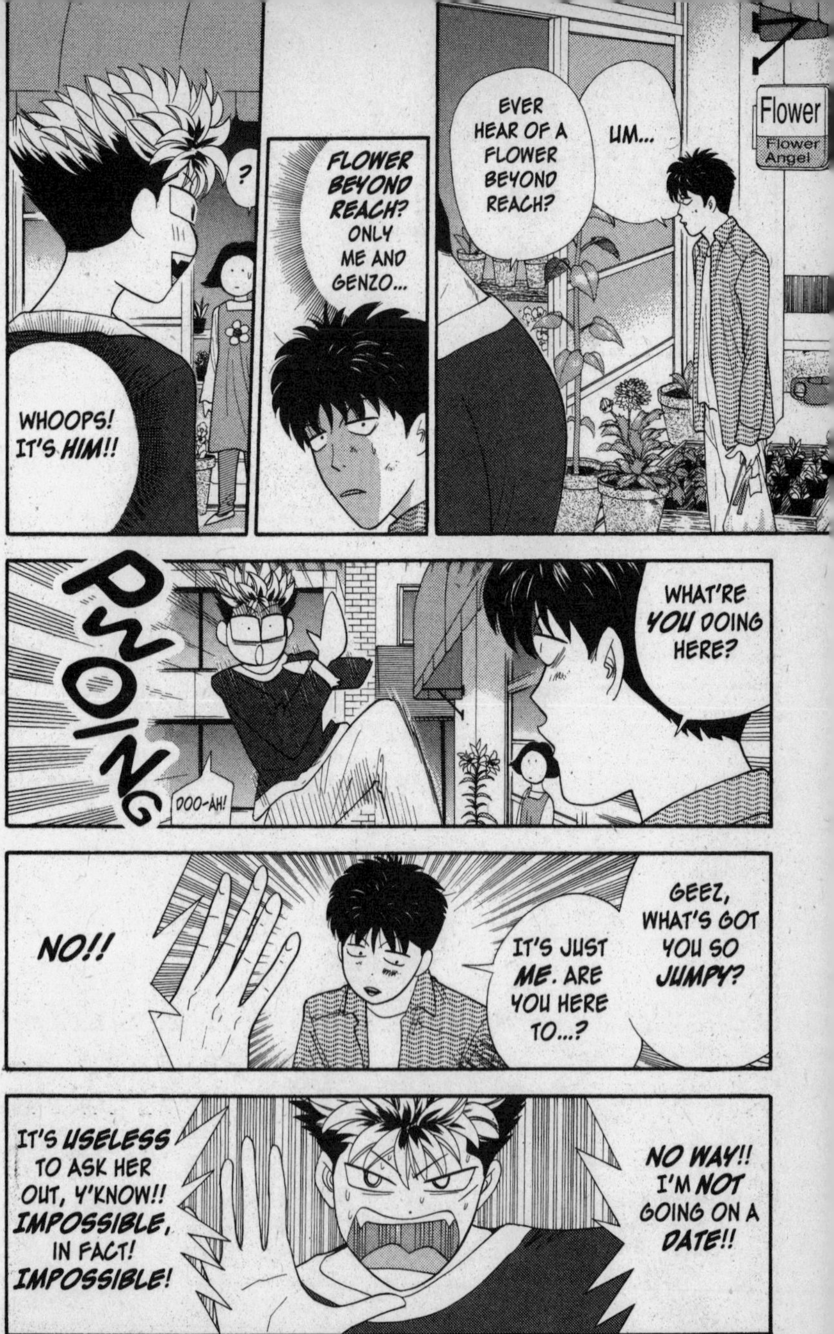
Flower
Flower Angel
UM...
EVER HEAR OF A FLOWER BEYOND REACH?
FLOWER BEYOND REACH? ONLY ME AND GENZO...
?
WHOOPS! IT'S HIM!!
WHAT'RE YOU DOING HERE?
PWOING
DOO-AH!
GEEZ, WHAT'S GOT YOU SO JUMPY?
IT'S JUST ME. ARE YOU HERE TO...?
NO!!
NO WAY!! I'M NOT GOING ON A DATE!!
IT'S USELESS TO ASK HER OUT, Y'KNOW!! IMPOSSIBLE, IN FACT! IMPOSSIBLE!

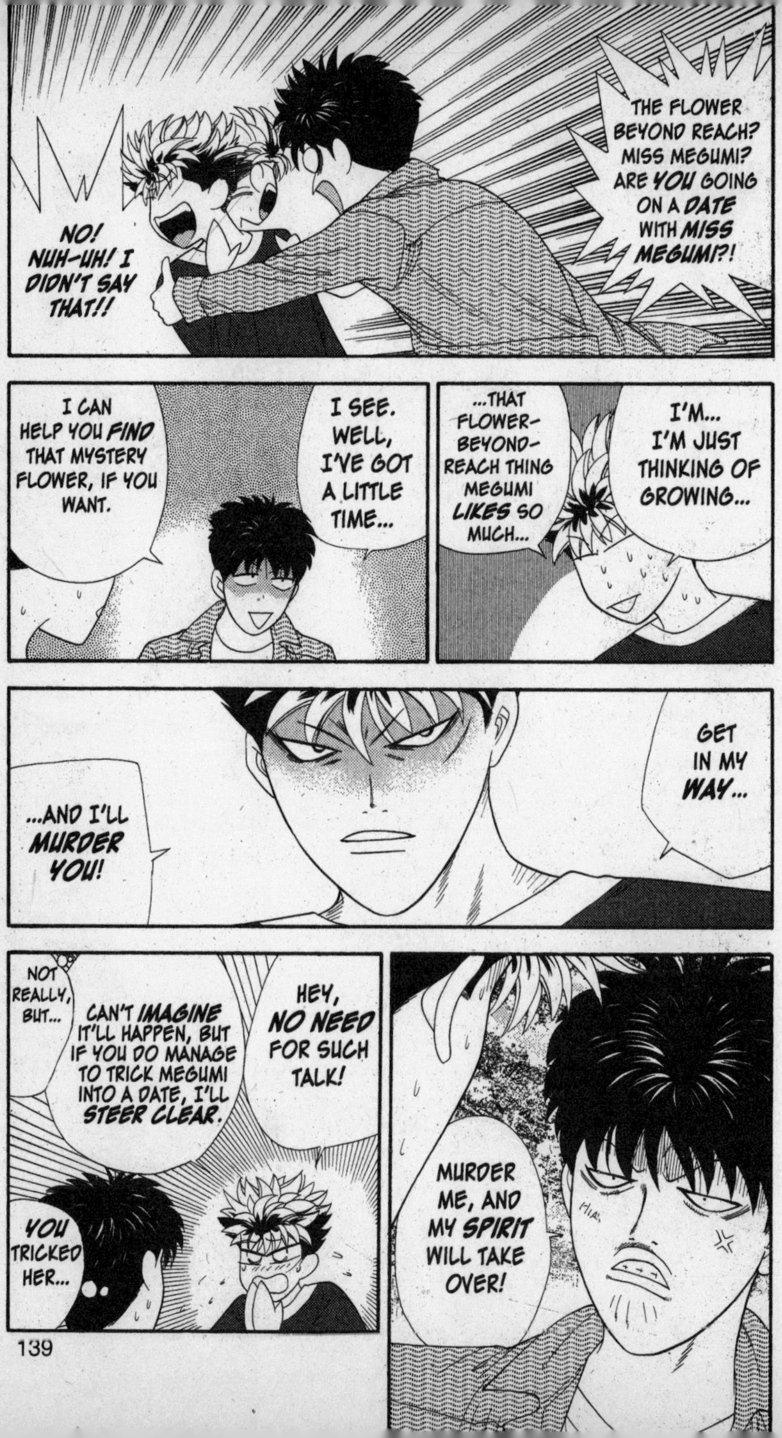
THE FLOWER BEYOND REACH? MISS MEGUMI? ARE YOU GOING ON A DATE WITH MISS MEGUMI?!
NO! NUH-UH! I DIDN'T SAY THAT!!
I'M... I'M JUST THINKING OF GROWING...
...THAT FLOWER-BEYOND-REACH THING MEGUMI LIKES SO MUCH...
I SEE. WELL, I'VE GOT A LITTLE TIME...
I CAN HELP YOU FIND THAT MYSTERY FLOWER, IF YOU WANT.
GET IN MY WAY...
...AND I'LL MURDER YOU!
MURDER ME, AND MY SPIRIT WILL TAKE OVER!
HEY, NO NEED FOR SUCH TALK!
CAN'T IMAGINE IT'LL HAPPEN, BUT IF YOU DO MANAGE TO TRICK MEGUMI INTO A DATE, I'LL STEER CLEAR.
NOT REALLY, BUT...
YOU TRICKED HER...

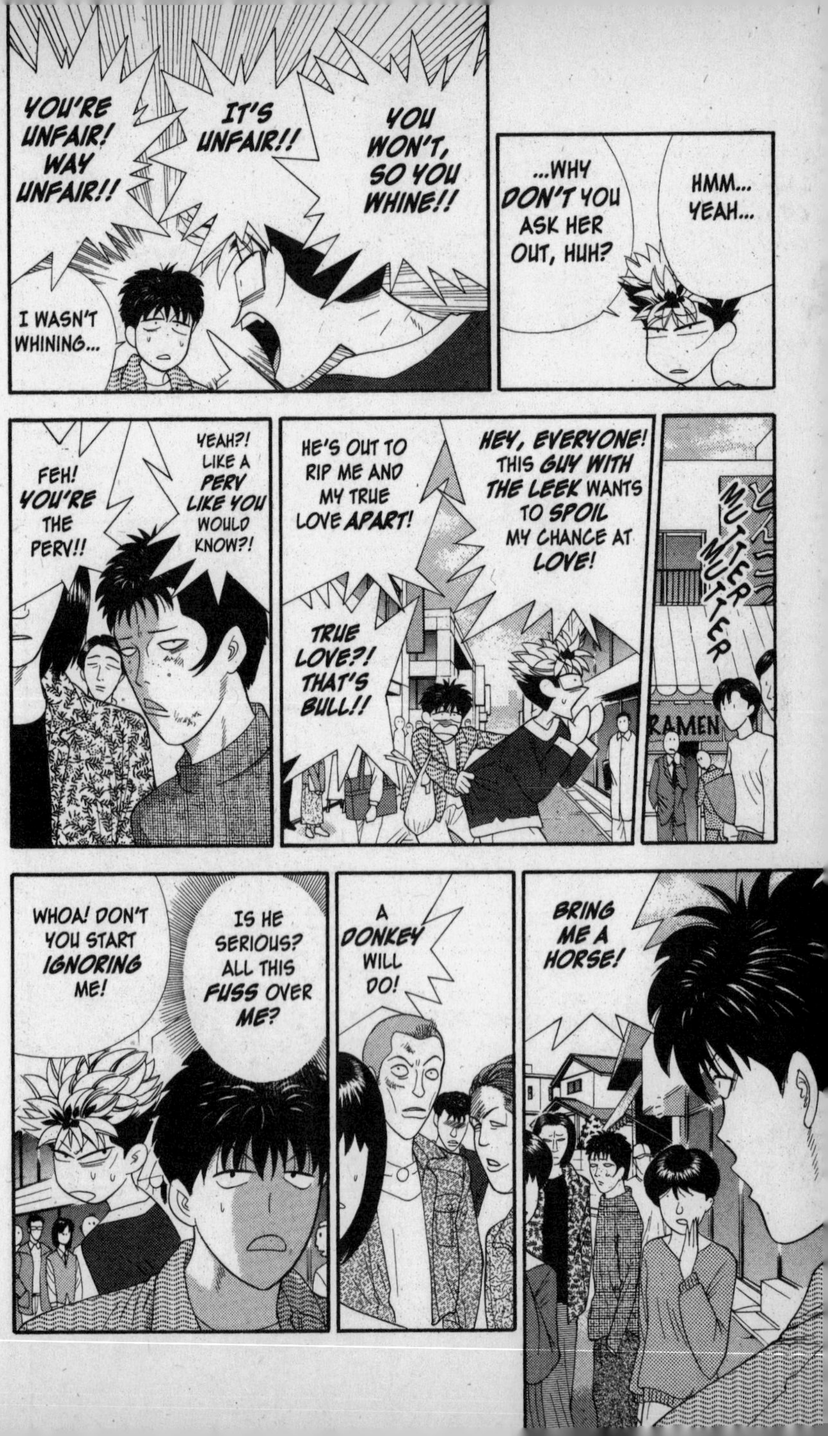
HMM... YEAH...
...WHY DON'T YOU ASK HER OUT, HUH?
YOU WON'T, SO YOU WHINE!!
IT'S UNFAIR!!
YOU'RE UNFAIR! WAY UNFAIR!!
I WASN'T WHINING...
MUTTER MUTTER
RAMEN
HEY, EVERYONE! THIS GUY WITH THE LEEK WANTS TO SPOIL MY CHANCE AT LOVE!
HE'S OUT TO RIP ME AND MY TRUE LOVE APART!
TRUE LOVE?! THAT'S BULL!!
YEAH?! LIKE A PERV LIKE YOU WOULD KNOW?!
FEH! YOU'RE THE PERV!!
BRING ME A HORSE!
A DONKEY WILL DO!
IS HE SERIOUS? ALL THIS FUSS OVER ME?
WHOA! DON'T YOU START IGNORING ME!

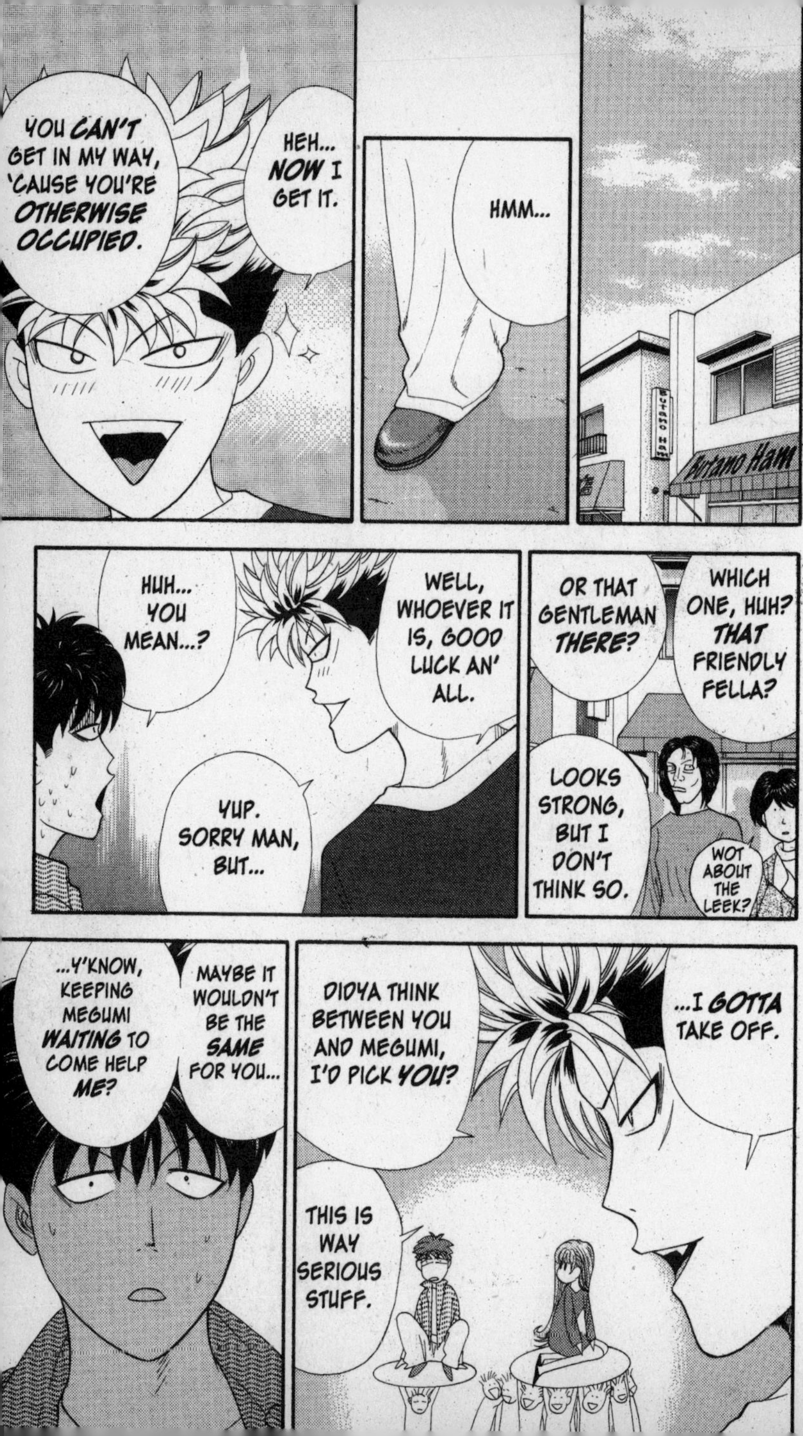
HMM...
HEH... NOW I GET IT.
YOU CAN'T GET IN MY WAY, 'CAUSE YOU'RE OTHERWISE OCCUPIED.
WHICH ONE, HUH? THAT FRIENDLY FELLA?
OR THAT GENTLEMAN THERE?
LOOKS STRONG, BUT I DON'T THINK SO.
WOT ABOUT THE LEEK?
WELL, WHOEVER IT IS, GOOD LUCK AN' ALL.
HUH... YOU MEAN...?
YUP. SORRY MAN, BUT...
...I GOTTA TAKE OFF.
DIDYA THINK BETWEEN YOU AND MEGUMI, I'D PICK YOU?
THIS IS WAY SERIOUS STUFF.
MAYBE IT WOULDN'T BE THE SAME FOR YOU...
...Y'KNOW, KEEPING MEGUMI WAITING TO COME HELP ME?

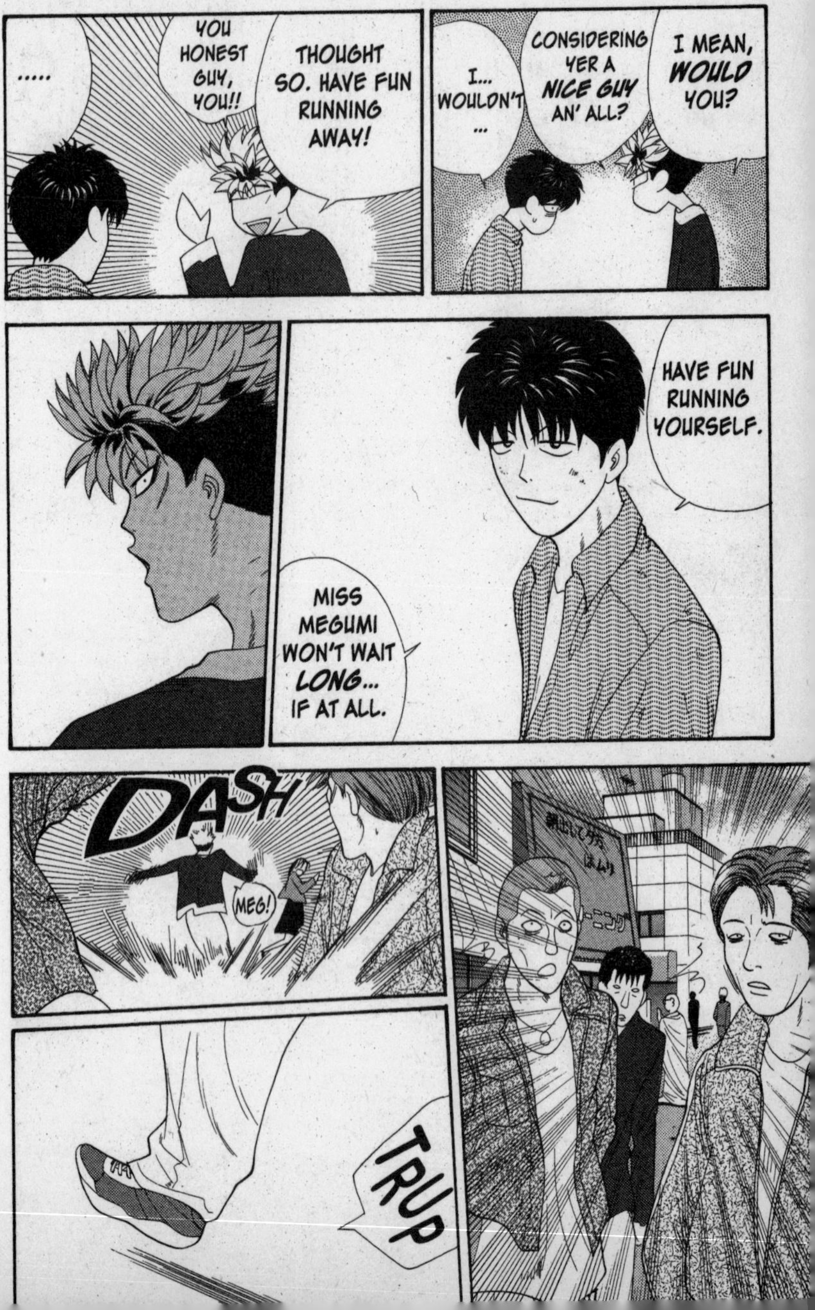
I MEAN, WOULD YOU?
CONSIDERING YER A NICE GUY AN' ALL?
I... WOULDN'T ...
THOUGHT SO. HAVE FUN RUNNING AWAY!
YOU HONEST GUY, YOU!!
.....
HAVE FUN RUNNING YOURSELF.
MISS MEGUMI WON'T WAIT LONG... IF AT ALL.
DASH
MEG!
TRUP

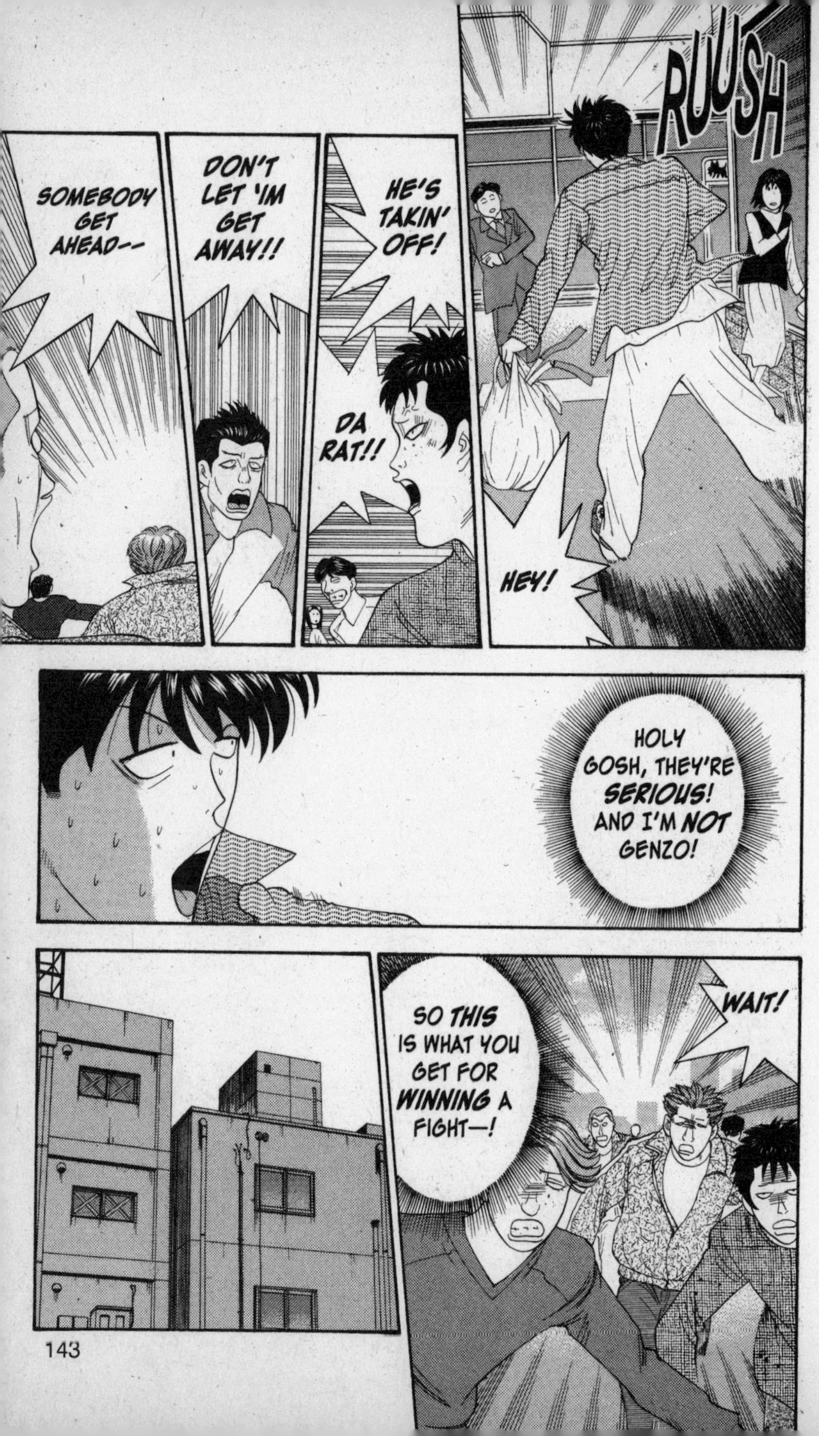
RUUSH
HEY!
HE'S TAKIN' OFF!
DA RAT!!
DON'T LET 'IM GET AWAY!!
SOMEBODY GET AHEAD--
HOLY GOSH, THEY'RE SERIOUS! AND I'M NOT GENZO!
WAIT!
SO THIS IS WHAT YOU GET FOR WINNING A FIGHT—!

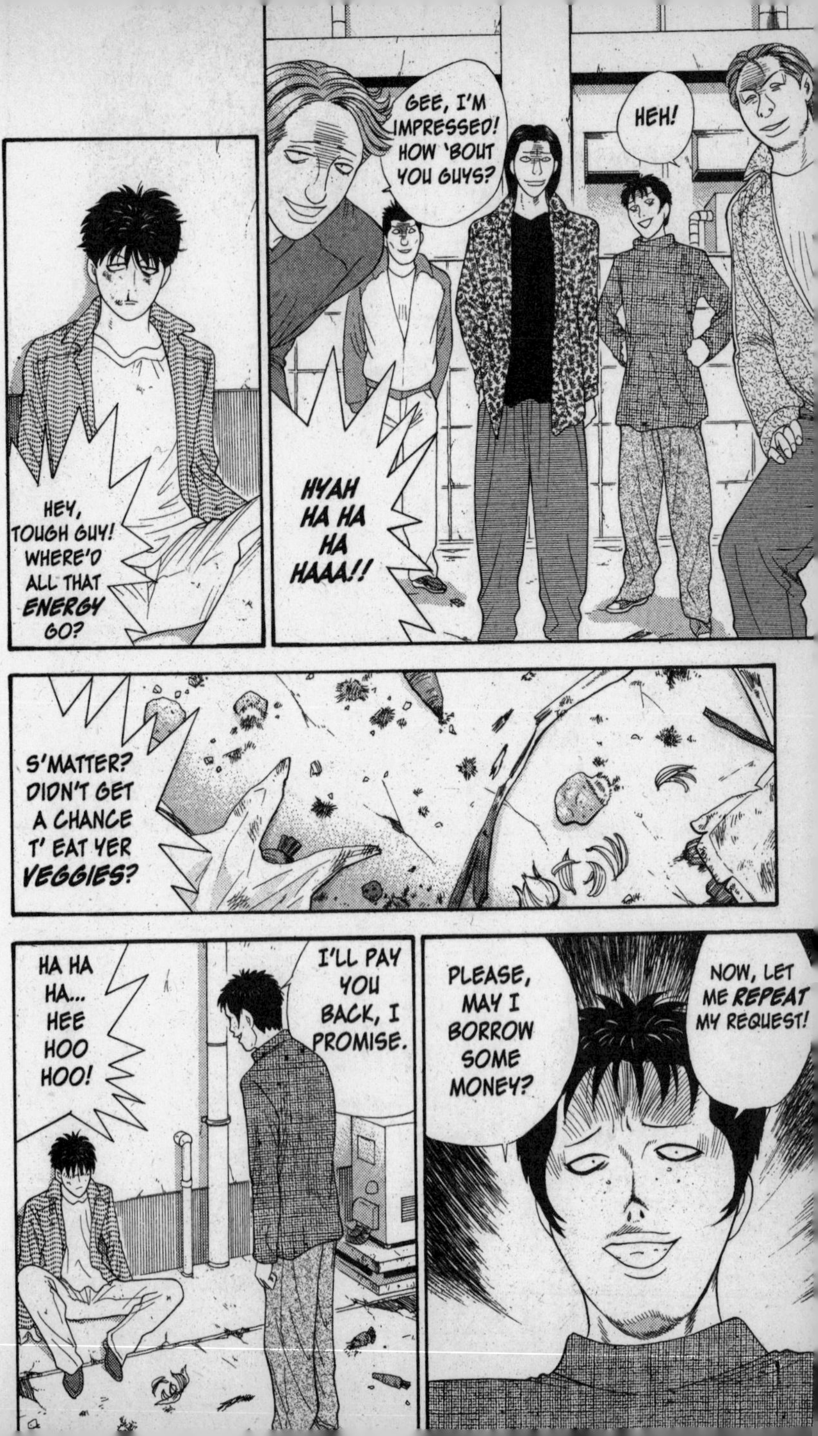
GEE, I'M IMPRESSED! HOW 'BOUT YOU GUYS?
HEH!
HYAH HA HA HA HAAA!!
HEY, TOUGH GUY! WHERE'D ALL THAT ENERGY GO?
S'MATTER? DIDN'T GET A CHANCE T' EAT YER VEGGIES?
NOW, LET ME REPEAT MY REQUEST!
PLEASE, MAY I BORROW SOME MONEY?
I'LL PAY YOU BACK, I PROMISE.
HA HA HA... HEE HOO HOO!

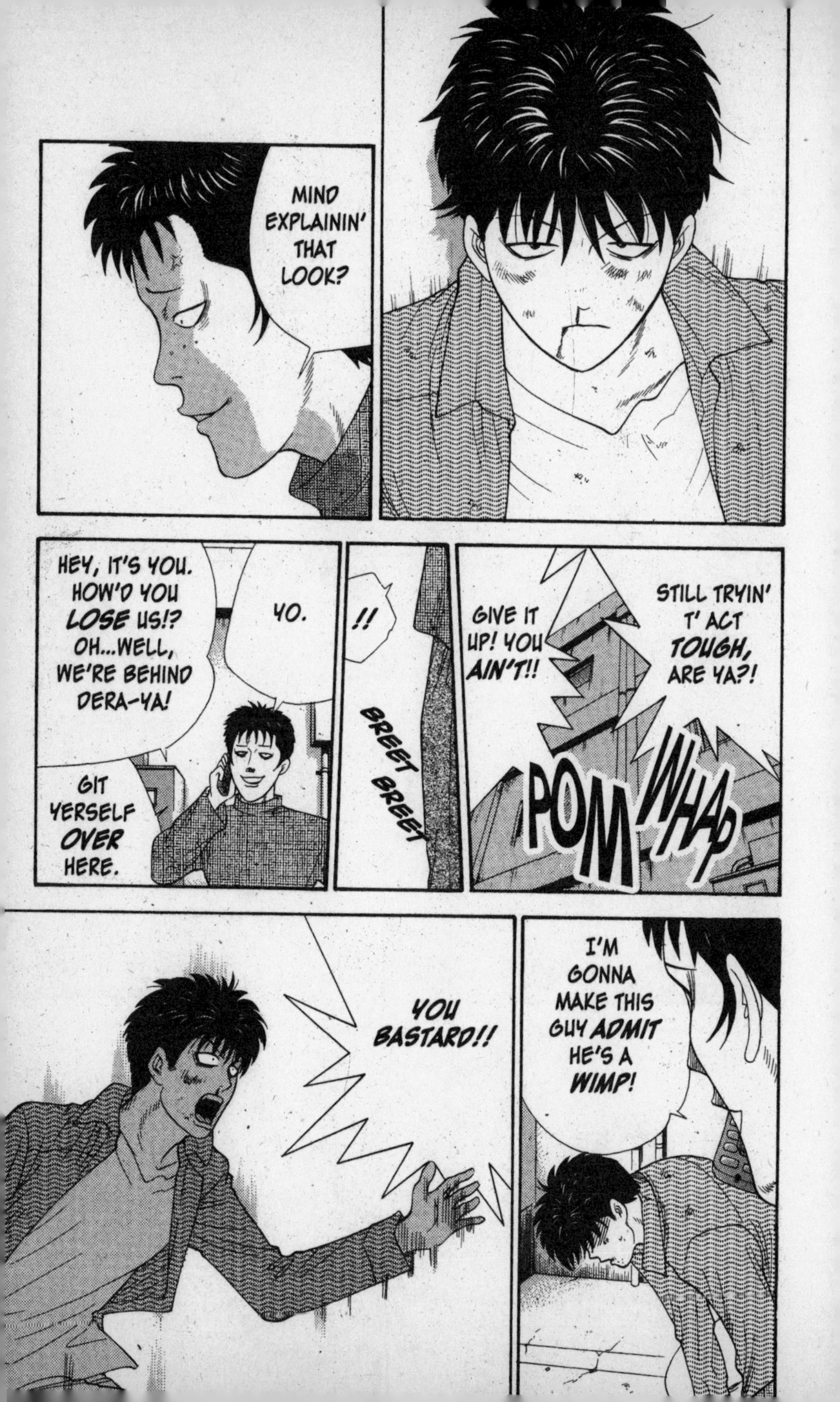
MIND EXPLAININ' THAT LOOK?
STILL TRYIN' T' ACT TOUGH, ARE YA?!
GIVE IT UP! YOU AIN'T!!
WHAP
POM
!!
BREET BREET
YO.
HEY, IT'S YOU. HOW'D YOU LOSE US!? OH...WELL, WE'RE BEHIND DERA-YA!
GIT YERSELF OVER HERE.
I'M GONNA MAKE THIS GUY ADMIT HE'S A WIMP!
YOU BASTARD!!

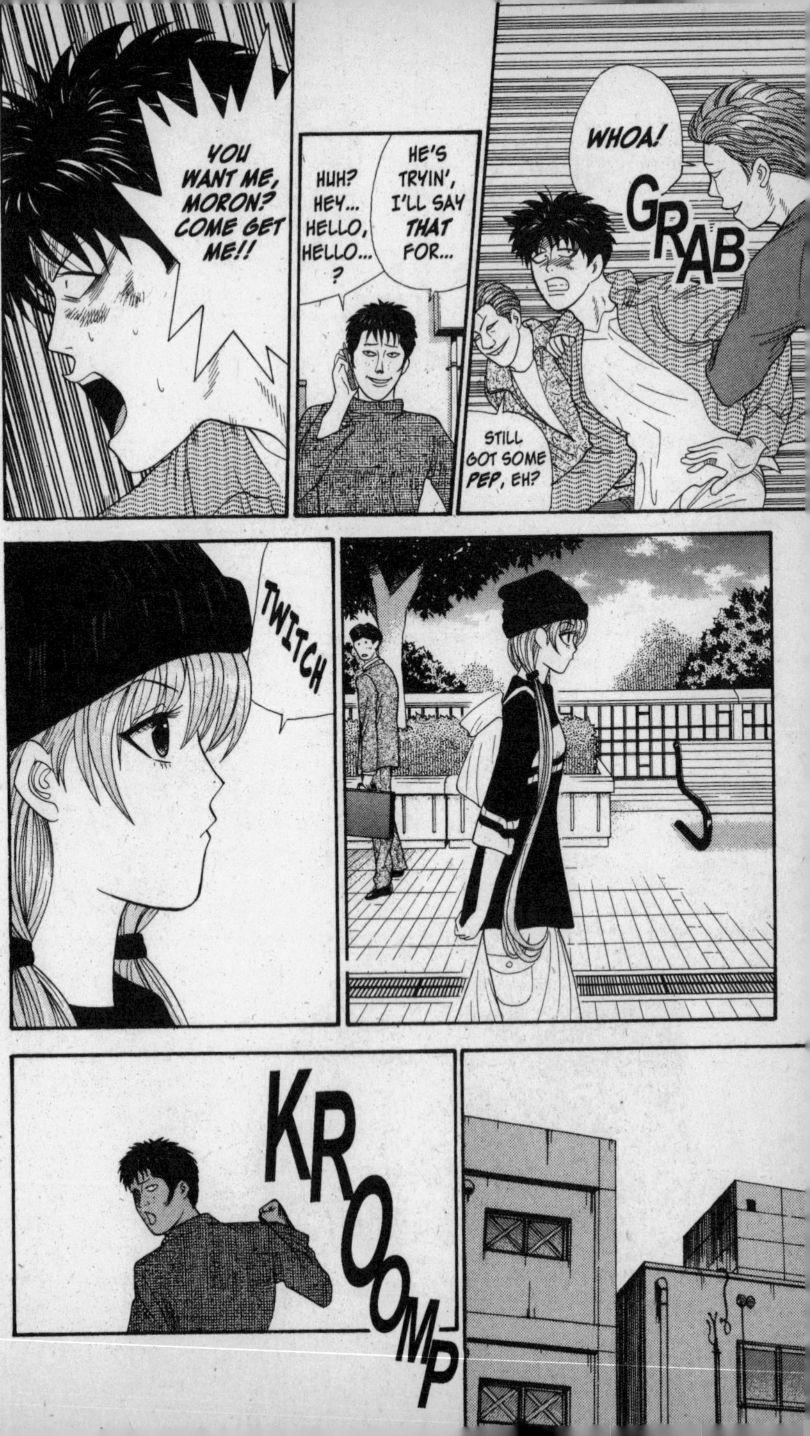
WHOA!
GRAB
STILL GOT SOME PEP, EH?
HE'S TRYIN', I'LL SAY THAT FOR...
HUH? HEY... HELLO, HELLO...?
YOU WANT ME, MORON? COME GET ME!!
TWITCH
KROOMP

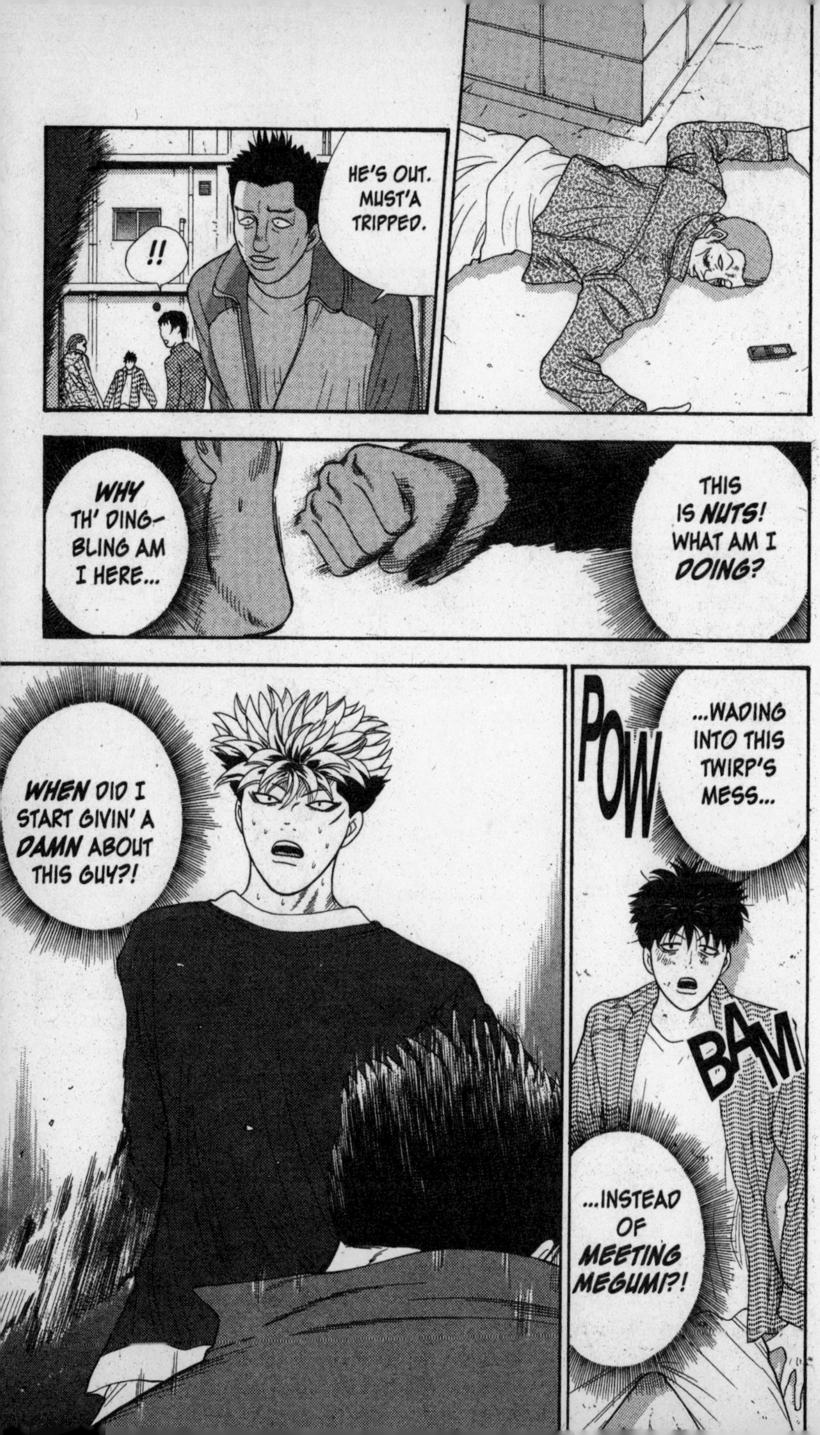

HE'S OUT. MUST'A TRIPPED.
!!
THIS IS NUTS! WHAT AM I DOING?
WHY TH' DING-BLING AM I HERE...
POW
...WADING INTO THIS TWIRP'S MESS...
BAM
...INSTEAD OF MEETING MEGUMI?!
WHEN DID I START GIVIN' A DAMN ABOUT THIS GUY?!

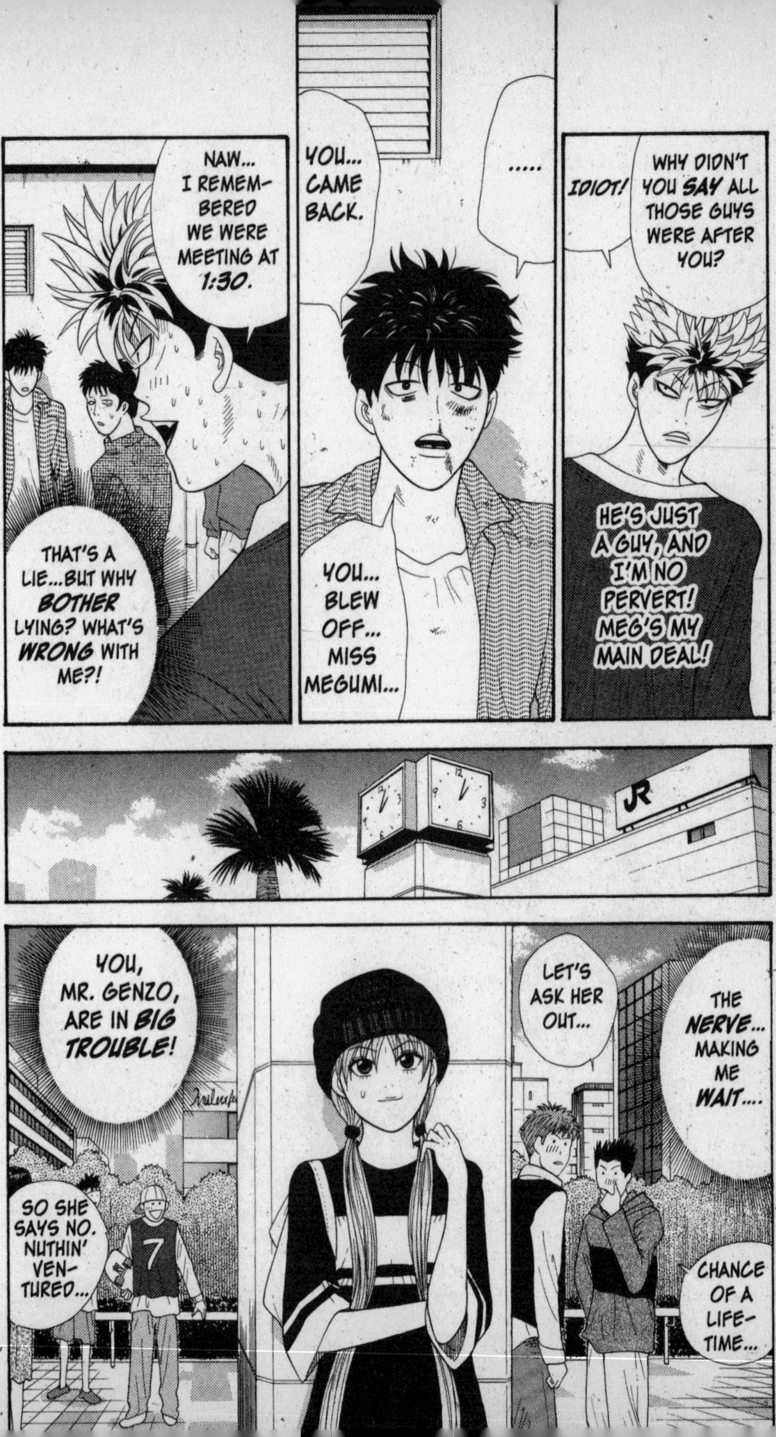
IDIOT!
WHY DIDN'T YOU SAY ALL THOSE GUYS WERE AFTER YOU?
HE'S JUST A GUY, AND I'M NO PERVERT! MEG'S MY MAIN DEAL!
.....
YOU... CAME BACK.
YOU... BLEW OFF... MISS MEGUMI...
NAW... I REMEMBERED WE WERE MEETING AT 1:30.
THAT'S A LIE...BUT WHY BOTHER LYING? WHAT'S WRONG WITH ME?!
JR
THE NERVE... MAKING ME WAIT....
LET'S ASK HER OUT...
CHANCE OF A LIFETIME...
YOU, MR. GENZO, ARE IN BIG TROUBLE!
SO SHE SAYS NO. NUTHIN' VENTURED...

Chapter 48: Reason for Being Late

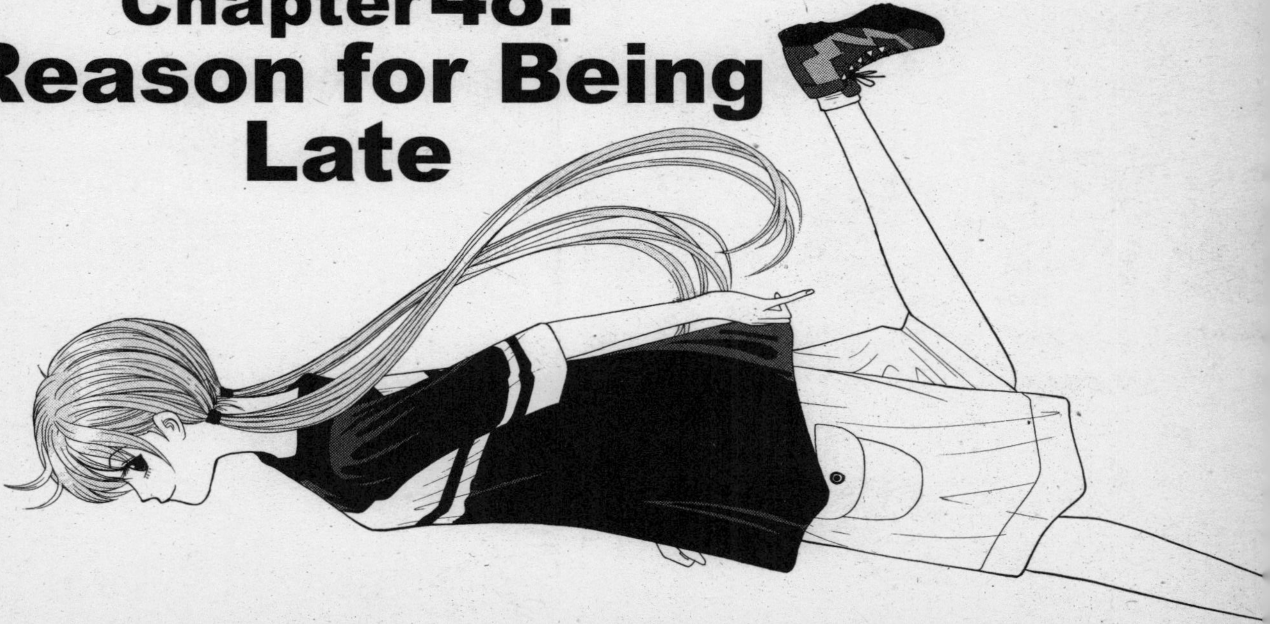

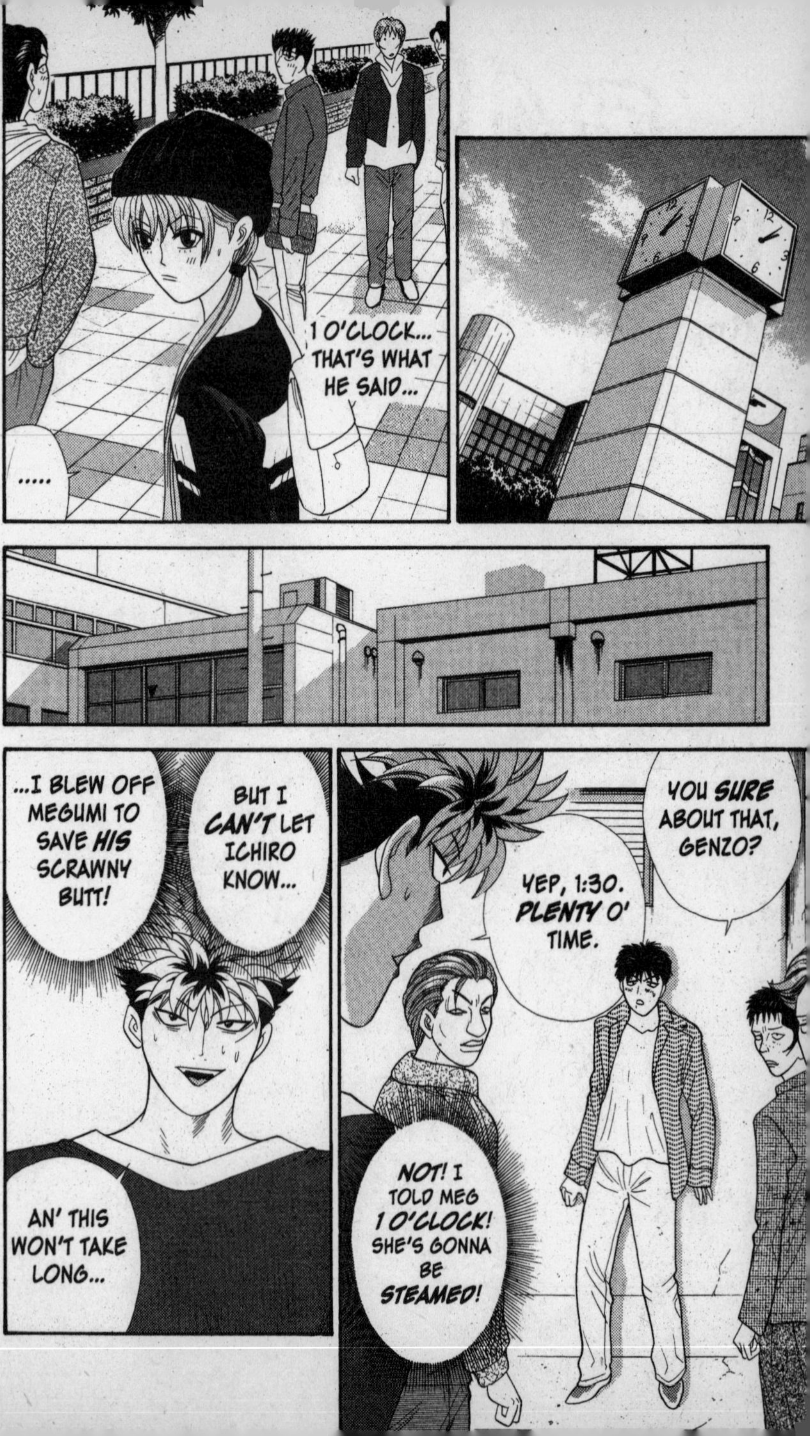
1 O'CLOCK... THAT'S WHAT HE SAID...
.....
YOU **SURE** ABOUT THAT, GENZO?
YEP, 1:30. **PLENTY** O' TIME.
NOT! I TOLD MEG **1 O'CLOCK!** SHE'S GONNA BE **STEAMED!**
BUT I **CAN'T** LET ICHIRO KNOW...
...I BLEW OFF MEGUMI TO SAVE **HIS** SCRAWNY BUTT!
AN' THIS WON'T TAKE LONG...

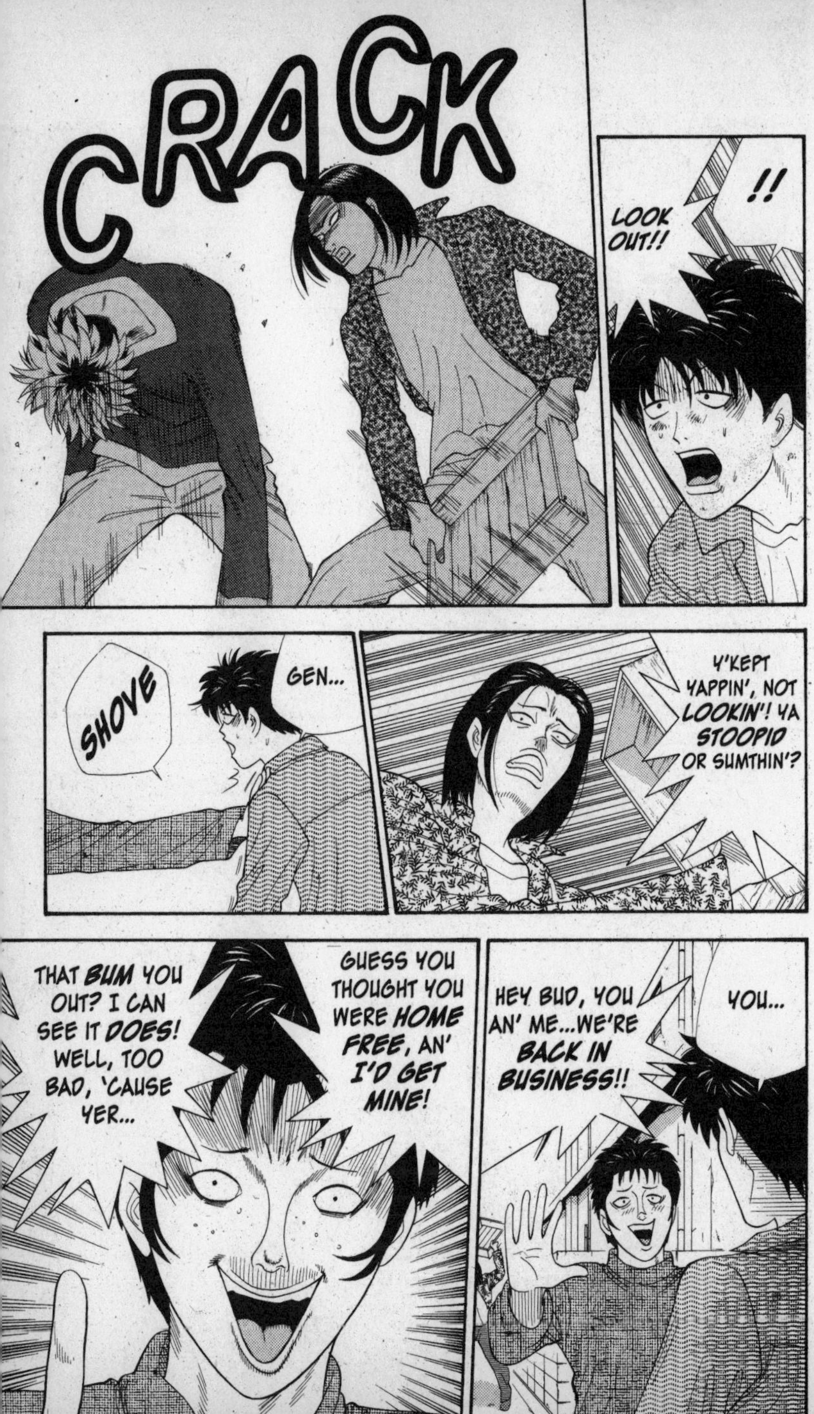
!!
LOOK OUT!!
CRACK
Y'KEPT YAPPIN', NOT LOOKIN'! YA STOOPID OR SUMTHIN'?
GEN...
SHOVE
YOU...
HEY BUD, YOU AN' ME...WE'RE BACK IN BUSINESS!!
GUESS YOU THOUGHT YOU WERE HOME FREE, AN' I'D GET MINE!
THAT BUM YOU OUT? I CAN SEE IT DOES! WELL, TOO BAD, 'CAUSE YER...

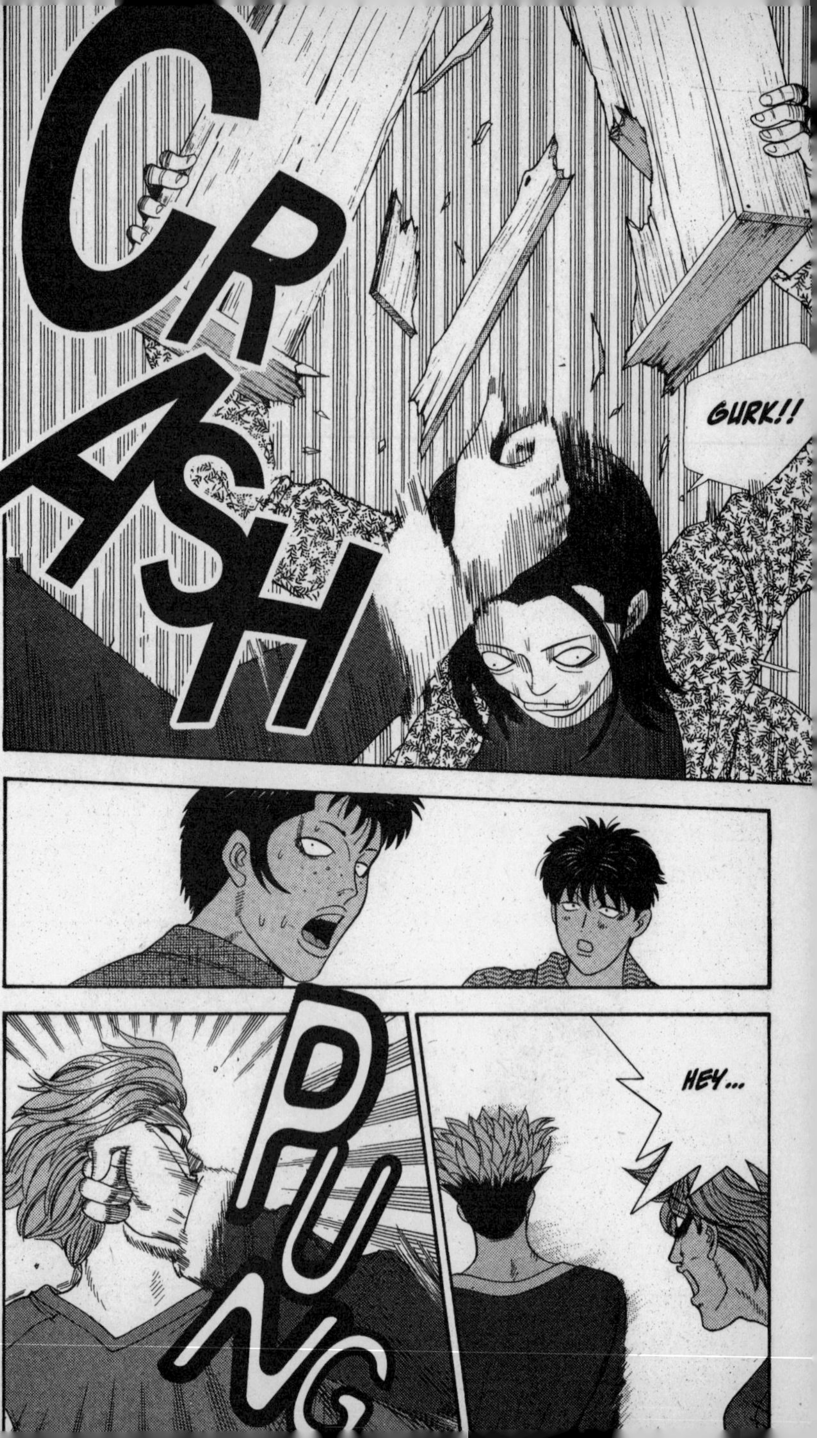
CRASH
GURK!!
HEY...
DUNG

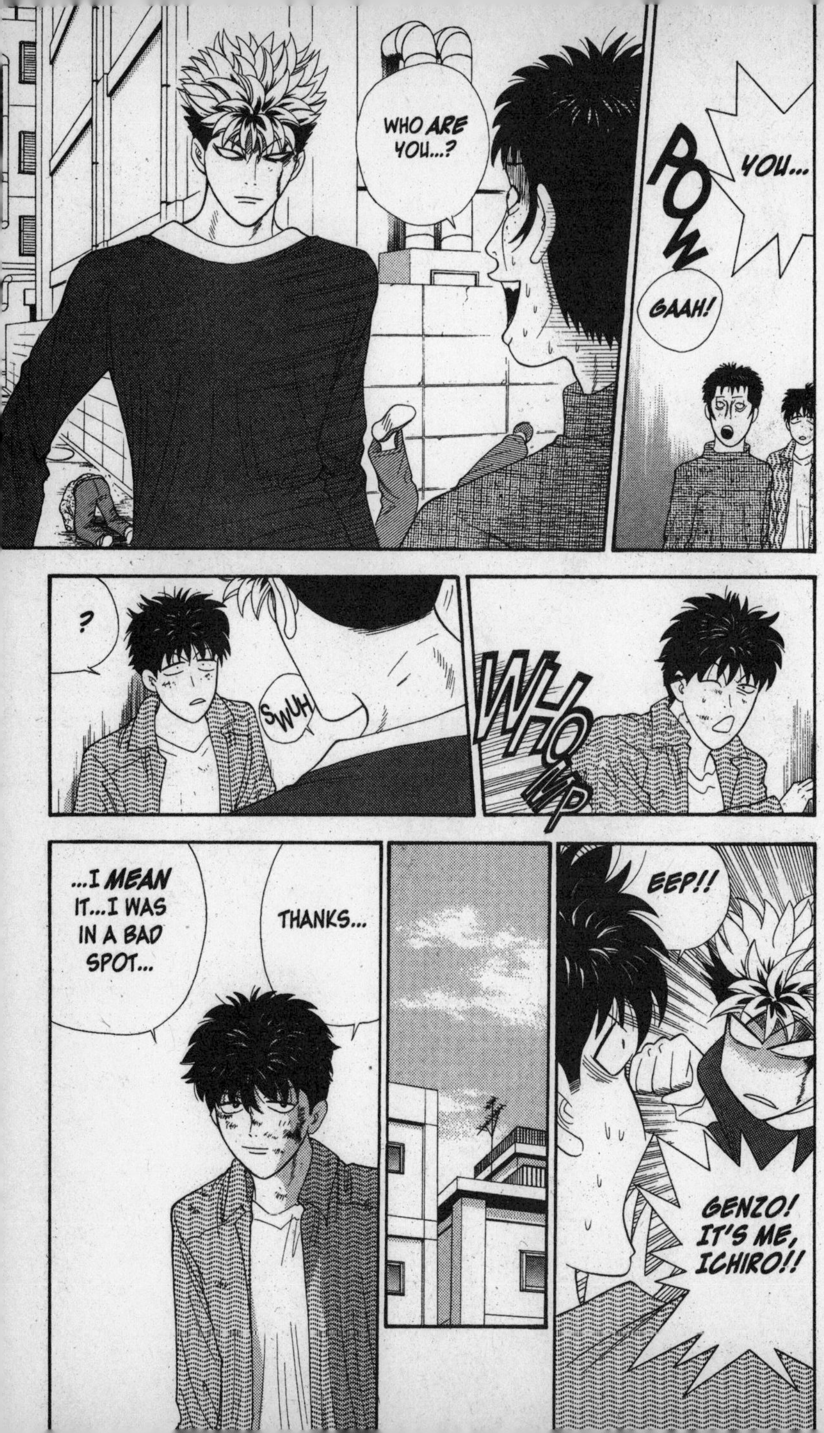
YOU...
POW
GAAH!
WHO ARE YOU...?
WHOMP
?
SWUH
EEP!!
GENZO! IT'S ME, ICHIRO!!
THANKS...
...I MEAN IT...I WAS IN A BAD SPOT...

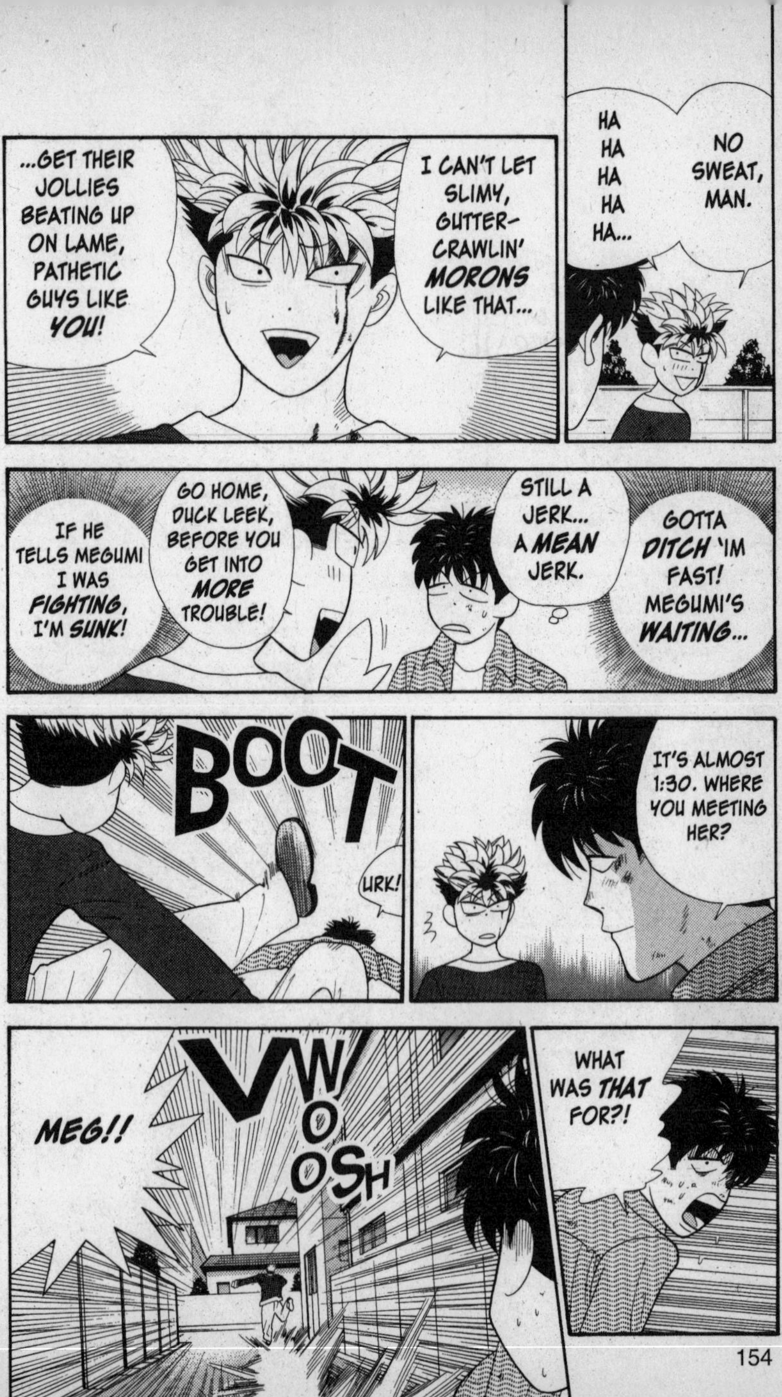
NO SWEAT, MAN.
HA HA HA HA HA...
I CAN'T LET SLIMY, GUTTER-CRAWLIN' MORONS LIKE THAT...
...GET THEIR JOLLIES BEATING UP ON LAME, PATHETIC GUYS LIKE YOU!
GOTTA DITCH 'IM FAST! MEGUMI'S WAITING...
STILL A JERK... A MEAN JERK.
GO HOME, DUCK LEEK, BEFORE YOU GET INTO MORE TROUBLE!
IF HE TELLS MEGUMI I WAS FIGHTING, I'M SUNK!
IT'S ALMOST 1:30. WHERE YOU MEETING HER?
BOOT
URK!
WHAT WAS THAT FOR?!
VWOOSH
MEG!!

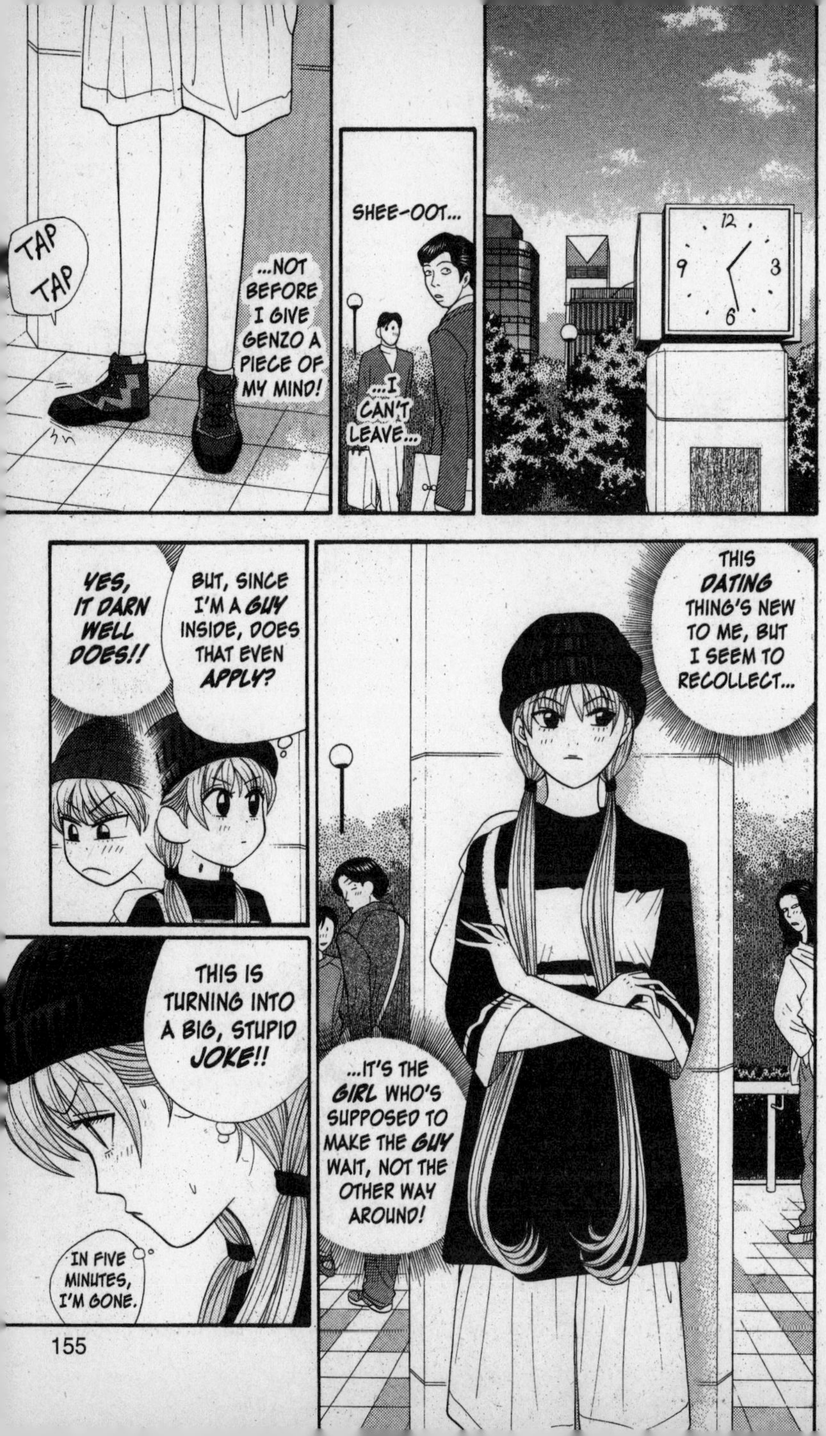
SHEE-OOT...
...I CAN'T LEAVE...
...NOT BEFORE I GIVE GENZO A PIECE OF MY MIND!
TAP TAP
THIS DATING THING'S NEW TO ME, BUT I SEEM TO RECOLLECT...
...IT'S THE GIRL WHO'S SUPPOSED TO MAKE THE GUY WAIT, NOT THE OTHER WAY AROUND!
BUT, SINCE I'M A GUY INSIDE, DOES THAT EVEN APPLY?
YES, IT DARN WELL DOES!!
THIS IS TURNING INTO A BIG, STUPID JOKE!!
IN FIVE MINUTES, I'M GONE.

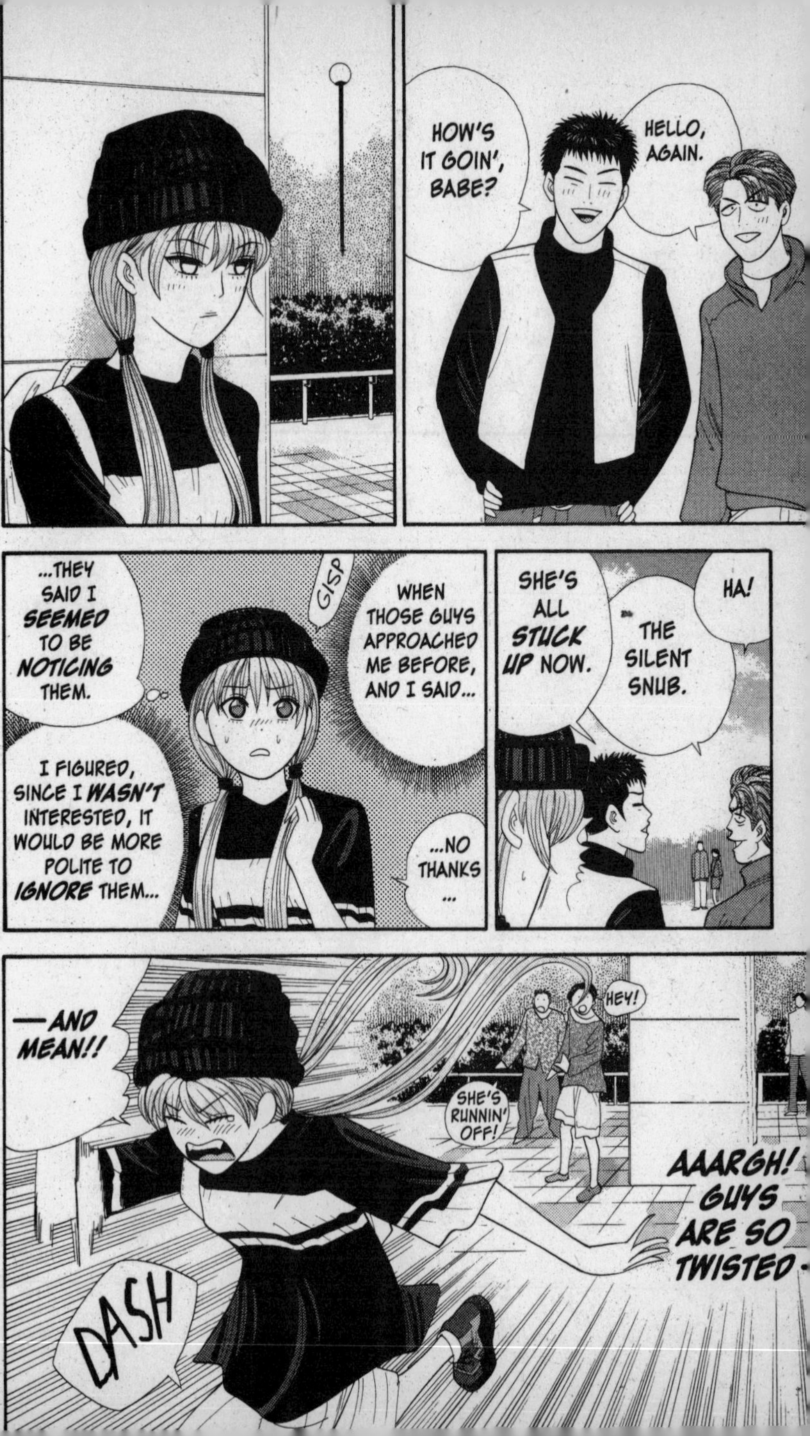
HELLO, AGAIN.
HOW'S IT GOIN', BABE?
HA!
THE SILENT SNUB.
SHE'S ALL STUCK UP NOW.
WHEN THOSE GUYS APPROACHED ME BEFORE, AND I SAID...
GISP
...THEY SAID I SEEMED TO BE NOTICING THEM.
...NO THANKS ...
I FIGURED, SINCE I WASN'T INTERESTED, IT WOULD BE MORE POLITE TO IGNORE THEM...
AAARGH! GUYS ARE SO TWISTED
HEY!
SHE'S RUNNIN' OFF!
—AND MEAN!!
DASH

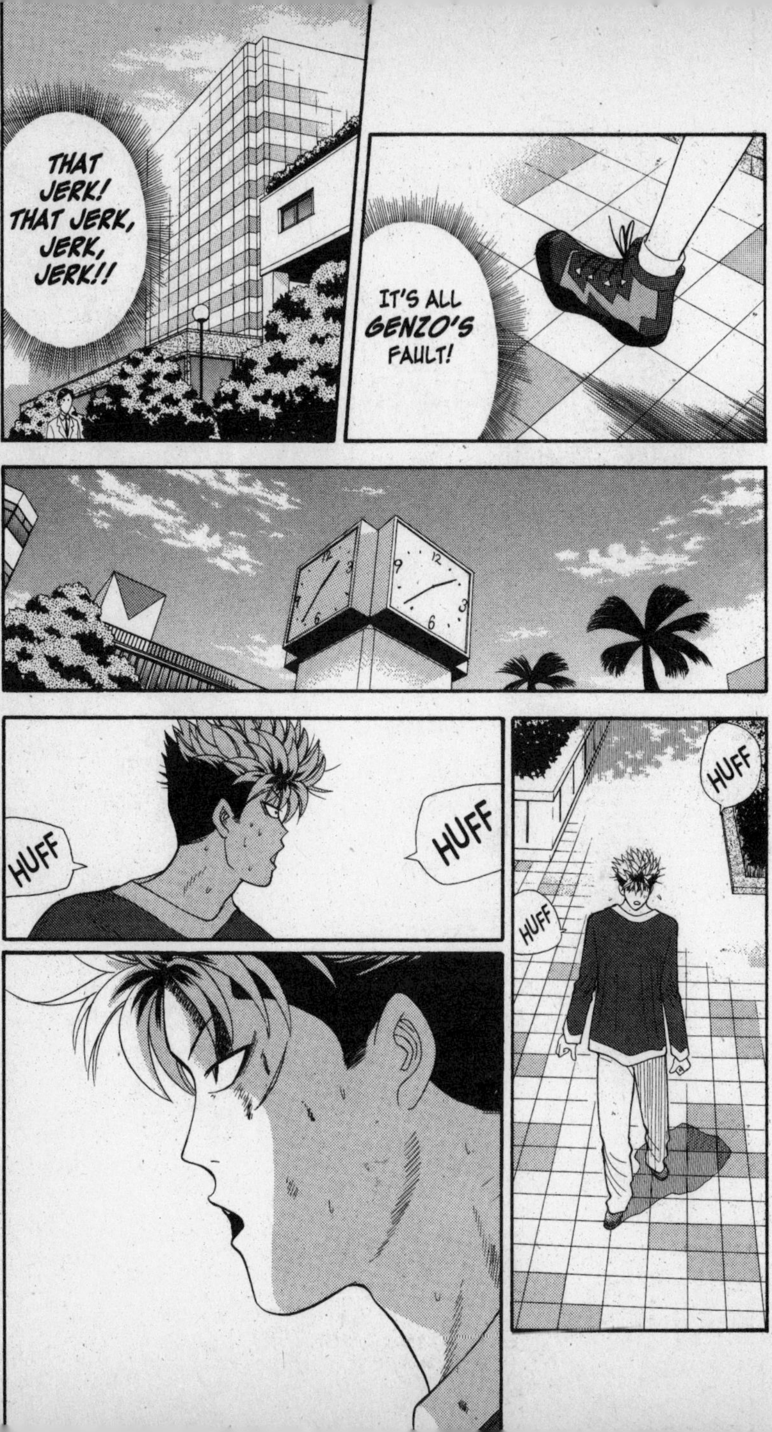
IT'S ALL GENZO'S FAULT!
THAT JERK! THAT JERK, JERK, JERK!!
HUFF
HUFF
HUFF
HUFF

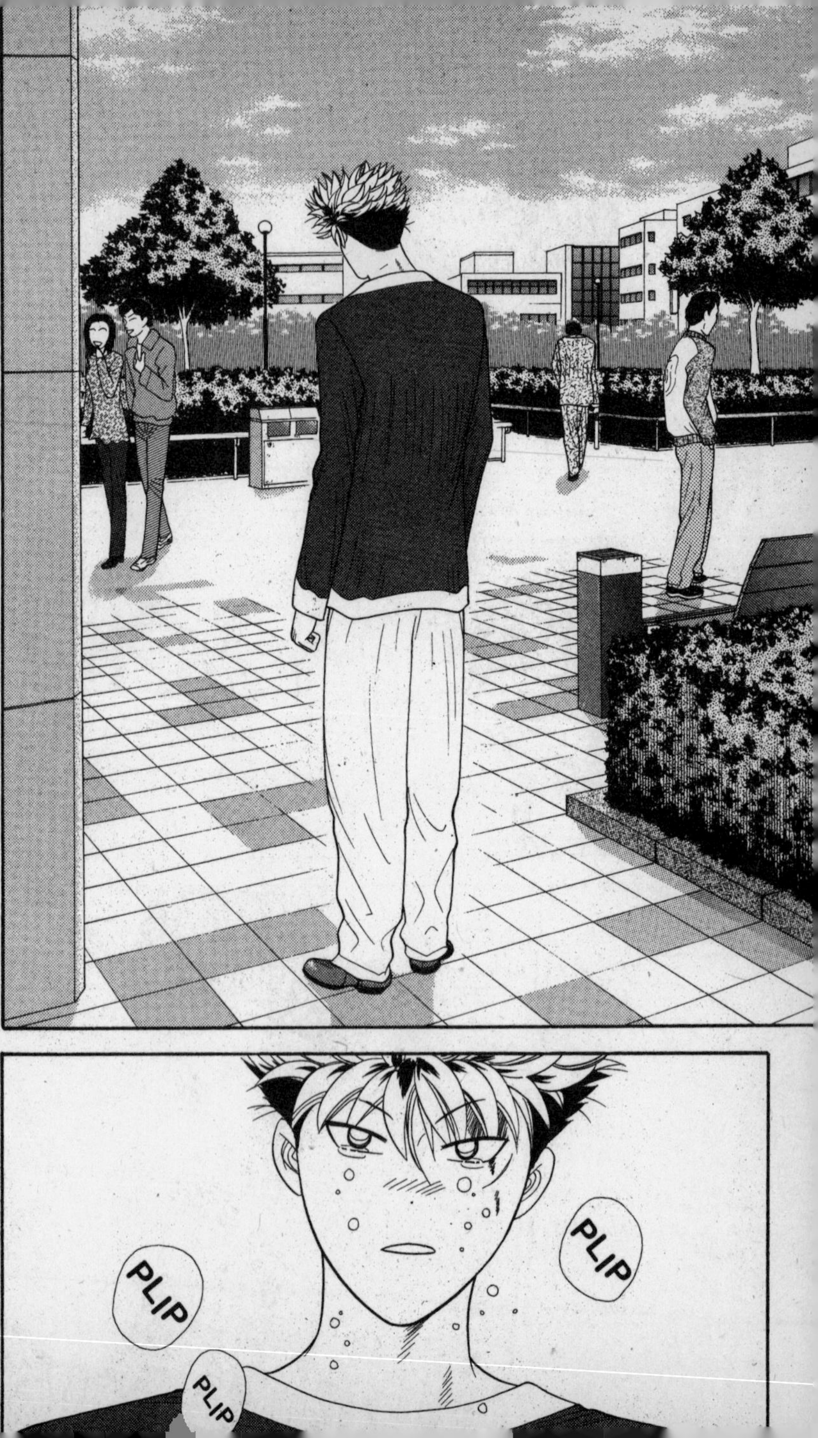
PLIP
PLIP
PLIP

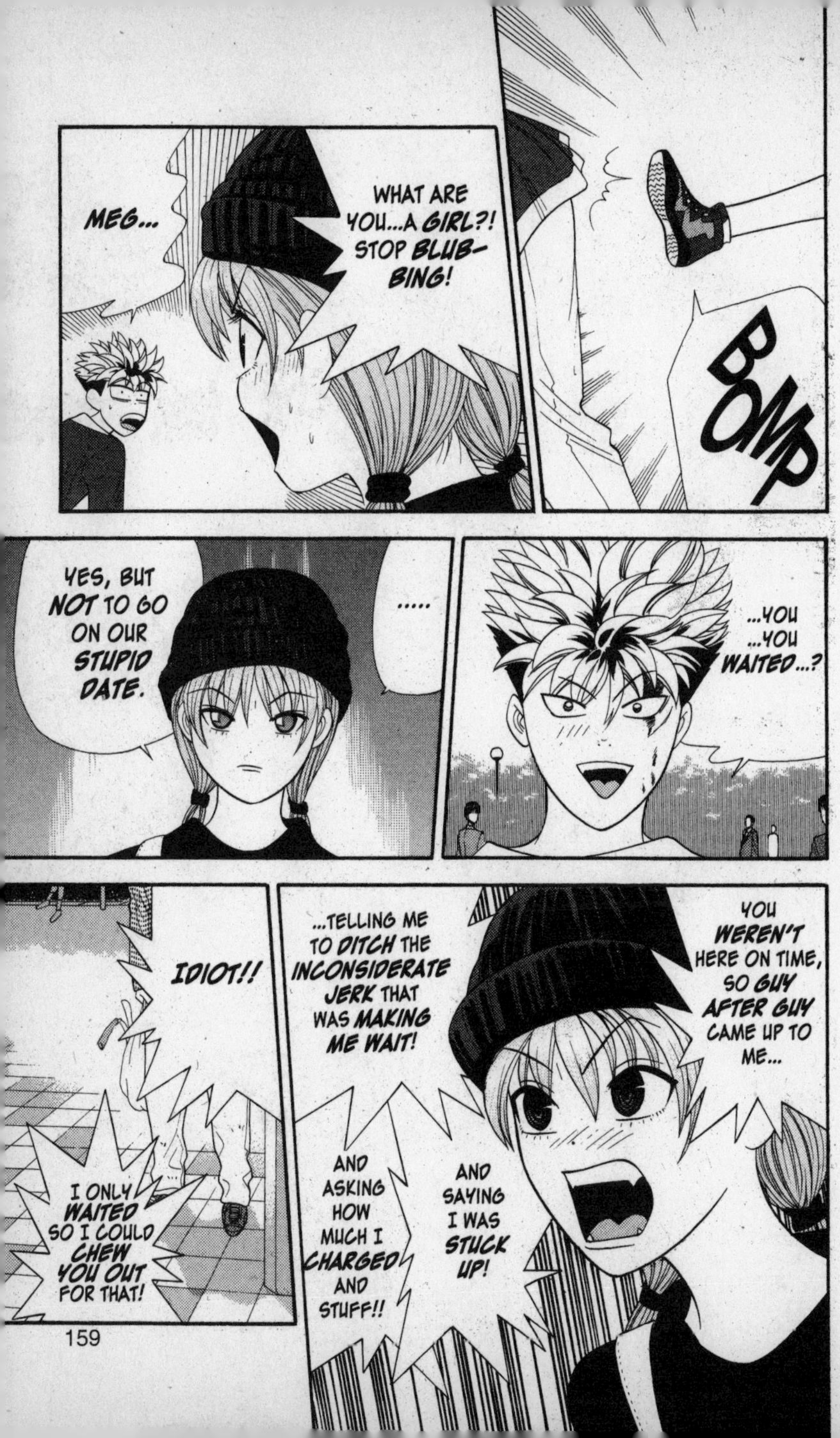
BOMP
WHAT ARE YOU...A GIRL?! STOP BLUBBING!
MEG...
...YOU ...YOU WAITED...?
.....
YES, BUT NOT TO GO ON OUR STUPID DATE.
YOU WEREN'T HERE ON TIME, SO GUY AFTER GUY CAME UP TO ME...
...TELLING ME TO DITCH THE INCONSIDERATE JERK THAT WAS MAKING ME WAIT!
AND SAYING I WAS STUCK UP!
AND ASKING HOW MUCH I CHARGED AND STUFF!!
IDIOT!!
I ONLY WAITED SO I COULD CHEW YOU OUT FOR THAT!

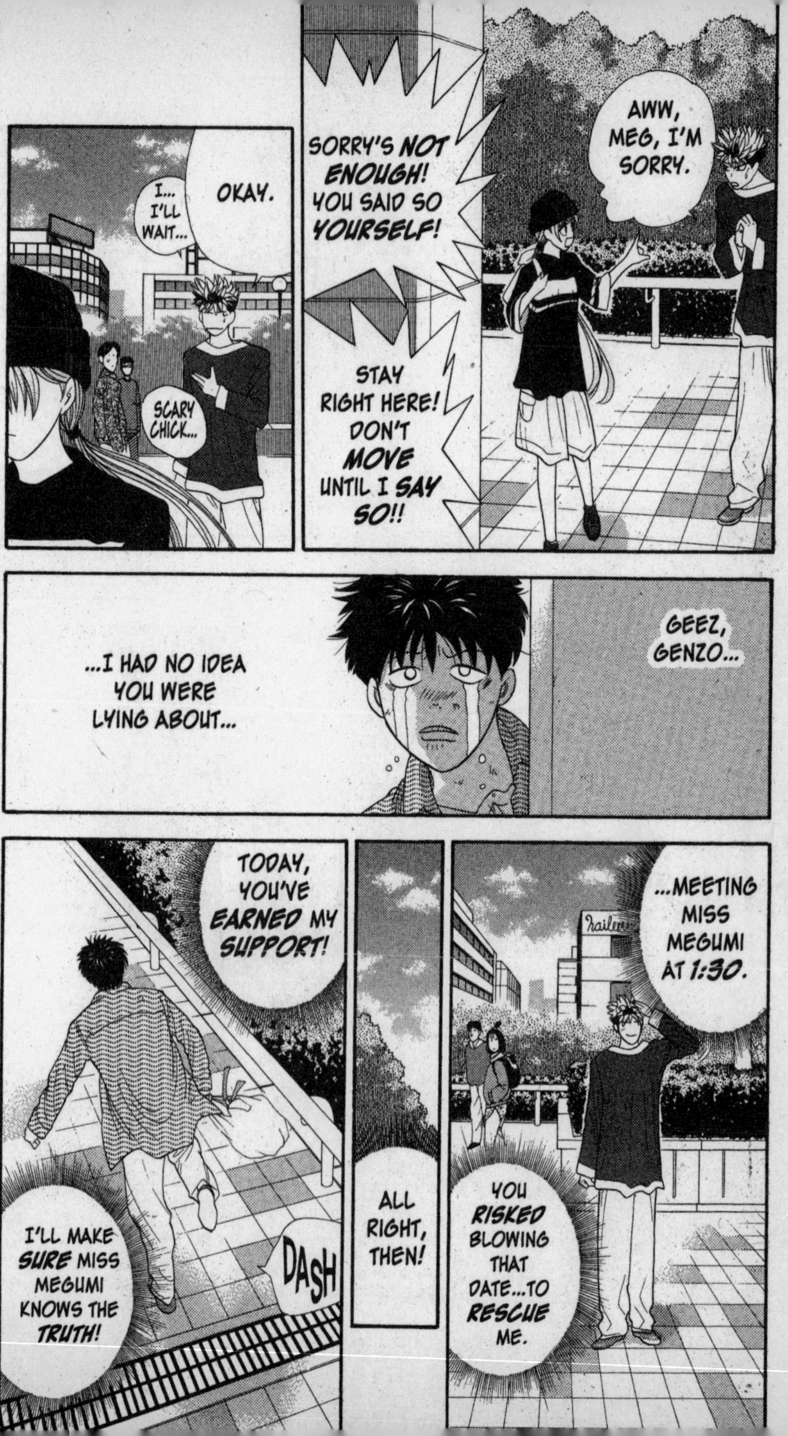
AWW, MEG, I'M SORRY.
SORRY'S NOT ENOUGH! YOU SAID SO YOURSELF!
STAY RIGHT HERE! DON'T MOVE UNTIL I SAY SO!!
OKAY.
I... I'LL WAIT...
SCARY CHICK...
GEEZ, GENZO...
...I HAD NO IDEA YOU WERE LYING ABOUT...
...MEETING MISS MEGUMI AT 1:30.
YOU RISKED BLOWING THAT DATE...TO RESCUE ME.
ALL RIGHT, THEN!
TODAY, YOU'VE EARNED MY SUPPORT!
I'LL MAKE SURE MISS MEGUMI KNOWS THE TRUTH!
DASH

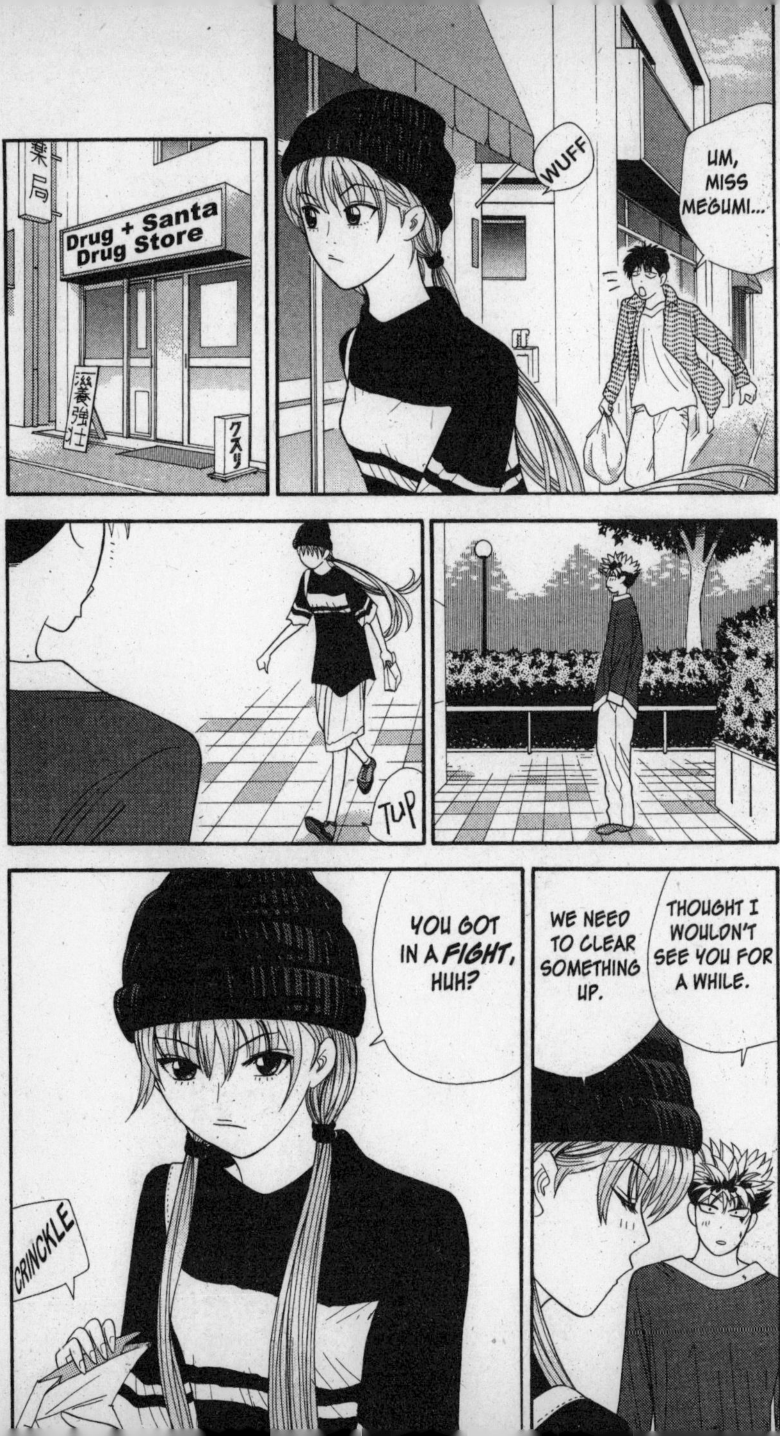
UM, MISS MEGUMI...
WUFF
Drug + Santa Drug Store
薬局
滋養強壮
クスリ
TUP
THOUGHT I WOULDN'T SEE YOU FOR A WHILE.
WE NEED TO CLEAR SOMETHING UP.
YOU GOT IN A *FIGHT*, HUH?
CRINCKLE

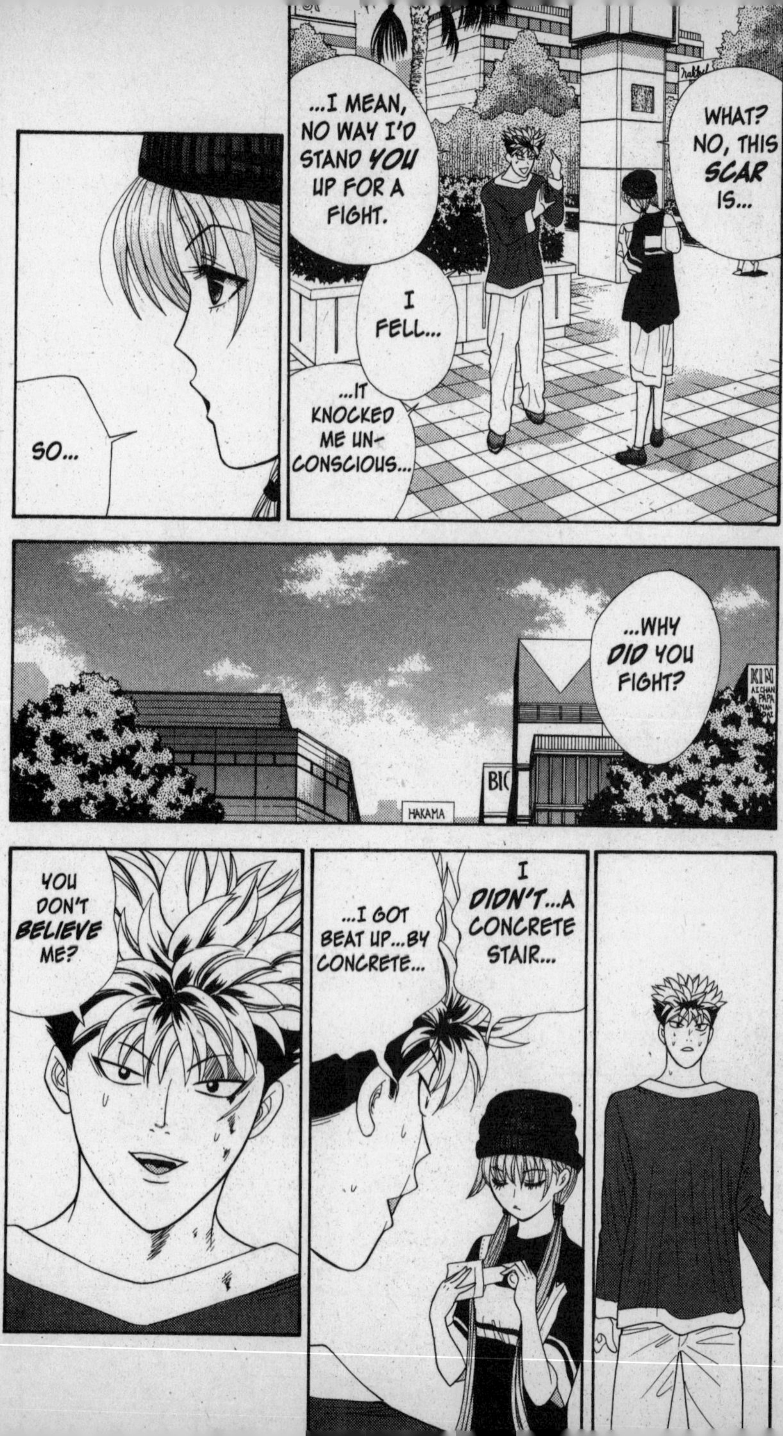
WHAT? NO, THIS SCAR IS...
...I MEAN, NO WAY I'D STAND YOU UP FOR A FIGHT.
I FELL...
...IT KNOCKED ME UN-CONSCIOUS...
SO...
...WHY DID YOU FIGHT?
HAKAMA
I DIDN'T...A CONCRETE STAIR...
...I GOT BEAT UP...BY CONCRETE...
YOU DON'T BELIEVE ME?

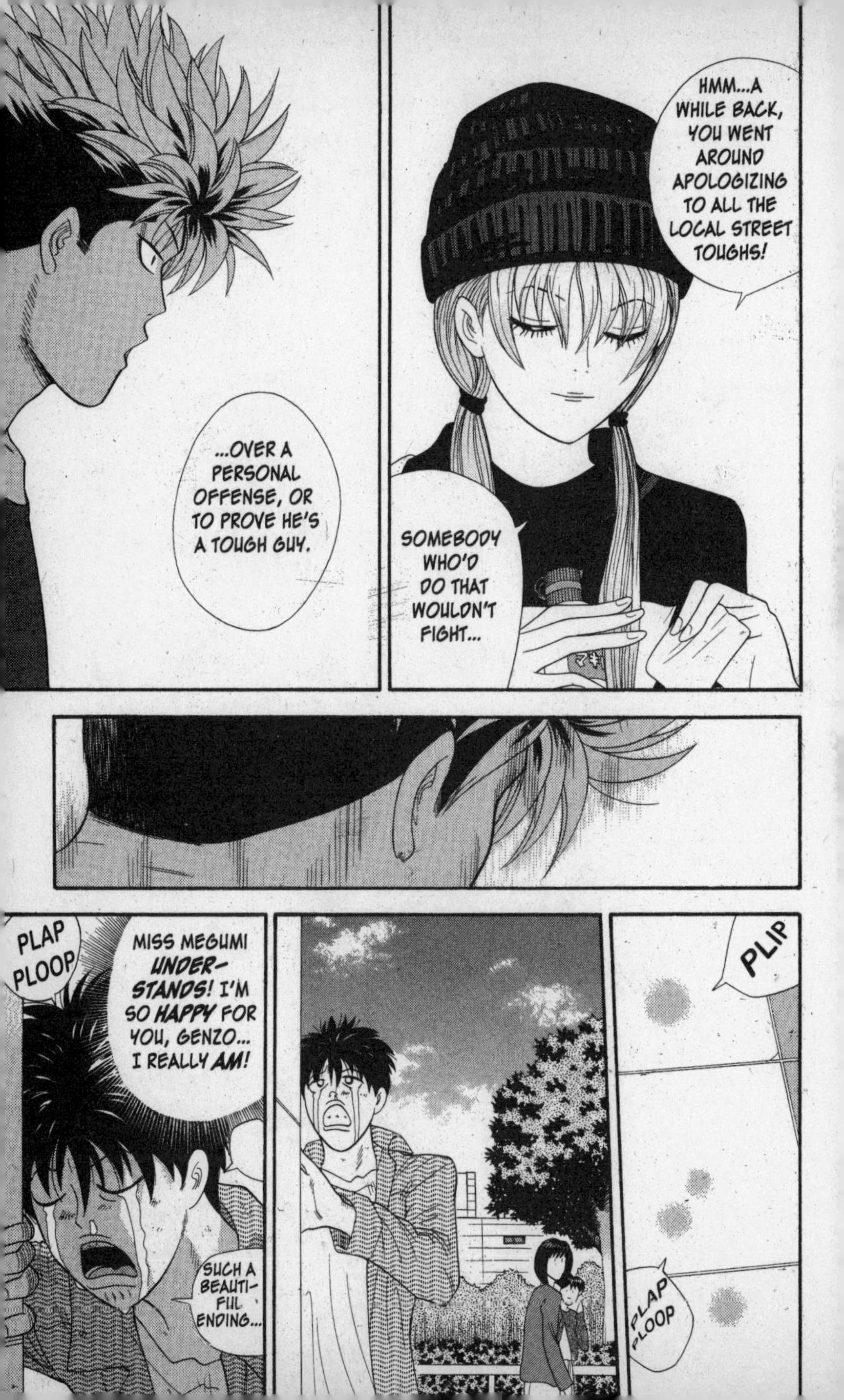
HMM...A WHILE BACK, YOU WENT AROUND APOLOGIZING TO ALL THE LOCAL STREET TOUGHS!
SOMEBODY WHO'D DO THAT WOULDN'T FIGHT...
...OVER A PERSONAL OFFENSE, OR TO PROVE HE'S A TOUGH GUY.
PLIP
PLAP PLOOP
MISS MEGUMI UNDER-STANDS! I'M SO HAPPY FOR YOU, GENZO... I REALLY AM!
PLAP PLOOP
SUCH A BEAUTI-FUL ENDING...

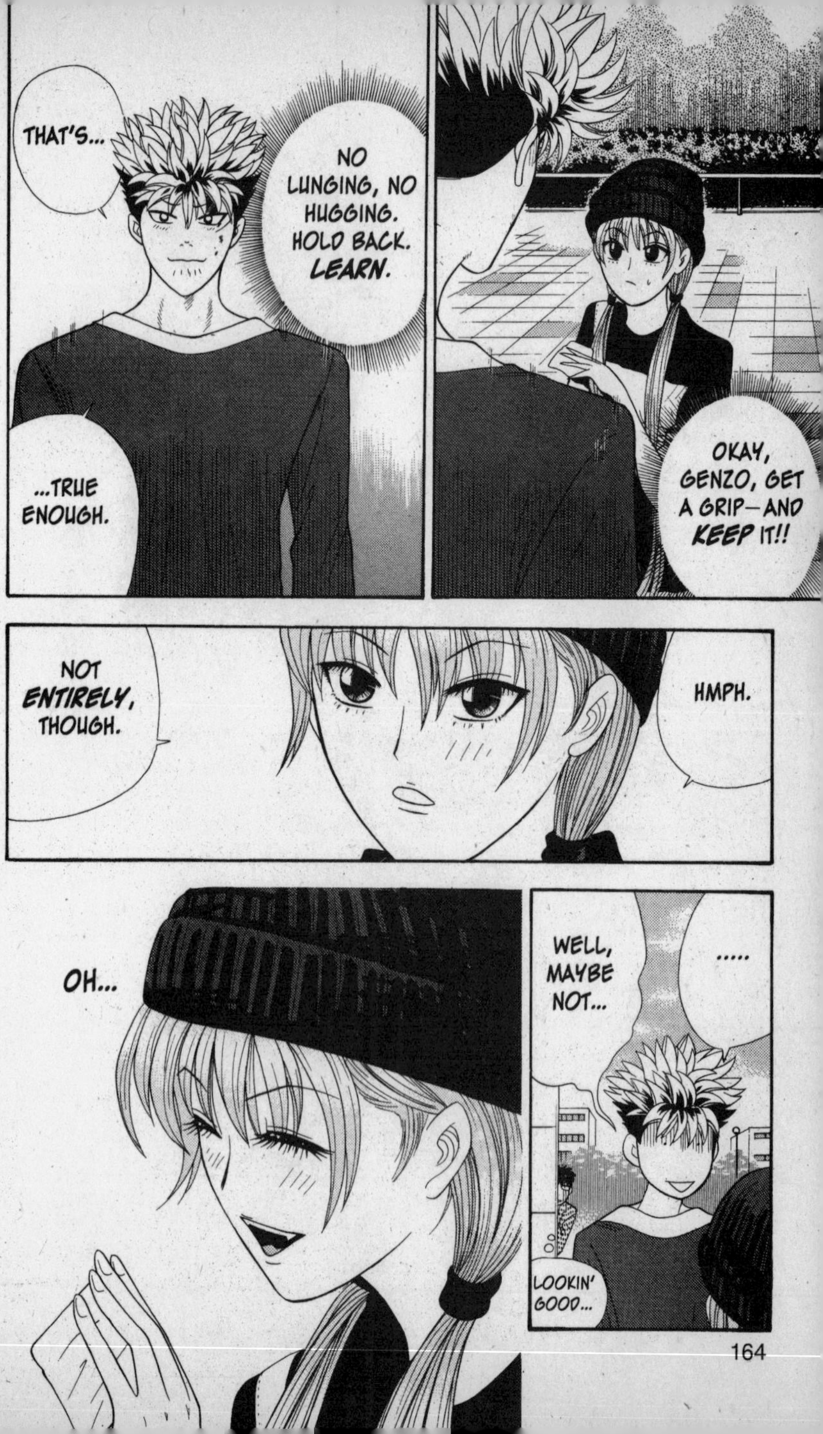
OKAY, GENZO, GET A GRIP—AND KEEP IT!!
NO LUNGING, NO HUGGING. HOLD BACK. LEARN.
THAT'S...
...TRUE ENOUGH.
HMPH.
NOT ENTIRELY, THOUGH.
.....
WELL, MAYBE NOT...
LOOKIN' GOOD...
OH...

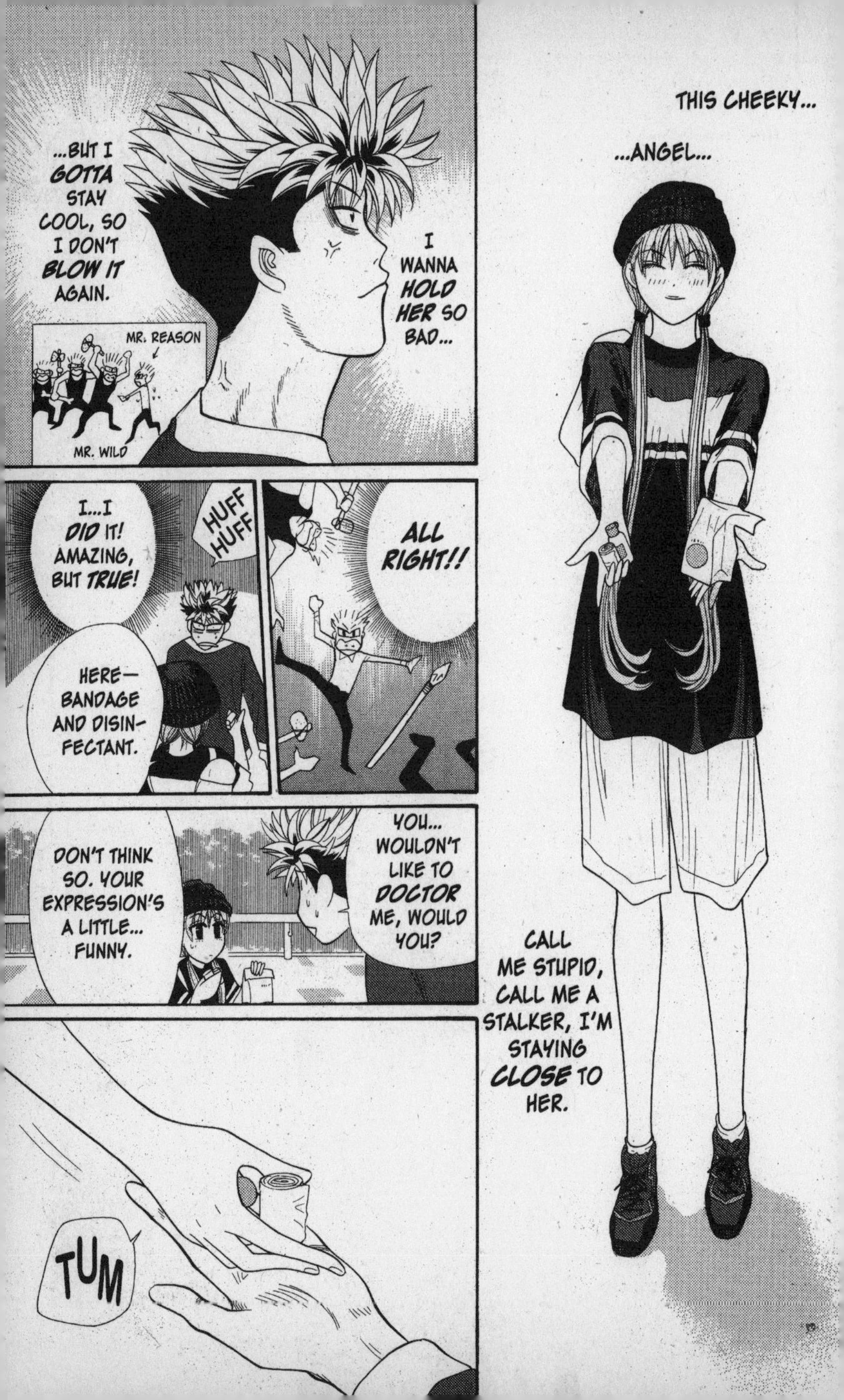
THIS CHEEKY...
...ANGEL...
CALL ME STUPID, CALL ME A STALKER, I'M STAYING CLOSE TO HER.
I WANNA HOLD HER SO BAD...
...BUT I GOTTA STAY COOL, SO I DON'T BLOW IT AGAIN.
MR. REASON
MR. WILD
ALL RIGHT!!
HUFF HUFF
I...I DID IT! AMAZING, BUT TRUE!
HERE— BANDAGE AND DISINFECTANT.
YOU... WOULDN'T LIKE TO DOCTOR ME, WOULD YOU?
DON'T THINK SO. YOUR EXPRESSION'S A LITTLE... FUNNY.
TUM

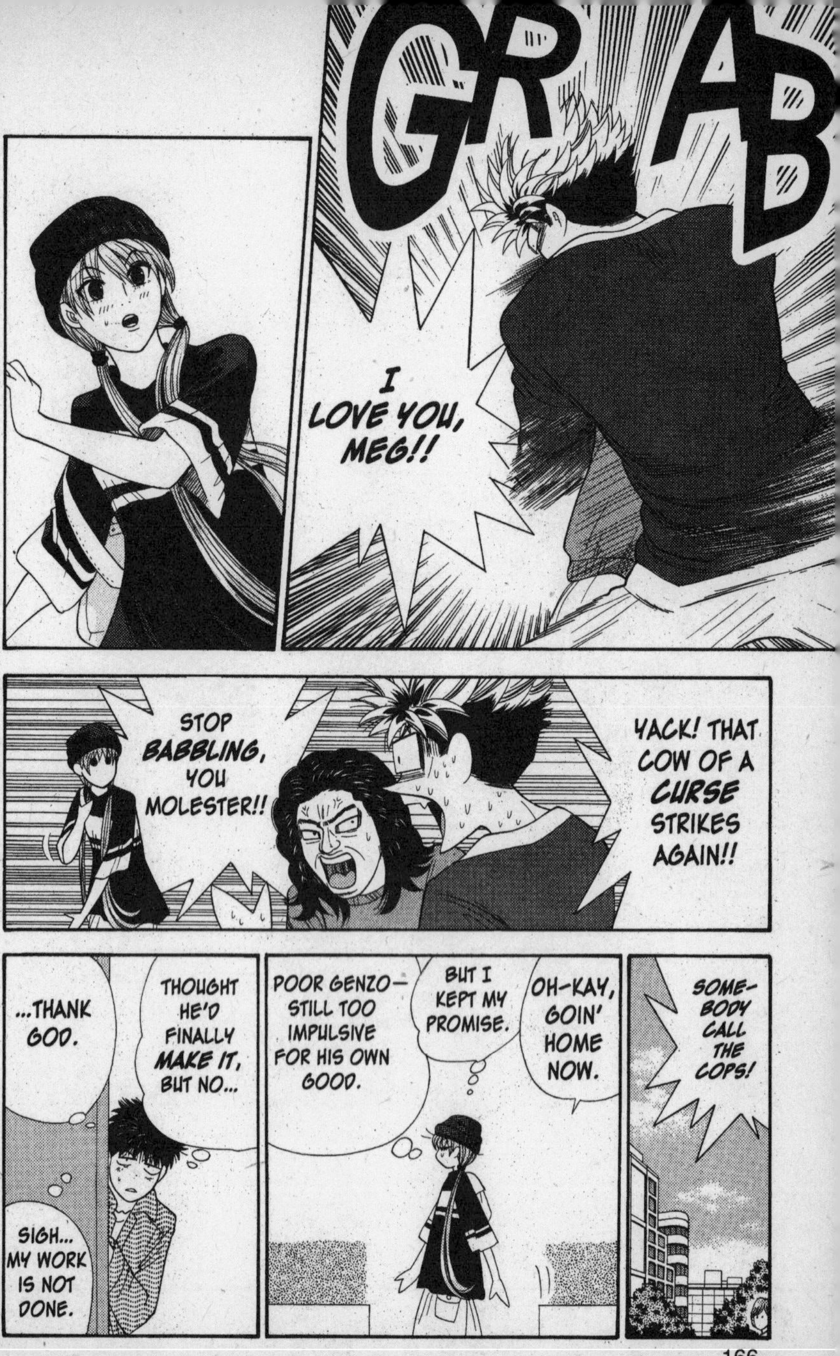
GRAB
I LOVE YOU, MEG!!
YACK! THAT COW OF A CURSE STRIKES AGAIN!!
STOP BABBLING, YOU MOLESTER!!
SOME-BODY CALL THE COPS!
OH-KAY, GOIN' HOME NOW.
BUT I KEPT MY PROMISE.
POOR GENZO— STILL TOO IMPULSIVE FOR HIS OWN GOOD.
THOUGHT HE'D FINALLY MAKE IT, BUT NO...
...THANK GOD.
SIGH... MY WORK IS NOT DONE.

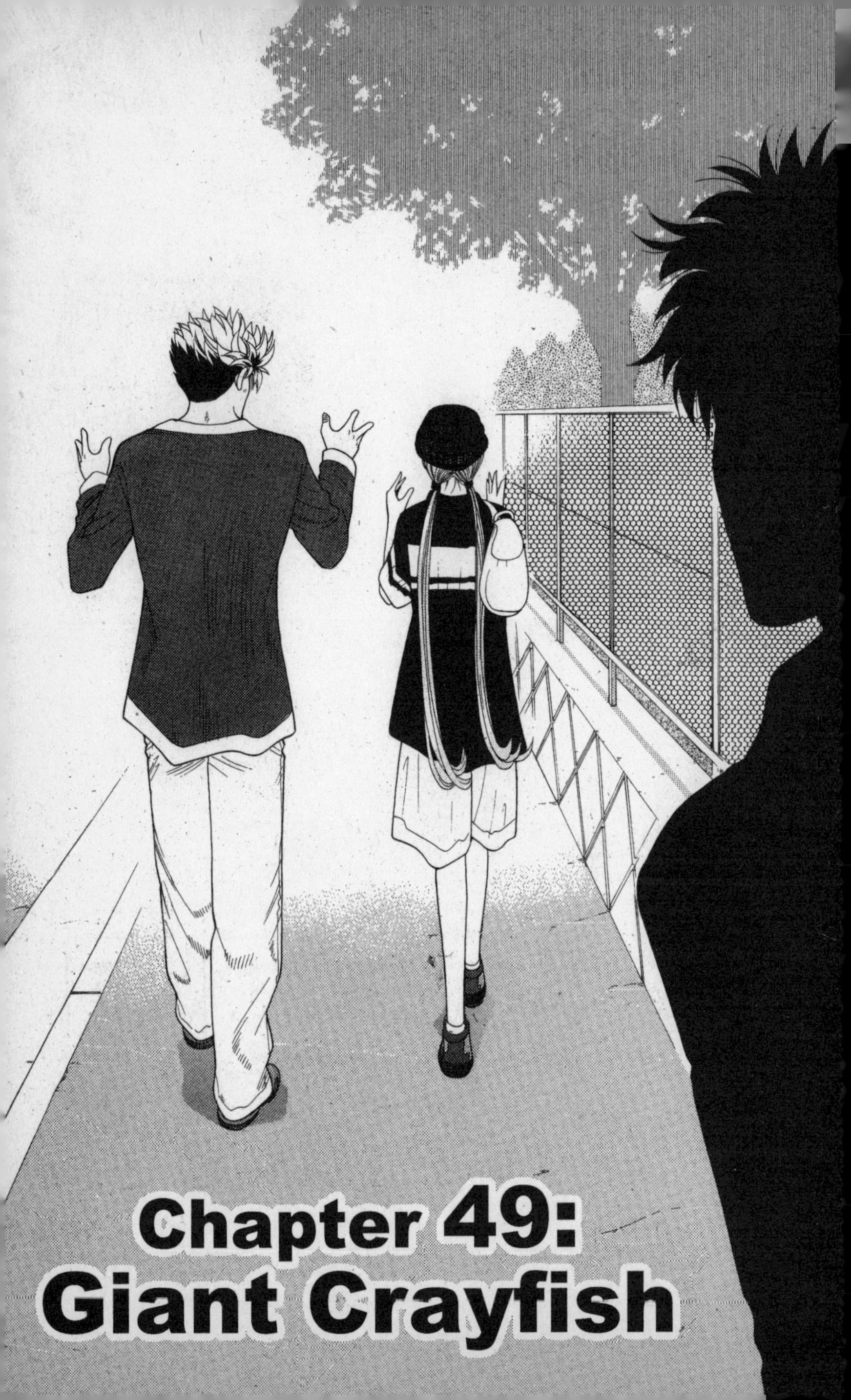
Chapter 49:
Giant Crayfish

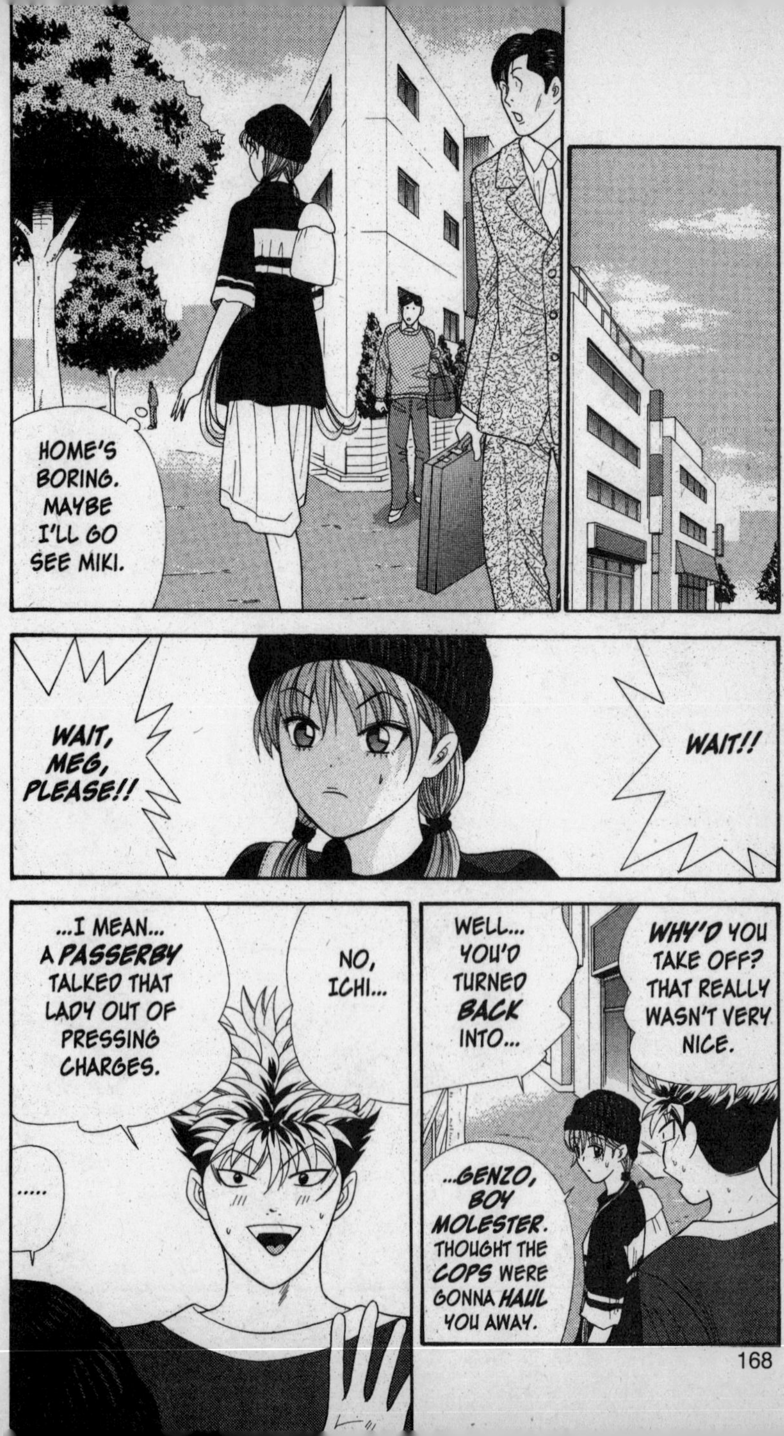
HOME'S BORING. MAYBE I'LL GO SEE MIKI.
WAIT!!
WAIT, MEG, PLEASE!!
WHY'D YOU TAKE OFF? THAT REALLY WASN'T VERY NICE.
WELL... YOU'D TURNED BACK INTO...
...GENZO, BOY MOLESTER. THOUGHT THE COPS WERE GONNA HAUL YOU AWAY.
NO, ICHI...
...I MEAN... A PASSERBY TALKED THAT LADY OUT OF PRESSING CHARGES.
.....

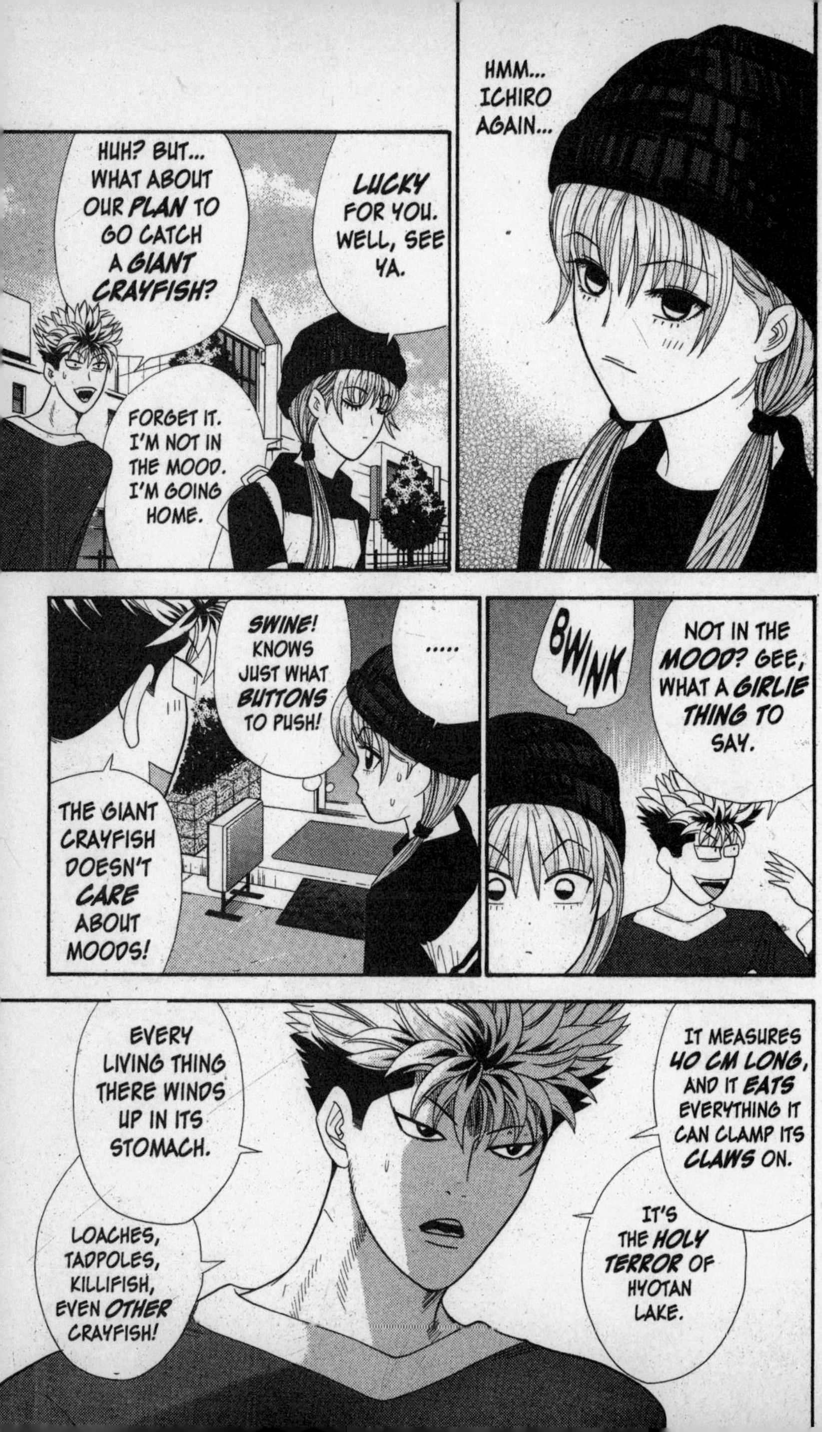
HMM... ICHIRO AGAIN...
LUCKY FOR YOU. WELL, SEE YA.
HUH? BUT... WHAT ABOUT OUR PLAN TO GO CATCH A GIANT CRAYFISH?
FORGET IT. I'M NOT IN THE MOOD. I'M GOING HOME.
BWINK
NOT IN THE MOOD? GEE, WHAT A GIRLIE THING TO SAY.
.....
SWINE! KNOWS JUST WHAT BUTTONS TO PUSH!
THE GIANT CRAYFISH DOESN'T CARE ABOUT MOODS!
IT MEASURES 40 CM LONG, AND IT EATS EVERYTHING IT CAN CLAMP ITS CLAWS ON.
IT'S THE HOLY TERROR OF HYOTAN LAKE.
EVERY LIVING THING THERE WINDS UP IN ITS STOMACH.
LOACHES, TADPOLES, KILLIFISH, EVEN OTHER CRAYFISH!

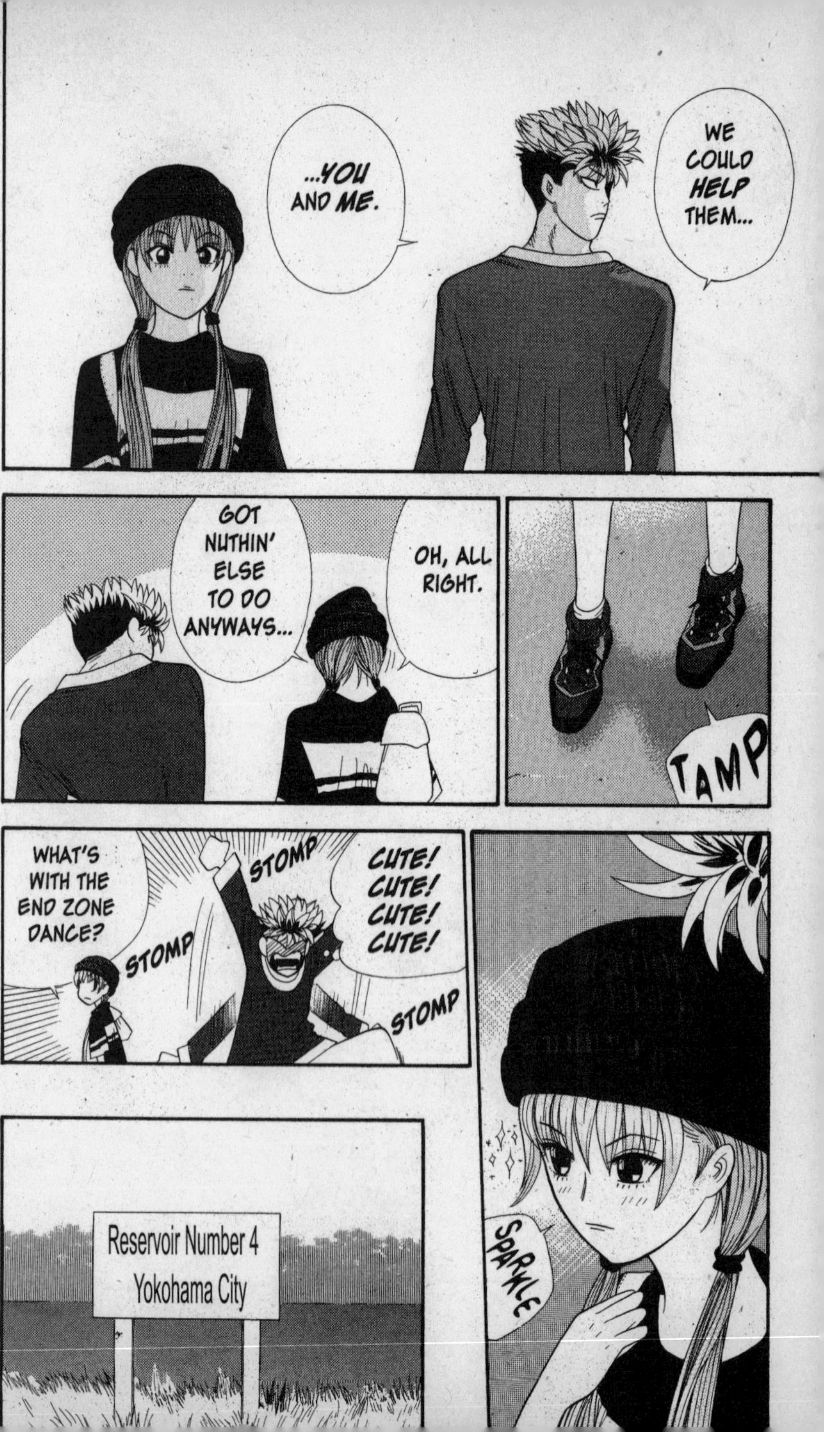
WE COULD HELP THEM...
...YOU AND ME.
TAMP
OH, ALL RIGHT.
GOT NUTHIN' ELSE TO DO ANYWAYS...
SPARKLE
CUTE! CUTE! CUTE! CUTE!
STOMP
WHAT'S WITH THE END ZONE DANCE?
STOMP
STOMP
Reservoir Number 4
Yokohama City

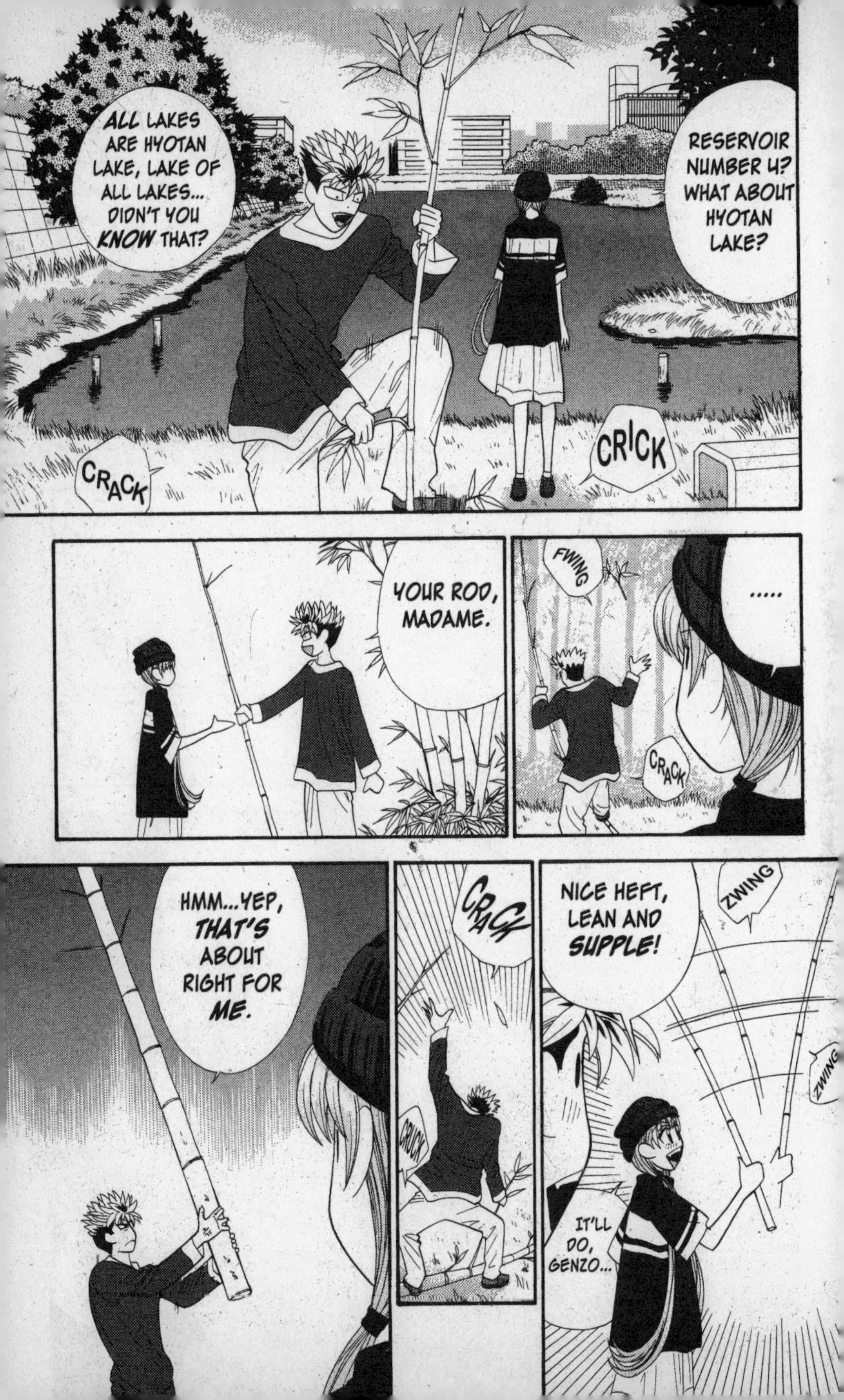
RESERVOIR NUMBER 4? WHAT ABOUT HYOTAN LAKE?
ALL LAKES ARE HYOTAN LAKE, LAKE OF ALL LAKES... DIDN'T YOU KNOW THAT?
CRICK
CRACK
.....
FWING
CRACK
YOUR ROD, MADAME.
NICE HEFT, LEAN AND SUPPLE!
ZWING
ZWING
IT'LL DO, GENZO...
CRACK
CRICK
HMM...YEP, THAT'S ABOUT RIGHT FOR ME.

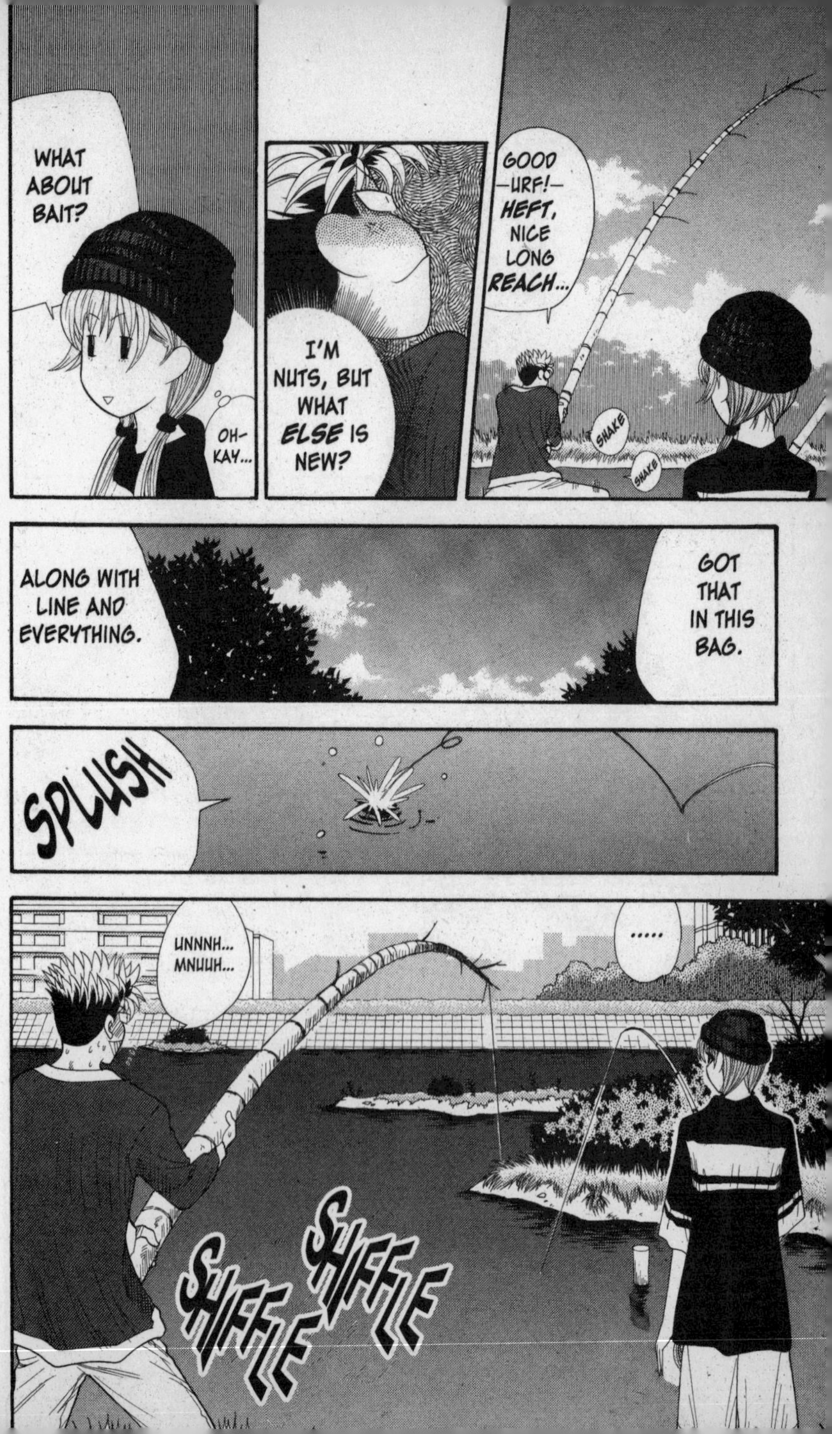
GOOD —URF!— HEFT, NICE LONG REACH...
SHAKE
SHAKE
I'M NUTS, BUT WHAT ELSE IS NEW?
OH-KAY...
WHAT ABOUT BAIT?
GOT THAT IN THIS BAG.
ALONG WITH LINE AND EVERYTHING.
SPLUSH
.....
UNNNH... MNUUH...
SHUFFLE
SHUFFLE

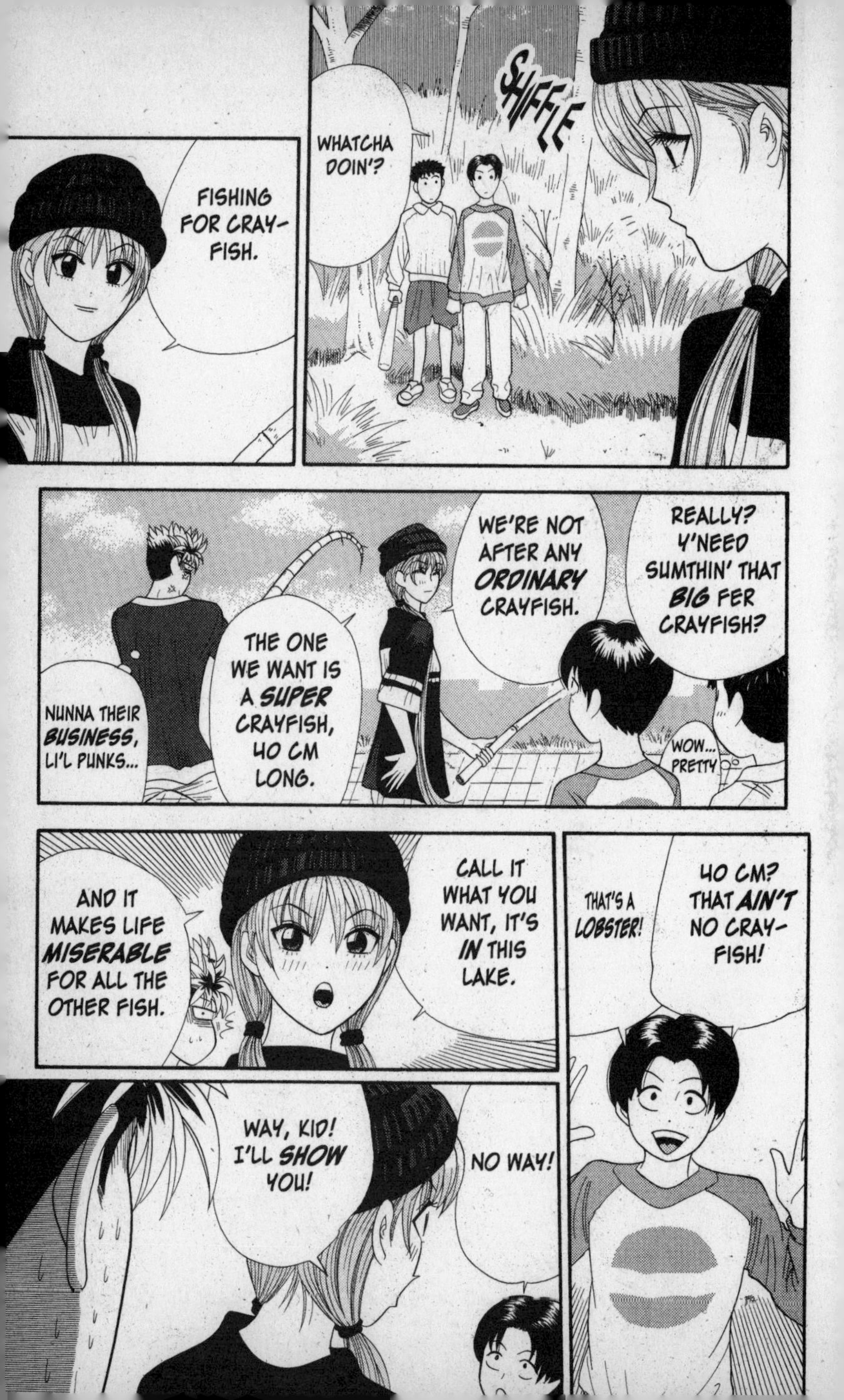
SHUFFLE
WHATCHA DOIN'?
FISHING FOR CRAY-FISH.
REALLY? Y'NEED SUMTHIN' THAT BIG FER CRAYFISH?
WE'RE NOT AFTER ANY ORDINARY CRAYFISH.
WOW... PRETTY
THE ONE WE WANT IS A SUPER CRAYFISH, 40 CM LONG.
NUNNA THEIR BUSINESS, LI'L PUNKS...
40 CM? THAT AIN'T NO CRAY-FISH!
THAT'S A LOBSTER!
CALL IT WHAT YOU WANT, IT'S IN THIS LAKE.
AND IT MAKES LIFE MISERABLE FOR ALL THE OTHER FISH.
NO WAY!
WAY, KID! I'LL SHOW YOU!

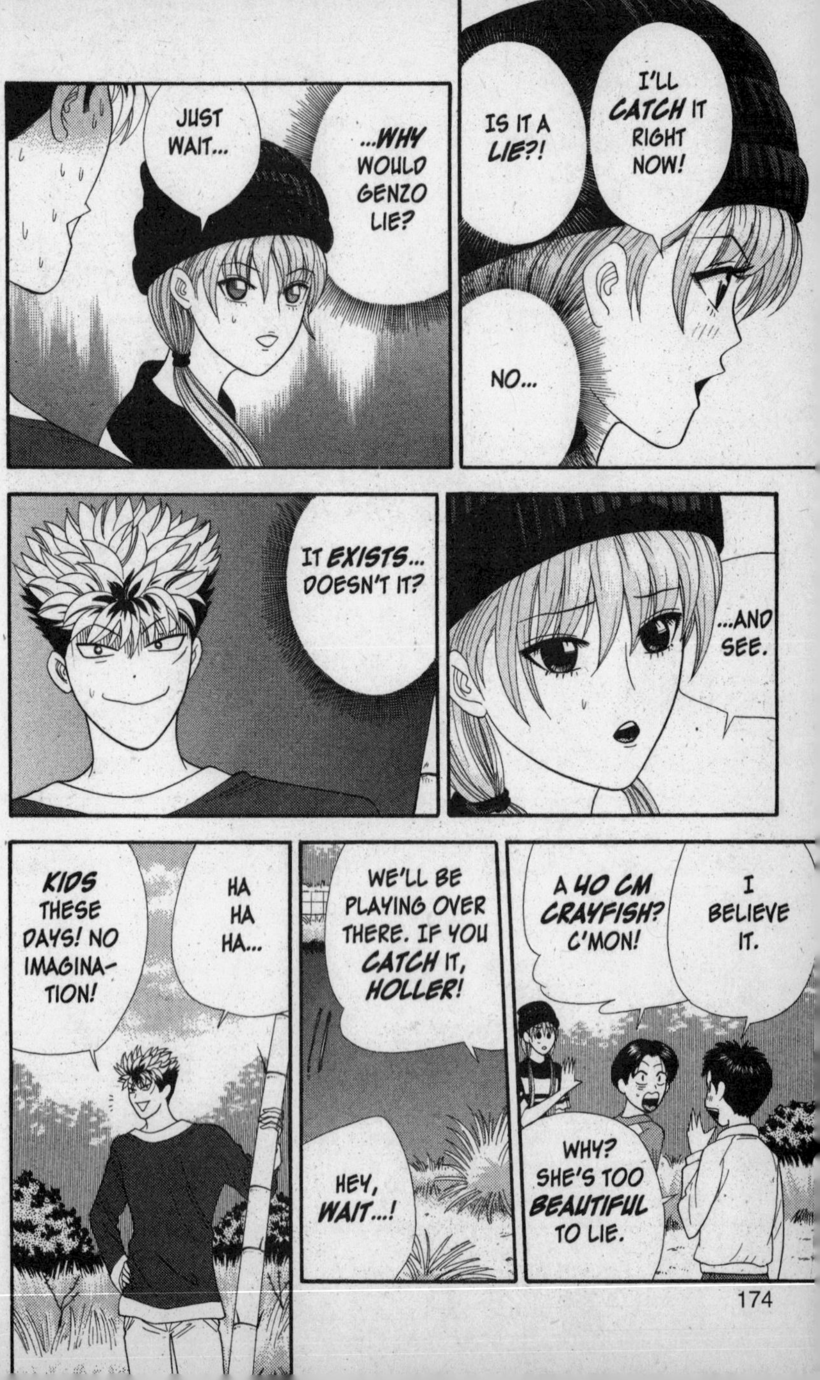
I'LL CATCH IT RIGHT NOW!
IS IT A LIE?!
NO...
...WHY WOULD GENZO LIE?
JUST WAIT...
...AND SEE.
IT EXISTS... DOESN'T IT?
I BELIEVE IT.
A 40 CM CRAYFISH? C'MON!
WHY? SHE'S TOO BEAUTIFUL TO LIE.
WE'LL BE PLAYING OVER THERE. IF YOU CATCH IT, HOLLER!
HEY, WAIT...!
HA HA HA...
KIDS THESE DAYS! NO IMAGINATION!

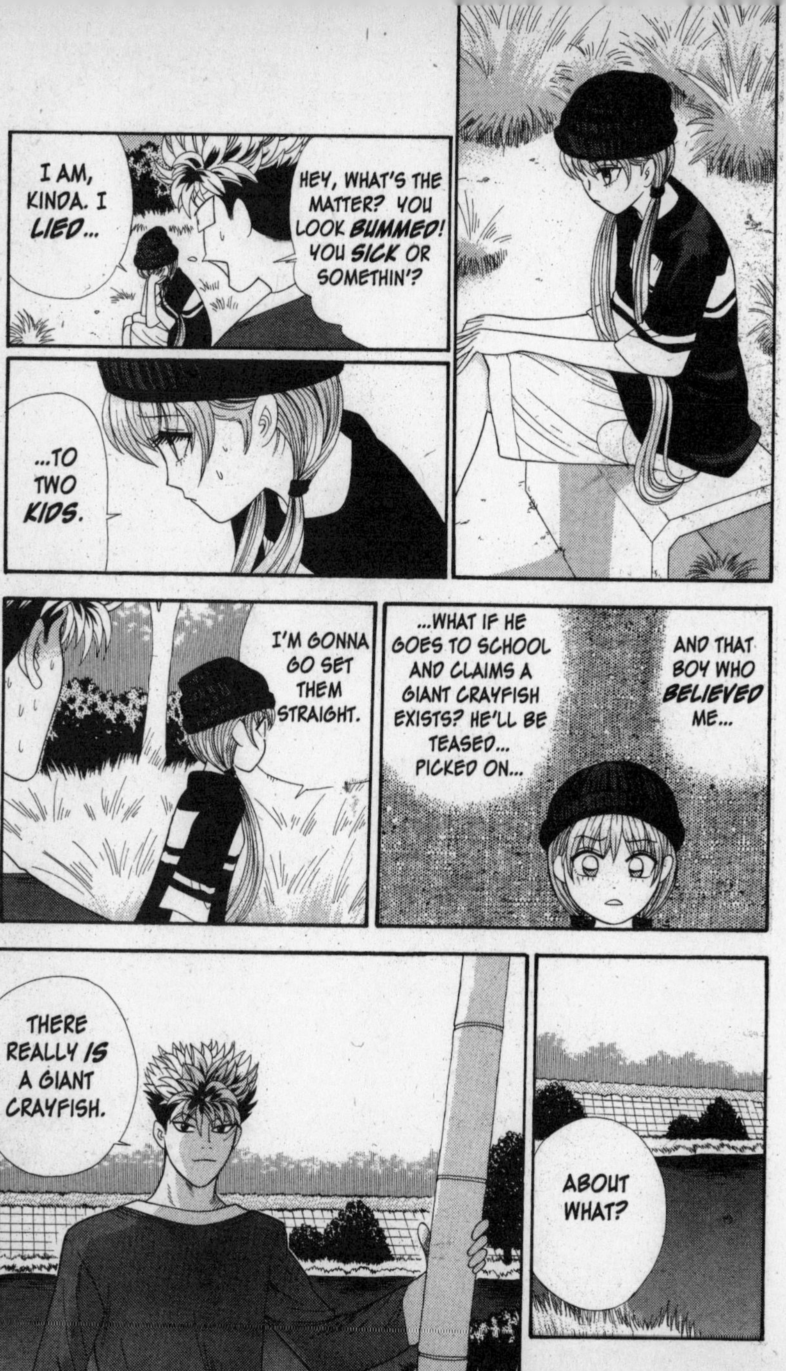
HEY, WHAT'S THE MATTER? YOU LOOK BUMMED! YOU SICK OR SOMETHIN'?
I AM, KINDA. I LIED...
...TO TWO KIDS.
AND THAT BOY WHO BELIEVED ME...
...WHAT IF HE GOES TO SCHOOL AND CLAIMS A GIANT CRAYFISH EXISTS? HE'LL BE TEASED... PICKED ON...
I'M GONNA GO SET THEM STRAIGHT.
ABOUT WHAT?
THERE REALLY IS A GIANT CRAYFISH.

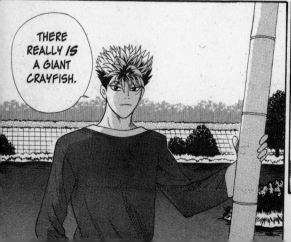

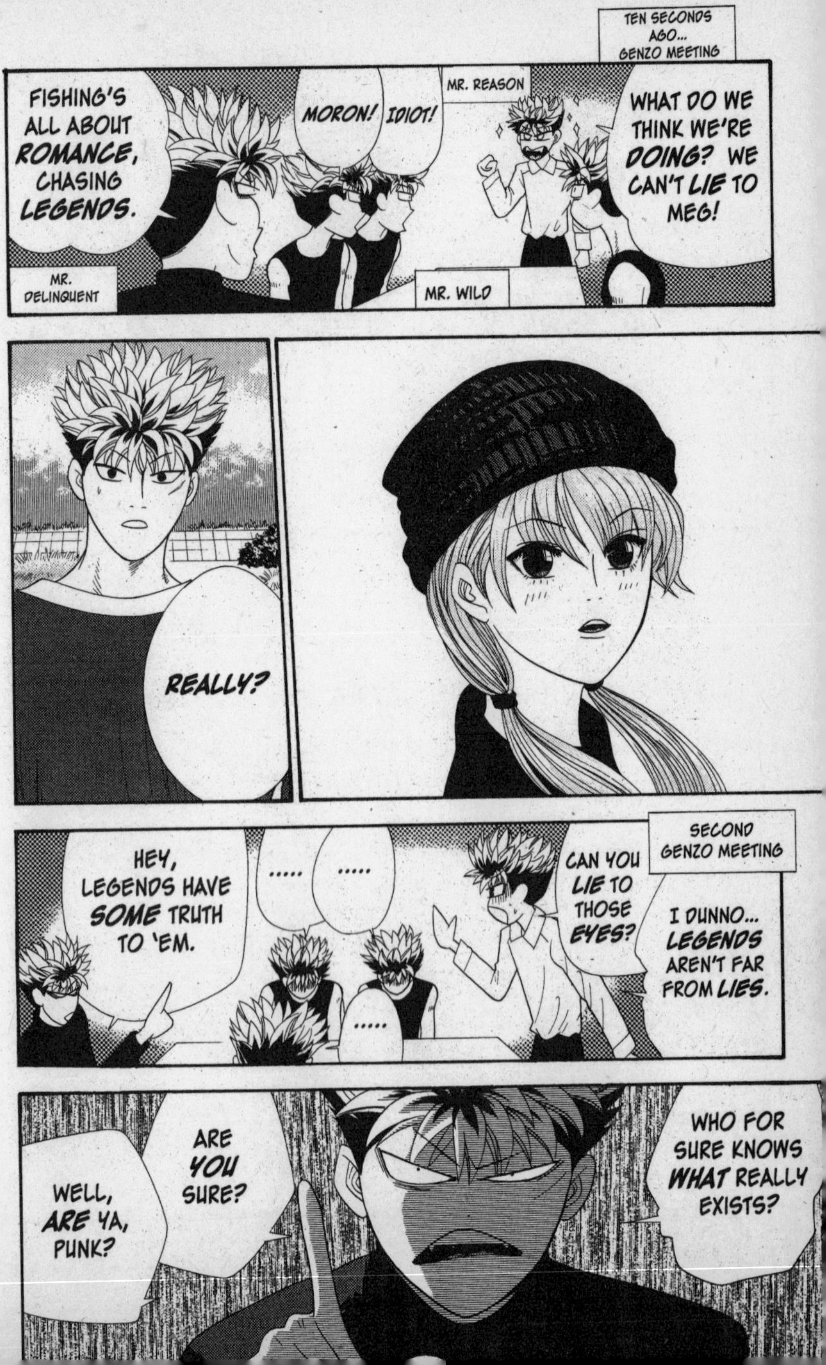
TEN SECONDS AGO... GENZO MEETING
WHAT DO WE THINK WE'RE DOING? WE CAN'T LIE TO MEG!
MR. REASON
IDIOT!
MORON!
FISHING'S ALL ABOUT ROMANCE, CHASING LEGENDS.
MR. WILD
MR. DELINQUENT
REALLY?
SECOND GENZO MEETING
I DUNNO... LEGENDS AREN'T FAR FROM LIES.
CAN YOU LIE TO THOSE EYES?
.....
.....
HEY, LEGENDS HAVE SOME TRUTH TO 'EM.
.....
WHO FOR SURE KNOWS WHAT REALLY EXISTS?
ARE YOU SURE?
WELL, ARE YA, PUNK?

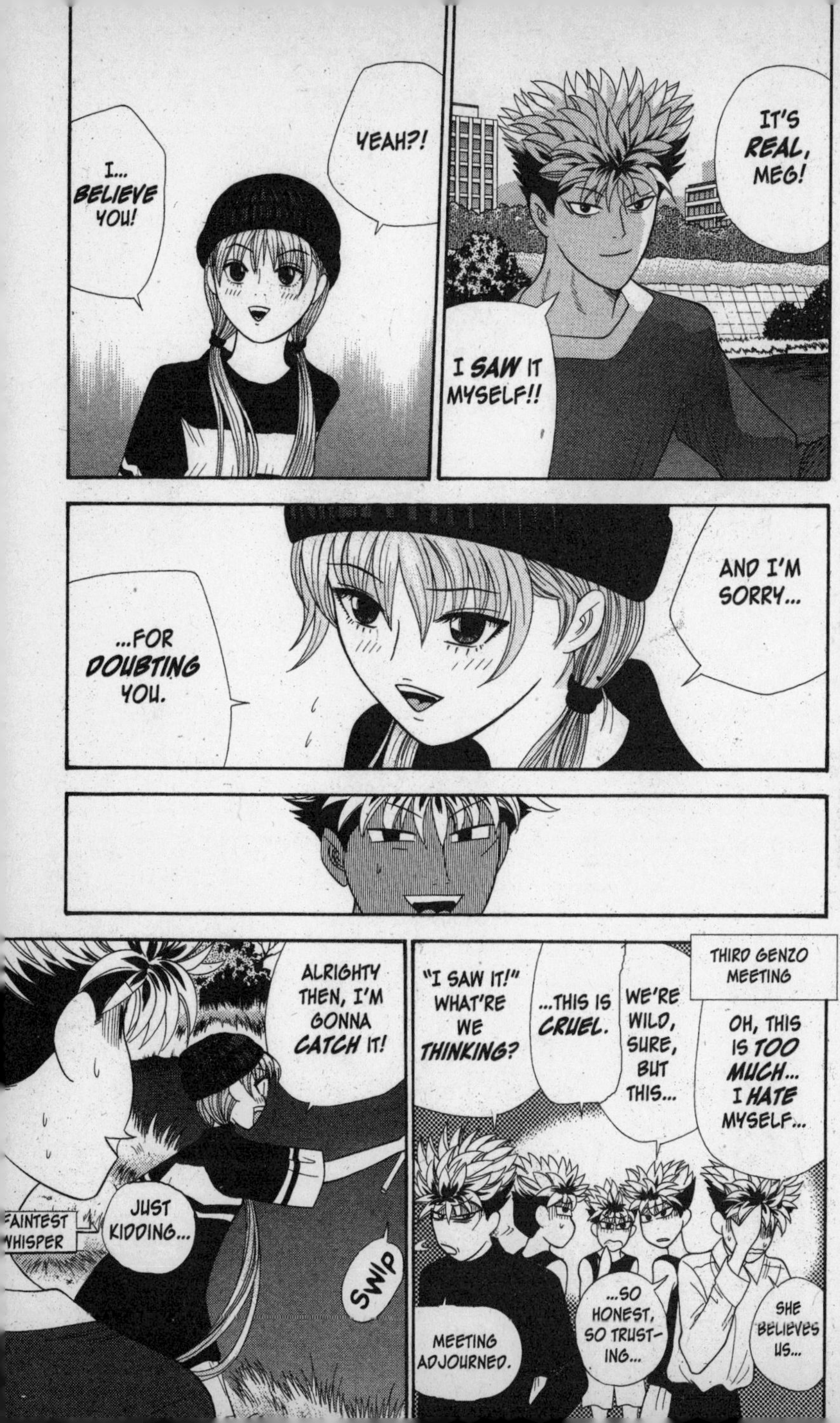
IT'S REAL, MEG!
I SAW IT MYSELF!!
YEAH?!
I... BELIEVE YOU!
AND I'M SORRY...
...FOR DOUBTING YOU.
THIRD GENZO MEETING
OH, THIS IS TOO MUCH... I HATE MYSELF...
WE'RE WILD, SURE, BUT THIS...
...THIS IS CRUEL.
"I SAW IT!" WHAT'RE WE THINKING?
SHE BELIEVES US...
...SO HONEST, SO TRUSTING...
MEETING ADJOURNED.
ALRIGHTY THEN, I'M GONNA CATCH IT!
SWIP
JUST KIDDING...
FAINTEST WHISPER

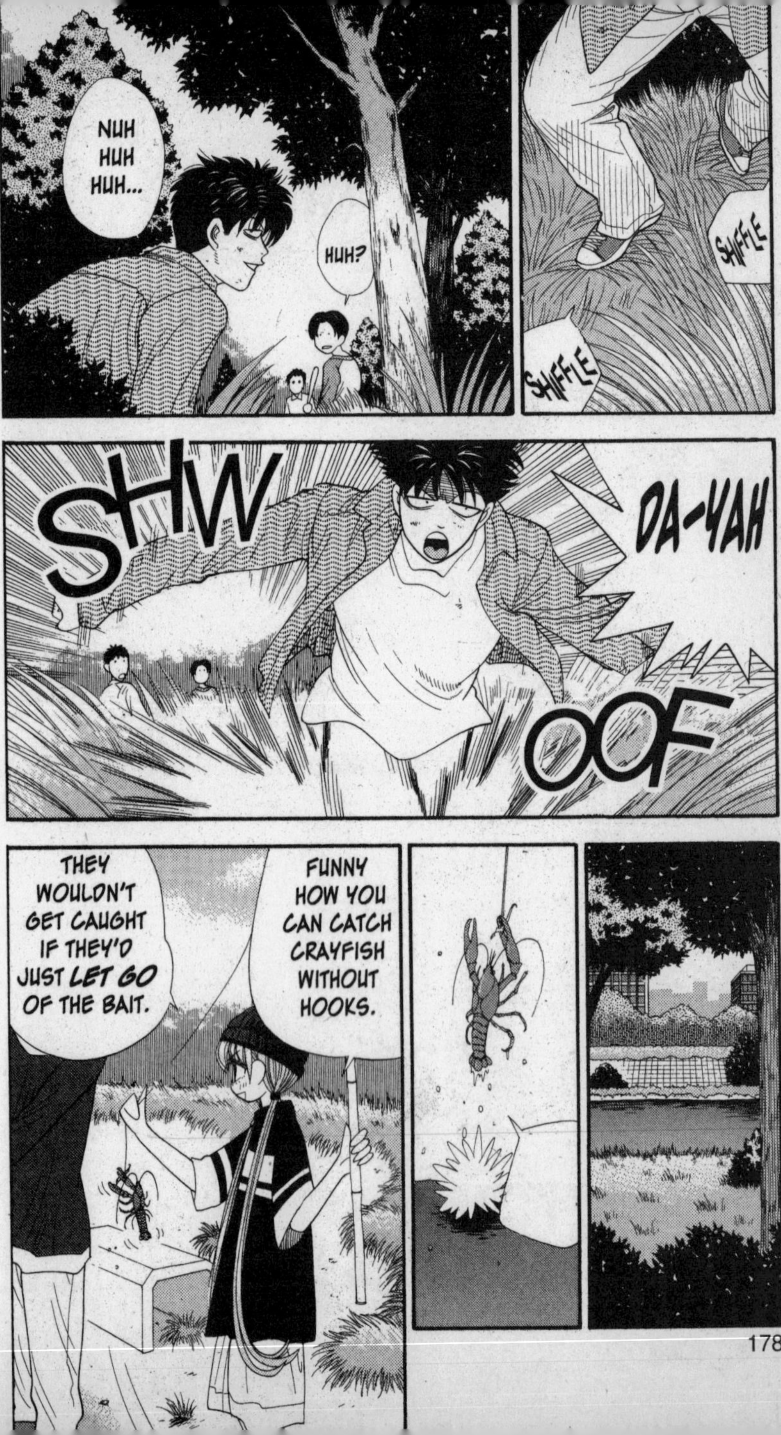
SHIFFLE
SHIFFLE
NUH HUH HUH...
HUH?
DA-YAH
SHW
OOF
FUNNY HOW YOU CAN CATCH CRAYFISH WITHOUT HOOKS.
THEY WOULDN'T GET CAUGHT IF THEY'D JUST LET GO OF THE BAIT.

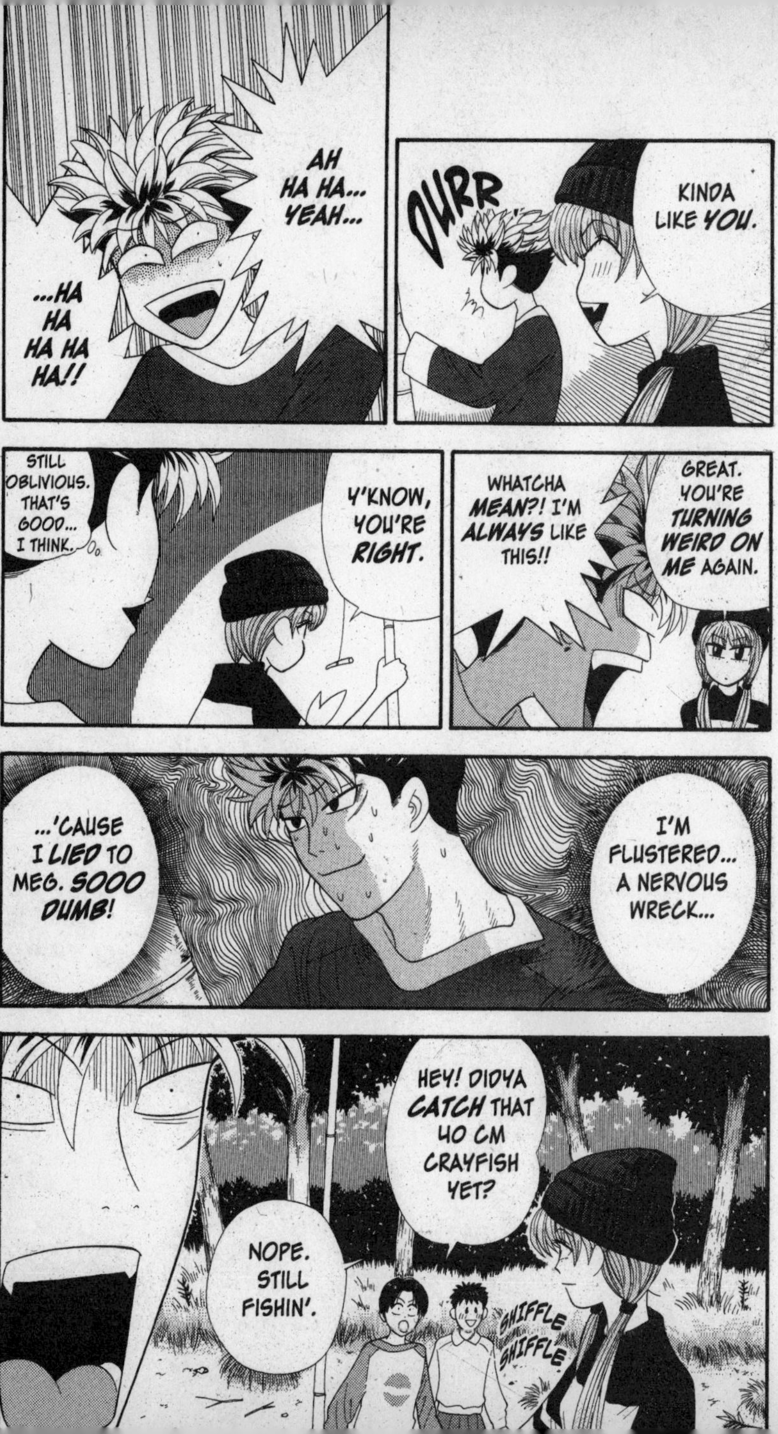
DURR
KINDA LIKE YOU.
AH HA HA... YEAH...
...HA HA HA HA HA!!
GREAT. YOU'RE TURNING WEIRD ON ME AGAIN.
WHATCHA MEAN?! I'M ALWAYS LIKE THIS!!
Y'KNOW, YOU'RE RIGHT.
STILL OBLIVIOUS. THAT'S GOOD... I THINK.
I'M FLUSTERED... A NERVOUS WRECK...
...'CAUSE I LIED TO MEG. SOOO DUMB!
HEY! DIDYA CATCH THAT 40 CM CRAYFISH YET?
SHIFFLE SHIFFLE
NOPE. STILL FISHIN'.

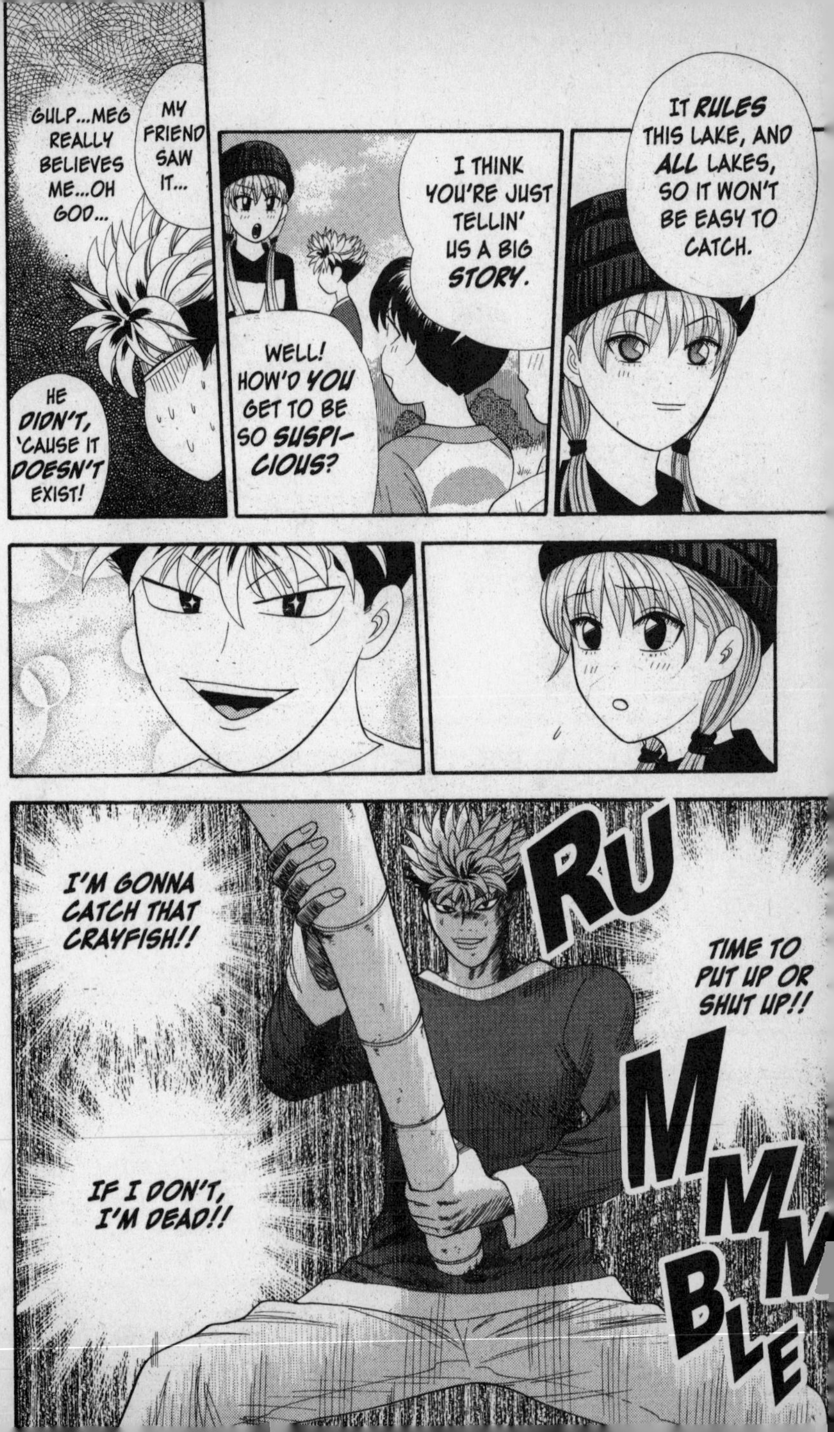

IT RULES THIS LAKE, AND ALL LAKES, SO IT WON'T BE EASY TO CATCH.
I THINK YOU'RE JUST TELLIN' US A BIG STORY.
WELL! HOW'D YOU GET TO BE SO SUSPICIOUS?
MY FRIEND SAW IT...
GULP...MEG REALLY BELIEVES ME...OH GOD...
HE DIDN'T, 'CAUSE IT DOESN'T EXIST!
RUMMMBLE
TIME TO PUT UP OR SHUT UP!!
I'M GONNA CATCH THAT CRAYFISH!!
IF I DON'T, I'M DEAD!!

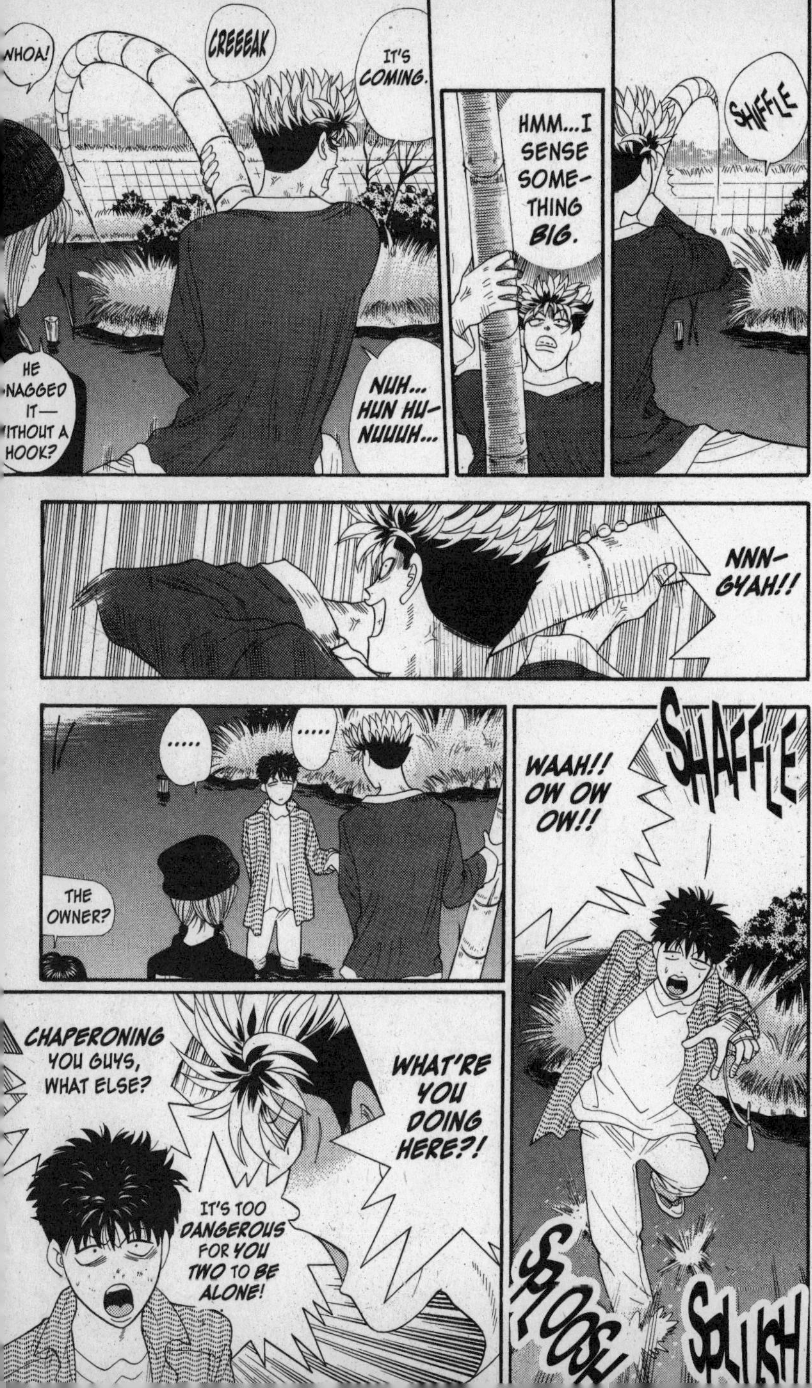
SHIFFLE
HMM...I SENSE SOME-THING BIG.
IT'S COMING.
CREEEAK
WHOA!
NUH... HUN HU-NUUUH...
HE NAGGED IT— ITHOUT A HOOK?
NNN-GYAH!!
SHAFFLE
WAAH!! OW OW OW!!
SPLISH
SPLOOSH
.....
.....
THE OWNER?
WHAT'RE YOU DOING HERE?!
CHAPERONING YOU GUYS, WHAT ELSE?
IT'S TOO DANGEROUS FOR YOU TWO TO BE ALONE!

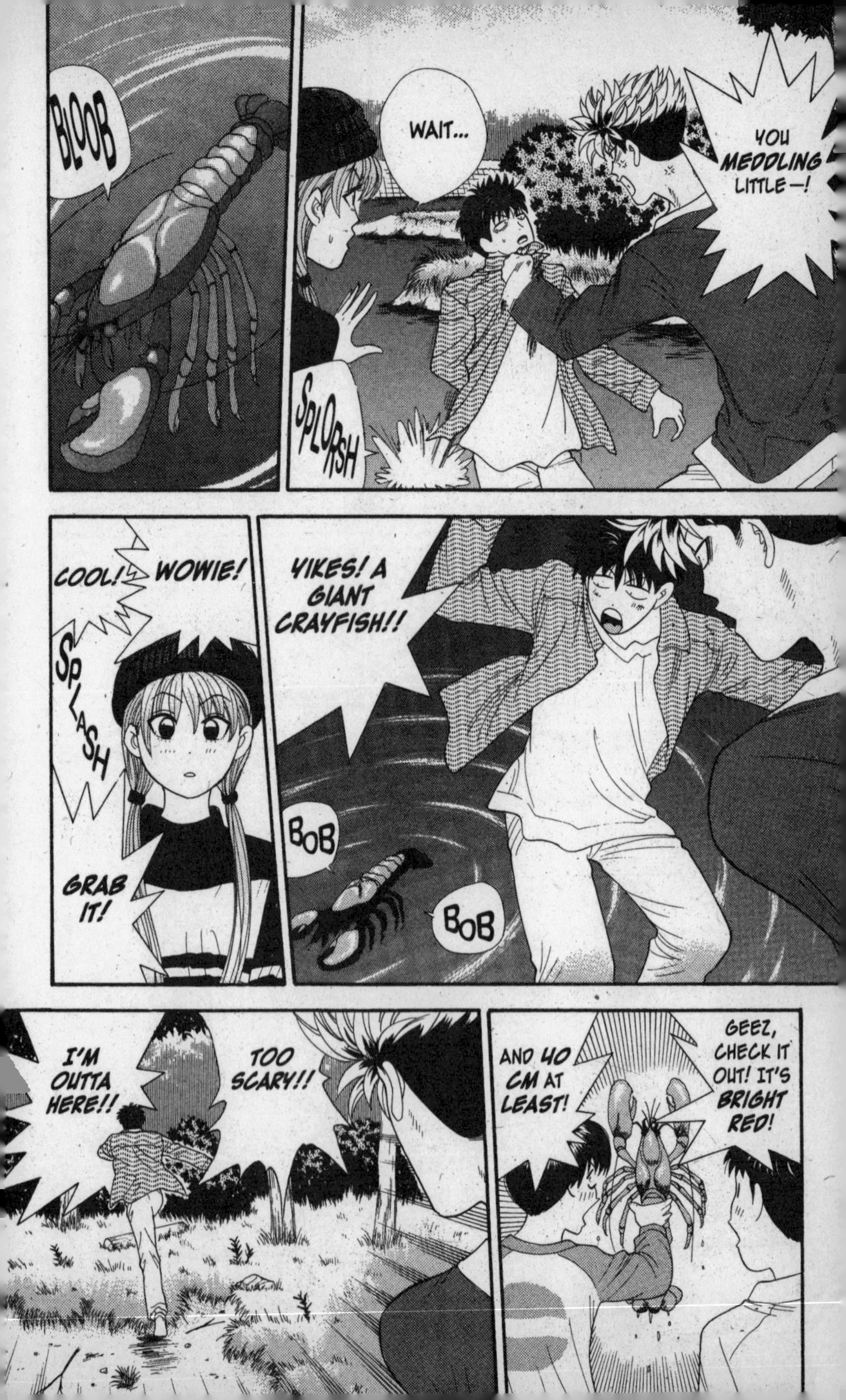
YOU MEDDLING LITTLE—!
WAIT...
SPLORSH
BLOOB
YIKES! A GIANT CRAYFISH!!
BOB
BOB
WOWIE!
COOL!
SPLASH
GRAB IT!
GEEZ, CHECK IT OUT! IT'S BRIGHT RED!
AND 40 CM AT LEAST!
TOO SCARY!!
I'M OUTTA HERE!!

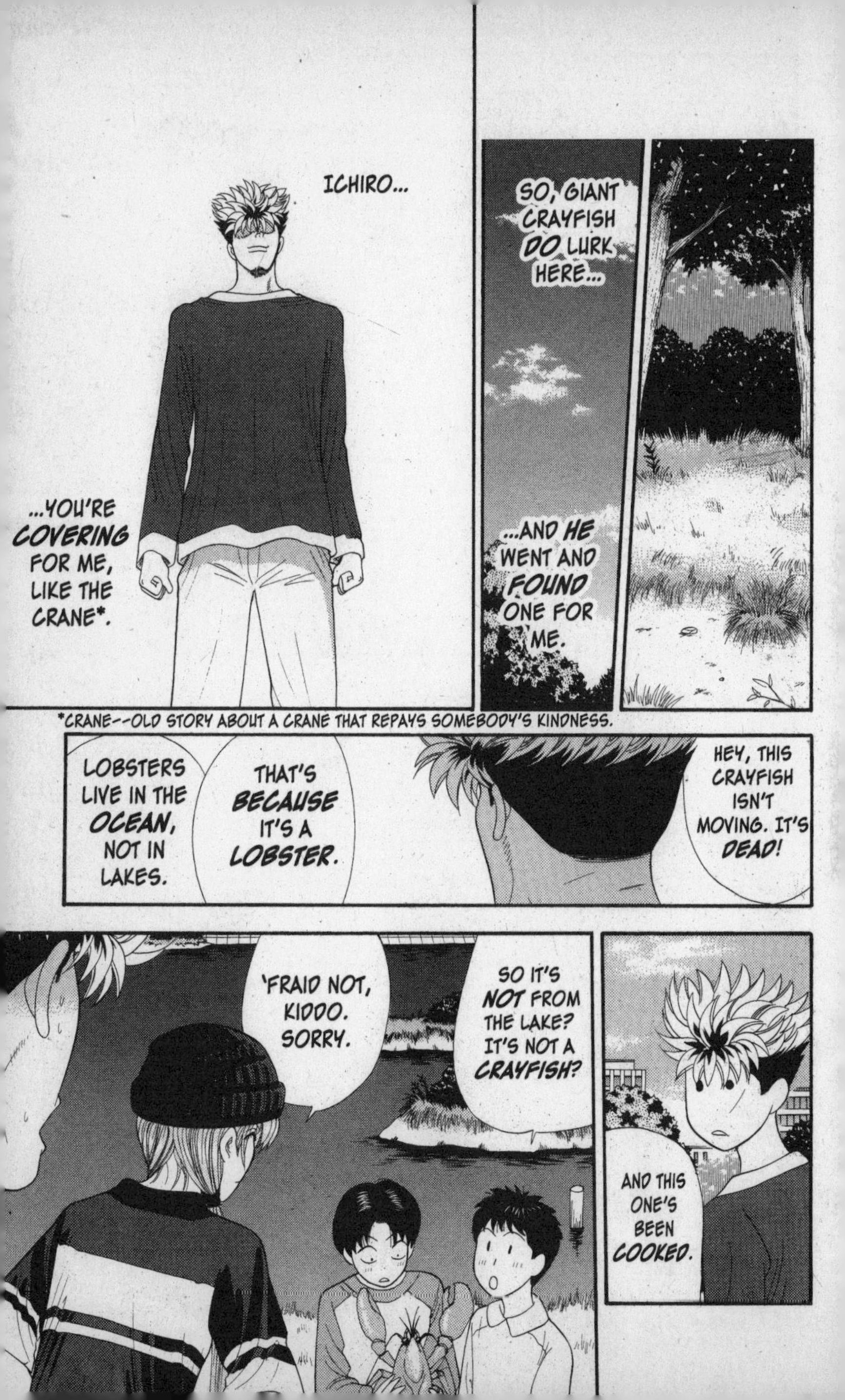
SO, GIANT CRAYFISH DO LURK HERE...
...AND HE WENT AND FOUND ONE FOR ME.
ICHIRO...
...YOU'RE COVERING FOR ME, LIKE THE CRANE*.
HEY, THIS CRAYFISH ISN'T MOVING. IT'S DEAD!
THAT'S BECAUSE IT'S A LOBSTER.
LOBSTERS LIVE IN THE OCEAN, NOT IN LAKES.
AND THIS ONE'S BEEN COOKED.
SO IT'S NOT FROM THE LAKE? IT'S NOT A CRAYFISH?
'FRAID NOT, KIDDO. SORRY.

*CRANE--OLD STORY ABOUT A CRANE THAT REPAYS SOMEBODY'S KINDNESS.

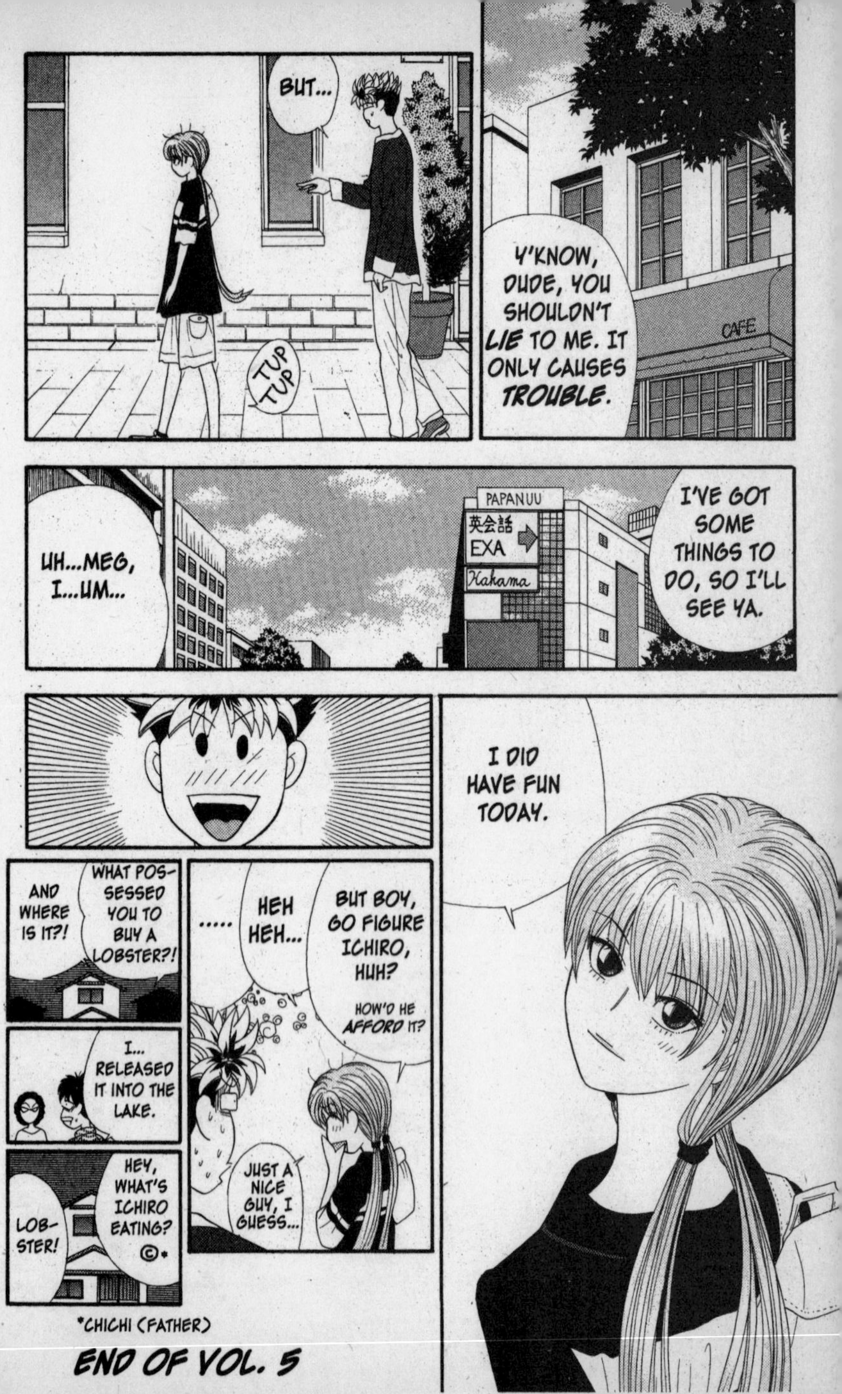
Y'KNOW, DUDE, YOU SHOULDN'T LIE TO ME. IT ONLY CAUSES TROUBLE.
CAFE
BUT...
TUP TUP
I'VE GOT SOME THINGS TO DO, SO I'LL SEE YA.
PAPANUU
英会話 EXA
Kakama
UH...MEG, I...UM...
I DID HAVE FUN TODAY.
BUT BOY, GO FIGURE ICHIRO, HUH?
HEH HEH...
.....
HOW'D HE AFFORD IT?
JUST A NICE GUY, I GUESS...
WHAT POS-SESSED YOU TO BUY A LOBSTER?!
AND WHERE IS IT?!
I... RELEASED IT INTO THE LAKE.
HEY, WHAT'S ICHIRO EATING? ©*
LOB-STER!

*CHICHI (FATHER)

END OF VOL. 5

EDITOR'S RECOMMENDATIONS

More manga!
More manga!

If you enjoyed this volume of

Cheeky Angel

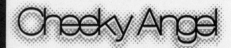

then here's some more manga you might be interested in.

Flowers & Bees
by Moyoco Anno

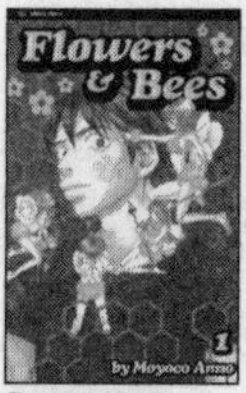

Flowers and Bees
© 2000 Moyoco Anno/Kodansha Ltd.

Flowers and Bees
Masao Komatsu might deem himself a complete and utter loser, but high-school life is never terrible enough that it can't get any worse. Gorgeous sisters Kiyoko and Harumi Sakurai are more than happy to bring out what's left of this shell of a young man—with each and every visit Masao pays to the World of Beautiful Men, the men's beauty salon they own!

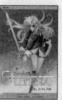

UTENA

Revolutionary Girl Utena
© 1996 SAITO CHIHO/IKUHARA KUNIHIKO & BE-PAPAS/Shogakukan, Inc.

Revolutionary Girl Utena
Still searching for the mysterious prince who saved her life as a young lass, Utena must bear her biggest cross yet—the romantic gestures of Akio Ohtori. Can she trust the self-confident and obviously more experienced older man? After one night of heated love, Utena prays the overwhelming dominance of tender emotions will alter her destiny forever.

Wedding Peach

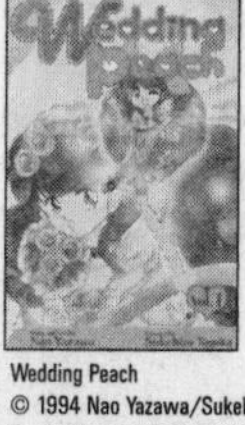

Wedding Peach
© 1994 Nao Yazawa/Sukehiro Tomita/Tenyu/Shogakukan, Inc.

Wedding Peach
Wedding Peach is about a first-year middle-school student Momoko Hanasaki and her friends Yuri and Hinagiku, who transform into demon-slaying supercharged angels when they aren't busy ogling the strapping captain of their soccer team.

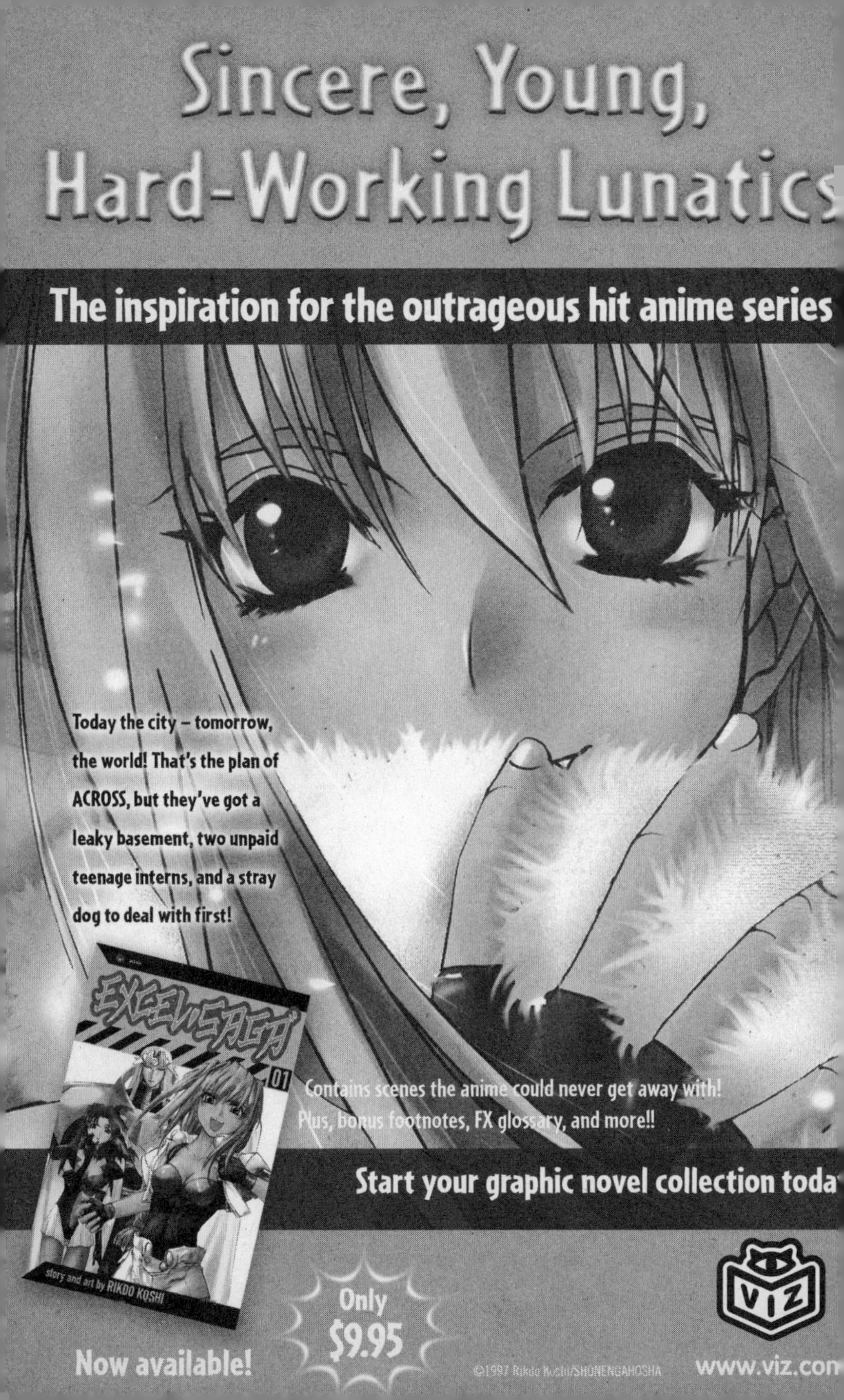
Sincere, Young, Hard-Working Lunatics
The inspiration for the outrageous hit anime series
Today the city – tomorrow, the world! That's the plan of ACROSS, but they've got a leaky basement, two unpaid teenage interns, and a stray dog to deal with first!
01
story and art by RIKDO KOSHI
Contains scenes the anime could never get away with! Plus, bonus footnotes, FX glossary, and more!!
Start your graphic novel collection toda
Only $9.95
Now available!
©1997 Rikdo Koshi/SHONENGAHOSHA
www.viz.con

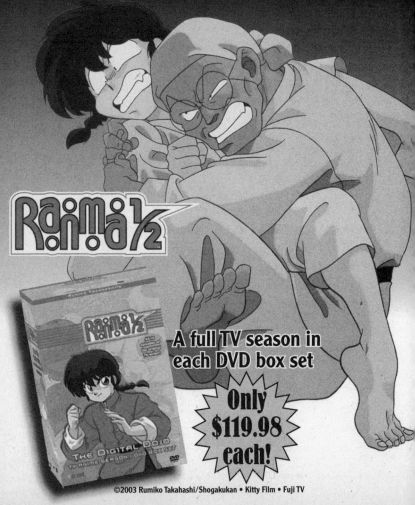

www.viz.com

store.viz.com

All New ACTION Graphic Novels!

action

All books starting at $7.95!

The latest volumes now available in stores:

Battle Angel Alita, Vol. 8
Case Closed, Vol. 4
Cheeky Angel, Vol. 5
Excel Saga, Vol. 11
Firefighter!, Vol. 10
MegaMan NT Warrior, Vol. 6 *

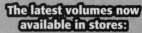

* Also available on DVD from VIZ

COMPLETE OUR SURVEY AND LET US KNOW WHAT YOU THINK!

☐ Please do NOT send me information about VIZ products, news and events, special offers, or other information.

☐ Please do NOT send me information from VIZ's trusted business partners.

Name: _____

Address: _____

City: _____ **State:** _____ **Zip:** _____

E-mail: _____

☐ Male ☐ Female **Date of Birth** (mm/dd/yyyy): ___ / ___ / ___ (Under 13? Parental consent required)

What race/ethnicity do you consider yourself? (please check one)

☐ Asian/Pacific Islander ☐ Black/African American ☐ Hispanic/Latino

☐ Native American/Alaskan Native ☐ White/Caucasian ☐ Other: _____

What VIZ product did you purchase? (check all that apply and indicate title purchased)

☐ DVD/VHS _____

☐ Graphic Novel _____

☐ Magazines _____

☐ Merchandise _____

Reason for purchase: (check all that apply)

☐ Special offer ☐ Favorite title ☐ Gift

☐ Recommendation ☐ Other _____

Where did you make your purchase? (please check one)

☐ Comic store ☐ Bookstore ☐ Mass/Grocery Store

☐ Newsstand ☐ Video/Video Game Store ☐ Other: _____

☐ Online (site: _____)

What other VIZ properties have you purchased/own? _____

_____

How many anime and/or manga titles have you purchased in the last year? How many were VIZ titles? (please check one from each column)

ANIME	MANGA	VIZ
☐ None	☐ None	☐ None
☐ 1-4	☐ 1-4	☐ 1-4
☐ 5-10	☐ 5-10	☐ 5-10
☐ 11+	☐ 11+	☐ 11+

I find the pricing of VIZ products to be: (please check one)

☐ Cheap   ☐ Reasonable   ☐ Expensive

What genre of manga and anime would you like to see from VIZ? (please check two)

☐ Adventure   ☐ Comic Strip   ☐ Science Fiction   ☐ Fighting

☐ Horror   ☐ Romance   ☐ Fantasy   ☐ Sports

What do you think of VIZ's new look?

☐ Love It   ☐ It's OK   ☐ Hate It   ☐ Didn't Notice   ☐ No Opinion

Which do you prefer? (please check one)

☐ Reading right-to-left

☐ Reading left-to-right

Which do you prefer? (please check one)

☐ Sound effects in English

☐ Sound effects in Japanese with English captions

☐ Sound effects in Japanese only with a glossary at the back

THANK YOU! Please send the completed form to:

VIZ Survey
42 Catharine St.
Poughkeepsie, NY 12601

All information provided will be used for internal purposes only. We promise not to sell or otherwise divulge your information.